Lexicographica Graeca

Lexicographica Graeca

Contributions to the lexicography
of Ancient Greek

JOHN CHADWICK

CLARENDON PRESS · OXFORD
1996

Oxford University Press, Walton Street, Oxford OX2 6DP

Oxford New York
Athens Auckland Bangkok Bombay
Calcutta Cape Town Dar es Salaam Delhi
Florence Hong Kong Instanbul Karachi
Kuala Lumpur Madras Madrid Melbourne
Mexico City Nairobi Paris Singapore
Taipei Tokyo Toronto

and associated companies in
Berlin Ibadan

Oxford is a trade mark of Oxford University Press

Published in the United States
by Oxford University Press Inc., New York

British Library Cataloguing in Publication Data
Data available

Library of Congress Cataloging in Publication Data
Lexicographica graeca: contributions to the lexicography of
ancient Greek / John Chadwick.
Includes bibliographical references
1. Greek language—Dictionaries—English. 1. Title
PA445.E5C58 1996 483'.21—dc20 96-13436
ISBN 0-19-814970-0

1 3 5 7 9 10 8 6 4 2

Typeset by Regent Typesetting, London
Printed in Great Britain on acid-free paper by
Bookcraft (Bath) Ltd., Midsomer Norton

PREFACE

I AM surprised at my own boldness—temerity might be a better word—in embarking on the compilation of this collection of notes, and even more so at the results. I had long been aware of the defects in the famous Lexicon of Liddell–Scott–Jones, but I did not expect that my efforts to improve the treatment of a few words would lead me to propose new interpretations of many passages. Some of these suggestions will inevitably be rejected and may even be disproved, but I believe the method which underlies them is still valid. It is time to stop worshipping this ancient monument and to replace it with more modern structures.

I have expressed my view of lexicography in the Introduction which forms the first part of this book. All I need to do here is to record my grateful thanks to all those who have contributed, wittingly or unwittingly, to these notes. My major debt is to my friend and colleague of many years, Dr John T. Killen, who has spent many hours discussing with me the problems I have encountered; and has then, at no little expense of time and labour, read through and criticised the drafts of this book. Without his encouragement and help I doubt if I should ever have ventured on this enterprise.

As I have explained, the book arose from working on the new supplement to Liddell and Scott as a member of the British Academy's Committee appointed to supervise the project. I am indebted to the other members of this Committee and especially to its Editor, Mr P. G. W. Glare, and his principal assistant Dr Anne Thompson; both of these spent a lot of time discussing problems with me, and called my attention to matters that would otherwise have escaped my notice. They are of course not in any way responsible for what appears in this book.

I have also been able to consult a wide range of colleagues, especially those at Cambridge. I should like to thank in particular Professor A. Morpurgo Davies, Professor P. E. Easterling, Mr G. P. Fitzgerald, Professor L. A. Moritz, Mr J. Morrison, and Dr D. N. Sedley.

Finally I am indebted to the Delegates of Oxford University Press for undertaking to publish a book which is not a dictionary but a contribution to Greek lexicography, and for allowing me to use the Supplements to Liddell and Scott, which are its copyright; and to Miss H. O'Shea and her staff, who have helped and encouraged me greatly in preparing this book and seeing it through the press.

JOHN CHADWICK

Faculty of Classics
University of Cambridge
August 1995

INTRODUCTION

Νᾶφε καὶ μέμνασ' ἀπιστεῖν. EPICHARMUS 13

This book is the product of a lifetime of Greek studies, but its immediate origin lies in work undertaken over the last ten years or so. During this period I have been a member of a Committee established in 1980 by the British Academy, to oversee their project for a new Supplement to the Greek Lexicon of Liddell and Scott. When drafts of this Supplement were circulated to the Committee for their comments, I read through these with some care and made a large number of suggestions for improvements. I am gratified to see that most of these have been accepted by the Editor, Mr P. G. W. Glare, and incorporated in the final version.

The nature of a Lexicon of course precludes any discussion of the validity of an entry. Dictionaries are inevitably compiled on a 'take-it-or-leave-it' principle; either you accept what you are told or you do not. Lack of space precludes discussion of doubtful points, nor can all the argumentation on which the entry is based be included. Thus a new suggestion which I made sometimes appears in the New Supplement, but without the arguments which justify it. It therefore seemed to me appropriate to write for publication a longer note explaining and commenting on the bald statement in the Lexicon. A good example is my note on Ϝαγάνω, a mysterious Boeotian word which has baffled commentators for a long time.

In other cases I objected to the interpretation offered by the Supplement entry. These were often entries taken over from the 1968 Supplement, which I have been forced to evaluate as amateurish and in places incompetent. All too often the information given is incomplete, inaccurate or misleading, and great efforts have been made in the New Supplement to check and revise these entries. Some of these corrections formed the subject of notes which I wrote, and some of the more interesting ones have been included in this book.

But even more frequent were the cases where the alterations proposed by the Supplement led me to study carefully the article in the main Lexicon. It became clear, as I had long suspected, that many of the longer articles were unsatisfactory and needed to be rewritten. In writing my comments for the Supplement I duly noted this fact, and in some cases recommended suppressing a correction in the Supplement, not because it was wrong, but because it did little but draw attention to underlying defects in the main Lexicon. I have selected a number of these words for a more extended treatment. I am not, however, so much concerned to demonstrate the faults as to offer suggestions on how the treatment of the word could be improved. Some of these notes amount to little short of a revision of the whole article; but it must always be remembered that a complete rewriting would demand far more time than I have been able to give.

The list of words treated is inevitably eclectic. It would be possible to increase the size of this book many times, if time and energy permitted. Thus the absence of a note does not imply that I approve the treatment the word has received in the lexica, nor are all the notes complete in themselves. It is my hope that the demonstration of the faults to be corrected and the methods to be employed in their correction will serve others as an example and a spur to future work of this kind.

In order to trace the more remote origins of this book I feel the need to insert an autobiographical digression. I hope I may be forgiven for approaching this subject from a personal angle, but I believe this may be not uninteresting and at the same time demonstrate how the strong ideas I hold on the subject developed. I have observed that lexicographers are regarded by scholars in general in two ways. In rare cases the author of an outstanding dictionary is treated with the utmost marks of distinction, as having achieved something beyond the powers of ordinary mortals. I need only instance Sir James Murray, the first editor and in large measure progenitor of *A New English Dictionary*, now known as *The Oxford English Dictionary*. To this class we may perhaps assign Henry George Liddell and Robert Scott, who established the leading dictionary of ancient Greek. On the other hand, the lexicographer is more often regarded as a competent, but not original researcher, whose business it is to discover what others have written about a word and organise their opinions into a form easy to consult. This divergence is partly due to the two different methods of making a dictionary, which will be the main subject of this preliminary essay.

My first acquaintance with large-scale dictionaries was the result of an excellent classical education which I received at my public school. For the last three years of my school career I was constantly to use the *Greek–English Lexicon* of Liddell and Scott, in the seventh or eighth editions, and the *Latin Dictionary* of Lewis and Short. The shortcomings of the latter were in some cases only too apparent, and we struggled to overcome them; but I have no doubt we were often misled in our attempts to write Latin by their treatment of certain words, especially those with many meanings. At the time the ninth edition of Liddell and Scott's Lexicon was still in progress, and could only be used for the earlier part of the alphabet. But I think we had already observed, or had it pointed out to us by our admirable Greek teacher, Mr (later Professor) G. E. Bean, that this was rarely superior to the eighth edition, except by its inclusion of many obscure authors, papyri, and inscriptions which are of little use to students of classical literature. It was not until after 1946 that I began regularly to consult the ninth edition, at a time when my interests in Greek had begun to range more widely.

In the meantime my undergraduate years at Cambridge were interrupted by five years of war service in the Royal Navy, a part of which was devoted to manual labour of a sort unconducive to any kind of study. But at a later stage I was fortunate enough to be recruited by the intelligence division of the Navy. It can hardly still be regarded as a betrayal of a state secret to reveal that in this I acquired a practical knowledge of low-grade cryptography. Much has been published about the British success in breaking the system of high-grade encipherment used by the German armed forces, which enabled our intelligence apparatus to predict enemy dispositions and operations. Relatively little has been said about the penetration of the low-grade ciphers used by all combatants for local messages, usually of little more than transitory importance. However, even these, if they can be deciphered fast enough, may provide information of tactical significance, and occasionally allow inferences to be made about more important matters.

For these more immediate messages a method of encipherment needs to be employed which can be used on a small ship or in the field, where a cipher-machine might be difficult to employ and would run the risk of falling into enemy hands. A frequent method is to have a code-book, a kind of small dictionary containing the words most often needed for the purpose envisaged, which equates each word with a numerical group, usually of four or five digits. The message is encoded by substituting the numerical groups for the words of the original. The code-book also includes a decoding section, in which the groups are listed in numerical order with the meaning for each. In practice such code-books are rarely used in this simple fashion, except for the lowest grade of operational messages; the encoded text is normally reciphered by another procedure, which does not need to be described here. The first task of the cryptographer is therefore to strip off the recipherment and recover the plain encoded text.

When confronted with this situation I could not at first see how it was possible to proceed to the second stage, the reconstruction of the code-book so as to recreate the original message. But having seen it done, I found myself able to apply the method and make progress towards the decipherment of an unknown code-book. The essence of the method is simply to study the contexts in which each group, that is, word, is used; this frequently leads to a determination of the class of word being studied and eventually to recognition of the actual word. Now it should be obvious that the same method can be applied to an unknown language, and, provided there are enough texts and enough time, it is always (in theory) possible to reconstruct the meaning of texts written in an unknown language. *A fortiori* the contextual method can be employed to determine the meaning of an unknown word in a known language. All that is needed is a sufficient number of examples of the word in different contexts.

Before I left the Intelligence organisation at the end of the war in 1945, I had begun to look around for possible employment, once I had been able to return to Cambridge and complete my first degree. At this stage I came across an officer in the Army Intelligence Corps, Captain James M. Wyllie, who had in peace-time been a lexicographer. He had been working in Oxford on a completely new Latin Dictionary, and needed to recruit suitable scholars for a resumption of this project once the war was over. He was sufficiently interesting for me to enter into an understanding that on finishing at Cambridge I would go to Oxford to work for the Clarendon Press under his direction.

Thus in the summer of 1946 I became a professional lexicographer and continued in this employment for six years. The *Oxford Latin Dictionary* was eventually published in parts between 1968 and 1982. By working on it I not only learned a great deal about the Latin language and its literature, but what I have always regarded as even more important, the practice of lexicography.

Wyllie was perhaps not the ideal teacher, but I should like to take this opportunity of recording my debt to the training in lexicography I received from him. He had himself been trained by Sir William Craigie, one of the editors of the *Oxford English Dictionary*, and was thus an inheritor of the Oxford lexicographic tradition. Strangely, none of the great English lexicographers of that period seems to have thought it worth while to compile a manual for the use of their successors; the tradition was handed down by word of mouth and is now in danger of becoming lost. At all events, it is clear that the discoveries and methods of the English lexicographers were never studied by classical scholars, and when the results appeared in the *Oxford Latin Dictionary* few classicists were able to appreciate the changes. Our task was not to revise Lewis and Short, but to create a new dictionary by the study of vast numbers of examples of usage which had already been collected. Needless to say it was often necessary to refer to the Greek Lexicon, and to the trained eye some of its faults were obvious.

But it was also clear to me that, despite the manifest differences imposed by the language being recorded, the principles to be applied remained the same, whatever the language. At one period I organised a Seminar at Cambridge on lexicography, which attracted the interest of several linguistic faculties, and this too confirmed the universality of the principles I was advocating. Indeed, the editor of an Italian dictionary lamented that I had not given these talks much earlier, since I had supplied the answers to some of the problems she and her colleagues had been forced to solve by trial and error. On another occasion I was asked by a publisher to write a report, strictly from the lexicographic point of view, on a dictionary of Malay, a language of which I knew nothing. At the same time, and without my knowledge, the same request was made to the editor of a German dictionary. When the publisher received our reports, he was surprised to find that we had both picked on the same points to criticise.

Nor does it matter, as is often asserted, whether the dictionary is unilingual, with its definitions in the same language, or bi-lingual, with definitions framed in another language. Of course a pocket dictionary will show a great deal of difference; but in any major dictionary the definition needs to be spelled out fully, and a series of translation-equivalents must be considered inadequate. Herein lies one of my major criticisms of Liddell and Scott.

The discrimination of senses and the framing of accurate definitions are the essentials of the semantic classification of words; and the way in which words are extended to new contexts and transferred to new situations appears to be the same in all languages. I am fortunate in having been able to test this outside the Indo-European family of languages, since at one stage I acquired an elementary acquaintance with Japanese.

But it was my training in Oxford which enabled me to see the faults of LSJ. I regretted that we were not working on a similar dictionary of classical Greek; but I was well aware that this would have taken an even greater organisation than had been assembled for Latin, since Greek literature is far more extensive and covers a much longer period.

Another result of this period of my life was the discovery of the fascination of lexicography. Contrary to the general opinion that it is a laborious and repetitive task, I soon found that it was one of the most interesting occupations I have ever tried, so that even now I cannot let it alone. Every word is different and raises different problems requiring difficult judgments and decisions. After leaving Oxford for a teaching post at Cambridge I was able to continue my interest in the Latin Dictionary; and at a later stage I compiled a special lexicon to a Neo-Latin writer of the eighteenth century, which is I believe the first attempt to produce any dictionary of the modern use of Latin.

When in 1979 the subject of a new supplement to Liddell and Scott's *Greek–English Lexicon* was mooted, I pointed out that what was more needed than another supplement was a thorough revision; but although my objections fell on deaf ears, I was included in the Committee set up to oversee this project. It will not therefore be surprising if I say that I have reservations about the value of this work, useful as it will be to editors of papyri and inscriptions.

*   *   *   *   *

But at this point we need to rehearse briefly the history of Greek lexicography in England from the first edition of Liddell and Scott's *Greek–English Lexicon* in 1843. It is recorded that an Oxford bookseller realised the need for a Greek–English lexicon and persuaded two brilliant young graduates to make a translation of the Greek–German Lexicon of Passow. In doing so they began to notice its deficiencies and read some of the standard authors to add more examples and improve the discrimination of senses. Thus even their first edition was an improvement on the original. Further editions followed, and these culminated in the publication in 1882 of the seventh edition. The eighth edition of 1897 was little more than a corrected reprint of this.

It was a remarkable achievement of Victorian scholarship and has served generations of students as a guide to a very rich and complex language. It is safe to say that no two scholars are ever likely to undertake again such a daunting task; and we must remain for ever indebted to them for having pioneered an extended lexicon with full references to all the quotations. But Greek studies made rapid progress around the end of the last century and the beginning of the present by the discovery and publication of vast numbers of papyri and inscriptions. Progress was also made in the editing and elucidation of the literary texts, and in the understanding of the history of the language and its dialects.

The mantle of Liddell and Scott was now assumed by H. (later Sir Henry) Stuart Jones, who began collecting materials for a new edition. But after his election to the Camden Chair of Ancient History at Oxford, he found an assistant in the person of Roderick McKenzie, Fellow of St John's College. It seems likely, and I have been told it as a fact, that the bulk of the laborious task of preparing the ninth edition fell to him. It appeared in parts between 1925 and 1940 under the name of H. Stuart Jones 'with the assistance of R. McKenzie', and is known Germanically as Liddell–Scott–Jones. The abbreviation LSJ is now hallowed by usage, so it is adopted here, though I have often wondered whether LSM might not be fairer. Stuart Jones died before the last part was published, and McKenzie too did not live to see it published.

I have discussed LSJ in a long article published in *BICS* 1994, 1–11, and I do not propose to repeat my strictures here. The basic fault was the decision to treat the sheets of the eighth edition as a first proof, and to make corrections and insertions on these. This effectively prevented any attempt to modernise the style or to recast the structure of the articles; only such corrections and additions as could be entered in the margins were admitted. The results are everywhere obvious, and the increase in both the number of entries and the diversity of senses over the immense period regarded as Ancient Greek render the new lexicon less rather than more serviceable for the average user. It is all too often forgotten that a dictionary is a tool, and needs therefore to be designed with the user in mind; what is suitable for a student will not serve an advanced scholar and vice versa.

Another fault of LSJ was the editors' failure to keep the etymological notes up to date. By 1925 a great deal was known on that subject which could not have appeared at least in the earlier editions of Liddell and Scott. One can only suppose that Stuart Jones and McKenzie were not interested in this aspect of their work; but since it often has implications for the development of senses, it was obviously important not to keep quoting discarded theories. The same attitude to linguistic matters is to be seen in the treatment of defective verbs, which are only used in certain tenses. LSJ still offers an article with the impossible lemma *εἴδω to contain the aorist εἶδον; but the perfect οἶδα was given its own entry because of its specialised meaning. Equally modern Greek is ignored, and one has the impression that the editors were probably ignorant of it, since it sometimes explains late forms which puzzled them. In this at least the New Supplement is an improvement, and I have commented in these notes on a few points where the modern language is helpful.

But the relentless pressure of newly published material did not abate, and in due course a Supplement was put in hand under the direction of E. A. Barber. He was assisted by a small team, which at one time included Paul Maas, one of the distinguished band of classical scholars forced to leave Germany by the Nazi government. Since I knew him personally during my employment in Oxford, I have no doubt that he cannot have been responsible for the faults of this Supplement, which appeared, after his death, in 1968. I have also criticised this Supplement in the article just mentioned as an incompetent production, unworthy both of Liddell and Scott and of the Oxford tradition of lexicography. Some of its faults will become evident in the notes which make up this book, and the alert reader will have no difficulty in discovering more for himself.

However, I was not myself aware of the general level of incompetence it displayed, when work began on a new Supplement, since I assumed that the errors I had detected were not typical. The Committee rightly took the decision to incorporate the old Supplement in the new, rather than give the user three alphabets to consult. What we did not realise was that by so instructing the Editor, we laid upon him the obligation to mix his work with another's and thereby to assume responsibility for both. When drafts of the new work combined with the entries of the old Supplement were circulated, it quickly became apparent that many of the old entries required amendment, and most of them needed to be fully checked and revised. Thus the scale of the Editor's task was more or less doubled; and the Committee was unable to provide him with the expert assistance he needed to complete the job in the time allotted.

Essentially a Supplement is intended to add new information to that contained in the main dictionary; it cannot and should not attempt to correct major faults in the original. Here we encounter the problem that its Editor cannot ignore a minor mistake when he can easily print a correction. This can often be effected by saying 'for ... read ...' or perhaps 'transfer this example from sense 2 to sense 3'. But suppose he now wishes to delete an example; it is easy enough to make the entry 'delete ...', but this will leave the reader wondering what has caused this change of opinion. Sometimes it is possible to add 'see ...', referring the reader to a different lemma, where the form in question is now treated. Lack of space normally prevents giving references to discussion of the point. So in reading drafts of the Supplement, I have often noted against such entries 'Why?'

An alternative method is to write an article to replace the existing one. In the New Supplement these are introduced with the sign + preceding the key-word. These must be written in the same 'style' as the main dictionary; by style we mean the standard arrangement of the article, what information is given and in what order and what abbreviations are used. Any significant change may confuse the user, and will cause problems if at a later stage the new entries are merged with the main text. Now that dictionaries are beginning to be published in electronic form on a disk that can be read by a computer, this is a real possibility, and thought needs to be given to the direction which further developments should take.

The temptation is to include every new piece of information instead of evaluating its usefulness and discarding those which cannot justify the space they occupy. I will quote one sample from the 1968 supplement:

'˟προσ[**]απλομένου, part. of unknown verb, *rely upon*, οὐδενὶ τεκμηρίῳ, UPZ 161. 67 (ii BC).'

It seems to be true that there is no known verb which could be restored so as to make sense in this context, and *rely upon* is a possible meaning for the medio-passive form. If the reading were complete, it would therefore merit consideration for inclusion, though its very incompleteness makes it impossible to enter in the alphabetical sequence in such a way that, if it subsequently appears complete, it could easily be matched with this entry. But when a completely new word appears in a papyrus, the wary editor will consider whether it may not be the result of a mistake. In this case a plausible emendation would be to transpose two letters and to fill the gap with one instead of the presumed two letters, to restore it as προσθαλπομένου. The active προσθάλπω is quoted by LSJ from Josephus as meaning *comfort, encourage*, a sense well attested for the simple θάλπω; and 'encouraged by no evidence' will clearly make sense. I should not recommend adding this to the evidence for προσθάλπω, but this possibility is enough to prove that the Supplement entry relies upon no satisfactory evidence. This is a blatant example of the inclusion of virtually worthless information, but there are many more entries of very questionable value. I shall discuss a possible method of dealing with such material in the last section of this Introduction (pp. 27–30).

A special problem is posed by the words and forms now known from the Greek dialects. Where a word is also used by the κοινή, it is normally entered under that form, and the variants are then listed, with cross-references where necessary. But there are cases where a dialect uses, not a variant form, but a different lexical item to express the same concept. For instance, πεδά in some dialects replaces μετά, not only as a preposition, but also in compounds. The temptation, to which LSJ at least partly succumbed, is to treat πεδά as a dialect form of μετά—a solution which might be acceptable in a small-scale dictionary, but ought never to appear in a major work.

Another problem is that of deciding where a new form should be entered. The editor of the 1968 Supplement found evidence for the West Greek form of κλειστός written in inscriptions as *ΚΛΑΙΚΤΟΣ*, and entered it as κλαϊκτός. This is a possible interpretation of the spelling, since Attic κλείς is contracted from *κλαϝίς, a form now attested by a Mycenaean compound. However, the West Greek form of κλείς is *ΚΛΑΙΞ*, and evidence that it contracted to a long diphthong is available from Theocritus (15. 33). It is therefore likely that *ΚΛΑΙΚΤΟΣ* should be treated alphabetically according to LSJ's rules as κλᾳκτός; and in fact it is entered in LSJ as such with reference to the same two inscriptions, though in one case to a different edition of it.

Words which have no equivalent in Attic or the κοινή are very difficult to handle. An addition to the vocabulary is the Cretan word *ϝΑΔΑ*, a noun from the root of ἁνδάνω meaning 'decision.' There is a rule, which I believe should now be changed, that ϝ is ignored in the alphabetical ordering of words. So should this appear as *ἁδή, which is what we should expect if it occurred in Attic; or as *ἁδά, or even *ἀδά? Anyone encountering the word for the first time will not know where to look for it, and the simplest solution would be to allow ϝ the status of a letter, inserted in the alphabet after *E*, and place ϝαδά there, unless and until a form without ϝ is found.

It is obvious that most of the entries in LSJ are basically sound. We might wish to improve the typography and style, to bring the references into line with modern editions, and so on. In a number of cases the wording of the equivalents is old-fashioned (and unnecessarily prudish); but the translations offered are for the most part acceptable. This is because the majority of entries relate to special terms with restricted usage. A minority of words, regarded as dictionary entries, are those which have a high frequency of occurrence in a running text, and it is these which have the largest number of uses or meanings. It is my considered judgment that most of the longer entries in LSJ now require more than cosmetic surgery, and many need to be completely rewritten.

If I have not attempted this, it is because it would require far more time and resources than I have at my disposal. Even the task of looking up all the references given by LSJ is very tedious.

To extend the search to other sources would vastly increase the time needed, and would require the assistance of a number of highly trained helpers. Nor am I convinced that the results would always justify the expenditure of energy. But I hope that enough new ideas are presented here to demonstrate that lexicography, so far from being a derivative science, can lead to new interpretations.

The idea of the lexicographer as innovator may seem to contradict his basic function as a recorder. He takes a particular language at a particular period and records the usage of its vocabulary as evidenced by the literature or other materials on which it is based. If the material is restricted, as for instance to a single author, there is no reason why he should not list every example, though even here the commonest words will demand a more summary treatment. In most cases he has to make a selection, and to arrange the different usages into a coherent pattern. The nature of the dictionary demands that these be reduced to a unidimensional sequence; but he knows very well that the true relationship of the senses is too complex to be represented by less than a three-dimensional model. The figure of a tree, with a root sending up a trunk which branches in all directions, each branch sending out smaller boughs and finally twigs, would be hard enough to represent in a linear sequence. But the senses of a complex word can sometimes be shown to have undergone mutual influence, as if the branches have not simply diverged, but at a later stage merged again. In his arrangement at least the lexicographer may be forced to innovate.

The essential factor to be considered here is that senses do not exist in isolation. The average speaker of a language is often unaware that he is using words in different senses; he may unwittingly extend the meaning of a word, and at this point he may be accused of misusing it. But if his extension of the meaning serves a useful purpose, it is likely to be imitated and a new sense will develop; but it will be related to other senses of the word, and the arrangement of the senses in a dictionary should, so far as possible, mirror the word's development. If the material is plentiful enough it may be possible to show the developments taking place chronologically; but in many cases several senses had developed before the language was recorded, and we can only arrive at an archetypal meaning by conjecture. I shall revert to this later.

There is, however, another way in which the lexicographer can be an innovator. But the discussion of this must be postponed until we have dealt with the two basic methods of making a dictionary.

The first, the traditional and almost universal method is take another man's dictionary and use it as the basis for one's own. It may need to be expanded to allow a wider scope, or abbreviated by the omission of matter judged irrelevant to a more limited purpose. But in essence the framework is taken over and used as the scaffolding on which to build. Unless he practises outright plagiarism, he is unlikely to be accused of infringing copyright; and it is often possible to use dictionaries which have lost this protection. Raids on other dictionaries will usually go undetected, and the resulting compilation (a revealing word to those who know its etymology) will seem all the larger and more impressive.

One obvious consequence of this proceeding is the emergence of what are called *ghost-words*. This term was coined in the 19th century to describe words which appear in dictionaries, being often copied from one to another, but have never had any real currency in the language. The original entry is usually the result of a mistake of some kind, but once accepted it continues to appear in lexica until someone has the patience to re-examine the evidence. I believe I have detected one such in LSJ under the heading ἤρυς, on which a note will be found in this book. But I have no doubt that there are many more awaiting exposure.

A similar chain of events has been initiated by Hesychius and the other ancient lexicographers. We are often indebted to him for information that we should otherwise never have had. The Mycenaean word *e-ru-mi-ni-ja* would have remained obscure, but for his entry: ἐλύμνιαι· δοκοὶ ὀροφηναί. It must have remained in use late enough for Hesychius' source to have recorded it; but it has not so far been detected in any literary text or inscription. But undoubted successes like this must not induce us to believe everything Hesychius tells us. Some entries are plainly wrong, or partially wrong, as when he gives a series of synonyms, only some of which appear to be correct. And the text is often too corrupt for any emendation to carry conviction. In this case the accent is improbable, and should be corrected, as in the new Supplement. It is regrettable that Latte's edition has proved little more satisfactory than its predecessors. I have noted under ἐνδαής an instance where his emendation is unnecessary and in my judgment unconvincing.

There is now a tendency to record every word or meaning found in the ancient lexicographers as if it were a valid addition to our knowledge of the language. Of course the advanced scholar needs to know what the ancients said about the word; but he also needs to be able to compare this with the positive evidence for the word's usage. LSJ has all too often entered the opinion of an ancient scholar as a positive fact, when research and judgment lead us to believe that it was an erroneous or at least misleading view. Moreover the meanings offered in antiquity have often been allowed to influence the structure of the Lexicon entry. It is my contention that the structure of meanings must be educed by the lexicographer from the material at his disposal, otherwise a preconceived pattern may distort the interpretation of passages. It must never be forgotten that the recording of dubious material takes up a great deal of space, which might be better occupied by clearer definitions and examples.

A much more intractable problem is posed by difficult passages in well-known authors. It is clear that the lexicographer will here consult the collective wisdom of commentators and translators; and if they disagree, he must make a choice. Sometimes it is possible to add the note: 'also interpreted as ...'; but if he regularly hedges his bets in this way, it will increase the length of the lexicon without any compensating advantage, for the average user, especially the student, will be less well placed to make a judgment than the lexicographer. Moreover, he will encounter passages where his experience and overview of the word's usage lead him to adopt an interpretation differing from that of the experts. A number of such passages are discussed in this book, and I have been able to be audacious precisely because this is not a dictionary, but a collection of contributions towards the production of an improved Greek lexicon. Some of my suggestions will undoubtedly be rejected by the consensus of opinion; but it will have done no harm to initiate a discussion. Some expert on animal behaviour may be able to explain what Homer meant by applying the epithet ἀραιός to wolves' tongues; but until it has been shown that it is unlikely to mean *narrow*, the commentators will continue to accept that meaning.

Perhaps I may quote here an example of a problem which

frequently confronts the lexicographer, and especially when revising an earlier edition. From time to time new interpretations of familiar passages are published, and these obviously need to be considered for inclusion in the Lexicon. It is easy enough to copy a correction proposed; it is far more difficult to decide whether the correction is plausible enough to be given the support of a major dictionary.

I should like to take as a specimen a well-known passage in Hesiod, which has given both ancient and modern commentators much trouble. It is the description of a winter's day:

ἤματι χειμερίῳ ὅτ᾽ ἀνόστεος ὃν πόδα τένδει
ἔν τ᾽ ἀπύρῳ οἴκῳ καὶ ἤθεσι λευγαλέοισιν. Hes. *Op.* 524–5.

The traditional view is that ἀνόστεος is a poetic expression or *kenning* for the octopus or squid, who in winter 'gnaws his foot in his fireless house and wretched home' (H. G. Evelyn-White, Loeb). Much debate has raged over the natural history of these creatures, and this has been allowed to obscure the absurdity of calling its undersea lair 'a fireless house', not to mention the improbability of a landsman such as Hesiod being familiar with the curious behaviour of sea creatures. It is at least clear that τένδει nowhere else occurs in Greek literature, except in passages which are clearly imitations of this, so that we cannot verify the assertion of ancient scholars that it means 'gnaw'. Nor has much attention been paid to the use of ὃν with πόδα, though it is well known that Greek idiom demands that 'his foot' be expressed with the definite article, unless it is emphatic. Does Hesiod therefore imply that in summer the octopus has other feet to nibble?

Now in 1986 an Italian scholar, E. Campanile, published a new interpretation of this passage in the Festschrift presented to E. Risch of Zürich (*O-o-pe-ro-si,* ed. A. Etter (Berlin, 1986) 355–62). Building on the demonstration by C. Watkins, *Étrennes Lejeune* (Paris, 1978) 231 ff. that 'the boneless one' is well known in other languages as a poetic expression for the *membrum virile*, he showed that the passage makes good sense on this basis, if τένδει means 'stretches' (cf. τείνω, Latin *tendo*) and πόδα means 'extremity' as it does in other contexts. As he points out, it was an ancient belief, to which Hesiod subscribed (cf. *Op.* 582–8), that sexual activity was strongest for males in the winter and for females in the summer. Whether this reinterpretation is right or not need not concern us here. But the lexicographer has to make up his mind when he comes to the relevant words. Should he delete the old explanation of each and insert the new; leave it unchanged, thus tacitly dismissing the new one; or hedge his bets with some such formula as 'Previously taken as … but now interpreted as …'? In various forms this problem is constantly arising; for other examples see my notes on ἀγαπητός, τάλας.

Another hazard encountered is the notes sent to the publisher by well-meaning amateurs. By 'amateurs' I mean of course people with no lexicographic training; they may be, and often are, scholars of distinction in their own fields. The 1968 Supplement suffered badly at the hands of an expert on the Septuagint, who seems to have assumed that the Greek word selected by the translators of iii BC must have the meaning which modern scholarship attributes to the corresponding Hebrew expression. No allowance seems to have been made for simple misunderstanding of the Hebrew, with the consequence that the Greek word has been tortured to make it conform to the Hebrew, and a number of non-existent senses have been created for the Greek words. In such cases the editor of a supplement must be prepared to investigate these cases for himself, and to form his own judgment about the meaning intended by the writer, which may or may not accurately reflect the meaning of the original. The lexicographer is always grateful for a note of new references, and he will note what is said about them; but if he is wary, he will not accept anything he is told until he has verified it for himself.

There is, however, also the problem of the editorial mistake. If the first publication of a new document incorrectly identifies a word, it is very hard for the lexicographer to escape from the wrong path. An amusing example which I have included in this book is the verb δισκυρέω, alleged to occur in one inscription. The solution is obvious enough when pointed out, but it involves supposing a grammatical blunder by the writer, for which I have not yet found a parallel. No wonder, since if it occurred in a transmitted text it would have been eliminated by a copyist or editor; it will therefore be difficult to parallel until we have all inscriptions and papyri available for electronic search.

It is the function of the lexicographer to record how the vocabulary of a language is normally used. He cannot predict the abnormal, catachrestic or poetic uses to which a word may be put. He ought not therefore to make his articles collections of famous cruces, though he cannot afford to ignore them. When the *Oxford Latin Dictionary* was in progress, we discussed whether a special sense of *lacrima* should be inserted to accommodate Vergil's *sunt lacrimae rerum*; it was decided that it should be treated as a poetic usage, which did not acquire any subsequent currency in the language. Had it done so, it would have required a new sense.

I turn now to the second method of making a dictionary. This is the only method which can be used in a case where there is no previous dictionary to use as a basis, but it is equally applicable to cases where such predecessors exist. It consists of two steps.

The first step is to assemble a representative collection of examples of each word. In the case of a lexicon to a single author, this will comprise all the examples in the corpus in question. In the case of a larger corpus some selection is inevitable, and the texts need to be read by someone able to judge whether a usage has already been adequately exemplified. But if, as in the case of ancient Greek literature, the corpus is enormous, then the collection of examples will become an immense task, only to be attempted by a major project employing a large staff. However, in the case of ancient Greek we already have an excellent collection, because LSJ draws on the stock of examples built up over a century and a half of research. There are, however, still a number of technical works, especially of later date, which have not been adequately covered. For some words the examples quoted give an inaccurate picture of the word's usage; for instance, if it is common in early verse, it may then not be sufficiently exemplified from prose authors. I have noted some cases where later developments have been ignored, but I do not claim to have searched later literature for them.

The collecting of examples has now been much facilitated by the IBYCUS computer system, and further improvements are promised which will allow inflected forms to be recovered. The danger here is the weight of material thus made available; it can easily take a day's work to scan the material for one word. It is therefore best to keep this weapon in reserve and use it selectively, as I have done in compiling these notes. It is also possible to make use of the special lexica to individual authors; but I think it is dangerous to allow these to determine the interpretation of passages, since their editors inevitably have a restricted view of the language.

It is theoretically possible to use a computer merely to record the next stage, the sorting of the examples. There is no way the computer can perform this operation, though programs may be devised in future which will assist the expert judgment which constantly needs to be applied. The difficulty here is to have a large number of examples simultaneously available for inspection, which would require a large screen, and the ability to move rapidly forwards and backwards. I was taught to perform this operation by the use of paper slips, each containing one example of the word, which can be shuffled and rearranged manually. The manipulation of a large pile of slips can be simplified by the use of a sorting box: a box with slots of appropriate size to hold the slips, arranged with the top slanting away from the user, so that the upper part of the top slip in each compartment is visible. Any notes and the apparent meaning can then be written at the top of the slip, and further examples of the same usage can be filed behind this, so that the heading remains always visible. It would be interesting to see if the experts can devise a computer program which would replicate this simple device.

It is most useful to arrange the slips in the chronological order of authors; obviously, the productive period of one author's life may overlap that of another, so that the order will be in part arbitrary. This will enable the examples as quoted in the dictionary to follow the chronological order, but only once they have been separated into their proper senses. It has become fashionable for dictionaries to be 'constructed on the historical principle'. While this is a desirable aim for the purpose of historical linguistics, it is not clear that this is the need most often to be met by a general dictionary. The order of the senses should be that which displays most easily to the user the various ways in which the word is used, and it will often be best served by making the earliest uses stand first in the final ordering of senses.

But the historical principle must never be allowed to take precedence over utility. A dictionary is a tool, and it must be adapted to the needs of its users. A lawn-mower is not a suitable tool for cutting hair, nor is a pair of scissors a suitable tool for mowing grass. I am a confirmed utilitarian in my view of dictionaries, and this implies that their merits are relative. Long ago I devised a simple formula for estimating the efficiency of a dictionary:

$$\text{EFFICIENCY} = \frac{\text{USEFULNESS}}{\text{WEIGHT}}$$

This implies that a book weighing 2 kilograms must be twice as useful as one weighing 1 kilogram to be as efficient, a condition rarely met by the dictionaries which go on increasing in size, like Liddell and Scott. The concept of USEFULNESS also involves the prospective user. The multi-volume major dictionary is no use to the traveller who wants to discover what is on the restaurant menu; nor is the pocket dictionary he needs much use to the translator of technical works. Part of the trouble with LSJ, and even more with its Supplements, is that no attempt has been made to define the user for whom the work is created. The editor of a new inscription or a papyrus may well want to know whether such a word, form or spelling has ever occurred elsewhere; but much of the information he needs is useless for the average reader of Greek texts, and ought to be consigned to a special lexicon of record. Inclusion of material of this kind simply makes the Lexicon too big to handle and too expensive for all but the experts to buy. I shall have something to say on the future of Greek lexicography at the end of this essay.

But to revert to the historical principle, it is often apparent that such respected works as the *Oxford English Dictionary* produce improbable results by its over-rigid application. For example, the adjective *soft* happens to be used in Anglo-Saxon as an epithet of sleep, and this has caused the dictionary to place first in its order of senses *producing agreeable or pleasant sensations*. It so happens that the purely physical sense *yielding to the touch* is attested only much later; but I should have thought it was self-evident that the first sense is a transference to the immaterial world of the second, purely material, sense. This can be contrasted with the more intelligent arrangement adopted by LSJ s.v. μαλακός, where μαλακῷ ... ὕπνῳ (Il. 10. 2) is correctly placed in sense **II**. In an ideal world, the material sense would also have appeared in extant Anglo-Saxon literature; but it is still possible for the lexicographer to modify the data produced by his chronological arrangement so as to present a logical ordering of senses, in which each can be seen to develop from a preceding sense. As I said before, it is not possible to represent the full range of meanings in a single linear order, for the real development is almost always more complex.

The lexicographer confronted by a pile of examples illustrating a particular word must begin by assuming that he does not know its meaning. He is thus in the same position as the cryptographer engaged in breaking a code-book. He must determine the meaning by reference to the context. If enough examples are available, he will in due course discover what meaning will fit all the contexts; if some offer a wide range of possibilities, others will narrow it down, until a satisfactory definition emerges.

If the word has only one meaning, what is sometimes called *monosemy*, this may emerge from only a few examples. But this is rare, since *polysemy,* the simultaneous existence of a number of meanings, is the general rule. Where the word is used in a few quite different contexts, it will then be useful to sort the examples by context. But context alone is sometimes inadequate to reveal the true meaning; LSJ often groups together examples which share the same context, although the specific meaning may be different. It is often also possible to sort by construction (e.g. the grammatical case or the preposition used with a verb, or the class of substantive such as noun of action, abstract, material object, etc.) Here too the grammatical classification needs to be subordinated to the semantic one. LSJ all too often gives a separate section to the middle voice of a verb, although many of the examples repeat senses already shown to exist in the active or passive. In dealing with prepositions which are construed with three cases, this may be a useful first division; but even here some overlapping of senses is inevitable. Generally speaking, words which have a basic physical or material sense tend to acquire by transference non-physical or metaphorical senses. One of LSJ's frequent faults is a failure to distinguish these, especially when a corresponding English term has the same extension.

It is often necessary to go through the examples a number of times, looking for the groupings which will gradually emerge. At this stage a provisional definition needs to be framed. This should be, if necessary, a lengthy phrase which accurately defines the examples grouped together *and excludes all others*. It is the failure to observe the second part of this prescription which so often vitiates the definitions found in a dictionary. It must be observed that LSJ rarely attempts to give a real definition; it is more often content to pile up English words which will serve as translation-equivalents, and then when other examples are found which require a different translation to add this, even if the new quotation does not in fact fall under the definition to be deduced from the earlier ones.

One feature of the definition has long been recognised as essential: that the phrase adopted be capable of insertion into any of the examples without changing the meaning of the whole. Thus an adverb must not be defined by an adjectival expression (even though English usage may require that substitution in translating), an active verb must not be defined in its passive application, and so on. This seems too obvious to be worth mentioning, but the rule is in fact all too often overlooked.

Equally the definition must not contain elements which are represented by other features in the context. A fault in LSJ is failure to allow for the semantic value of the present-tense system, which was perhaps less well understood in the nineteenth century. For an example, see ἐμβατεύω in LSJ; this is correctly defined as *step in* or *on*. But then the meanings *frequent* and *haunt* are added, because they are called for by some of the contexts in which the verb is used in the present tense. Where it is in the aorist, this sense is inappropriate, and new translations such as *enter* have been added. The correct method is of course to begin with the meaning as deduced from the aoristic use, which is aspectually neutral. Then, if needed, a special sense can be created for uses confined to the present system. Some of the problems raised by LSJ's treatment of ἀγοράζω are due to this failure to observe the component of meaning conveyed by the aspect of the verb (see the note on this word). Similar aspectual considerations underlie the problem of defining the meaning of ὀπυίω, which has been much misunderstood (see the note on βινέω).

The contextual method alone can take us far, as my cryptographic experience proved to me. But in real languages there is another way of approaching the meaning, at least in the great majority of cases. There are very few words which are lexically isolated, words such as English *kiosk, penguin, zenith*. Nearly all words belong to 'families'; verbs normally have nouns of action derived from them, like πρᾶξις from πράσσω, and nouns often have denominative verbs, like δουλόω from δοῦλος or βαρύνω from βαρύς. In fact a language which had many words not belonging to a family would be extremely hard to learn or understand. Compound words are a special case, since they belong to two (or more) families. Not all compounds beginning ὑπο- have the same component of meaning; but there is at least a restricted range of meanings which this prefix can convey.

It follows that the determination of meaning in most cases depends upon combining the contextual with the kinship clues, so as to find an acceptable meaning. If a word has a sense which appears to be unconnected by any plausible line of development from another established sense, it is at once suspect. But it is not therefore to be discarded as incorrect. It may have acquired its sense by the suppression of the links which led back to another attested sense; it is not easy to find evidence for the stages by which κοντός acquired the sense of *hymn* required by the derivative κοντάκιον of modern Greek. Some words have been borrowed from other languages, or simply invented. A stock example of invention is *gas*, a term coined to express a new concept by a Dutch chemist, though he admitted that even this is distantly related to Greek χάος (since Dutch *g* = [ɣ]), so it is not entirely isolated; and it has of course acquired its own family in modern usage. A good example of a Greek word which, although belonging to a numerous family, displays even at the earliest stage three quite separate lines of development is σταθμός. In my discussion of this I have endeavoured to suggest a possible starting-point from which these are derived, though this must remain conjectural.

The family resemblance may of course be misleading. Dictionaries often assume that a word must have an 'etymological' meaning; that is to say, the meaning which other members of the family suggest, or in the case of a compound, its two members. Although this is generally true, there are plenty of words which do not obey the rule. For instance συκοφάντης ought to be the equivalent of ὁ τὰ σῦκα φαίνων; in practice it never is, though why it developed the sense of 'informer' we shall probably never know. The ancient explanations are fairly obviously *ad hoc* inventions. LSJ often begins an article with this theoretical meaning but without quoting any example.

Another hazard which interferes with the logical inference from kinship is the fortuitous resemblance between two words which have in fact no affinity. An excellent example of this is the English word *outrage*. Most English-speakers would have no hesitation in relating this to *out,* which forms compounds such as *output,* and *rage,* thus suggesting a meaning of *excessive fury.* In fact the word is a loan from French, where *outrage* is the phonetic development of late Latin **ultraticum* (cf. Italian *oltraggio*).

These are less easy to detect in Greek, but I have pointed out an example in εἰκῇ, which has a sense in which it acquires the same meaning as εἰκότως, although its etymology is fairly certainly different. A much more complicated example is ἔχω, which is probably a conflation of two verbs: one from **segh-* meaning *hold,* and another from **wegh-* meaning *carry.* Once the digamma of Ϝέχω had been lost, and the operation of Grassmann's law had removed the initial aspirate of **ἔχω,* the two verbs became indistinguishable, and the senses *hold* and *carry* could be conflated, as in expressions like ἦλθεν ἔχων.

It happens not infrequently that in the early stages of contextual analysis, one or two examples are recalcitrant and cannot be fitted into the emerging pattern of meanings. Such cases may of course be a warning that the pattern is false and needs to be modified; but there is also the possibility that the interpretation of these examples is incorrect. Some of the notes in this book will illustrate the way in which taking the lexicographic view, that is to say, regarding the example in the light of all the other information about the word's usage, may lead to a reinterpretation. The lexicographer is, if not better equipped to interpret a particular text, at least in a special position as having in front of him a much larger collection of examples than is normally available to the editor of the text. It is rather the difference between an aerial view and one which is confined to a single viewpoint on the ground.

A constant problem to guard against is the proliferation of meanings. It might be possible to defend the thesis that every time a word is used its meaning is minimally different; but even if true, this would hardly be helpful to the users of a dictionary. In practice many examples of a word's use are so much alike as to be virtually identical, and it is this which enables the lexicographer to group the examples under mutually exclusive definitions. It is often tempting to create a new sense to accommodate a difficult example, but we must always ask first, if there is any other way of taking the word which would allow us to assign the example to an already established sense. We need the lexicographic equivalent of Occam's razor: *sensus non sunt multiplicandi praeter necessitatem.*

As I have remarked in several of my notes, there may be no reason
why a proposed sense should not exist, but is there any reason why
it must exist?

I have no illusions about the popularity of my work, for I have
frequently had occasion to attack long-established interpretations
and eminent commentators. I am not unaccustomed to presenting
unpopular views, and I have lived long enough to see some of them
adopted as the current orthodoxy. I have therefore no hesitation in
putting forward my own interpretations, even though I am well
aware that other scholars will reject them. But I think some at least
will survive criticism, and it will have done no harm to open up the
debate. But at this point I should like to record an experience that
I had more than forty years ago, when I was working on the
Oxford Latin Dictionary.

   It fell to me to prepare the first draft of the article on *ineptus,* a
fairly straightforward word applied to persons or their actions and
roughly corresponding to English *foolish*. However, there was one
passage which did not fit this meaning, the famous poem of
Catullus (17) which begins:

> O colonia quae cupis ponte ludere longo
> et salire paratum habes sed uereris inepta
> crura ponticuli axulis stantis in rediuiuis
> ne supinus eat ...

The omission of any punctuation is deliberate. *Inepta* is interpreted by virtually all dictionaries and commentaries as meaning
badly fitted together, which is the expected 'etymological' sense; as
the *Thesaurus Linguae Latinae* puts it, '*i.q. male aptus.*' But here
my principle came into effect; why are there no other examples of
this meaning? Could it have any other sense here? The answer is
that so long as *inepta* is associated with *crura* in the next line, this
must be the meaning. However, I observed that there was an
idiom in which *ineptus* was closely associated with a verb and in
agreement with its subject, to describe the folly of the action
indicated by the verb. A good example, although rather later in
date, is from Persius, who states that freedom is not conferred by
the wand waved by the lictor in the ceremony of manumission:

> hic hic quod quaerimus, hic est,
> non in festuca, lictor quam iactat ineptus.

Pers. 5. 175.

This does not mean 'in the wand waved by the fool of a lictor', but 'in the wand which the lictor, fool that he is, waves'. There are other examples of this idiom. Once this is appreciated, we can see that it will fit very neatly in Catullus too; *inepta* is not accusative plural neuter, but nominative singular feminine agreeing with *colonia*. Thus it means 'you are afraid, fool that you are, of the supports of the bridge'.

I was very pleased with this discovery, and wrote it up in a note which I intended to send for publication to one of the periodicals. But before doing so, I took the precaution of showing it to a few Latinists of my acquaintance, and was shocked to find that they all rejected it out of hand. They had been reading Catullus for years, and they knew that he used the word in this out-of-date sense. I, as a young and unknown lexicographer, could not possibly know better than the distinguished line of commentators who had long ago decided the correct interpretation. Now in publishing this book I am aware that I am in the same position again, except that I am now rather better known, and people are more inclined to treat my opinions seriously. Even so, I prophesy with assurance that many of the new ideas to be found in these pages will be attacked and rejected simply because they are not what everyone expects to find. I believe, however, that there are enough un-prejudiced scholars around to study my work on its own merits, and to decide for themselves whether or not my ideas are, if not a final solution, at least a contribution towards that end.

I must say a few words about the presentation of these notes. In most cases they arose from observing a fault in LSJ or the Supplements, but all too often it proved impossible to correct one fault without discovering others. In some cases I was simply unhappy with the information given, without having any specific complaint, and the easiest way to satisfy myself was to attempt a reconstruction of the article in the form imposed by the material. Accordingly I took all the references in LSJ and trans-ferred them to separate slips; these were then sorted by author and arranged in a roughly chronological sequence. This had the effect of shuffling the slips and removing the former order, so that I could devise my own without prejudice. Each passage had to be looked up and a sufficient quotation written out on the slip, with enough context to ensure the meaning could be grasped.

These quotations then formed the basis of the note, being suitably abbreviated.

Where coverage by this means appeared to be inadequate I supplemented the references by resorting to special lexica, the IBYCUS machine, and other sources. But I make no claim to have been exhaustive in my search for new examples, for to achieve complete coverage would have been a task beyond my powers and resources. I submit, however, that I have in some cases improved considerably on LSJ, finding sense which its editors had failed to discover.

The quotations are given at greater length than is possible in a lexicon. LSJ gives vast numbers of references without any quotation, and in such cases I have supplied these; where I have given only a reference, it may be assumed that this is merely a further example of a usage already exemplified. But I do not claim that this is the main purpose of my discussion; I am merely presenting the evidence which is not visible in LSJ to justify the new analysis which I am presenting.

As in LSJ the reference is to the line or point at which the word in question occurs, even if several lines are quoted. I have copied the system of abbreviations familiar from LSJ, not because I think it is a good one, but because it would be laborious to the writer and tedious to the reader to change it. In a few cases I have expanded the abbreviation to make it clearer or corrected strange aberrations like its practice of writing Lxx for *Septuaginta*. I have in many cases supplied references to more up-to-date editions, but I have not attempted the enormous task of imposing a new standard throughout. I have added in some cases the initial of the Editor to demonstrate the edition I used. I have in appropriate cases added subsection numbers to the references.

I have not concerned myself with questions of authenticity, though this is a subject which needs to be investigated for any new lexicon. I have, generally speaking, followed the conventions of LSJ and thus continue to refer to, e.g., the *Prometheus Vinctus* as A. *Pr.* or the *Rhesus* as E. *Rh.*, without meaning to imply that I accept these works as authentic. Likewise it must always be remembered that Hp. stands for the *Hippocratic Corpus* and it must not be interpreted as the work of the historical Hippocrates. In a few cases where it might be significant, I have enclosed the abbreviation of the author's name in square brackets. All abbreviations should be resolved by the use of the appropriate indexes in LSJ. I have occasionally quoted inscriptions from L. H. Jeffery, *The Local Scripts of Archaic Greece* under the abbreviation *LSAG*.

It is generally agreed that the etymological notes of LSJ, mostly copied from earlier editions, are unreliable and sometimes worthless. I have not attempted to put a broom to this corner of the stables. Where I have inserted notes on etymological matters, this is because I think there is something to be added to what the reader will find in the standard etymological dictionaries, in particular, H. Frisk, *Griechisches etymologisches Wörterbuch,* (*GEW*) and P. Chantraine, *Dictionnaire étymologique de la langue grecque,* (*DELG*). Some of my suggestions in this field are very tentative and must not be taken as representing anything but my own opinion; but they are included in the hope that they will stimulate debate and illustrate the possibility of further improvements by the use of my methods.

In consulting these notes the reader will need to have the appropriate page of LSJ before him, and I have not repeated information, such as that on forms, which is to be found there. My purpose has been primarily to investigate the semantic range of the word, not to rewrite the Lexicon. If these notes have any virtue, it is that of being independent of the centuries of tradition which have choked the free exercise of judgment and cluttered our editions with useless erudition. As I have said, I have a poor opinion of most of the notes on words which have been handed down to us from antiquity, and I believe they have exerted far too great an influence on modern commentators. The effort of making an unprejudiced analysis of the meanings of a word is considerable; small wonder that most scholars have found it easier to rely on another's opinion, especially if enshrined in the dense print of a lexicon. But the iconoclast runs the risk of damaging fine structures; it is easier to pull down false idols than to erect noble images in their place. These notes are not finished pieces of a new lexicon, but drafts *in usum lexicographorum,* which will, I hope, be of interest to Greek scholars generally.

What still needs to be done in Greek lexicography? Or more practically, what should be the aims of the present generation of Greek scholars? Many projects have been started which never got beyond *alpha.* The *Lexicon der frühgriechischen Epos* started out on such a scale that it would have taken a century or more to complete, and it would have produced a virtually unusable book. Vast indexes of this sort can now be better accommodated on electronic systems equipped with rapid retrieval devices. But even so, the concept of a *Thesaurus Linguae Graecae* is flawed, simply because the resultant work, however stored, will be too large and complex for the average user to consult. Here again, the dictum that the dictionary is a tool must not be forgotten.

It is difficult to see how any increase in the length of LSJ can be justified. It is already less efficient than the eighth edition of Liddell and Scott; and the combination of LSJ with a large Supplement will make it still more unwieldy. The new Greek–Spanish Dictionary of F. R. Adrados (*DGE*) is also adding to its length by including many proper names; this is still too incomplete to have been much used in this book. The extra entries in the New Supplement will for the most part be of use only to a few epigraphists, papyrologists, and linguists. There is no case at all to be made for an indefinite expansion of the book in printed form, but a master index of the total vocabulary of the language is certainly needed. Thus we have arrived at the parting of the ways: the total lexicon must henceforth be kept in electronic form, so that additions and corrections can be regularly entered, and the dubious words which have so far failed to gain acceptance can be listed with references, in the hope that they may be matched with new discoveries. A continuously progressive lexicon should be created, probably at one location with on-line facilities for consultation at a distance. There need be no limit on its size, provided that access always remains rapid.

But whatever the future of personal computers, it is hard to imagine that we shall ever be able to dispense with the printed book. For most purposes small-scale dictionaries will always be needed. This means that the Lexicon must become more selective, and since the principal users will be students, its coverage needs to be slanted to give prominence to the authors most often studied in schools and university courses. There will always be some users whose needs are different, and a number of different lexica might be edited to serve particular needs. Theological students might require a lexicon which treats especially the Septuagint and the New Testament. Most students of classics concentrate on early epic and lyric, Attic tragedy, Herodotus, Thucydides, Xenophon,

Aristophanes, and the Attic orators, together with Plato and a selection of other fourth- and third-century writers. Some works of Aristotle are widely read, but I suspect that most of that vast corpus is rarely read except by specialists. The later historical writers, such as Polybius and Plutarch's *Lives*, are needed, but probably not Josephus and Strabo. It must constantly be remembered that every author who is added to the list will add several pages to the volume, and the resulting enlargement must be valuable enough to justify the additional weight (i.e. length, work needed for editing, and price).

It is relatively easy to reduce the scale of a good large dictionary, but there is no way a good dictionary can be created out of a bad one. There is now a project to produce a revised edition of the *Intermediate Greek Lexicon* compiled by Liddell himself and published in 1889. This was of course based on the seventh edition of the main lexicon, with only slight additions for the benefit of students. It is to be hoped that in revising this some attention will be paid to the structure of the major articles, which naturally share the faults of their model. A really good lexicon to the major classical authors will do more to keep alive the study of ancient Greek than a dozen supplements, thesauri or other large-scale works. It is my hope that the notes in this book will provide, not only a framework which can be adapted for a few of the more difficult words, but also a model which can be followed by my successors.

Lexicography is not, or should not be, a solo effort. It needs the co-operation of a team which can work together following the same principles and methods. Major projects on ancient Greek are now probably beyond the resources of any one country. We may applaud the valiant attempt of our Spanish colleagues to produce a new Greek-Spanish Lexicon; it will be most welcome, if it is ever completed, but I know I shall not live to see that day. We need to concentrate on smaller projects which can be realised in a more practical period; though good lexicography being the hard taskmaster that it is, we must not expect good work to be produced to a demanding schedule.

Whatever the future holds, I hope that these notes will provide an incitement and a starting point for further work, perhaps not only on ancient Greek, but other languages too. In conclusion I can only revert to the quotation from Epicharmus, which I put at the head of this essay. The essential precept to bear constantly in mind is the need for exercising sober judgment, and adopting a sceptical attitude towards every assertion which cannot be proved by satisfactory evidence. This is true of all forms of scholarship, but it is never more necessary than in the practice of Greek lexicography.

ἀάατος

1 There appear to be only four examples of the word, one in the Iliad, two in the Odyssey in identical contexts, and one in Apollonius Rhodius. In the Iliad the third syllable has a long vowel, elsewhere it is short; but Homer has often enough variations in scansion for this not to be a good argument for a different meaning. The problem therefore is to find a meaning which satisfies all four contexts, and suits the etymology; or if this is impossible, suspicion must fall on the passage in Apollonius, since this is likely to be the result of a misunderstanding of a Homeric use.

2 It is generally agreed that ἀάατος is a negative adjective formed from ἀάω; and whatever its etymology this verb always means *lead into error, mislead*. The sense *hurt, damage* is quoted by LSJ without any example and appears to be a purely etymological speculation. Thus ἀάατος ought to mean *which cannot be led into error, infallible*. This is evidently true of the water of Styx, which will invariably detect a false oath.

ἄγει νῦν μοι ὄμοσσον ἀάατον Στυγὸς ὕδωρ. Il. 14. 271.

So too the contest of the bow is an infallible test for the suitors, because only the true owner has the knack of stringing it.

κατ᾽ αὐτόθι τόξα λιπόντε,
μνηστήρεσσιν ἄεθλον ἀάατον. Od. 21. 91; 22. 5.

(The first reference is defective in LSJ).

3 This meaning, however, is impossible in the fourth passage.

πυγμαχίην, ᾗ κάρτος ἀάατος ᾗ τε χερείων. A. R. 2. 77.

The sense here must be *invincible*, probably due to a misinterpretation of the context in the Odyssey. This note explains the rewriting of this entry in the New Supplement.

ἀγαπητός

1 The adjective appears first in Homer and continues in use down to the present day. It cannot be divided from the verb ἀγαπάω, which never occurs in the Iliad, but only in the Odyssey (21. 289; 23. 214). The more common Homeric verb is ἀγαπάζω. But the obvious explanation of these verbs as denominatives from ἀγάπη runs into the difficulty that the noun does not seem to be attested before iii BC, though its restriction to Judaeo-Christian writers has been disproved (see C. H. Turner, in 3 below). It has therefore been suggested that ἀγάπη is a back-formation from the verb, though this seems unlikely, when verbs in -άω are mainly restricted to denominatives from a-stems.

2 Ἀγάπη, perhaps under the influence of Hebrew 'aḥᵃbāh (Schwyzer, *Gram.* i. 39), became the ordinary word for *love* of all kinds. But it may, as the derivatives show, have originally been restricted to non-sexual love, especially parental affection. It would seem to have replaced the old-fashioned word στοργή, more or less restricted to poetry and high-flown prose. Similarly στέργω is replaced by ἀγαπάω, and στερκτός (only once, in Sophocles *OT* 1338) by ἀγαπητός. Thus ἀγαπάω took over not only the basic meaning of στέργω *feel affection for* (a person), but also the secondary meaning *tolerate cheerfully, be content with* (a situation). This therefore is to be expected also in ἀγαπητός:

κακὸν ἀγαπητὸν ἐν ἐκείνῳ τῷ χρόνῳ. And. 3. 22.

ἀγαπητὸν δ' ἦν τὸ μὴ καὶ προσαπολέσθαι σεσυλημένον.
J. *BJ* 5. 10. 3 [=5. 438].

3 So far there is no problem. But when we turn to LSJ we find as sense **I** of ἀγαπητός 'that wherewith one must be content ... hence of only children.' It should be observed that the corresponding meaning of ἀγαπάω only appears as sense **III**; but if the verbal adjective showed this semantic development, we should expect to find the same in the verb. Part I of LSJ was published in 1925, but a possible explanation of this inversion did not appear until 1926, when C. H. Turner published an article entitled Οὗτός ἐστιν ὁ υἱός μου ὁ ἀγαπητός in *Journal of Theological Studies*, 27. 113–29. He began by quoting the new Lexicon, which he regarded as justifying his claim that the Gospel phrase meant 'This is my *only* son.'

It should be observed that LSJ did not in fact say this; it appears merely to have called attention to the obvious fact that only children are especially dear to their parents, and it is therefore not surprising if in many instances ἀγαπητός is used of only children. Indeed it could be argued that LSJ did not intend their formulation to be read as implying the sense *only*, since they were at pains to define it as *that with which one must be content*, and it would be absurd to suppose that God regarded Jesus Christ as 'the son I have to be content with'. *DGE* goes so far as to begin its meanings with '*único y amadísimo, querido* de hijos únicos'.

4   The early examples of ἀγαπητός confirm that it does not mean *only* (of children). Eurycleia addresses Telemachus:

> πῇ δ' ἐθέλεις ἰέναι πολλὴν ἐπὶ γαῖαν
> μοῦνος ἐὼν ἀγαπητός.   Od. 2. 365.

The epithet μοῦνος would be otiose, if ἀγαπητός meant the same. It is evident that it means 'being greatly loved because you are an only son'. Turner quotes a number of later passages where ἀγαπητός is coupled with μονογενής: e.g. a variant text in LXX *Jd.* 11. 34 has:

> καὶ αὔτη (*sc.* ἡ θυγάτηρ) μονογενὴς αὐτῷ ἀγαπητή, καὶ οὐκ
> ἔστιν αὐτῷ πλὴν αὐτῆς.

Another reading omits ἀγαπητή, but if it is read this is precisely similar to the Homeric example; μονογενής gives the reason why she was beloved. Turner quotes a number of similar passages, apparently being unaware that the presence of another word meaning *only* demonstrates that ἀγαπητός cannot have this sense. In order to prove his contention, he would need to produce an example where ἀγαπητός alone means *only;* and this he fails to do. It is a good example of what my old lexicographic mentor, J. M. Wyllie, named 'contextual contamination'. It is all too easy to suppose that a word has a meaning which is in fact conveyed by other elements in the context.

5   Take for example the New Testament use:

> ἔτι ἕνα εἶχεν, υἱὸν ἀγαπητόν.   *Ev. Marc.* 12. 6.

There too the presence of ἕνα proves that ἀγαπητόν does not

convey that meaning. It is also interesting to compare Matthew's quotation with the original passage of Isaiah, as given by the Septuagint:

τὸ ῥηθὲν διὰ Ἡσαίου τοῦ προφήτου λέγοντος, Ἰδού, ὁ παῖς μου, ὃν ᾑρέτισα· ὁ ἀγαπητός μου, εἰς ὃν εὐδόκησεν ἡ ψυχή μου. *Ev. Matt.* 12. 18.

Ἰσραὴλ ὁ ἐκλεκτός μου, προεδέξατο αὐτὸν ἡ ψυχή μου.
LXX *Is.* 42. 1.

The Septuagint appears to ignore the phrase ὁ ἀγαπητός μου.

6   The explanation of the curious and misleading arrangement in LSJ would appear to be the 'historical principle', which was trumpeted by the *New English Dictionary* as its major achievement. It is the simple theory that if you place first in a dictionary the senses which are attested earliest, you will get a chronological picture of the word's semantic development. Given a common word and large quantities of material for all periods, this is broadly true. But alas, we rarely have enough material for the earliest periods, and it is quite possible that Homer used the word only in a sense which must logically have been secondary. The discovery of Mycenaean Greek has demonstrated that words which we have otherwise only attested from post-Homeric sources were in fact in use five centuries before Homer. It is therefore important that the lexicographer should arrange the senses in a logical order of development, rather than following blindly the historical principle.

ἀγοράζω

1   I have already discussed this word briefly (*BICS* 1994, 4), but I believe it requires a longer discussion, especially to correct a false impression of its use in Thucydides 6. 51. 1. I observed that two of the senses given by LSJ were in fact identical: **1** is '*frequent the ἀγορά*', **3** is '*haunt the ἀγορά*'. It is hard to see how these can be distinguished. In fact sense **3** appears to have started from a scholiast on Ar. *Ach.* 720, who defines ἀγοράζειν as ἐν τῇ ἀγορᾷ διατρίβειν, adding that Corinna criticised Pindar for using it on the grounds that it was an Atticism. From this note LSJ constructed a sense

which it attributes to Corinna and Pindar, although in neither case
are the actual words given by the scholiast. The only genuine
quotation is that from Ar. *Eq.* 1373, which is certainly not to be
distinguished from sense 1 (see 5 below).

2   No one doubts that hanging around the ἀγορά was a common
enough activity in Greek cities. As the main open space at the
heart of a city, it was there that men gathered to talk, in much the
same way as today the same function is discharged by the cafés
surrounding the main square. But it is far from certain that this
meaning was ever conveyed by the verb ἀγοράζω, for the leading
example of this use quoted by LSJ is, to say the least of it, highly
questionable.

3   Herodotus in a passage describing how the Egyptians invert all
the normal customs of human behaviour says:

> αἱ μὲν γυναῖκες ἀγοράζουσι καὶ καπηλεύουσι, οἱ δὲ ἄνδρες
> κατ᾽ οἴκους ἐόντες ὑφαίνουσι.   Hdt. 2. 35. 2.

There is a contrast between the women going out and the men
staying at home, whereas in Greece women stay at home and do
the weaving, and men go out and engage in small-scale trade
(καπηλεύουσι). What does ἀγοράζουσι add to this picture? Surely
it makes the point that in Egypt it is the women who do the
shopping, the implication being that in Greece this is done by
men. Strange as it may seem to us, it was the inevitable consequence of the strict rule that respectable women were not seen in
public unless escorted. So what Herodotus is saying here is that
Egyptian women go to market and engage in trade. It is certainly
no evidence for a sense = ἐν ἀγορᾷ διατρίβειν.

4   LSJ give a second reference for this alleged sense:

> παρὰ τοῦτον (sc. the king of Barca) ἀπικνέεται, καί μιν
> Βαρκαῖοί τε ἄνδρες καὶ τῶν ἐκ Κυρήνης φυγάδων τινὲς
> καταμαθόντες ἀγοράζοντα κτείνουσι.   Hdt. 4. 164. 4.

Here too it is possible that ἀγοράζοντα means 'spending time in
the market-place.' But it is equally plausible to imagine that
his enemies were informed (καταμαθόντες) that he was shopping
in the market, and took the opportunity to assassinate him. The

assumption seems to have been made that anyone as important as
a tyrant, even when fleeing for his life, would not have done his
own shopping. But without knowing what he was shopping for, we
cannot judge this argument. It is surely possible that he was in the
ἀγορά for the normal purpose of making a purchase.

5   The same argument applies to the prohibition of ἀγοράζειν by
boys under the age of puberty in Aristophanes:

> οὐδ' ἀγοράσει γ' ἀγένειος οὐδεὶς ἐν ἀγορᾷ.
> — ποῦ δῆτα Κλεισθένης ἀγοράσει καὶ Στράτων;
>   Ar. Eq. 1373–4.

It could be argued that the prohibition is of idling in the market-
place, and the interlocutor misunderstands it to mean *do one's
shopping*. But if ἀγοράσει means *spend time in the* ἀγορά, why is it
necessary to add the words ἐν ἀγορᾷ? This must mean that ἀγοράσει
here has a more general sense, presumably 'no one without a beard
is to shop in the market-place'. Hence the question ποῦ δῆτα ...
'Where then are K. and S. to do their shopping?' is a serious
question, and the humour consists in grouping these persons
among the ἀγένειοι.

6   Even clearer is the example from Aristophanes' *Acharnians*:

> ἐγὼ δὲ κηρύττω τοῖς Πελοποννησίοις ...
> πωλεῖν ἀγοράζειν πρὸς ἐμέ, Λαμάχῳ δὲ μή.   Ar. Ach. 625.

Here the proclamation is that they are to sell and buy πρὸς ἐμέ. In
other words ἀγοράζειν is treated as a verb of motion, *go and buy*.

7   Very similar is the following:

> οἷον τοῦ ἐλθεῖν ἀπὸ τύχης εἰς τὴν ἀγορὰν καὶ καταλαβεῖν ὃν
> ἐβούλετο μὲν οὐκ ᾤετο δέ, αἴτιον τὸ βούλεσθαι ἀγοράσαι
> ἐλθόντα.   Arist. Ph. 196ᵃ5.

The motive which took him to the market-place was his wish to
buy something, and meeting the man he was looking for there was
an accident. There is no evidence here for a sense *frequent the
market-place*.

8   Less certain, but I think clearly of the same type, is another line of Aristophanes:

καὶ φορήσω τὸ ξίφος τὸ λοιπὸν ἐν μύρτου κλαδί,
ἀγοράσω τ᾽ ἐν τοῖς ὅπλοις ἑξῆς Ἀριστογείτονι.
                                                Ar. Lys. 633.

It would be possible to understand ξίφος as the object of both verbs, but it is more likely that ἀγοράσω is here intransitive, 'do my shopping'.

9   The New Supplement adds an unusual example of the verb being used to mean *hold a meeting, meet in assembly*. An Athenian tribe is to be asked to vote ὅταν ἀγοράζει (= -ζηι) *SEG* 3. 115. 18 (iv BC).

10   So far in all examples ἀγοράζω is intransitive, but the more frequent use is as a transitive verb. This can have two meanings, one of which develops naturally from the other. The earlier sense logically must be *to go to market for*. This occurs frequently in military writers, of soldiers obtaining their provisions. Ancient armies had no standing arrangements for commissariat, and the troops were expected to feed themselves by purchasing, or in some circumstances seizing, local produce. The presence of ἐκ in the following example demonstrates the sense the verb must bear:

ἐκ ταύτης (τῆς πόλεως) οἱ στρατιῶται ἠγόραζον τὰ ἐπιτήδεια.
                                                X. *An.* 1. 5. 10.

The troops were in the habit of going to get supplies from this city. Greek as usual says *from,* where in English we should say *in.* The middle voice is also employed with hardly any distinction in sense:

τὰ δ᾽ ἐπιτήδει᾽ ἀγοράζεσθαι (ἡ δ᾽ ἀγορὰ ἦν ἐν τῷ βαρβαρικῷ στρατεύματι) καὶ συσκευάζεσθαι. X. *An.* 1. 3. 14.

Here the parenthetic remark about the location of the market shows clearly that the verb means *to go to market for.*

11   From this naturally arises the use when the verb describes merely the act of purchase. This is the sense in which the word has come down to Modern Greek, and it answers exactly to English

buy. This predominates in usage, at least from iv BC, and hardly
needs to be exemplified:

ἃ αὐτῇ τῇ ἀνθρώπῳ ἠγοράσθη.   D. 59. 46.

ἔξον αὐτῇ βελτίω πρίασθαι τῆς αὐτῆς τιμῆς, τοῦτον ἠγόρασεν.

D. 21. 149.

It can even be used of buying immaterial things, such as contracts:

οἱ μὲν γὰρ ἀγοράζουσι παρὰ τῶν τιμητῶν (*sc. the Roman
censors*) αὐτοὶ τὰς ἐκδόσεις.   Plb. 6. 17. 4.

12   In the light of this revision of the usage we can now approach
the disputed passage:

καὶ λέγοντος τοῦ Ἀλκιβιάδου, καὶ τῶν ἐν τῇ πόλει πρὸς
τὴν ἐκκλησίαν τετραμμένων, οἱ στρατιῶται πυλίδα τινὰ
ἐνῳκοδομημένην κακῶς ἔλαθον διελόντες, καὶ ἐσελθόντες
ἠγόραζον ἐς τὴν πόλιν.   Th. 6. 51. 1.

The situation described is the effort made by the Athenian expedi-
tion in Sicily to bring Catana over to their side in the attack on
Syracuse. The Catanians refused to admit the army to the city, but
they received a delegation of its officers, and gathered in the
Assembly to hear a speech by Alcibiades. While he was speaking,
the troops discovered a postern gate which had been poorly walled
up, and managed to get it open without attracting attention.
Herwerden proposed deleting ἐς τὴν πόλιν as superfluous; Gomme,
Andrews, and Dover thought ἐσελθόντες might be deleted. But
ἀγοράζω can be used as a verb of motion, so no change is required:
'on entering they went shopping in the town.'

13   At least it is clear that ἀγοράζω is here intransitive, and is used
with ἐς implying motion, exactly like πρὸς ἐμέ in Ar. *Ach.* 625 (see
6 above). There would be no difficulty in guessing the purpose for
which the troops entered the city, were it not for the tradition,
faithfully reported by LSJ, that ἀγοράζω here means *to occupy the
market-place*. Now if this were a clandestine attempt to capture the
city while the citizens were engaged in holding an assembly, it is
curious that Thucydides does not make this clear. In fact, the
whole tone of the narrative implies that this was a casual operation
conducted by the troops on their own initiative, while their officers
were absent. The imperfect ἠγόραζον implies that it took place

gradually, as small numbers of men made their way in. It should now be clear that this was no military operation, but the usual habit of troops on campaign to go looking for provisions in the local market. Their aim was not to exert pressure on the Catanians, for if so, they would have moved quickly to surround the ἐκκλησία; they merely made their way to the market to obtain τὰ ἐπιτήδεια. The result of this action was misinterpreted by the Syracusan party in Catana, which fled at once, leaving the city in the hands of the pro-Athenian party.

14 The senses of this verb should therefore be arranged as follows:

1 (intr.) *go to market, go shopping.*
2 (tr.) *go to market for, buy in a market.*
3 (tr.) *purchase, buy.*
4 (intr.) *hold a meeting, meet in assembly.*

ἀλανής

1 Hesychius has the entries: ἀλανές· ἀληθές and ἀλανέως· ὁλοσχερῶς· Ταραντῖνοι. The adverb is found in an Elean inscription (Schwyzer 412) of vi BC in the form ἀϝλανέος.

2 The etymology of this word is worth a comment, since it could well be identical with ἀολλής. This is believed to be from *ἀ-ϝολνής with Aeolic -ολ- from -l̥- and -λλ- < -λν-, cf. ὀφέλλω. The base form will be a neuter s-stem *welnos, so the compound *sm̥-wlnēs will account for both ἀολλής and ἀ(ϝ)λανής. Elean is a psilotic dialect.

3 The same etymon may perhaps survive in Latin *uolnus*, which might represent an earlier *uelnos. A semantic development would need to be postulated, the basic meaning *pressure* developing to the result of pressure, bruising, and then extended to any kind of injury. A possible Greek cognate is οὐλή, which might be an earlier *ϝολσᾱ. Both would be enlargements of the root *wel-, cf. εἰλέω, probably from *ϝελνέω (see *DELG*).

ἄμαχος

This is defined by LSJ as meaning '*without battle*. **I** *with whom no one fights, unconquerable* ... *irresistible* ... **II** *Act.*, *not having fought, taking no part in the battle* ... **2** *disinclined to fight, not contentious.*' This needs regrouping under the following definitions:

1 *that cannot be fought, irresistible,* used of persons, hands, natural forces, etc.; also of grief, behaviour, etc.: ἄλγος A. *Ag.* 733; ἄμαχος τρόπος Men. *Dysc.* 869.

b (of places) *unsuitable for fighting, impregnable*: ἀπότομός τε γάρ ἐστι ταύτῃ ἡ ἀκρόπολις καὶ ἄμαχος Hdt. 1. 84. 3.

2 *unrivalled in its class, unsurpassable*: ἐγὼ γάρ σε συγκατεῖρξα τούτῳ τῷ ἀμάχῳ πράγματι (of a woman) X. *Cyr.* 6. 1. 36; γεωργός Men. *Dysc.* 775.

3 *not fighting*: X. *Cyr.* 4. 1. 16, *HG* 4. 4. 9; *not given to contention*: *1 Ep. Ti.* 3. 3.; *Ep. Tit.* 3. 2.

4 (of a victory) *gained without fighting*: νίκη Eun. *VS* p. 472B.

ἄνερμα

The New Supplement contains the entry:

ἄνερμος, ον, unexpld. wd., neut. pl. subst., ἄνερμα τοῦ ἱ[ερ]οῦ ἀργύρου *IG* 2².1544.24 (Eleusis, iv BC)

The explanation of this word was proposed by me some years ago, but has not been accepted by the Editor. It appears in a catalogue of objects dedicated in a temple, the previous entries being of silver and each followed by a weight. Here too a weight is given, so it is presumably a silver object. But there is nothing to confirm that it is neuter plural; it might just as well be singular, in which case it will fit into the common class of neuter nouns in -μα derived from verbs. The verb may well be compounded with ἀνα-, so what is needed is a verb with the root -ερ-. Since presents in -ω are largely the product of a suffix *-yō, the present tense may be εἴρω (cf. . e.g. σπείρω, σπέρμα), listed by LSJ as εἴρω (A) and almost certainly for *εἴρω (cf. Lat. *series*, etc.). In fact the compound ἀνείρω exists, defined by LSJ as '*fasten on* or *to, string*'; and there is an example from a Delos inscription of ἐνώτια ἀργυρᾶ ἀνειρμένα. It should be obvious that ἄνερμα is *that on which objects are threaded*, here probably a silver chain or wire used to attach the objects to a temple wall.

ἀντίον, ἀντία

1 The use of the neuter of ἀντίος as an adverb requires some comment, especially in view of the discussion to which it has given rise in Hes. *Op.* 481. It is sometimes constructed with a genitive or less often dative, as if it were in the process of becoming a preposition. But semantically this usage is not really distinct from the purely adverbial, and the examples can be conveniently discussed together.

2 The primary sense is *in a position opposite the face of the speaker*:

> αὐτὸς δ’ ἀντίον ἷζεν.   Od. 14. 79, cf. 17. 334.

Closely allied to this is its use with verbs of speaking:

> τὸν δ’ αὖ Νεστορίδης Πεισίστρατος ἀντίον ηὔδα.
> Od. 15. 48 et passim.

With genitive, *opposite to, facing*:

> ἀντίον ἀκραέος Ζεφύρου τρέψαντα πρόσωπα.   Hes. *Op.* 594.
> τὰς δὲ καμήλους ἔταξε ἀντία τῆς ἵππου.   Hdt. 1. 80. 4.
> ἀντίον δὲ τοῦ μεγάρου.   Hdt. 5. 77. 3.

3 A more developed sense is where it means not simply *facing*, but *in the presence of* (Latin *coram*). With genitive:

> μέγα δὲ δμῶες χατέουσι
> ἀντία δεσποίνης φάσθαι καὶ ἔκαστα πυθέσθαι.   Od. 15. 377.
> ἐντειλάμενος μηδένα ἀντίον αὐτῶν μηδεμίαν φωνὴν ἱέναι.
> Hdt. 2. 2. 2; cf. 7. 209. 2.

4 A natural development is to mean *in opposition to, against*:

> ἢ πολὺ λώϊόν ἐστι κατὰ στρατὸν εὐρὺν Ἀχαιῶν
> δῶρ’ ἀποαιρεῖσθαι ὅς τις σέθεν ἀντίον εἴπῃ.   Il. 1. 230.

This clearly means not 'in your presence', but 'in opposition to you'. Similarly:

πῶς δὲ σὺ νῦν μέμονας, κύον ἀδεές, ἀντί' ἐμεῖο
στήσεσθαι;   Il. 21. 481.

Μεγάβυζος, ὃς ἐν Αἰγύπτῳ ἀντία Ἀθηναίων καὶ τῶν
συμμάχων ἐστρατήγησε.   Hdt. 3. 160. 2.

With dative:

Λακεδαιμόνιοι δὲ ἢν ἴωσι ἀντία Πέρσῃσι ἐς μάχην.
Hdt. 7. 236. 3.

οὐκ ἐρίζων ἀντία τοῖς ἀγαθοῖς.   Pi. P. 4. 285; cf. N. 1. 25.

5   We can now turn to the Hesiod passage mentioned, which describes the unsatisfactory results of ploughing too late in the season:

ἥμενος ἀμήσεις ὀλίγον περὶ χειρὸς ἐέργων,
ἀντία δεσμεύων κεκονιμένος, οὐ μάλα χαίρων,
οἴσεις δ' ἐν φορμῷ.   Hes. Op. 481.

The traditional interpretation of this passage is: 'You will do your reaping sitting down [because the stalks are so short] and gather little in your hand, binding [the sheaves] with their ends facing opposite ways, covered in dust, no pleasant task, and you will bring them [home] in a skep.' (A *skep* is the technical term for the large wicker basket used by farmers for carrying bulky loads, so this implies that there will be not enough for a waggon-load.) The meaning attributed to ἀντία here, *facing opposite ways,* comes from the *Scholia vetera,* quoted by M. L. West *ad loc.*: τὰ γεννήμα⟨τά⟩ σου ἀντ⟨ί'⟩ ἀλλήλων δεσμεύσεις διὰ τὴν βραχύτητα· τὸ γὰρ ἐπίμηκες ἐν τῷ μέσῳ δεσμεῖται. Here ἀντία plainly means 'facing each other', but the presence of ἀλλήλων is crucial. It is less clear why the shortness of the stalks makes this necessary. But West has an answer: 'The ἐλλεδανοί with which they were bound ... would slip off if the straw was too short, unless the sheaf was made with ears at both ends.' This might be true, but it does not fit the following clause of the *Scholion:* 'for an elongated object is tied in the middle'. Whether the ears are at one end or both, the sheaf will still be ἐπίμηκες. Perhaps the idea is that by this alternating arrangement the effective length of the sheaf will be increased.

6 But just because the editors have, in some cases reluctantly, accepted this ancient interpretation, this does not make it the correct one. We must ask ourselves: is this a plausible meaning for ἀντία, and are there other examples to confirm it? It would seem clear that there are no parallels, at least in early Greek. So perhaps we should look for a simpler explanation.

7 I believe the solution to this problem lies in determining where the emphasis falls. Obviously ἥμενος at the beginning of 480 is emphatic: 'you will sit down to reap'; and ἐν φορμῷ in 482: 'you will do your carting in a skep' [i.e. one man will be able to carry the whole crop]. The curious sense given to ἀντία assumes that it too is emphatic; but I think the emphasis falls better on κεκονιμένος: 'you will get covered in dust as you do your binding'. If we suppose that ἀντία merely describes the normal (indeed, only) way to bind sheaves, we can give it its proper meaning: *in a facing direction, straight ahead*. If you are sitting down with the stalks of corn across your knees, there is only one way you can bind them, at right angles to the way they lie, which is correctly described from the speaker's point of view as *straight ahead*. It is therefore unnecessary to invent a new and unparalleled sense for the word on the basis of this passage. Of course, if satisfactory parallels can be found, this may change the balance of probability. But I believe that the simple, straightforward and obvious meaning must always be chosen, until it can be shown to be inappropriate to the passage.

ἄντομος

1 This word is known from only two sources, the *Tabulae Heracleenses* (Schwyzer 62, 63), a long inscription of iv BC recording the operations of boundary commissioners, and the lexicon of Hesychius. There would have been no problem in determining its meaning and etymology, but for the information supplied by the lexicographer. It is certainly true that Hesychius preserves for us a number of rare words which would otherwise be unknown. But he often offers for his entries meanings which cannot be supported by known usage, and these must remain doubtful. Indeed, it is often possible to see that his synonyms are, if not wrong,

sometimes only half-right. Thus we ought in a case like this to rely much more on the evidence of usage than on ancient testimony.

2 The sense of the word is easy to deduce from passages such as these:

συνεμετρήσαμες δὲ ἀρξάμενοι ἀπὸ τῶ ἀντόμω τῶ hυπὲρ Πανδοσίας ἄγοντος τῶ διατάμνοντος τώς τε hιαρὼς χώρως καὶ τὰν Ϝιδίαν γᾶν ἐπὶ τὸν ἄντομον τὸν ὁρίζοντα τώς τε τῶ Διονύσω χώρως καὶ τὸν Κωνέας hο Δίωνος ἐπαμώχη.

1. 12, 13.

τετάρτα μερὶς ἀπὸ Ϝικατιδείω μᾶκος μὲν ἀπὸ τῶ ἀντόμω τῶ ἐς πόταμον ἄγοντος ποτὶ τὰν πόθοδον τὰν πὰρ τὰς ἀμπέλως ἄγωσαν, εὖρος ... κτλ. 2. 93.

These make it clear that an ἄντομος is a visible linear feature separating one plot from another, and distinguished from an access road (πόθοδος). As such, we might think of a fence or hedge; but in open country it is the usual practice simply to leave a narrow strip of uncultivated ground to serve as a marker. This is presumably what ἄντομος means, and its technical name in English is *baulk*.

3 The etymology is also clear. It is a dialect form of *ἀνάτομος, with apocope of the preposition, probably an adjective in origin, implying a suppressed substantive. But the meaning *cut off* or *dissected* is inappropriate. More likely therefore we should treat the compound as active in sense, meaning *divider;* cf. τέμνω **II 4** in LSJ and section 16 of my note on this word.

4 The Hesychius entry reads:

ἀντόμους· σκόλοπας· Σικελοί.

Pointed stakes might of course make up a fence, and these too would serve to mark a boundary. But it is unlikely that the lands described in the *Tabulae* would all be fenced. Rather it seems as if this is an etymological deduction from ἄντομος as meaning *cut up,* i.e. sharpened. Whether such a sense existed or not, it is impossible to tell. But the attested use of the word can now be accepted, and the lexicographer's note held in limbo until an example is found to confirm it.

ἀπέχω

1 LSJ gives as sense **IV** '*have* or *receive in full*'. The examples quoted are:

ἐπειδὴ δὲ ἀνεγνώσθη (ἡ ἐπιστολή), Ἀπέχετε, ἔφην, τὴν ἀπόκρισιν, καὶ λοιπὸν ὑμῖν ἐστι βουλεύσασθαι.

Aeschin. 2. 50.

ἐπεσσομένοισιν ὁρᾶσθαι
ἡ γρηῢς μαστῶν ὡς ἀπέχει χάριτας. Call. *Epigr.* 50 Pf.

τὸ χρέος ὡς ἀπέχεις, Ἀσκληπιέ ... γιγνώσκειν.
Ibid. 54 Pf.

ἀμὴν λέγω ὑμῖν, ἀπέχουσιν τὸν μισθὸν αὐτῶν.
Ev. Matt. 6. 2.

ὁ γὰρ ἐν γάμῳ παρορῶν τὸ καλὸν οὐ τέκνων ἕνεκα δῆλός ἐστιν, ἀλλ᾽ ἡδονῆς ἀγόμενος γυναῖκα, τόν τε μισθὸν ἀπέχει, καὶ παρρησίαν αὐτῷ πρὸς τοὺς γενομένους οὐκ ἀπολέλοιπεν, οἷς αὐτὸ τὸ γενέσθαι πεποίηκεν ὄνειδος. Plu. *Sol.* 22. 4.

ὥστε καὶ αὐτὸν ... ὁμολογῆσαι τὸν καρπὸν ἀπέχειν τῶν ... ποιηθέντων. Plu. *Them.* 17.

τὸ δ᾽ ἀπέχοντα τῇ φύσει τὸ μέτριον καὶ πεπληρωμένον ἐπιδράττεσθαι τῶν τοιούτων. Plu. 2. 124e.

ἀπέχω παρ᾽ ὑμῶν τὸν φόρον τοῦ ἐλα[ι]ουργίου.
BGU 612. 2 (i AD).

The New Supplement adds:

Θηβαῖοι μὲν ἀπέχουσι τὰ οἰκεῖα, Φωκεῖς δὲ ἅπαντα ἀπολωλέκασι. D. *fr.* 23 S.

2 There is nothing in any of these examples to suggest that payment is made *in full*. But in every case the present tense describes the result of a past action, and it is clear that in Plu. *Sol.* 22. 4 and in the new example from the fragment of Demosthenes it is coupled with a perfect. In other words ἀπέχω functions as the perfect of ἀποδέχομαι, just as ἔχω often means 'to have acquired' and so 'to possess'. The definition should therefore be emended to read: *to have received*.

ἁπλόος

1   An inscription from Miletus of iii AD (*SEG* 30. 1352) mentions that:

τῆς ἐπιγραφῆς ἁπλοῦν ἀπετέθη εἰς τὸ ἀρχεῖον.

Clearly this means that a text of the inscription was deposited in the archives; but what sort of text is so described? Surely it was the *original*, from which the inscription was engraved.

2   LSJ quotes:

χαρίσασθαι μὲν αὐτῇ τὰς ἐκ Περγάμου βιβλιοθήκας, ἐν αἷς εἴκοσι μυριάδες βιβλίων ἁπλῶν ἦσαν. Plu. *Ant.* 58.

This can hardly mean, as LSJ state, 'rolls *containing a single author*', since each major author would have been represented by a number of rolls (Homer by 48, Thucydides by 8, for instance). It is more likely to mean 'excluding duplicates', because a large number could easily be achieved by counting separately each copy of a book. The modern equivalent would be '200,000 *titles*'.

ἀραιός

1   The first sense given by LSJ is '*thin, slender ... narrow ... meagre*'. This is a remarkably vague sense for a word which is usually much more precise. Sense **II** then begins 'later, of the substance of bodies, *of loose texture*'. What does 'later' mean? Sense **I** includes examples from Homer, Hesiod, Xenophon, Aristotle, Nicander, and Plutarch. So it can hardly mean later than all of these writers, since it begins with the Presocratics, Anaximenes, Melissus, and Anaxagoras. Any attempt to sort out this muddle needs to begin by choosing clear and unambiguous examples; then, once the pattern has been established, we may be able to see where the passages cited in sense **I** fit.

2   There can be little doubt that the predominant sense of the word is *having gaps or intervals*, for as LSJ rightly records it is frequently used as the opposite to πυκνός. The Presocratics used it as a technical term for *rarefied* forms of matter, and this usage continues in later Greek, as for instance:

ἀναθυμίασις ... νέφους ἀραιοτέρα. Arist. *Mu.* 394ᵃ21.

In more general terms it means *of loose texture*, for instance in the medical writers of parts of the body:

τὰ δὲ πυκνά τε καὶ τεθηλότα, τὰ δὲ σπογγοειδέα καὶ ἀραιά.
Hp. *VM* 22.

ὁκόσοισι δὲ (δέρματα) χαλαρὰ καὶ ἀραιά, σὺν ἱδρῶτι τελευτῶσιν. Hp. *Aph.* 5. 71.

ἁπαλὸν γὰρ καὶ ἀραιὸν χρῆμά ἐστιν ὁ πλεύμων.
Hp. *Nat. Puer.* 24.

It can be used of anything *loosely structured*, for instance:

εἴρια, ἅτε ἀραιά τε καὶ μαλθακὰ ἐόντα. Hp. *Mul.* 1. 1.

σπόγγοις ἀραιοῖς. D. S. 3. 14.

Here it is not merely an epithet of sponges, but designates those which are especially loose. Of plants:

τὰ μὲν στερεὰ καὶ πυκνὰ ἐν τοῖς ξηροῖς φυτεύειν, τὰ δ' ἀραιὰ καὶ ὑγρὰ ἐν τοῖς μαλακωτέροις καὶ ἐφυγροτέροις.
Thphr. *CP* 2. 4. 7.

3 Arising naturally from this is the use in the plural to mean *having gaps between them, widely spaced, sparse*:

καὶ γὰρ ἀσθενεῖς αἱ τρίχες καὶ ἀραιαὶ καὶ βραχεῖαι τὸ πρῶτον ἅπασιν ἐπιγίγνονται τοῖς παιδίοις. Arist. *Col.* 797ᵇ27.

καὶ γὰρ ταῦτα (sc. *water and air*) εἶναι δοκεῖ μέλανα, βάθος ἔχοντα, διὰ τὸ παντελῶς ἀραιὰς ἀνακλᾶσθαι τοὺς ἀκτῖνας.
Ibid. 791ᵃ27.

νέφεσι δὲ πυκνοῦσι τὸν οὐρανὸν καικίας μὲν σφόδρα, λὶψ δὲ ἀραιοτέροις. Arist. *Mete.* 364ᵇ25.

The last passage is translated by H. D. P. Lee (Loeb) 'Caecias fills the sky with thick clouds, Lips with thinner.' But πυκνοῦσι goes with both winds; 'both Caecias and Lips cover the sky thickly with clouds, but in the case of Lips these are more widely spaced.' There is a good example from Pollux quoting Aristotle:

Ἀριστοτέλης δέ φησι ... τοὺς μὲν ἔχοντας πυκνοὺς καὶ συνεχεῖς τοὺς ὀδόντας, μακροβίους· τὸ ἐναντίον δέ, ὅποσοι ἀραιούς. Poll. 2. 94.

4   As noted by LSJ (**II 2**), ἀραιός is used by military writers to
mean *in open order*:

> τό τε ἀραιότατον, καθ' ὃ ἀλλήλων ἀπέχουσι κατά τε μῆκος
> καὶ βάθος ἕκαστοι πήχεις τέσσαρας καὶ τὸ πυκνότατον ...
>
> Ascl. Tact. 4. 1.

But as we shall see, further examples of this use have already
appeared in sense **I**.

5   It is a general rule that words which describe spatial arrangement can also be used to show arrangement in time; for instance,
before, πρό, etc. mean both *in front of* and *previous to*. Thus we
should expect to find ἀραιός meaning also (of events) *occurring at
intervals, intermittent*. Again the medical writers offer the best
examples:

> τούτῳ πνεῦμα διὰ τέλεος, ὥσπερ ἀνακαλεομένῳ, ἀραιόν,
> μέγα.   Hp. *Epid.* 1. 26. α'.

This describes a comatose patient in a terminal illness: 'his breathing throughout was as if he had to summon it up, with pauses
between deep breaths.' So of the pulse:

> εἰ μὲν οὖν μείζους εἶεν οἱ τῶν ἡσυχιῶν χρόνοι τοῦ κατὰ φύσιν,
> ἀραιὸν ὀνομάζουσιν τὸν σφυγμόν· εἰ δὲ ἐλάττους, πυκνόν.
>
> Gal. 9. 444.

In other contexts:

> τοιαύτας καὶ τὰς φωνὰς συμβαίνει γίγνεσθαι προσπιπτούσας
> πρὸς τὴν ἀκοήν, οἷον ἀραιὰς ἢ πυκνὰς, ἢ μαλακὰς ἢ σκληρὰς,
> ἢ λεπτὰς ἢ παχείας.   Arist. *Aud.* 803ᵇ28.

This is listed by LSJ in sense **IV** under the heading *scanty, few and
far between,* together with the hair of young children and the rays
reflected off water, both of which are spatial.

6   Having established this pattern, we can now turn to LSJ's
sense **I**, and some other alleged senses. In the Iliad ἀραιός is four
times used of parts of the body; three of these are easy, the fourth
is more difficult to explain. Athena is being bitchy about the
wound Aphrodite has received from Diomedes, and cattily
suggests it was a scratch from a brooch:

> πρὸς χρυσῇ περόνῃ καταμύξατο χεῖρα ἀραιήν.   Il. 5. 425.

This is not *slender* (LSJ) or *dainty* (Rieu), but is strongly derogatory, more like English *flabby*. It also has a suggestion of weakness, and this too is obvious in the description of Hephaistos with his brawny arms but withered legs:

ὑπὸ δὲ κνῆμαι ῥώοντο ἀραιαί.
Il. 18. 411, cf. 20. 37.

7 The fourth example is different. It occurs in the long simile about the wolves which have brought down a deer and then go in a pack to drink at a spring:

καί τ᾽ ἀγεληδὸν ἴασιν ἀπὸ κρήνης μελανύδρου
λάψοντες γλώσσῃσιν ἀραιῇσι μέλαν ὕδωρ,
ἀκρόν, ἐρευγόμενοι φόνον αἵματος. Il. 16. 161.

The translators and commentators offer such versions as *narrow*, *slender*, *thin* (Willcock). But wolves' tongues are not, so far as I can discover, notably narrow. They might be described as *thin* in the sense of lacking thickness, or we might suppose that the word is again used in the sense of *flabby*. But Homeric similes are usually the result of careful observation and accurate description. What would be most noticeable about the tongues of a pack of wolves which were lapping the surface of a pool? Surely the fact that they were in constant motion, coming and going. They would thus be *intermittent*, a sense we have already established for this word at a later date. Perhaps the best translation would be *flickering*.

8 We come now to the only example of the word in the Odyssey, where it occurs in the description of the harbour of the Laestrygonians:

ἔνθ᾽ ἐπεὶ ἐς λιμένα κλυτὸν ἤλθομεν, ὃν πέρι πέτρη
ἠλίβατος τετύχηκε διαμπερὲς ἀμφοτέρωθεν,
ἀκταὶ δὲ προβλῆτες ἐναντίαι ἀλλήλῃσιν
ἐν στόματι προὔχουσιν, ἀραιὴ δ᾽ εἴσοδός ἐστιν. Od. 10. 90.

The scene is clear: the harbour is surrounded by high cliffs on both sides, and headlands jut out facing each other at its mouth, and the entrance is ἀραιή. The description goes on to relate how the water inside was never rough, so all the other captains brought their ships inside; only Odysseus had his ship tied to a rock outside, so that when they were attacked he could cut the rope and escape.

The translation *narrow* looks at first sight inescapable. But if the original meaning was, as I have suggested, *having gaps,* then perhaps it was intended to mean 'the entrance is the gap between them'. The passage can hardly be assigned to the same sense as Aphrodite's hand or the wolves' tongues.

9 Hesiod uses the adjective once, to describe ships. The context is unhelpful, because it occurs in his calendar of lucky and unlucky days:

τετράδι δ' ἄρχεσθαι νῆας πήγνυσθαι ἀραιάς.   Hes. *Op.* 809.

This is not a stock epithet, but it too has been taken as meaning *narrow.* But what are these narrow ships? Certainly not the ordinary merchant ship of Hesiod's time. The epithet would only be suitable for a warship, which cannot be Hesiod's meaning. It is so inappropriate as a descriptive epithet it must surely have some more functional meaning. Now πήγνυσθαι is certainly the word for building a ship; cf. the noun ναυπηγός. But its basic meaning is *fasten together,* the vital carpentry which creates a ship. The first stage is lay a keel, then to fit to this ribs and connect them with stringers, the longitudinal members; at this stage the outline of the ship is clearly visible, but it lacks the planking of the hull. It is therefore a mere skeleton, which could quite properly be described as *having gaps.* It would make sense if Hesiod recommended the fourth as a suitable day for making a start on constructing the framework of ships. Even if this explanation seems too far-fetched, *narrow* cannot be right, nor is Mazon's *sveltes* (Budé) any better.

10 There is another passage in early epic ignored by LSJ, but which certainly requires a commentary. This is in the Homeric hymn to Hermes, and is part of the description of how he carried off the cattle of Apollo. Being well aware that they would leave tracks, especially in the sandy place they had to cross, Hermes used short baulks of timber to lengthen his legs, so that he would not leave tracks recognisable as those of a small boy. It is necessary to quote a long section:

τὰ δ' ἄρ' ἴχνια δοιὰ πέλωρα
οἷά τ' ἀγάσσασθαι καὶ ἀγανοῦ δαίμονος ἔργα.
τῇσιν μὲν γὰρ βουσὶν ἐς ἀσφοδελὸν λειμῶνα
ἀντία βήματ' ἔχουσα κόνις ἀνέφαινε μέλαινα·   345

αὐτὸς δ᾽ οὗτος ὁ δεκτός, ἀμήχανος, οὔτ᾽ ἄρα ποσσὶν
οὔτ᾽ ἄρα χερσὶν ἔβαινε διὰ ψαμαθώδεα χῶρον·
ἀλλ᾽ ἄλλην τινὰ μῆτιν ἔχων διέτριβε κέλευθα
τοῖα πέλωρ᾽ ὡς εἴ τις ἀραιῇσι δρυσὶ βαίνοι.   h. Merc. 349.

The beginning of line 346 is corrupt and some editions print αὐτὸς
δ᾽ ἐκτὸς ὁδοῦ, τις, but whatever the reading it will not affect the
general picture. Hermes took care not to walk on his feet or his
hands when crossing the sandy spot. But he pressed deeply tracks
such as a monster might make (πέλωρα), 'as if someone walked on
ἀραιῇσι timbers.' This clearly refers, though I have been unable to
find this explanation in translations and commentaries, to the use
of wooden stilts. The effect of these is to lengthen the stride and,
owing to the extra weight, to make deep impressions (διέτριβε);
thus anyone studying the tracks might well conclude that the
cattle-rustler was not a boy, but a large monster. The epithet
ἀραιῇσι is transferred from the prints to the objects which made
them, but it clearly means *widely spaced,* a characteristic of tracks
left by a person on stilts. This explanation of διέτριβε seems to me
preferable to that offered by the New Supplement, for I do not see
how '*space out* tracks' could be extracted from this verb, although
it would suit my interpretation of the passage.

11   We come now to the later examples assigned by LSJ to sense
I. In Nicander the adjective is applied to the belly:

ἐπεὶ διὰ μητρὸς ἀραιήν
γαστέρ᾽ ἀναβρώσαντες ἀμήτορες ἐξεγένοντο.   Nic. Th. 133.

There seems no reason why this should not refer to the flabby
structure of the belly, as in the medical examples quoted above;
and the same would hold for LSJ's sense **V**, where the feminine is
apparently used alone with the same sense (Ruf. *Onom.* 171). In
fact Nicander is fond of ἀραιός; there are five more examples in the
Theriaca, only one of which is quoted by LSJ (**II 1 b**) as meaning
empty when applied to blisters. Here too there is no reason why it
should not mean *flabby,* which empty blisters are.

12   In this section LSJ add with 'cf.' a passage of Theocritus
which calls for discussion:

ἐγὼ δέ σε τὸν καλὸν αἰνέων
ψεύδεα ῥινὸς ὕπερθεν ἀραιῆς οὐκ ἀναφύσω.   Theoc. 12. 24.

The sense is plainly: 'if I call you beautiful, I shall not be proved a liar.' The scholia tell us that ψεύδεα are spots or pimples which appear on the faces of liars. Gow (ad loc.) debates whether ὕπερθεν means *on* the nose or *above* the nose, and opts for the latter. But if it means on the forehead there is little point in adding an epithet to the nose; so I should prefer to take it as meaning *on,* i.e. sticking up from, the nose. Gow has a learned note, expanded in *JHS* 71 (1951), 81, explaining that a sharp nose was regarded as a sign of honesty, and ἀραιή meaning *thin* might be regarded as the same as ὀξεῖα. However, as we have seen, there is no evidence for the sense *thin, slender,* but we have for *flabby.* Surely this is the meaning intended; spots are typical of loose, flabby flesh.

13   I discussed earlier the military use of ἀραιός to mean *widely spaced* of men in battle formation. It is hard to understand why LSJ inserted in sense **I** instead of **II 2** the examples from Xenophon and Plutarch, which must be quoted:

> αἱ δὲ παραγωγαὶ ὥσπερ ὑπὸ κήρυκος ὑπὸ τοῦ ἐνωμοτάρχου λόγῳ δηλοῦνται ⟨καὶ⟩ ἀραιαί τε καὶ βαθύτεραι αἱ φάλαγγες γίγνονται. X. *Lac.* 11. 6.

> ἀραιὰν τὴν φάλαγγα τῶν ὁπλιτῶν ἐπὶ πλεῖστον ἀνάγων τοῦ πεδίου. Plu. *Crass.* 23.

These appear to be classified as *narrow* by LSJ, which might fit the Xenophon passage, if as they suggest βαθύτεραι is taken as its direct opposite. But it is clear from the passage of Asclepiodotus quoted above (4) that the spacing of men in a *phalanx* can vary laterally and longitudinally. The line becomes sparse by increasing the distance to left and right of each man, deeper by increasing the distance between the lines. The Plutarch example cannot of course mean *narrow;* the line was extended so as to cover most of the plain.

14   This leaves us with only one further example of sense **I**:

> χρὴ δὲ καὶ τὰς ἐγκύους ἐπιμελεῖσθαι τῶν σωμάτων, μὴ ῥαθυμούσας μηδ' ἀραιᾷ τροφῇ χρωμένας.

> Arist. *Pol.* 1335ᵇ13.

It is of course possible that Aristotle meant *meagre* as LSJ translates; but since this sense has not been proved to exist, it would obviously be preferable to assign it to a well-attested sense, namely *intermittent* (see 5 above). Pregnant women are not to get slack and skip meals.

15   There remains sense **VI** 'of the voice, *thin*' in Theocritus. If *meagre* of food were established, *thin* or *feeble* of the voice would be possible. But without that support I think we should look for another explanation of the passage in the Hylas epyllion:

τρὶς μὲν Ὕλαν ἄυσεν, ὅσον βαθὺς ἤρυγε λαιμός·
τρὶς δ᾽ ἄρ᾽ ὁ παῖς ὑπάκουσεν, ἀραιὰ δ᾽ ἵκετο φωνά
ἐξ ὕδατος, παρέων δὲ μάλα σχεδὸν εἴδετο πόρρω.

                                          Theoc. 13. 59.

Here the last clause obviously means that a person standing very close perceived the voice as distant; hence the idea that ἀραιά means *faint*. But would Theocritus have repeated the idea so blatantly? Surely it is much better if we can give a different sense to ἀραιά, so that the last clause adds something more to the picture. Since the call came and was answered three times, it is quite possible that the adjective means *sounding at intervals*, i.e. with a gap in time between each reply. A new sense at least needs far better evidence than this to be acceptable and an isolated example should in preference be attached to a well-known sense.

16   In conclusion I give the scaffolding on which I would construct a new Lexicon article on this word. The numbers in brackets refer to the sections above where the examples are quoted and discussed.

> **1** *containing spatial discontinuities or gaps, loosely structured, of loose texture* (2). **b** of parts of the body, *lacking firmness, flabby* (6, 11, 12). **c** of a gap, *narrow*.
> **2** in plural, *having gaps intervening, widely spaced, sparse* (3, 10). **b** in military use, *in open order* (4, 13).
> **3** *occurring at intervals of time, intermittent* (5, 14, 15). **b** *appearing and disappearing, flickering* (7).

17   Finally, a speculation about the etymology. The scansion in Homer suggests that the word may have had Ϝα-, though no proof of this has been found. If so, it is tempting to think that Latin *uarius* might be a cognate, if it means *discontinuously coloured,*

patchy. Greek does not show this development, which is covered by another word, αἰόλος. The connexion has not hitherto been evident, owing to the failure to grasp the basic meaning of ἀραιός.

ἀργύριος

LSJ recorded this as an Aeolicism in Alcman (the up-to-date reference is 1.55 P). It is well known that Aeolic has adjectives of material with the suffix -ιος replacing the more usual -εος. In the 1968 Supplement Aeolic was changed to Laconian, in accordance with the modern view that most of Alcman's dialect forms are taken from early Laconian. But the editor failed to remember that in Laconian εο > ιο, so that this is not a separate formation, but merely a dialect modification of the familiar ἀργύρεος, ἀργυροῦς. In the New Supplement it has been moved to this article. It should also be added that ἀργύριον πρόσωπον can hardly mean *a silver face*, but it is a poetic extension, probably *shining like silver, silvery*.

ἁρπακτός

LSJ gives as sense **2** '*to be caught*, i.e. *to be got by chance, hazardous*' in Hesiod. The passage runs:

> εἰαρινὸς πέλεται πλόος· οὔ μιν ἔγωγε
> αἴνημ', οὐ γὰρ ἐμῷ θυμῷ κεχαρισμένος ἐστίν
> ἁρπακτός· χαλεπῶς κε φύγοις κακόν.   Hes. *Op.* 684.

The translators and commentators are unanimous in agreeing that ἁρπακτός here means *snatched*, i.e. executed rapidly in the intervals of bad weather. See Sinclair, Evelyn-White; 'il faut en saisir l'instant' Mazon (Budé). West's note on line 320 emphasises correctly that the word means *snatched*, and not *to be snatched* as Mazon's translation seems to imply, but fails to explain in what respect, since in the other use it is applied to property. It is obvious that LSJ's explanation is unsatisfactory and needs to be changed as in the New Supplement.

ἀσσκονικτεί

1 This word appears on a ἁλτήρ found at Olympia and inscribed in the Laconian alphabet of vi BC. It is clear from parallels that this form is a variant of the regular ἀκονιτεί, meaning 'without raising the dust', i.e. 'without much effort'. The problem is to explain the form, which Hansen (*CEG* 372) regards as not yet solved. The full text reads:

Ἀκματίδας Λακεδαιμόνιος νικον ἀνέθεκε τὰ πέντε ἀσσκονικτεί.

2 There are two details which require explanation: the -σ- which apparently precedes the root of κόνις, and the presence of an intrusive -κ- before -τει. The doubling of the -σ- in this position is frequent in inscriptions; cf. Ἀσσκληπιός. But there seems to be no trace of a form *σκόνις, with the doubtful exception of the Modern Greek σκόνη. However, variants with and without this 'movable' s- do occur, often visible only in cognates in other languages, such as Gk. σχίζω, Sanskrit *khidati*. But this is usual only where Sanskrit has *kh, ph* answering to Gk. χ, φ. Attempts have been made (as in the 1968 Supplement to LSJ) to invoke σκορακίζω as a parallel; but this is simply due to the loss of an initial vowel in allegro pronunciation, being derived from ἐς κόρακας as an imprecation. A similar oath (ἐ)ς κόνιν might perhaps have been used by wrestlers attempting to throw their opponent, but remains unattested.

3 But whatever the origin of the σ-, the -κ- also demands explanation. Adverbs of this type are formed from adjectives in -τος, though ἀκόνιτος is recorded only at a late date (Q. Smyrnaeus 4. 319). So ἀσσκονικτεί demands a stem *σκονικ- meaning *dust*. This can be explained by supposing that in Laconian the i-stem had been extended by a velar. This is exactly what happened in West Greek to *κλαϝίς, which can be reconstructed both from Mycenaean *ka-ra-wi-po-ro* = /klāwiphoros/ and from the probable Latin loan-word of very early date *clāuis*. This in Attic–Ionic received a dental extension (κλείς, κλειδός, κληΐς, κληΐδος). At Epidaurus and elsewhere we have κλαιξ, κλαικος, probably with a long diphthong (i.e. κλᾷξ). It would thus seem likely that the Laconian for *dust* had the form *σκόνιξ, σκόνικος.

ἀτεχνῶς

The adjective ἀτεχνής is hardly recorded before late Greek, so it has been generally assumed that ἀτεχνῶς is not the adverb from it, but is from ἄτεχνος (Plato onwards), with shift of accent. See e.g. Schwyzer, *Gram.* ii 414. The new example of Ionic ἀτεχνεως in an inscription of iv BC from Olynthus (*TAPhA* 65 (1934), 105; see the New Supplement) must reopen this question, for this can only come from ἀτεχνής. It is thus clear that its absence from the record of classical Greek is probably an accident, and the theory of an aberrant accent can be abandoned.

ἄχυρον

1   There is considerable confusion about this simple word due to a faulty definition in LSJ, which reads: '*chaff, bran, husks* left after threshing or grinding'. This omits to mention the chief waste product of threshing, *straw*, but this is almost always what ἄχυρα means.

2   The clearest evidence can be found in a passage of Xenophon:

> ἂν μὲν βραχὺς ᾖ ὁ κάλαμος τοῦ σίτου, ἔγωγ', ἔφην, κάτωθεν
> ἂν τέμνοιμι, ἵνα ἱκανὰ τὰ ἄχυρα γίγνηται. X. *Oec.* 18. 2.

In a discussion about reaping the question is how near the ground the stalk should be cut; so if the stalks are short, the cut should be made low, so as to yield sufficient *straw*. It is obvious that *chaff* makes no sense here. Similarly:

> συνάξει τὸν σῖτον αὐτοῦ εἰς τὴν ἀποθήκην, τὸ δὲ ἄχυρον
> κατακαύσει πυρὶ ἀσβέστῳ. *Ev. Matt.* 3. 12.

A disputed passage of Theocritus needs to be mentioned here.

> σῖτον ἀλοιῶντας φεύγειν τὸ μεσαμβρινὸν ὕπνον·
> ἐκ καλάμας ἄχυρον τελέθει τημόσδε μάλιστα.
> Theoc. 10. 49.

This passage has caused commentators and lexicographers much perplexity; see Gow *ad loc.* and the New Supplement. It is generally agreed that the sense of the couplet is that threshing is

best done at midday. As Gow notes, the same idea is expressed by
Vergil:

> et medio tostas aestu terit area fruges.   *G.* 1. 298.

The main purpose of threshing is to separate the edible grain from
the by-product, straw; hence this is what we should expect ἄχυρον
to mean in this context. If so, it is at first sight surprising that the
grain is not given prominence. In fact it is the first word, but Gow
misses the point by translating 'thresh the corn'. Now if σῖτος here
is grain, it follows that the verb must mean 'produce by threshing',
a perfectly proper sense for a denominative verb. The first line will
therefore translate 'when threshing out the grain forgo your sleep
at midday'; and the second line will give the reason for this. Since
τημόσδε μάλιστα implies that this is the best time of day for the
operation, it follows that the first four words of the second line
must be an 'elegant variation' on the theme of threshing. If ἄχυρον
means, as this note will demonstrate, straw, the line will translate:
'this is the best time of day to get the straw from the stalk' or 'turn
the stalk into straw'. In either case this simply repeats the idea
expressed by σῖτον ἀλοιῶντας. The καλάμα, like the κάλαμος in the
Xenophon passage quoted above, will refer to the stalk as cut still
bearing the ear. For this cf.

> ἧς τε πλείστην μὲν καλάμην χθονὶ χαλκὸς ἔχευεν,
> ἄμητος δ' ὀλίγιστος.   Il. 19. 222.

There is therefore no need to invent a new sense to accommodate
this passage.

3   This sense can be confirmed by the various uses to which this
material is put. A primary use is as fodder for animals.
Theophrastus discussing the effect of a certain crop on horses:

> οἱ ἵπποι ἐσθίοντες τὸ πρῶτον διεφθείροντο, κατὰ μικρὸν δὲ
> οὖν ἐθισθέντες ἐν ἀχύροις οὐδὲν ἔπασχον.
>
> > Thphr. *HP* 4. 4. 9.

For sheep:

> πιαίνει δὲ τὰ πρόβατα θάλλος, κότινος, ἀφάκη, ἄχυρα ὁποῖα
> ἂν ᾖ.   Arist. *HA* 596ª25.

Theophrastus similarly remarks on the difference between barley
and wheat straw as fodder:

ἴδιον δὲ καὶ τὸ ἄχυρον τοῦ κριθινοῦ τὸ πύρινον, ἐγχυλότερον γὰρ καὶ μαλακώτερον. Thphr. *HP* 8. 4. 1.

In the Septuagint:

καὶ λέων ὡς βοῦς φάγεται ἄχυρα. LXX *Is*. 11. 7.

4 Another obvious use is in the making of mud-bricks, again well exampled from the Septuagint, e.g.:

διδόναι ἄχυρον τῷ λαῷ εἰς τὴν πλινθουργίαν. LXX *Ex*. 5. 7

This is necessary equally to explain a reference in Hippocrates:

κροκύδας ἀπὸ τῶν ἱματίων ἀποτιλλούσας καὶ καρφο-
λογεούσας καὶ ἀπὸ τῶν τοίχων ἄχυρα ἀποσπώσας.
Hp. *Prog*. 4.

And the same applies to the derivative ἀχύρωσις applied to the making of swallows' nests:

οἷον πρῶτον ἐπὶ τῶν ὀρνίθων ἡ τῆς χελιδόνος σκηνοπηγία· τῇ γὰρ περὶ τὸν πηλὸν ἀχυρώσει τὴν αὐτὴν ἔχει τάξιν.
Arist. *HA* 612ᵇ22.

In all these cases straw rather than chaff is clearly meant.

5 It can also be used to deaden sound. Though here chaff is a possible meaning, one wonders if it would have been available in sufficient quantities, whereas straw plainly would have been.

ὅταν τελευτήσῃ βασιλεύς ... ἀχύρῳ ἡ ἀγορὰ καταπάσσεται.
Arist. *fr*. 611. 60.

Cf. the use of ἀχυρόω:

διὰ τί, ὅταν ἀχυρωθῶσιν αἱ ὀρχῆστραι, ἧττον οἱ χόροι γεγώνασιν; Arist. *Pr*. 901ᵇ30.

6 The same argument holds when it is used as stuffing; Herodotus describes how at the funeral of a Scythian king human victims and horses are sacrificed:

ἐξελόντες αὐτῶν τὴν κοιλίην καὶ καθήραντες ἐμπιμπλᾶσι ἀχύρων καὶ συρράπτουσι. Hdt. 4. 72. 2.

Or again when in a fable of Aesop the mice made spears and chariots of this material:

οἱ δὲ μύες δόρατα καὶ ἅρματα ἐξ ἀχύρων λαβόντες.

Aesop. 40.

7 In a fragment of Antiphanes we have a case where it appears to be used to adulterate porridge:

τὸ δεῖπνόν ἐστι μᾶζα κεχαρακωμένη
ἀχύροις, πρὸς εὐτέλειαν ἐξωπλισμένη. Antiph. 225. 2 K–A.

Here we might expect *chaff* to be used, but the strange word κεχαρακωμένη *equipped with sharp stakes* surely implies that pieces of straw were also included in the unappetising mixture.

8 The best evidence for *chaff* or *bran* is in the derivatives:

τοῦ ἀλεύρου τὸ ἀχυρωδέστατον ἀποκαίεται.

Arist. *Pr.* 928^{a}20.

This certainly refers to the waste product of grinding or milling, not threshing. It would appear that the Greeks did not clearly distinguish these.

9 Other derivatives point clearly in the direction of *straw*. An ἀχυροβολών is unlikely to be a *barn for chaff* (LSJ), but must be for *straw*. Similarly such words as ἀχυρηγέω refer to the carting of *straw*.

10 We may thus conclude that *straw* ought to be the first meaning, with *chaff* not clearly distinguished from it. The same inference can be drawn from Aristophanes' figurative use:

τοὺς γὰρ μετοίκους ἄχυρα τῶν ἀστῶν λέγω. Ar. *Ach.* 508.

This is simply the worthless part of anything.

βάπτω

1 The danger of using translations instead of definitions is well demonstrated by LSJ's treatment of this word. The New Supplement has done much to improve this, but the easiest way to show how to rearrange it is to sketch out a replacement article.

2   The basic sense is *to plunge* or *dip* (in a yielding medium,
usually but not necessarily a liquid):

> ὡς ὅτ᾽ ἀνὴρ χαλκεὺς πέλεκυν μέγαν ἠὲ σκέπαρνον
> εἰν ὕδατι βάπτῃ ψυχρῷ μεγάλα ἰάχοντα
> φαρμάσσων.   Od. 9. 392.

With εἰς:

> εἰς πῦρ αὐτὸ ἐντίθησιν, μετ᾽ ἐκεῖνο δὲ εἰς ὕδωρ βάπτει.
>   Pl. *Ti.* 73e.

> τὸν χόρτον εἰς μέλι βάπτοντες διδόασιν ἐσθίειν.
>   Arist. *HA* 605^{a}29; cf. *de An.* 435^{a}2.

3   This leads naturally to the use which emphasises the result of
immersion, *to make wet:*

> τἄρια | βάπτουσι θερμῷ.   Ar. *Ec.* 216.

Here the absence of a preposition indicates that θερμῷ is the
instrument: 'they wet the fleeces with hot water.' Likewise:

> ᾗ μελαγχόλους
> ἔβαψεν ἰοὺς θρέμμα Λερναίας ὕδρας.   S. *Tr.* 574.

So with no dative:

> χιτῶνα τόνδ᾽ ἔβαψα.   S. *Tr.* 580.

Possibly also:

> κουράλλιον ... ἔξαλον γινόμενον καὶ βαπτόμενον ἤτοι
> πηγνύμενον.   var. lectio in Dsc. 5. 121.

LSJ take this as meaning *become hard;* but it is more likely that it
refers to hardening (πηγνύμενον) as a result of being alternately
exposed to the air and then wetted again. Also with ἀπό introducing the instrument:

> καὶ βάψει ὁ ἱερεὺς τὸν δάκτυλον ἀπὸ τοῦ αἵματος τοῦ μόσχου.
>   LXX *Le.* 4. 17.

A special sense of this means *to baptize:*

> ὅταν δ᾽ ἀναλάβῃ τὸ πάθος τὸ τοῦ βεβαμμένου καὶ ἠρημένου,
> τότε ... ἔστι τῷ ὄντι ... Ἰουδαῖος.   Arr. *Epict.* 2. 9. 20.

4 Both of these usages reappear in a group of examples where the object is a weapon. One can *plunge* a weapon in an enemy's body:

φάσγανον εἴσω
σαρκὸς ἔβαψεν. E. *Ph.* 1578.

ὁ μὲν εἰς τὰ πλευρὰ βάψας τὴν αἰχμήν, ὁ δ᾽ εἰς τὰς λαγόνας.
D. H. 5. 15. 2.

But one can also *wet* one's sword with blood:

μαρτυρεῖ δέ μοι
φᾶρος τόδ᾽ ὡς ἔβαψεν Αἰγίσθου ξίφος. A. *Cho.* 1011.

Here there is also an allusion, as so often in poetry, to another sense (see 6 below).

γυνή ...
δίθηκτον ἐν σφαγαῖσι βάψασα ξίφος. A. *Pr.* 863.

Even clearer is this example:

ἔβαψας ἔγχος εὖ πρὸς Ἀργείων στρατῷ; S. *Aj.* 95.

i.e. 'did you get your spear properly bloodied?' LSJ has of course failed to see the distinction, and added the Septuagint example quoted in 3 above because blood is involved; but there of course the object is a finger.

5 Another special use is where the object is a bucket or similar container, which is dipped in a liquid in order to draw it up:

σὺ δ᾽ αὖ λαβοῦσα τεῦχος, ἀρχαία λάτρι,
βάψασ᾽ ἔνεγκε δεῦρο ποντίας ἁλός. E. *Hec.* 610.

Cf. Antiph. 25, Thphr. *Char.* 9.8. A different sense, but clearly derived from this is: *to draw* (a liquid) *by dipping*:

ἄνθ᾽ ὕδατος τᾷ κάλπιδι κηρία βάψαι. Theoc. 5. 127.

6 Equally special is the use: *to dip in a colouring medium, dye*:

εἵματα ... βεβαμμένα. Hdt. 7. 67. 1.
οἱ βαφῆς, ἐπειδὰν βουληθῶσι βάψαι ἔρια ὥστ᾽ εἶναι ἁλουργά.
Pl. *R.* 429d.

κύλικες ... βάπτονται ἐς τὸ δοκεῖν εἶναι ἀργυραῖ.
Ath. 11. 480e.

This is also used humorously in a figure by Aristophanes, with internal accusative:

ἵνα μή σε βάψω βάμμα Σαρδιανικόν.   Ar. *Ach.* 112.

βέβαπται βάμμα Κυζικηνικόν.   Ar. *Pax* 1176.

7 The intransitive uses, listed by LSJ under **B**, have the general sense: *to plunge oneself*:

ἐὰν βάπτωσιν (ἐγχελεῖς) εἰς ψυχρόν.   Arist. *HA* 592ᵃ18.

Of a ship:

καὶ ναῦς γὰρ ἐνταθεῖσα πρὸς βίαν ποδὶ
ἔβαψεν, ἔστη δ' αὖθις, ἢν χαλᾷ πόδα.   E. *Or.* 707.

Of the sun:

εἰ δ' ὁ μὲν ἀνέφελος βάπτῃ ῥόου ἑσπερίοιο.   Arat. 858.

Also in the middle voice:

ἤ που καὶ ποτάμοιο ἐβάψατο (κορώνη).   Arat. 951.

It is also used with an accusative, presumably internal rather than objective:

νῆα ... βάπτουσαν ... κῦμα κυρτόν.   Babr. 71. 2.

βαρέω

1 Here is a case where the historical principle would be helpful, if correctly applied. The earliest use is the aberrant perfect participle βεβαρηώς, followed by the corresponding perfect passive βεβαρημένος. The finite verb does not appear until much later, apart from the example quoted from Sappho, which needs further discussion (see 5 below). It would seem best to deal with this problem by making separate entries for the perfect participles, with cross-references. The meaning is regularly *oppressed,* and needs no further discussion.

2 The verb βαρέω seems to have arisen by back-formation from βεβαρημένος. It is found in the perfect indicative passive in the *Placita Philosophorum* under the name of Democritus, but the

wording is probably due to Plutarch, and cannot be used to prove an early date. There are a number of entries throughout LSJ quoted from fragments of early writers which are not in fact verbatim quotations, but later paraphrases. The failure to distinguish between these and genuine quotations seems to be a feature of the ninth edition. There is another example in the present passive in Hippocrates, but in the fourth book περὶ νούσων, which is certainly not one of the earlier parts of the Corpus, and is very hard to date. A more reliable example, again passive, is in Parthenius (i BC) and I have not found the active before Josephus (i AD); it becomes common from ii AD. This chronological distribution strongly supports the idea that it arose from the regular use of the perfect passive βεβαρημένος.

3 The verb is occasionally used literally to mean *weigh down*:

οἱ μέν τινες αὐτὴν μίτραις ἀνέδουν, οἱ δὲ ζώναις αἷς βαρηθεῖσα ἡ παῖς διὰ πλῆθος τῶν ἐπιρριπτομένων ἀπεπνίγη. Parth. 9. 8.

In the two following examples the context is figurative:

καὶ τὸν τῦφον ἀπόρριψον ... καὶ τὴν ὑπεροψίαν· βαρήσει γὰρ τὸ πορθμεῖον συνεμπεσόντα. Luc. D. Mort. 4. 14.

ἐπλανᾶτο περιφερομένη πανταχόσε ἡ τῆς δίκης ῥοπὴ ὅπῃ ἂν αὐτὴν βαρήσας ὁ πλείων χρυσὸς ἀνθέλκειν ἰσχύοι.
Procop. Arc. 14. 10.

4 The normal sense is *oppress, make uncomfortable, bother*; in the passive:

τὴν κεφαλὴν βαρέεται. Hp. Morb. 4. 49.

οὔκουν ἑκάτερον ὑμῶν ἰδίᾳ δεῖ βαρεῖσθαι δι᾽ ἡμᾶς.
Diog. Oen. 64.

οὗτοι, οἷς βαροῦνται. M. Ant. 8. 44.

αὐτὸς δὲ βαροῦμαι τῷ ἐκφορίῳ. P. Giss. 6. 7 (ii AD).

ὁ παραπλοῦς ... ὀχληρότατός ἐστιν καὶ καθ᾽ ἑκάστην ἡμέραν βαροῦμαι δι᾽ αὐτόν. P. Oxy. 525. 3. (ii AD).

In the active:

οὐδὲ τὸ πᾶν ἔθνος ἐβάρει ταῖς εἰσφοραῖς. J. BJ 2. 14. 1.

τὰ γὰρ ἕτερα ἀναλώματα ... ἑαυτοῖς ἐλογισάμεθα, ἵνα μὴ τὴν πόλιν βαρῶμεν. IG 14. 830. 15 (Puteoli).

τὸ δημόσιον ἰσχυρῶς τῇ τῶν χρημάτων ... αὐξήσει
βεβαρηκέναι ἔφη. D. C. 78. 17. 3.

There is an example of the middle quoted from Herodian the
historian of iii AD:

ἐβαροῦντο ... αὐτῶν αὐτὴν τὴν εὐγένειαν. Hdn. 8. 8. 1.

The verb continued in use as late as vi AD, and survives into
Medieval and Modern Greek, where however it has developed the
sense of *strike*.

5 The only item in the inventory which does not fit this pattern
is the alleged example from Sappho:

πόλλα δὲ ζαφοίταισ᾿, ἀγάνας ἐπι-
μνάσθεισ᾿ Ἄτθιδος ἰμέρῳ
λέπταν ποι φρένα κ[.]ρ‿ –βόρηται.
    Sappho, *Supp.* 25 (=fr. 96) 17.

This has traditionally been explained as an Aeolic form for
βαρεῖται, with ορ for αρ and athematic inflexion. LSJ quotes it as
κῆρ ... βόρηται, which can be translated 'the heart is oppressed',
but it leaves φρένα with no plausible construction. Moreover, as
D. L. Page (*ad loc.*) points out, words from this root appear in
Lesbian poetry in the form βαρ-, not βορ-. There has been much
discussion of this passage and various reconstructions have been
proposed. But perhaps the verb is incomplete and it is the end of
a compound such as θυμοβορέω, though this is found only in the
active. At all events this is hardly sufficient evidence to prove that
the development of the finite verb, which all other evidence places
relatively late, occurred as early as the beginning of vi BC. This is
one of numerous cases where the Lexicon ought to suspend judgment until clearer evidence is available, and it should at any rate
only be quoted as a dubious suggestion.

βαρύς

1 An adjective as common as this is peculiarly difficult to handle,
for there must be thousands of examples of the word in Greek
literature, and to analyse them all would be immensely time-

consuming; hence all I can attempt is a re-ordering of the material supplied by LSJ. Taken individually each example might suggest a plausible meaning; but the result of such an approach is to spread the range of meanings so wide it becomes extremely vague. LSJ not only used the English *heavy* in a number of different senses, but adds (*inter alia*) *bushy, pregnant, slow, grievous, oppressive, unwholesome, indigestible, violent, grave, ample, severe, stern, overbearing, important, difficult, strong, deep, bass, low.* Most of these sound appropriate in the context in which they appear; but the user of the Lexicon may well wonder what is the difference between *grave* and *stern, oppressive* and *overbearing* and so on. We all know that Homer uses the word to describe groaning; but does he mean *low-pitched* or *violent* or what? The only way to elucidate the many problems LSJ has left unresolved or solved in an arbitrary fashion is to analyse again the whole collection of material. The treatment of adverbs is always difficult. In a small dictionary it is sufficient to list the forms under the adjective and leave the exact meaning to be inferred. But in a major dictionary, and especially where the usage of the adverb has special features, I believe that adverbs should have separate entries. I have therefore kept βαρέως with its comparative and superlative separate; but the adverbial use of the neuter can still appear under the adjective.

2   A simple principle may be used to find the starting-point: we need to choose the simplest and most obviously material sense, from which the others may have arisen by transference. Hence we shall agree with LSJ in beginning with *heavy in weight*. It is interesting that under its opposite, κοῦφος, LSJ allowed the historical principle to outweigh logic; *light in weight* appears only as sense **I 4**, because it is absent from Homer and early literature. I should add to the definition the word *relatively;* a heavy child may still weigh less than a light man. The examples of this sense are few in LSJ, and the first offered (Hdt. 4. 150. 3) does not belong here; see 6 below. It is often paired with κοῦφος:

βαρύτερα πρὸς κουφότερα καὶ θάττω πρὸς τὰ βραδύτερα.
Pl. *R.* 438c; cf. *Tht.* 152d; Arist. *Cael.* 310ᵇ25.

ὁ δ᾽ Ἀμίλκας ἦγε μὲν τὴν πορείαν πρώτους ἔχων τοὺς ἐλέφαντας ... τελευταῖα δὲ τὰ βαρέα τῶν ὅπλων.
Plb. 1. 76. 3.

This last example was placed by LSJ in sense **II 3** 'of soldiers, *heavy-armed*'. But since it refers to ὅπλα it cannot fall under that heading; the fact that 'heavy weapons' imply the men who carried them does not give βαρύς here a new sense. As we shall see, the alleged military sense does not exist.

3 Another clearly physical sense is when it is used of parts of the body to mean *well developed, heavy* :

ἦ καὶ ἐπ᾽ ἀργυρέῃ κώπῃ σχέθε χεῖρα βαρεῖαν. Il. 1. 219.

τοὺς μὲν ὑπερσιτήσαντες ὀφρύς τε δηλώσει βαρεῖα καὶ κοῖλον ἄσθμα. Philostr. *Gym.* 48.

Both of these are included by LSJ under **I 1**. See also under 11 below.

4 To this can be attached as a sub-sense the use of the feminine to mean *pregnant*. There appears to be only one example so far recorded, but it would not be surprising; cf. Latin *grauida*: *P. Goodsp. Cair.* 15. 15 (iv AD).

5 Closely allied to this, but distinct enough to rank as a sub-sense, is *of heavy construction, massive*. This is not recognised by LSJ, and the first example is new; there are probably more to be found:

τὸ ἥκιστα ἡμῖν σύμφορόν ἐστι νέας ἔχουσι βαρυτέρας καὶ ἀριθμὸν ἐλάσσονας. Hdt. 8. 60. a.

ὁρῶντες δὲ τὴν τῶν Ἀκραγαντίνων πόλιν εὐφυεστάτην οὖσαν πρὸς τὰς παρασκευὰς καὶ βαρυτάτην ἅμα τῆς αὑτῶν ἐπαρχίας, εἰς ταύτην συνήθροισαν τά τε χορήγια καὶ τὰς δυνάμεις. Plb. 1. 17. 5.

The second example is quoted by LSJ (**II 2**) as meaning *important, powerful*, but no supporting evidence is quoted for such a meaning, and it is not clear why a politically influential city should be preferred as a base of operations for an army. What a general would look for is a city with good fortifications enclosing a large space, and this is precisely what Akragas offered. According to Walbank 'it contained 900 acres'.

6 Another physical sense is when it is used of persons or their attributes to indicate lack of agility (as opposed to κοῦφος in the sense of *nimble*). It might be defined as *weighed down, heavy-laden, burdened:*

πρεσβύτερός τε ἤδη εἰμὶ καὶ βαρὺς ἀείρεσθαι 'slow to stir myself'. Hdt. 4. 150. 3.

καὶ ζῶντα καὶ θάλλοντα κοὐ νόσῳ βαρύν. S. *Tr.* 235.

βαρεῖαν ἄψοφον φέρει βάσιν. S. *Tr.* 966.

οἱ δὲ σὺν γήρᾳ βαρεῖς. S. *OT* 17.

κελεύω τοὺς θωρακοφόρους ἡγεῖσθαι ὅτι τοῦτο βαρύτατόν ἐστι τοῦ στρατεύματος. τοῦ δὲ βαρυτάτου ἡγουμένου ἀνάγκη ῥᾳδίως ἕπεσθαι πάντα τὰ θᾶττον ἰόντα. X. *Cyr.* 5. 3. 37.

In the last example βαρύτατος was twice emended by Hirschig to βραδύτατος, a conjecture adopted by Marchant in OCT. One cannot help feeling that if this sense had been properly identified, there would have been no temptation to emend. LSJ places this in the military sense *heavy-armed* (**II 3**), a sense which now depends upon one passage, which will be shown to be at least very dubious (see below). There are two other examples of this attributable to old age (Ael. *VH* 9. 1, App. *Mac.* 14), and one to drink:

βαρεῖς ὑπὸ τῆς μέθης ὄντες. Plu. 2. 596a.

7 A different but still physical sense is *causing physical distress, offensive, unpleasant.* These examples are not distinguished by LSJ from those where the distress is mental (sense **I 2**):

ὀδμὴν παρεχόμενον βαρεῖαν. Hdt. 6. 119. 3.

νόσου βαρείας. S. *Ph.* 1330.

λέγεται βαρὺ τὸ χωρίον (*sc.* τὰ ἀργύρεια) εἶναι.
X. *Mem.* 3. 6. 12.

To this might be added: of food *heavy on the stomach*:

ὁ δ᾽ ἐγκρυφίας ἄρτος βαρὺς δυσοικονόμητός τε διὰ τὸ ἀνωμάλως ὀπτᾶσθαι. Ath. 3. 115e.

Here LSJ gives the meaning as *indigestible* (**I 2**) ignoring its own translation of δυσοικονόμητος as *hard to digest*. It is reasonable to assume that if a Greek writer coupled two epithets he intended them to convey a more precise meaning than if he had used only one.

8 Next we shall place *causing mental distress, hard to bear, grievous, burdensome*. There are too many examples to quote in full, but I give a selection:

Ζεύς με μέγα Κρονίδης ἄτῃ ἐνέδησε βαρείῃ.
Il. 2. 111; cf. 10. 71.

ἔριδα ῥήγνυντο βαρεῖαν. Il. 20. 55.

Κλῶθες ... βαρεῖαι. Od. 7. 197.

βαρεῖα˙ μὲν κῆρ τὸ μὴ πιθέσθαι,
βαρεῖα δ᾽ εἰ τέκνον δαΐξω.
A. Ag. 206; Pers. 1044; Th. 332, 767; Supp. 415.

βαρεῖαν ὁ ξένος φάτιν
τήνδ᾽ εἶπ᾽. S. Ph. 1045.

βαρεῖαν ἡδόνην νικᾶτέ με
λέγοντες. S. OC 1204.

ἀπέχθειαι ... χαλεπώταται καὶ βαρύταται. Pl. Ap. 23a.

πόλεμος ... ὅμορος καὶ βαρύς. D. 18. 241.

ἀφήκατε τὰ βαρύτερα τοῦ νόμου. Ev. Matt. 23. 23.

9 As applied to persons (or gods), *severe, stern, difficult:*

ὡς οὑπιτιμητής γε τῶν ἔργων βαρύς. A. Pr. 77.

Ζεύς τοι κολαστὴς τῶν ὑπερκόμπων ἄγαν
φρονημάτων ἔπεστιν, εὔθυνος βαρύς. A. Pers. 828.

τοιαῦτ᾽ ἀνὴρ δύσοργος, ἐν γήρᾳ βαρύς
ἐρεῖ, πρὸς οὐδὲν εἰς ἔριν θυμούμενος. S. Aj. 1017.

This last is placed by LSJ with the other examples of old age producing physical infirmity, but the context makes it clear that this refers rather to the severity of judgment which often marks old age.

δυσμενῆ γὰρ καὶ βαρύν σ᾽ ηὕρηκ᾽ ἐγώ. S. OT 546.

Here too surely belongs the following new example, Aeschines' description of Demosthenes:

ἀφόρητον ὄντα καὶ βαρὺν ἄνθρωπον. Aeschin. 2. 21.

ἧττον ἔσῃ βαρὺς τοῖς συνοῦσι καὶ ἡμερώτερος. Pl. Tht. 210c.

οἱ δυνάμενοι ... καὶ σεμνότεροι καὶ βαρύτεροι.
Arist. Rh. 1391ᵃ27.

Κύπρι βαρεῖα,
Κύπρι νεμεσσατά, Κύπρι θνατοῖσιν ἀπεχθής.   Theoc. 1. 100.
ἐπεὶ δ' οὐκ ἐμετρίαζον ἀλλ' ἦσαν ὑπερήφανοι καὶ βαρεῖς.
Plu. 2. 279c.

10   When applied to actions rather than agents, it can be defined as *causing concern, alarming, serious*:

δεισάντων φθόγγον τε βαρὺν αὐτόν τε πέλωρον.   Od. 9. 257.

The voice of the Cyclops might well have been *basso profundo* ; but in the context it is surely its effect on the hearers that is important.

ὅρκος γὰρ οὐδεὶς ἀνδρὶ φηλήτῃ βαρύς.   S. *fr.* 933.

ἀγγελίαν ... φέρων ... καὶ χαλεπὴν καὶ βαρεῖαν, ἣν ἐγώ ... ἐν
τοῖς βαρύτατ' ἂν ἐνέγκαιμι.   Pl. *Cri.* 43c.

βαρέα αἰτιώματα καταφέροντες.
Act. Ap. 25. 7; cf. *2 Ep. Cor.* 10. 10.

11   A different line of development, harking back to the material senses, can be placed next: *intense, violent, profound*. I should place here the examples of groans and other lamentations.

βαρέα στενάχοντα.   Il. 8. 334; Od. 8. 95, 534.

βαρὺ δ' ἀμβόασον οὐράνι' ἄχη.   A. *Pers.* 572.

βαρεῖα τηλόθεν αὐδά.   S. *Ph.* 208.

ἠχὼ βαρεῖα προσπόλων ἀφίκετο.   E. *Hipp.* 791.

Perhaps we should place also here the things or actions which display violence, such as hands or blows:

οὔ τις ... σοὶ ... βαρείας χεῖρας ἐποίσει.   Il. 1. 89.

τυπάδι βαρείᾳ.   S. *fr.* 844.

It is used of anger:

ὀργῇ βαρείᾳ.   S. *Ph.* 368.

μῆνιν βαρεῖαν.   S. *OC* 1328.

Here too I think we should place a rather difficult example:

αἱ γὰρ βαρεῖαι πλησμοναὶ τῶν σκυλακίων διαστρέφουσι τὰ
σκέλη, ⟨τοῖς⟩ σώμασι νόσους ἐμποιοῦσι.   X. *Cyn.* 7. 4.

LSJ places this example in **I 2**, between *unwholesome* and *indigestible;* but it is evident that overfeeding is bad for puppies for the reasons given. The effect of βαρεῖαι is surely to intensify the force of πλησμοναί. Here too we may place:

λάθρη μὲν γελάοισα, βαρὺν δ' ἀνὰ θυμὸν ἔχοισα.

Theoc. 1. 96.

if θυμός here means 'anger'. But if it means 'the seat of the emotions', 'heart', then perhaps this should be referred to the sense described in 9 above, though this seems to be otherwise restricted to persons. Here too we must apparently place the following, translated *ample* by LSJ (**I 4**):

βαρυτάτην εὐδαιμονίαν τοῖς ἀρχομένοις παρέξειν.

Hdn. 2. 14. 3.

But this seems to me such an extraordinary expression, verging on an oxymoron, that I should be tempted to emend to βαθυτάτην.

12   Then we come to another physical sense, but of a quite different type, where it is applied to sounds. In this case its opposite is not κοῦφος but ὀξύς, which shows clearly that it means *low-pitched, deep*. LSJ's addition of *strong* as the first equivalent in this sense is unfortunate, because it suggests loudness. The problem here concerns the nature of the Greek word-accent. It is now generally accepted that the accent of Attic Greek and hence the κοινή was one of pitch, not stress. But we know that in the course of time pitch was replaced by stress, though it is extremely hard to fix an accurate date for this change. Much of the confusion in the language used by grammarians may be due to their description of the contemporary stress accent by the terms inherited from their predecessors to describe pitch. A βαρὺς τόνος was in origin a syllable pronounced with no rise in pitch, so that every unaccented syllable could be (and sometimes was) marked with the grave accent. Since the subject has been fully discussed and elucidated by W. S. Allen in *Vox Graeca* (Cambridge, 1968) 106–24, I do not propose to do more than quote a few examples of this use of βαρύς.

13   Of sounds, *low-pitched, deep*. Explaining the difference between Διὶ φίλος and the proper name Δίφιλος Plato says:

ἀντὶ ὀξείας τῆς μέσης συλλαβῆς βαρεῖαν ἐφθεγξάμεθα.

Pl. *Cra.* 399b; cf. *Prt.* 332c.

Of a musician:

ὀξυτάτην καὶ βαρεῖαν χορδὴν ποιεῖ.   Pl. *Phdr.* 268e.

Hippocrates notes the association of low-pitched voices with damp climates:

φθέγγονται βαρύτατοι ἀνθρώπων.   Hp. *Aër.* 15.

Aristotle speaks of the variations in pitch by an orator:

πῶς ... δεῖ χρῆσθαι ... τοῖς τόνοις, οἷον ὀξείᾳ (φωνῇ) καὶ βαρείᾳ καὶ μέσῃ.   Arist. *Rh.* 1403ᵇ30.

In word-accent again, he explains the difference between οὗ and οὐ, remarkably ignoring the presence of the aspirate in one:

οὐ γὰρ ταὐτὸ σημαίνει ὀξύτερον, τὸ δὲ βαρύτερον ῥηθέν.
Arist. *SE* 178ᵃ3.

This example proves that he is not talking about what we call an acute accent, but about the pitch of a circumflex accent, which rises higher than an unaccented syllable.

14   The adverb βαρέως is not common, but it is used in its literal sense:

ἐρόμενος εἰ οἷόν τε ταχὺ βραδέως ἢ κοῦφον βαρέως ... γίγνεσθαι.   Pl. *Tht.* 189d.

It is also found meaning *with difficulty*:

εἰδὼς ὅτι τὰ παλαιότατα τῶν νοσημάτων ... βαρύτατα ὑπακούει.   Hp. *Prorrh.* 2. 39.

This example is placed by LSJ, with no indication that it is adverbial, in sense **III 1** 'of sound', where it is quoted simply as 'βαρύτατα ὑπακούειν, of diseases'. It is hard to imagine how they translated the passage, where ὑπακούω plainly means 'respond to treatment'. Another example, given by LSJ a special section (**III 3**) and defined as *slowly,* probably belongs here:

ἵνα ... τῆς λείας βαρέως ἐπισπωμένης ταχεῖα παραγωγὴ γίνηται.   Hero, *Aut.* 26. 6.

If the counterweight (λεία) is pulled hard, the picture unrolls quickly. (Incidentally neither this sense of λεία nor its use in geometry appears in LSJ.)

15 An adverbial sense corresponding to the sense of βαρύς discussed in 11 above is to be expected, *intensely, violently*. The only example offered by LSJ (**III 1**) is:

ἐκ δὴ τούτων ἐπένθει βαρύτατα καὶ δριμύτατα ἤλγει.

Ael. *VH* 12. 1.

I suspect that further research would produce more examples.

16 A sense corresponding to 7 above is not unexpected, *severely, sternly*:

αἰεὶ γὰρ βαρέως εἶχε πρὸς τὴν ὁμιλίαν.   Arist. *Pol.* 1311ᵇ9.

Perhaps we can place here the dubious reading:

ὁ δὲ τὴν ὕβριν ἀταράχως καὶ βαρέως ἔφερεν.   D. S. 26. 2.

Here βαρέως is a conjecture for .αρεως, but other emendations have been proposed. LSJ quotes it as meaning '*bear with dignity*'.

17 In other contexts it appears to mean *with annoyance, angrily*:

οἱ δὲ Ἕλληνες βαρέως μὲν ἤκουσαν ...   X. *An.* 2. 1. 9.

βαρυτέρως ἐναντιωθῆναι.   LXX *3 Ma.* 3. 1.

This is also used in the phrase βαρέως φέρειν or ἔχειν:

Δαρεῖος δὲ κάρτα βαρέως ἤνεικε ἰδὼν ἄνδρα δοκιμώτατον λελωβημένον.   Hdt. 3. 155. 1.

βαρέως φέρων εἶπε ...   Hdt. 5. 19. 1.

τὸ γὰρ πλῆθος οὐχ οὕτω τῶν ἀρχῶν ἀγανακτεῖ στερούμενον ὡς ἔχει βαρέως ὑβριζόμενον.   Arist. *Rh. Al.* 1424ᵇ5.

ὁ Πόπλιος βαρέως μὲν ἔφερεν ἐπὶ τῷ μὴ ... παρηρῆσθαι τὴν χορηγίαν.   Plb. 15. 1. 1.

18 Naturally the adverb is used of the pitch of sounds, *low*:

οἱ αἰάζοντες βαρύτερον αὐλοῦσιν.   Arist. *GA* 788ᵃ22.

Equally with respect to word-accent, i.e. *without rise of pitch*:

ἀμυγδάλην μὲν (λέγει) τὸν καρπὸν βαρέως, ὃ ἡμεῖς οὐδετέρως ἀμύγδαλον λέγομεν.   Ath. 2. 53b.

19   Finally a conspectus of the meanings as they might appear in
a revised Lexicon. The numbers refer to the paragraphs above.

   1 *relatively heavy in weight* (2).
   2 of parts of the body, *well-developed, heavy* (3); of women,
     pregnant (4). **b** *of heavy construction, massive* (5).
   3 *weighed down, heavy-laden, burdened* (6).
   4 *causing physical distress, offensive, unpleasant* (7).
   5 *causing mental distress, hard to bear, grievous* (8).
   6 of persons, *severe, stern, difficult* (9).
   7 *causing concern, alarming, serious* (10).
   8 *intense, violent, profound* (11).
   9 of sounds, *low-pitched, deep* (12, 13).

20   βαρέως, adv.

   1 *heavily* (14).
   2 *with difficulty* (14).
   3 *intensely, violently* (15).
   4 *severely, sternly* (16).
   5 *with annoyance, angrily* (17).
   6 *at a low pitch* (18).

βινέω

1   There is an excellent formula to be found in English dictionaries for dealing with the notorious 'four-letter' words: 'not in
polite use'. LSJ never thought of making such a comment, being
content as a rule with their *sens. obsc.*, which is appropriate to call
attention to a *double entendre,* but fails to indicate the register of
speech to which the word belongs. There is no doubt that βινέω
was avoided by all respectable writers; it is not merely absent from
all serious verse and histories; it does not occur in such works as
Theophrastus' *Characters* or the *Mimes* of Herondas. It was even
banished from Menander, who appears only to have used a derivative (ὑποβινητιῶντα βρώματα, *fr.* 462. 11). It is at home only in
Aristophanes, Archilochus, and Hipponax.

2   Explicit evidence for the opprobrium attached to the word
comes from no less an authority than Cicero:

cum loquimur 'terni', nihil flagitii dicimus; at cum 'bini', opscenum est.   Cic. *ad Fam.* 9. 22. 3.

He goes on to point out that obscenity is, as we should say, language-specific. If you think only in Latin, there is nothing improper about *bini;* but if you know also Greek, it can be interpreted as βίνει, which is. This remark is instructive as proving that ι and ει were to Cicero pronounced alike and could be equated with Latin long ῑ. The Greek form intended is presumably imperative, for in the indicative βινεῖ the position of the Greek accent would have inhibited the comparison.

3   There are, however, two further points about this word which can be made without embarrassment. It is alleged by Solon *fr.* 52b R that it means *to have illicit intercourse with* (a woman), being opposed to ὀπυίω, which therefore means *to have lawful intercourse with*.

4   Ὀπυίω is defined by LSJ as 'of the man, *marry, take to wife'* with the qualification that it is used by Homer only in the present and imperfect tenses. This restriction appears to be generally observed, a fact which may arouse our suspicion, as it would then be synonymous with γαμέω. A clue to its right meaning is supplied by a gloss of Hesychius, who equates an alleged form ὀπυόλαι with γεγαμηκότες. If this is a derivative or corruption of some form of ὀπυίω, it is clear that it describes the state of being married, not the process of becoming married. This is abundantly clear in the description of Nausikaa's brothers:

οἱ δύ' ὀπυίοντες, τρεῖς δ' ἠίθεοι θαλέθοντες.   Od. 6. 63.

An apparent exception has been noted in the Gortyn Law Code, where ὀπυίεν and the passive ὀπυίεθθαι used of the woman have been taken to mean *get married to*. In fact, the translation *be the husband (wife) of* is in all cases equally appropriate and there is no good evidence for the usual view. The whole subject has been admirably analysed and discussed at length by G. P. Edwards (*Minos* 20–2 (1987) 178–81). Once this is appreciated, the attempt to oppose ὀπυίω to βινέω may be dismissed as a typical effort by a grammarian to see distinctions that never existed.

5 A more important point concerns the etymology, not that I
think it solves the problem. Graffiti of vi and v BC from the
Athenian agora are reported by M. Lang (*Athenian Agora* C 2,
C 14) with the spelling *BEN*- for βιν-. This has been compared
with the alleged form in early Elean (*Inscr. Olymp.* 7 = Schwyzer
412):

αἰ δεβενεοι, ἐν τ' ἱαροῖ βοί κα θōά(δ)δοι καὶ κοθάρσι τελείαι.

It has been proposed to read αἰ δὲ βενέοι ἐν τ' ἱαροῖ, though it
hardly seems necessary to envisage expiation being laid down for
such a pollution of the temple. Other interpretations involving
emendation have been proposed, and this example should surely
remain suspect, since it is obviously not the kind of prohibition
normally found in laws.

6 In early Attic (and for that matter in early Elean) *BEN* can
stand for what would later have been written βην, βειν, or βεν.
There is no good reason to suppose that βῑν- could have replaced
βεν-, so the choice is presumably between βην- and βειν-. Now
there are two words, and a few proper names, which have ῑ even
in early Attic, where we should expect ει: χίλιοι and ἱμάτιον. The
tendency to close both ει and η seems to have been established at
an early date, especially as a sub-standard feature, as is shown by
schoolboys' spellings such as Διμοσθενις. In a word which certainly
belongs to the lower classes it is quite possible that what was
etymologically βεινέω became pronounced and hence written too as
βινέω.

7 This does not solve the problem of the etymology. The β- may
well be the product of a voiced labio-velar, cf. βίος. But there is no
obvious base of the type *gʷen- which will have yielded βειν-. A
connexion with γυνή (Boeotian βανά) is semantically attractive, but
the formation is still obscure; and in a 'popular' term of this kind
an unpredictable semantic development is not to be excluded. The
rhyme-words δινέω and κινέω may in any case have played a part in
its development.

βλεμεαίνω

1   The verb occurs five times in the Iliad; of Hector leading the
Trojans:

Ἕκτωρ δ' ἐν πρώτοισι κίε σθένεϊ βλεμεαίνων.   Il. 8. 337.

Similarly Il. 9. 237. Of Hephaistos:

Ἥφαιστος δ' ἅμα τοῖσι κίε σθένεϊ βλεμεαίνων.   Il. 20. 36.

and of a wild animal:

κάπριος ἠὲ λέων στρέφεται σθένεϊ βλεμεαίνων.
                              Il. 12. 42; cf. 17. 135.

οὔτε συὸς κάπρου ὀλοόφρονος, οὔτε μέγιστος
θυμὸς ἐνὶ στήθεσσι περὶ σθένεϊ βλεμεαίνει.   Il. 17. 22.

It is generally agreed that the verb is built upon an unattested
neuter s- stem *βλέμος (cf. μενεαίνω). The same etymon is required
by the negative adjective ἀβλεμής found in Nicander *Al.* 82,
Longinus 29. 1, and in the adverb in Panyasis (an obscure epic
poet). Ἀβλεμής is glossed in Hesychius as:

ἄτολμος, ἀτερπής, παρειμένος, οἳ δὲ κακός.

Cf. ἀβλεμές· ἀσθενές, φαῦλον. So if we could give the noun a meaning, we might solve the problem posed by its derivatives. Attempts
have been made (see *DELG*) to explain ἀ as ἁ-, ἁ- *copulativum*, but
a negative would be much more likely.

2   If we suppose then a substantive *βλέμος, the β is likely to be
the product of a labio-velar. This would allow us to associate it
with the family of βάλλω (<*g^wlyō) cf. formations like προβλής, as
built on a hystero-dynamic form with the enlargement -em-. In
fact the same type of enlargement will account also for βλέπω,
where the dialect form in γλεπ- may be a reminiscence of the labio-
velar. So *βλέμος might mean a *look* as something you throw. Sight
was until quite recently regarded as a power residing in the eye,
which sent out beams to detect an object, rather like radar. This
is apparent in standard phrases like French *jeter un coup d'œil*,
Mod. Gk. ρίχνω μια ματιά, and notice also phrases like βλέπειν νᾶπυ.
The intensive formation in -εαίνω (cf. μενεαίνω) ought therefore to
mean *darting fierce looks, glaring,* a sense which fits the Homeric

passages admirably. Wild animals certainly can be seen behaving like this. See now the New Supplement.

3 The compound ἀ-βλεμής should therefore properly mean *not glaring,* which would evolve naturally to *timid-looking.* This is exactly what Hesychius' ἄτολμος means, and with a little more extension his παρειμένος *slack* and κακός, if this means *cowardly.*

4 But adjectives of this kind regularly have 'passive' as well as 'active' senses, so ἀβλεμής could equally mean *not patently obvious.* The Nicander passage is regrettably obscure; Gow at one time (*CQ,* NS I (1951), 97) thought it here meant *ineffective.* But I believe the sense *insidious* would fit as well, if not better, and this can be accommodated in the semantic pattern just established. Similarly the adverb ἀβλεμέως πίνων would mean *drinking heedlessly,* taking no thought for the consequences. In the Longinus passage: ἡ περίφρασις ... ἀβλεμές προσπίπτει will mean 'falls so as to escape notice'. This explanation accounts for all the evidence, with the exception of Hesychius' gloss ἀτερπής.

γερός

1 An inscription of ii BC from Delos (*Inscr. Délos* 1417) has twice a phrase describing the condition in which a building is to be handed over by the contractor to the officials in charge of temples:

παραδώσει τοῖς ἐπὶ τὰ ἱερὰ γερὰ καὶ στεγνά.   C 58.

καὶ παραδ[ώ]σει τοῖς ἐπὶ τὰ ἱερὰ πάντα γερὰ καὶ στεγνὰ καὶ τεθυρωμένα.   C 89.

The remainder of the formula clearly means waterproof, i.e. roofed, and in the second case fitted with doors. So what can the adjective γερά mean? It must describe the building as in good condition for occupation. But *DGE* lists the word as of doubtful meaning, and the New Supplement only adds a reference to modern Greek γερός meaning *strong.*

2 The modern word is explained by etymologists (as Andriotes, Ἐτυμολογικὸν Λεξικόν) as a development of ancient ὑγιηρός, which

is phonetically acceptable and semantically plausible. But it might also phonetically continue ancient ἱερός, coexisting as a colloquial word with the learned form, which is restricted to the religious meaning. Now it is well known that in Hellenistic Greek γ was developing its modern value, as witness such forms as ὀλίος for ὀλίγος and ἀγώριν for ἀώριον, the origin of the modern word αγόρι 'boy'. The compound γερουσιάρχης is found also spelled ἱερουσι-άρχης. If this development had already occurred in colloquial speech by the middle of ii BC, it is possible that ἱερά and γερά were both being pronounced alike; but in both these examples τοῖς ἐπὶ τὰ ἱερά precedes, and it would obviously be impossible to write ἱερά twice consecutively with different meanings. Hence the substitution of γερά where a special sense is required. The required sense has been demonstrated in my note on ἱερός, paragraph 12. This will allow us to interpret γερά here as *which ought not to be violated*, i.e. *safe from intruders, secure,* which fits the context perfectly. The modern γερός may thus continue both ὑγιηρός and ἱερός in this special sense, either of which are consistent with the meaning *strong*.

γλεῦκος

The New Supplement has improved the treatment of this word, but by deleting the reference to *sweet wine* has concealed its etymological connexion with the adjective γλυκύς. It is of course the parallel substantive, formed with the *e*-grade, as ἔρευθος from ἐρυθρός, βένθος (the old form for βάθος) from βαθύς, etc. The Mycenaean form not only attests the antiquity of the sense *grape-juice*, but supplies valuable confirmation of the ultimate connexion of this adjective with Latin *dulcis*. There might therefore be a case, despite its late appearance, for putting *sweetness* as the first sense. However, in the passage quoted it appears to mean, not the abstract, but as might be expected, *the sweet stuff*.

> διὰ τί τὰ γλυκέα ἧττον δοκεῖ γλυκέα εἶναι θερμὰ ὄντα ἢ ὅταν
> ψυχθῇ; πότερον ὅτι ἅμα δύο αἰσθήσεις γίνονται ἀμφοῖν ... ἢ
> ὅτι καὶ τὸ γλεῦκος θερμόν. Arist *Pr.* 931ᵃ18.

The juice of ripe grapes is of course sweet, until fermentation has converted the sugar to alcohol.

γράφω

1 At first sight the LSJ article looks fairly convincing, and I thought it would need only minor modification. But the further my research progressed, the more I found needing changes, and I came to the conclusion that it requires extensive treatment. Even so, I am not sure if I have discovered all the ramifications of its senses, and I have not attempted to deal with all LSJ's examples. LSJ begins with the only two examples of the simple verb in Homer (ἐπιγράφω also occurs, in two different senses). The original meaning must have been *make a shallow cut in, scratch*:

> γράψεν δέ οἱ ὀστέον ἄχρις
> αἰχμὴ Πουλυδάμαντος.   Il. 17. 599.

With this we can compare the compound:

> Κτήσιππος δ' Εὔμαιον ὑπὲρ σάκος ἔγχεϊ μακρῷ
> ὦμον ἐπέγραψεν.   Od. 22. 280.

I have been unable to find any further example of this use.

2 LSJ, however, apparently in the conviction that writing was unknown to Homer, places here two more disputable examples. First the other example of ἐπιγράφω:

> ὅς μιν ἐπιγράψας κυνέῃ βάλε.   Il. 7. 187.

This describes the casting of lots, where each man scratches a mark on his lot before putting it in the helmet. If ἐπιγράψας meant merely 'scratched', it would be difficult for him to recognise his scratch again; it must therefore mean 'made a mark on', which does not of course imply the use of an organised graphic system. But the other is the famous passage in the story of Bellerophon, which has been discussed at immense length; a good summary of the arguments can be found in A. Heubeck, 'Die Schrift', *Archaeologia Homerica*, X. 132–40.

> πέμπε δέ μιν Λυκίηνδε, πόρεν δ' ὅ γε σήματα λυγρά,
> γράψας ἐν πίνακι πτυκτῷ θυμοφθόρα πολλά.   Il. 6. 169.

I disagree with LSJ's decision that this does not describe true writing for several reasons. There is now no doubt that knowledge of the Greek alphabet was widely diffused by the end of viii BC, so the practice of writing must have been known to the poet we call Homer. Secondly, Proitos would have needed his message to be unambiguous, if he hoped it would secure Bellerophon's murder; moreover, he can hardly have risked the message being intercepted by the messenger breaking the seal, unless of course he knew Bellerophon to be incapable of reading it. Thirdly, and this is the most telling reason, the object of γράψας is not σήματα, but θυμοφθόρα πολλά, which must denote a written message. This can therefore be left to a later section (see 7 below).

3   Arising from the scratching on the lot we can see that γράφω must have been used to mean *make a mark by scratching,* and this was then extended to *make any kind of visual mark.* So for example in geometry Euclid uses the phrase:

κύκλος γεγράφθω.   Eucl. 1. 1.

to mean 'let a circle be described', i.e. let a circular figure be drawn.

κύκλον γράψαι.   Gal. 1. 47.

But LSJ supplies no example of its use meaning to *draw* a letter of the alphabet. I have come across two and I have no doubt there are others to be found.

γράμματα γράφουσι καὶ λογίζονται ψήφοισι Ἕλληνες μὲν ἀπὸ
τῶν ἀριστερῶν ἐπὶ τὰ δεξιὰ φέροντες τὴν χεῖρα.
Hdt. 2. 36. 4.

The sutures in the skull are described by Hippocrates as T-shaped.

ὥσπερ γράμμα τὸ ταῦ γράφεται.   Hp. *VC* 1 (p.183, 7 L.)

It is important to notice that at this stage we are still not talking about the use of a graphic system, where letters are used to write a word. See further 6 below.

4   It is a small step from drawing a line to using drawn lines to make a picture. Hence we can place next the examples given by LSJ, still in sense **I 1**, under the heading '*represent by lines, draw, paint*'. I think *visually* should be added to the definition, and perhaps *delineate* would be better than *paint,* for a reason which will

appear. Visual lines may of course be made by the use of paint. But as usual LSJ has confused two different kinds of object. We must distinguish *making* a picture *by drawing* and *making a picture* of something. For the first:

μᾶλλον ἢ γεγραμμένην εἰκόν᾽ ἑστάναι. Ar. *Ra.* 538.

ὥσπερ γραφεὺς μηδὲν ἐοικότα γράφων. Pl. *R.* 377e.

if this means, as I believe, 'making drawings which in no way resemble (their subject)'. A more difficult example is:

εἰ ἡμᾶς ἀνδριάντα γράφοντας προσελθών τις ἔψεγε ...
Pl. *R.* 420c.

This is translated *paint* by LSJ s.v. ἀνδριάς, and the same translation was added by the 1968 Supplement s.v. γράφω. Since ancient statues were painted, this seems at first sight obvious. But this would be a surprising extension of the meaning. The nearest parallel seems to be:

τὰ ἐν γῇ εἴδη, ὁπόσα τοὺς λειμῶνας αἱ Ὧραι γράφουσι.
Philostr. Jun. *Im. Praef.*

This may refer to colouring, but is perhaps more generally *make into a picture*. I prefer therefore to take the Plato passage as meaning *delineate the features on*, for the context shows that it refers not to the whole statue, but the treatment of the eyes.

5   The next sense will therefore be *draw* or *paint a picture of, represent in a drawing*. This seems to have started with the drawing of living creatures, as is clear in early Greek art, where things are only drawn as a background or as incidental features in the picture. The phrase ζῷα γράφεσθαι is actually used with a second accusative describing the subject of the painting:

ζῷα γραψάμενος πᾶσαν τὴν ζεῦξιν τοῦ Βοσπόρου.
Hdt. 4. 88. 1.

From this the compound ζωγράφος 'painter' developed and its denominative verb ζωγραφέω. Plato can still use this etymology as an argument:

εἰ ἐτύγχανόν σε ἐρωτῶν τίς ἐστιν τῶν ζωγράφων Ζεῦξις, εἴ μοι εἶπες ὁ τὰ ζῷα γράφων ... Pl. *Grg.* 453e.

More commonly γράφω in this sense is followed by a predicate, *depict as*:

> κατά περ Ἕλληνες τὴν Ἰοῦν γράφουσι. Hdt. 2. 41. 2.

> ὁρῶν γῆς περιόδους γράψαντας πολλούς ... οἳ Ὠκεανόν ...
> ῥέοντα γράφουσι πέριξ τὴν γῆν. Hdt. 4. 36. 2.

> εἶδόν ποτ᾽ ἤδη Φινέως γεγραμμένας
> δεῖπνον φερούσας (Γοργόνας). A. *Eu.* 50.

> εἶτ᾽ οὐ δικαίως προσπεπατταλωμένον
> γράφουσι τὸν Προμηθέα πρὸς ταῖς πέτραις.
>   Men. *fr.* 718 (535 K.)

> τίς ἦν ὁ γράψας πρῶτος ἀνθρώπων ἄρα
> ἢ κηροπλαστήσας Ἔρωθ᾽ ὑπόπτερον;
>   Eub. 40.1 (ii p.164 Kock)

6   The fully developed sense *write*, i.e. use a graphic system, arises naturally out of the sense defined in 3 above. But here too we must make a distinction ignored by LSJ. We need first to distinguish a usage *cover with writing, inscribe*:

> καὶ σκῦλα γράψεις πῶς ἐπ᾽ Ἰνάχου ῥοαῖς; 'and how will you
> inscribe the spoils (dedicated) by the streams of Inachus?'
>   E. *Ph.* 574, cf. *Tr.* 1189.

> γράμματα δ᾽ ἐν φλοιῷ γεγράψεται. Theoc. 18. 47.

Here γράμματα means 'an inscription' and this must be separated from the use with the same object in D. 9. 41, where it means 'a document' (see 7 below).

> τοὺς ἔτι νηπιάχους γράψαν τεχνήμονες ἄνδρες
> αἰθομένῳ χαλκῷ. Opp.*C.* 1. 326.

This may be used in the passive with a retained accusative:

> ἐν τῷ προσώπῳ καὶ ταῖς χερσὶ γραφεὶς *(i.e. branded)* τὴν
> συμφοράν. Pl. *Lg.* 854d.

(Note that S. *Tr.* 157 cited by LSJ is actually an example of ἐγγράφω.) Also with predicate (cf. with 7 below):

> ἔλαφον ... ἄν ποτε Ταϋγέτα
> ἀντιθεῖσ᾽ Ὀρθωσίας ἔγραψαν ἱεράν. Pi. *O.* 3. 30.

Absolutely or intransitively, *write*:

> τοῖς μήπω δεινοῖς γράφειν τῶν παίδων. Pl. *Prt.* 326d.

Also *write* on a specified material:

πολλοὶ τῶν βαρβάρων ἐς τοιαύτας διφθέρας γράφουσι.
Hdt. 5. 58. 3.

7 Finally we come to the most common usage *record in writing, write down*. Here I would place first the Bellerophon passage (Il. 6. 169) quoted in 2 above. Later:

γράψας ἐς βυβλίον τὰ ἐβούλετο. Hdt. 1. 125 .2.
περὶ μὲν τῶν ματαίων πολλὰ αὐτοῖς γέγραπται.
X. *Cyn.* 13. 2.
τὰ δικασθέντα ... ἐν χρυσῷ πίνακι γράψαντες. Pl. *Criti.* 120c.
ὃς ἂν διαθήκην γράφῃ. Pl. *Lg.* 923c.

A proverbial expression for impermanence is 'to write on water':

οὐκ ἄρα σπουδῇ αὐτὰ ἐν ὕδατι γράψει μέλανι σπείρων διὰ καλάμου. Pl. *Phdr.* 276c.
ὅρκους ἐγὼ γυναικὸς εἰς ὕδωρ γράφω. S. *fr.* 811.
παίζεις ... ἢ καθ᾽ ὕδατος ... γράφεις. Luc. *Cat.* 21.

Equally it is used in a figure, as:

ἀνάγνωτέ μοι
Ἀρχεστράτου παῖδα, πόθι φρενὸς
ἐμᾶς γέγραπται. Pi. *O.* 10. 3.

This sense is also used in the middle voice, with the usual implication of personal involvement of the subject:

γενομένου γὰρ τέρατος φυλάσσουσι γραφόμενοι τὠποβαῖνον
'they make a written note and await the outcome'.
Hdt. 2. 82. 2.

ἐγραψάμην ... τότ᾽ εὐθὺς οἰκάδ᾽ ἐλθὼν ὑπομνήματα.
Pl. *Tht.* 143a.

συγγραφὴν ἐγράψαντο ὑπὲρ τούτων. D. 56. 6.

LSJ records the last of these as 'cause to be written', but there is no need to give this force to the middle. In figurative phrases:

τοιαῦτ᾽ ἀκούων ... ἐν φρεσὶν γράφου. A. *Ch.* 450.
καὶ τοῦτ᾽ ἐπίστω, καὶ γράφου φρενῶν ἔσω. S. *Ph.* 1325.

With a predicate it means also *record as*:

τοῦτον αἴτιον γράφω. 'I record him as responsible.'

Hdt. 7. 214. 3.

κληρονόμον ὃν ἂν ἀξιώσῃ γίγνεσθαι γραφέτω.   Pl. *Lg.* 923c.

Again intransitively or absolutely, *communicate in writing, write*:

ἐπισταμένοις δ' ὑμῖν γράφω ὅτι βραχεῖα ἀκμὴ πληρώματος.
'You know well what I am telling you, that a crew is only at its
peak for a short time.'   Th. 7. 14. 1.

With εἰς:

θαυμάζειν ... πῶς οὐ καὶ εἰς Διονύσιον γράφει.

Longin. 4. 3, cf. 1. 3.

λέγουσι ... τὴν Στρατονίκην ... γράψασαν ἐς τὸν ἄνδρα τοῦ
Κομβάβου κατηγορέειν.   Luc. *Syr. D.* 23.

A special sense is found in late papyri, *be the recorder* or *scribe of*:

τῷ γράφοντι τὸν Ὀξυρυγχίτ[ην].   *P. Oxy.* 239. 1 (i AD).

But as an intransitive verb there is a much earlier example, for
which I am indebted to *DGE*:

τὸνς δὲ στραταγὸνς, οἷς γράφει Δαμέας, ἀνγράψαι ἐνς τὰνς
στάλανς.   Schwyzer 90. 10 (Argos, iii BC).

8   As a sub-sense we may further distinguish the use to mean
compose, write a book, etc., where it sometimes means *write in prose*
as opposed to ποιέω *write in verse*:

δεῖ ... ἢ ποιεῖν ἢ γράφειν τι κεχαρισμένον τοῖς πολλοῖς.

Isoc. 2. 48.

τῶν πράξεων ὑπὲρ ὧν προῃρήμεθα γράφειν.   Plb. 1. 1. 4.

9   We can now distinguish a special usage where the verb means
lay down in writing, prescribe a command, rule, etc. This is particularly common in the perfect passive. This sense is ignored by LSJ
and some of the examples quoted here are new ones:

αἰ δὲ οἰ τίται μὲ Ϝέρκσιεν ἀι ἔγρα(τ)ται (= γέγραπται) 'if the
exactors have not acted as prescribed.'

Inscr. Cret. 4. 78. 7 (Schwyzer 175, v BC).

κατὰ τὰ ἐγραμμένα.   *Leg. Gort.* 3. 21.

ἐπιστέλλω σοι περὶ Περσῶν ᾗπερ γέγραπται. X. *Cyr.* 4. 5. 34.

νόμοι ... οὓς τὸ πλῆθος συνελθὸν καὶ δοκιμάσαν ἔγραψε.
$$\text{X. } \textit{Mem.} \text{ 1. 2. 42.}$$

τολμῶντα παρὰ τὰ γραφέντα δρᾶν. Pl. *Plt.* 295d.

With infinitive:

οὐκ εἰδότες ... ἄμμε πότμος
ἄντιν' ἔγραψε δραμεῖν ποτὶ στάθμαν 'not knowing what line
fate has ordained us to run along'. Pi. *N.* 6. 7.

10 Another special use is with a predicate where it means *write
down on a list, enrol*. This is usually in the middle:

ἕνα τῶν μαθητῶν ... καὶ ἐμὲ γράφου. Pl. *Cra.* 428b.

In the passive, *be enrolled*:

ὥστ' οὐ Κρέοντος προστάτου γεγράψομαι 'so I shall not be
enrolled as under the protection of Creon'. S. *OT* 411.

ἀφ' ἧς ἂν γράψηται 'from the time of his enrolment'.
$$\text{Pl. } \textit{Lg.} \text{ 850b.}$$

In the active:

ἐμὲ μὲν οὖν ... γράφε τῶν ἱππεύειν ὑπερεπιθυμούντων.
$$\text{X. } \textit{Cyr.} \text{ 4. 3. 21.}$$

11 Equally it is used of writing a formal proposal:

ψηφίσματ' οὐ γράφουσιν. Ar. *Nu.* 1429.

ἔγραψε γνώμην κατὰ τὸ Καννανοῦ ψήφισμα κρίνεσθαι τοὺς
ἄνδρας δίχα ἕκαστον. X. *HG* 1. 7. 34.

But more often the word for proposal is omitted, so that it
effectively means *propose*, with accusative and infinitive:

ἔγραψε Φιλοκράτης ἐξεῖναι Φιλίππῳ δεῦρο κήρυκα ...
πέμπειν. Aeschin. 3. 62.

ἀλλὰ τί ἐχρῆν με ποιεῖν; μὴ προσάγειν γράψαι τοὺς· ἐπὶ τοῦθ'
ἥκοντας ... ; D. 18. 28; 1. 19; 24. 83.

Also with περί:

οὕτως ... ἐδόκει γράφειν καὶ νομοθετεῖν περὶ τούτων.
$$\text{D. 24. 48.}$$

12 A further extension or sub-sense of this is with accusative, *propose* a course of action:

γράφειν πόλεμον. D. 10. 55.

γράφοντας εἰρήνην. D. 19. 55.

γράφοντα παράνομα 'making an illegal proposal'.
D. 18. 13.

This is also found in the middle:

ἐχρῆν σε ... πρῶτον μὲν πρόσοδον γράψασθαι πρὸς τὴν βουλήν, εἶτα τῷ δήμῳ διαλεχθῆναι. D. 24. 48.

With infinitive, in the active:

πολεμεῖν μὲν οὐ γράψεις. Din. 1. 70.

13 Then we have a usage which seems to be confined to the middle, though it can of course also be used in the passive. It begins as a special sense of *put in writing*, where the object is a formal accusation (γραφή) and the person accused is designated by a second accusative:

εἶτ' αὐτοὺς γραφὴν
διωκάθω γραψάμενος. Ar. *Nu.* 1482.

γραφὴν σέ τις, ὡς ἔοικε, γέγραπται. Pl. *Euthphr.* 2b.

ἐπὶ τὴν Μελήτου γραφὴν ἥν με γέγραπται. Pl. *Tht.* 210d.

From this it is an easy step to *make the subject of an accusation*:

οὗτος ἐγράψατο τὴν Χαβρίου δωρειάν. D. 20. 146.

Then with an object clause replacing the accusative:

ἐγράψατο
κύων Κυδαθηναιεὺς Λάβητ' Αἰξωνέα
τὸν τυρὸν ἀδικεῖν ὅτι μόνος κατήσθιεν. Ar. *V.* 894.

γεγραμμένος ταῦθ' ὡς οὐκ ἀληθῆ. D. 18. 59.

Absolutely ὁ γραψάμενος means *the accuser*:

τοὺς φεύγοντάς τ' ἐλεεῖν μᾶλλον
τῶν γραψαμένων. Ar. *V.* 881.

ὁ δὲ γραψάμενος Διώνδας τὸ μέρος τῶν ψήφων οὐκ ἔλαβεν.
D. 18. 222.

14   As a development from this the middle is used to mean *accuse*
a person, with the charge given in the genitive:

αἰσχροκερδείας οὖν αὐτὸν γραψάμενος.   Pl. *Lg.* 754e.

ταῦτ᾽ ἐστὶν ὧν οὐδὲν σὺ γέγραψαι.   D. 18. 119.

In the passive with retained accusative:

γραφεὶς τὸν ἀγῶνα τοῦτον 'being accused on this charge'.
D. 18. 103.

15   A scheme for a rationally arranged article might therefore run
thus:

    1 *make a shallow cut in, scratch* (1).
    2 *make* a visible mark, *describe* a line, etc. (3). **b** *write* a letter
      of the alphabet (3).
    3 *make* a visual representation (4).
    4 *draw* or *paint a picture of* (5).
    5 *cover with writing, inscribe* (6); (absol.) *write* on a specified
      material (6).
    6 *record in writing, write down* (7). **b** *be the scribe of* (7).
      c *compose, write* a book etc. (8)
    7 *lay down in writing, prescribe, ordain* a command, rule, etc.
      (9).
    8 *write down on a list, enrol* (10).
    9 *write* or *make* a formal proposal (11). **b** *propose* a course of
      action (12).
   10 (mid.) *put in writing, lodge* an accusation; (with two
      accusatives) *bring* an accusation *against* a person (13).
      b *accuse* a person.

διαβάλλω

1   The senses given by LSJ are as follows:

    I *throw* or *carry across.* **2** intr. *pass over, cross.* **3** *put*
      through.
   II *throw* with a play on sense V.
  III *set at variance, set against, bring into discredit*; Pass. *to be*
      at variance with; *to be filled with suspicion and resentment*
      against; *to be brought into discredit.*

    IV *put off with evasions.*
    V *attack* a man's character, *calumniate; accuse, complain of; reproach with.* **2** *misrepresent; speak* or *state slanderously; give hostile information.* **3** *lay the blame for* ... *on.* **4** *disprove.* **5** *declare spurious.*
    VI *deceive by false accounts, impose on, mislead.*
    VII *divert* from a course of action.
    VIII Med., *contract an obligation.*
    IX *throw* against a person (at dice).

It is fairly obvious that some of these senses, however justified in their context, do not form a coherent pattern and in some cases seem to overlap. Sense **IX**, if correctly so interpreted, belongs with the physical senses in **I**; and **IV** *put off* might well be grouped with **VII** *divert,* though in fact the existence of either of these is doubtful. **VII** has been deleted by the 1968 and the New Supplement, and various examples have been switched to other senses. Yet the overall picture is still very far from clear, and despite a good deal of research I am not confident that all the problems are solved. There still seem to be too many usages insufficiently exemplified, some perhaps because they belong to different periods in the development of the language. It is curious that the physical sense in classical Greek is more or less restricted to the nautical use, and was only later generalised.

2   We must begin with the physical sense, the earliest examples of which do not include any where it means literally *throw across.* The definition *relocate on the other side, move across* will cover the use in Herodotus:

    διέβαλον ἐκ τῆς Χίου τὰς νέας ἐς τὴν Νάξον.
                 Hdt. 5. 34. 2; 5. 33. 1.

The third is more difficult:

    καταγαγὼν ἐκ Χερρονήσου διαβαλὼν ἀγκυρίσας
    εἶτ' ἀποστρέψας τὸν ὦμον αὐτὸν ἐνεκολήβασας.   Ar. *Eq.* 262.

Since the two following participles refer to holds in wrestling, it is hard to resist the conjecture διαλαβών 'grasping him round the waist.' If διαβαλών is kept, it is more likely to belong in the sense discussed in 5 below.

3   Sense **2** is correctly given as 'intr. *pass over, cross*', in other words the intransitive meaning corresponding to 2 above, e.g.:

> ἐκ Πατρῶν ... πρὸς τὴν ἀντιπέρας ἤπειρον διαβάλλοντες ἐπ'
> Ἀκαρνανίας κατεῖδον τοὺς Ἀθηναίους προσπλέοντας.
>
>   Th. 2. 83. 3.
>
>   πρὶν λιπὼν Κάδμου πόλιν
> φυγῇ πρὸς Ἄργος διαβαλεῖν αὐθαίρετος.   E. *Supp.* 931.

However, it is not so simple to add here 'c. acc. spatii', since it could be reasonably argued that the accusative is here an object, and it would be better to add another transitive sense, *go across, traverse*:

> ἀθρόοις ἐπὶ ἄκραν Ἰαπυγίαν τὸν Ἰόνιον διαβαλοῦσιν.
>
>   Th. 6. 30. 1.

LSJ places this together with a very corrupt fragment of Aeschylus (*fr.* 69), a fragment of Old Comedy (Demetr. Com. Vet. 1) and the following:

> πῶς δ' αὖ γεφύρας διαβαλοῦσ' ἱππηλάται,
> ἢν ἄρα μὴ θραύσαντες ἀντύγων χοάς;   E. *Rh.* 117.

Here it seems simpler to take the verb as meaning *construct* or *throw* a bridge *across*. This could then be attached to the transitive uses in LSJ's **I 1** (2 above). It is possible that the literal sense of *throw* is also present in Ar. *Pax* 643, but this is better treated later (see 10).

4   Finally we come to *place* or *put through, insert*. Interestingly this seems to be absent from classical Greek, though there is no apparent reason for this.

> διαβαλόντα τῆς θύρας τὸν δάκτυλον.   D. L. 1. 118.

In passive participles:

> τύλος διαβεβλημένος διὰ τοῦ ῥυμοῦ διαμπάξ.   Arr. *An.* 2. 3. 7.
>
> αἵδε (*sc.* ἁλύσεις) εἰσὶν ἐκ κρίκων τινῶν κεχαλκευμέναι δι'
> ἀλλήλων διαβεβλημένων.   D. Chr. 30. 20.
>
> διαβληθέντων τῶν ἀγκώνων διὰ μέσων τῶν τόνων.
>
>   Hero, *Bel.* 101. 12.

5 At this point the orderly development of senses is abandoned, and no sort of pattern seems discernible. As a first stage of metaphorical development we need a sense *set on opposite sides* of a contest or argument, *make into an opponent*, where δια- has the force of separation:

> τούτου ἕνεκα ... τοῦ ἐμὲ καὶ Ἀγάθωνα διαβάλλειν.
> Pl. *Smp*. 222c; 222d.

> μὴ διάβαλλε ... ἐμὲ καὶ Θρασύμαχον ἄρτι φίλους γεγονότας.
> Pl. *R*. 498c.

Then with other constructions *set against*:

> τὸ διαβάλλειν ἀλλήλοις καὶ συγκρούειν καὶ φίλους φίλοις καὶ τὸν δῆμον τοῖς γνωρίμοις. Arist. *Pol*. 1313ᵇ16.

So probably:

> ἄπωθεν ἡμᾶς πρὸς ἐκεῖνα τὰ πάθη διαβάλλοντες 'distancing us as regards these emotions'. Plu. 2. 727d.

In this sense we can now include the examples of the middle quoted from Plutarch, where the contest is a game:

> τούτοις γὰρ ὥσπερ ἀστραγάλοις ... παίζουσα χρῆται καὶ διαβάλλεται πρὸς τοὺς ἐντυχόντας. Plu. 2. 148d; 272f.

6 Just as we have an intransitive literal sense (3 above), so there is probably one developed from this transferred sense, *be on the opposite side*:

> πέμπουσι ... οἱ Μυτιληναῖοι τῶν τε διαβαλλόντων ἕνα, ᾧ μετέμελεν ἤδη, καὶ ἄλλους. Th. 3. 4. 4.

This is translated by LSJ '*give hostile information*, without any insimulation of falsehood'. But it is hard to see that it means more than 'one of the opponents, who had already changed his mind'. At least, having no object, it ought not to be placed under **V 2** *misrepresent*. It is also found in the middle voice, with πρός:

> πρὸς ἐπιβουλεύοντα διαβάλλονται 'they take opposite sides to anyone plotting against them'. Arist. *Rh*. 1404ᵇ21.

7 From this it is an easy step to the sense *make an enemy of, denounce, discredit*:

> ἐλθόντες παρὰ βασιλέα διέβαλλον τοὺς Ἴωνας, ὡς δι' ἐκείνους ἀπολοίατο αἱ νέες. Hdt. 8. 90. 1.

διαβαλὼν αὐτοὺς ὡς οὐδὲν ἐν νῷ ἔχουσιν.   Th. 5. 45. 3.

ὡς τότε δυνάμενος ἢ ὡς νῦν διαβεβλημένος.   Lys. 7. 27.

With dative:

Μεγαβάτῃ διαβεβλημένος.   Hdt. 5. 35. 1; 6. 64.

ἵνα ... οἱ ... πολέμιοι τῷ Τισσαφέρνει ὡς μάλιστα διαβάλλοιντο.   Th. 8. 81. 2.

οὐδὲν οὖν ἔτι ὑπολείπεται ὅτῳ ἄν μοι δικαίως διαβεβλῆσθε.
                                                    And. 2. 24.

μή με διαβάλῃς στρατῷ
λέγονθ᾽ ἃ μὴ δεῖ.   S. Ph. 582.

ἐὰν δὲ ἀδύνατοι ἐκβάλλειν αὐτὸν ὦσιν ἢ ἀποκτεῖναι διαβάλλοντες τῇ πόλει.   Pl. R. 566b; also Ev. Luc. 16. 1.

With εἰς or πρός:

Πελοποννησίους διαβαλεῖν ἐς τοὺς ἐκείνῃ χρῄζων Ἕλληνας 'desiring to discredit the Peloponnesians in the eyes of the Greeks in that area'.   Th. 3. 109. 2.

διαβάλλων ... τοὺς Ἀθηναίους πρὸς τὸν Ἀρταφέρνεα.
                                    Hdt. 5. 96. 1; also Plb. 30. 19. 2.

It would seem possible to place among the first set of examples:

διαβάλλων με μίαν ἐκ μιᾶς.   SB 5343. 41 (ii AD).

This is translated by LSJ as *put off with evasions* (**IV**), but there is no reason why it should not be taken as 'denouncing me day after day'.

8   Where the object is a statement or opinion, the translation *denounce* might still hold good with the addition of *criticise*. This appears to be confined to later Greek:

τοῦτο τὸ ἔπος διαβάλλουσι καὶ τὴν περὶ Μουνύχου μυθολογίαν.   Plu. Thes. 34. 1.

δίκαιον γὰρ ἦν, οἶμαι, πρῶτον μὲν εἰπεῖν, ὑπὸ τίνων πιθανῶν ἀναπεισθεὶς ὁ Πλάτων οὕτως ἐδόξαζεν, ἔπειτα δὲ ἐξελέγξαι καὶ διαβαλεῖν αὐτά.   Gal. 5. 289; cf. 5. 480.

9   A further development is to *deceive, mislead*. This is clearly to be distinguished from the sense in 7 above, though the choice in some cases is not easy. This will also provide a better explanation

of the use of διάβολος to mean the *devil*; *deceiver* is surely a better starting-point than *slanderer*. Clear examples are:

τἆλλα ἐὼν σοφὸς καὶ διαβάλλων ἐκεῖνον εὖ, ἐν τούτῳ ἐσφάλη.
Hdt. 5. 50. 2.

Θεμιστοκλέης μὲν ταῦτα λέγων διέβαλλε, Ἀθηναῖοι δὲ ἐπείθοντο. Hdt. 8. 110. 1.

διέβαλλέ μ᾽ ἡ γραῦς (the uncouth complaint of the τοξότης).
Ar. *Th.* 1214.

This can be used with things as subject:

μάλιστα δ᾽ αὐτὸν διέβαλεν ἀνενεχθεῖσά τις ἐξ Ἀμφιλόχου μαντεία. Plu. 2. 563d.

In the passive:

εἰ γὰρ διαβέβληνται πανταχῇ τῷ σώματι. Pl. *Phd.* 67e.

ἀλλ᾽ ὅσαι δὴ ἔδοξαν πλείονα χρόνον δέκα μηνῶν ἔχειν ... κεῖναι διεβλήθησαν. Hp. *Nat. Puer.* 30 (p. 532 L).

The middle is used in much the same sense as the active, but as usual implying the involvement of the subject in the action, perhaps *deceive to one's own advantage*:

λέγων δὲ τοιάδε Ξέρξην διεβάλετο. Hdt. 9. 116. 2.

διαβάλλεταί σ᾽ ὁ θεῖος, ὦ πόνηρε σύ. Ar. *Av.* 1648.

We can perhaps classify here the problematic use in the Gortyn Law-Code, which editors have doubtfully taken to mean *defraud*. The context only indicates that it is an action which is likely to leave an heir with an obligation to fulfil:

αἰ ἀν[δ]εκσάμ[ε]νος ἒ̄ νενικαμένο[ς ἒ̄ ἐνκ]οιστὰν ὀπέλōν ἒ̄ διαβαλόμενος ἒ̄ διαϝειπάμενος ἀπο[θ]άνοι ... *Leg. Gort.* 9. 25.

There seems at least no reason to believe LSJ's doubtful suggestion (**VIII**) that it means *contract an obligation;* all the cases envisaged are of obligations, so something more specific must be intended.

10 To *assert falsely, allege*:

ἡ μὲν οὖν τότε συγχωρηθεῖσ᾽ εἰρήνη διὰ ταῦτ᾽, οὐ δι᾽ ἐμέ, ὡς οὗτος διέβαλλεν, ἐπράχθη. D. 18. 20.

With an internal accusative:

εἴ τι τῶν ἄλλων ὧν νυνὶ διέβαλλε καὶ διεξήει. D. 18. 14.

εἰ δὲ βουλεύων ἐγὼ προσάγειν τοὺς πρέσβεις ᾤμην δεῖν, τοῦτό μοι διαβάλλει. D. 18. 28.

ἃ μήτε προῄδει μηδεὶς μήτ᾽ ἂν ᾠήθη τήμερον ῥηθῆναι διαβάλλειν. D. 18. 225.

We can probably take in the same way this example from Aristophanes, though, as LSJ observes, the use of ἤσθιεν implies a new metaphor:

ἡ πόλις γὰρ ὠχριῶσα κἂν φόβῳ καθημένη,
ἄττα διαβάλοι τις αὐτῇ, ταῦτ᾽ ἂν ἥδιστ᾽ ἤσθιεν. Ar. Pax 643.

11 Perhaps we can add here an example where there is an object expressed, so that the verb means to *make the subject of a false allegation, misrepresent:*

ταύτην (sc. τὴν μαρτυρίαν) εἰς τὸν ὕστερον λόγον ὑπελίπετο, ὡς διαβαλεῖν τὸ πρᾶγμα ἐξ αὐτῆς δυνησόμενος. D. 28. 1.

LSJ places this on a par with D. 18. 225 (see 10), but in this case the object is the allegation.

12 To *blame* a person (for something), with dative:

τὴν ... ἀτυχίαν ᾗ με διαβάλλουσι. Antipho 2. 4. 4.

With εἰς:

αὐτὸ τοῦτο κατηγοροῦντος αὐτοῦ καὶ εἰς κιναιδίαν διαβάλλοντος. Luc. Demon. 50.

With πρός:

τοὺς ... διαβεβλημένους πρὸς αὐτὴν (sc. τὴν φιλοσοφίαν) παυστέον. Isoc. 15. 175.

πρὸς τὴν ὠμότητα τοῦ υἱοῦ διαβληθείς. Luc. Macr. 14.

πρὸς τὴν κακίαν διαβαλοῦμεν αὐτούς. Plu. 2. 809f.

This last example is classified by LSJ as *divert* from a course of action, but it is the direction towards which is emphasised, if this is what διαβάλλω means. There appears to be no good reason for separating this from the other two examples quoted. Also with ἐπί:

ἐπὶ βίῳ μὴ σώφρονι διαβεβλημένος.   Hdn. 2. 6. 6.

In the middle:

> διαβάλλεται ... ἐπὶ τῶν κυρτῶν κατόπτρων ὅταν ἐμφάσεις ποιῇ μείζονας ἑαυτῶν 'blame is laid on curved mirrors when they create enlarged images.' Plu. 2. 930b.

This last is given by LSJ in sense **V 4** *'disprove* a scientific ... doctrine' as an example of the passive. I am unable to make sense of the passage on that basis.

13   As a sub-sense of this we can attach a late usage, to *lay the blame for* a thing on someone:

> πολλοὶ τὸ πρᾶγμα ἐς βασιλέα διέβαλλον.   Procop. *Arc.* 22. 19.

Used intransitively it seems also to mean to *make a complaint*:

> περὶ ὧ ἀπέφαινεν ἠδικῆσθαι ὑπὸ σοῦ καὶ Δημητρίῳ ... ἠναγκάσθαι διαβαλεῖν.   *P. Teb.* 23. 4 (ii BC).

14   We may recapitulate the main senses thus:

1 *relocate on the opposite side, move across* (2). **b** *construct* or *throw* a bridge *across* (3).
2 intr. *pass over, cross*; tr. *go across, traverse* (3).
3 *place* or *put through, insert* (4).
4 *set on opposite sides* of a contest or argument, *make into an opponent, set against* (5). **b** intr. *be on the opposite side* (6).
5 *make an enemy of, denounce, discredit* (7).
6 *denounce, criticise* an opinion (8).
7 *deceive, mislead* (9). **b** *defraud* (9).
8 *assert falsely, allege* (10).
9 *make the subject of a false allegation, misrepresent* (11).
10 *blame* a person for something (12). **b** *lay the blame for* a thing on someone (12).

δίζημαι

Hesychius lists διττάμενον· ἀρνούμενον (Latte). For this ἀρνύμενον has also been proposed. It is possible to interpret this as a Cretan (or less likely Elean) form with -ττ- as the product of -dy-, cf.

φροντίττω, Τῆνα, ἀττάμιος. Thus if, as generally accepted (Frisk, Chantraine) δίζημαι is from *di-dyā-, a participle διττάμενος is to be expected. The meaning as given is inaccurate, but there are contexts in which either 'seeking' or 'achieving' would make sense.

διςκυροῦςι

SEG 32. 637 is a manumission document from Macedonia of iii AD. Part of it runs:

> ἀνεθόμην Ἀγα[θ]ήμερον κὲ Παράμονον παραμένουσί μοι τὸν
> τῆς ζωῆς χρόνον ὑπηρετούντων αὐτῶν τῇ θεῷ τὰς ἐθίμας
> ἡμέ[ρας]· τούτων οὐ διςκυροῦσι οὔτε μοι κληρονόμος οὔτε
> δανειςττής· εἰ δέ τις πειράσει, δίδωσι πρόστιμον ...

The editors have so presented the text, speculating about the meaning of the new verb διςκυρῶ. But a much easier solution is to divide the words

> οὐδὶς (= οὐδεὶς) κυροῦσι

The singular subject with a plural verb is poor grammar, but τούτων οὐδείς 'none of these' is plural in sense, if not grammatically. So too in English, however much purists frown, we often hear 'none of these are ...'. But is κυροῦσι from κυρέω or κυρόω? Although κυρέω is supposed to be a 'poetic' verb, it seems to offer better sense here, and it would not be the only example of a poetic word re-appearing in late prose. I suggest therefore the sentence might be translated: 'None of these are, as it happens, either a legatee of mine or a borrower from me.' This implies that the persons manumitted have no further claim on the manumitter or his estate.

ἔγρω

1 This word is recorded by LSJ as 'later form of ἐγείρω', which is true, but conceals the word's history. It is certainly so used by late authors, but it is surprising to find Homer (Il. 24. 789) added by the 1968 Supplement. The whole entry has now been deleted by the New Supplement. What has been overlooked is that the

normal epic (unaugmented) aorist middle of ἐγείρω is ἔγρετο and this form should not therefore have been quoted from Oppian as derived from ἔγρω. The same remark applies equally to the imperatives ἐγρέτω and ἔγρεσθε, which can and therefore presumably should be referred to ἐγείρω. The infinitive ἐγρέσθαι equally belongs to ἐγείρω (see LSJ), unless it is to be accented ἔγρεσθαι.

2   The facts are easy to establish. The aorist ἔγρετο was misinterpreted as an imperfect, and a present ἔγρεται, ἔγρονται was built on it; and from this a present indicative active ἔγρει. This allowed forms such as ἔγρετο, ἐγρέτω, ἔγρεσθε to be interpreted as passive instead of middle; but there is often little semantic difference between 'rousing oneself' and 'being roused'.

εἰκῇ, εἰκῆ

1   The meanings given in LSJ and the 1968 Supplement are as follows:

  I   *without plan* or *purpose, at random, at a venture.*
  II   *in vain.* 2 *without cause.*
  III   *slightly, moderately.*
  IV   *willingly, readily.*

The origin of the adverb is believed to be the dative of an obsolete substantive related to ἑκών. The spelling εἰκῆ is common in later authors.

2   All the translations given will make sense in certain examples. But the question the lexicographer must ask is: is it necessary to create five different meanings for the one word, and if so, are these the necessary five? Can we be sure that these are the meanings which can be proved to exist?

3   The first, which I would define more closely as *without plan, anyhow, at random,* is well attested, e.g.:

  ἔφυρον εἰκῇ πάντα. A. *Pr.* 450.

  εἰκῇ κράτιστον ζῆν, ὅπως δύναιτό τις. S. *OT* 979.

  αἳ δ' ἐν δρυὸς φύλλοισι πρὸς πέδῳ κάρα

εἰκῆ βαλοῦσαι. E. *Ba.* 686.

κράτιστον εἰκῆ ταῦτ' ἐᾶν ἀφειμένα. E. *El.* 379.

ὥσπερ σάρμα εἰκῆ κεχυμένον ὁ κάλλιστος κόσμος.

Heraclit. 47.

ὁμοῦ ταράττων τήν τε γῆν καὶ τὴν θάλατταν εἰκῆ.

Ar. *Eq.* 431.

οὐ μέντοι ... κεκαλλιεπημένους γε λόγους ... ἀλλ' ἀκούσεσθε
εἰκῆ λεγόμενα τοῖς ἐπιτυχοῦσιν ὀνόμασιν. Pl. *Ap.* 17c.

οὐκ εἰκῆ αὐτὸν (*sc.* τὸν σῖτον) ὅπου ἂν τύχωσιν ἀπέβαλον.

X. *Oec.* 20. 28.

πᾶσα φύσις ... οὐθὲν μὲν εἰκῆ ποιεῖ, ἔνεκα δέ τινος πάντα.

Arist. *Protr.* 23.

κρέμαται δὲ σὺν ἱστίῳ ἄρμενα πάντα
εἰκῆ ἀποκλασθέντα. Theoc. 22. 14.

4 The second well-attested meaning is ignored by LSJ, and only
superficially represented by the 1968 Supplement, quoting a
papyrus of i AD. This can be defined as *without thought for the
consequences, heedlessly, recklessly*. Translators have frequently
used such expressions in dealing with it. It seems to be especially
common in the Attic orators, and I have not yet detected examples
earlier than the end of v BC. A selection only is presented here:

οὐ χρὴ προσφέρειν τοῖς πλησίοισιν εἰκῆ
τὴν χεῖρ'. Ar. *Lys.* 471.

φοβοίμην ἂν αὐτοὺς καὶ αἰσχυνοίμην ἀπολιπὼν ταῦτα εἰκῆ
ἀπελθεῖν. X. *Cyr.* 5. 1. 23.

ἡ πόλις αὖ τούς τε νόμους ἀναγκάζει μανθάνειν καὶ κατὰ
τούτους ζῆν κατὰ παράδειγμα, ἵνα μὴ αὐτοὶ ἐφ' αὑτῶν εἰκῆ
πράττωσιν. Pl. *Prt.* 326d.

μή μοι οὕτως εἰκῆ, ὥσπερ τι ἠδικημένος ὑπό τινος, ἀλλὰ
προσέχων ἐμοὶ τὸν νοῦν ἀπόκριναι. Pl. *Hipp.* 225b.

ὁ γὰρ εἰκῆ τοῦτο καὶ πρὸς πολλοὺς πράττων καὶ μισθοῦ ...

Aeschin. 1. 52.

τοὺς εἰκῆ διδομένους στεφάνους. Aeschin. 3. 177.

τοὺς οὐδὲν ἀποδεξομένους τῶν εἰκῆ λεγομένων. Isoc. 4. 12.

πόλεις καὶ τηλικαύτας τὸ μέγεθος δυνάμεις οὕτως εἰκῆ τῷ
βαρβάρῳ παραδεδώκαμεν. Isoc. 4. 136.

ὧν νῦν ἀλογίστως καὶ λίαν εἰκῆ πολὺν ἤδη χρόνον

καταφρονοῦμεν.   Isoc. 8. 30.

τοῖς εἰκῇ καὶ φορτικῶς καὶ χύδην ὅ τι ἂν ἐπέλθῃ λέγουσιν.
        Isoc. 12. 24.

ἵνα μηδεὶς ἀδικῇ μηδένα τῶν ἐμπόρων εἰκῇ.   D. 33. 1.

ἢ ἃ ἔλεγες πρὸς τοὺς δικαστάς, εἰκῇ οὑτωσὶ λέγειν, ἢ περὶ
ὧν τὰς μαρτυρίας παρέσχον, οὕτως ἂν παρασχέσθαι.
        D. 48. 43.

τὸ μηθὲν εἰκῇ λέγειν ἀλλὰ μετὰ λόγου.   Arist. EE 1216ᵇ40.

5   As a development from this sense we can discern a special use
with verbs of believing, where it means *without good cause:*

ἀλλ᾿ οὐδὲ μετὰ πολλῶν μαρτύρων ἀποδιδοὺς εἰκῇ τις ἂν
ἐπίστευσεν.   D. 30. 20, cf. 28. 5.

μὴ τοῖς αἰτιωμένοις εἰκῇ πιστεύειν.   Isoc. 15. 157.

ἐκτὸς εἰ μὴ εἰκῇ ἐπιστεύσατε.   1 Ep. Cor. 15. 2.

This last example is listed by LSJ under the heading *in vain* (see
6 below), but it appears to be indistinguishable from the others.
This also appears in later Greek with other verbs:

οὐ γὰρ εἰκῇ τὴν μάχαιραν φορεῖ (ἡ ἐξουσία).   Ep. Rom. 13. 4.

ὧν οὐκ ἄν τις εἰκῇ καταφρονήσειεν.   Plu. Cam. 6.

6   The sense *in vain, to no purpose* has been proposed for *1 Ep.
Cor.* 15.2 quoted just above. Clearer examples are:

τοσαῦτα ἐπάθετε εἰκῇ; εἴ γε καὶ εἰκῆ.   Ep. Gal. 3. 4.

φοβοῦμαι ὑμᾶς, μή πως εἰκῇ κεκοπίακα εἰς ὑμᾶς.
        Ep. Gal. 4. 11.

εἰκῆ φυσιούμενος ὑπὸ τοῦ νοὸς τῆς σαρκὸς αὐτοῦ.
        Ep. Col. 2. 18.

7   There remain a few examples that cannot easily be accommodated in this scheme, and I believe we therefore need to establish
a new sense for them. It is quite clearly influenced by a paretymo-
logical connexion with εἰκός and corresponds closely in meaning to
εἰκότως. Even if its true etymology is different, this does not pre-
clude the development of its sense being influenced by a merely
apparent kinship. I propose therefore to add a new sense *as is*

likely, reasonably, probably. The best example is from the iv BC comic poet Antiphanes, listed by the 1968 Supplement to LSJ, but translated *of one's free will*.

> ὥστε μηδ' ἄν, εἰ χαλκοῦς ἔχων
> μυκτῆρας εἰσέλθοι τις, ἐξελθεῖν πάλιν
> εἰκῇ, τοσαύτην ἐξακοντίζει πνοήν.
> Antiph. 216. 7 (K–A) (= Athen. 14. 623a.)

But it is clear that what is being said here is that if anyone went in even equipped with nostrils of bronze, he would not come out again εἰκῇ. Clearly he would want to come out, but would not be able to. εἰκῇ serves to qualify the verb, stating that this would be the likely result; translate 'it is not likely he would come out again'. Once this sense is accepted other passages may be found to support it:

> τοιαύτας ἐπιβουλὰς ... οὐδ' ἂν κατὰ τῶν ἐχθίστων τις εἰκῇ
> ποιήσαιτο. Aeschin. 2. 22.

Another possible example:

> οἷσιν ἡ πόλις πρὸ τοῦ
> οὐδὲ φαρμακοῖσιν εἰκῇ ῥαδίως ἐχρήσατ' ἄν. Ar. Ra. 733.

8 It remains to examine the alleged example of the meaning *slightly, moderately*. The reference quoted is from Agatharchides, a geographer of ii BC, whose work is known only through two later summaries or paraphrases. It is therefore questionable whether the words quoted can legitimately be attributed to this author. Users of LSJ should always beware of believing in usages attributed to an author on the basis of a fragment. The passage in question runs:

> ἀφ' αἵματος καὶ γάλακτος ζῶσιν, εἰς ταὐτὸ μίξαντες καὶ
> κυλίσαντες ἐν ἀγγείοις εἰκῇ πεπυρωμένοις. Agatharch. 61.

The reason for so interpreting εἰκῇ is that the parallel version of this passage in Diodorus Siculus speaks of 'lightly cooking' (βραχὺν χρόνον ἐψήσαντες D. S. 3. 22. 2). But there is no other evidence to support this meaning, and it does not appear to fit the scheme of semantic development (see 9 below). It should be observed that ἀγγείοις πεπυρωμένοις can hardly mean 'heated vessels'; it ought to be 'fired', i.e. baked in a kiln. It is not impossible to take it as meaning 'vessels fired anyhow', i.e. they are not experts in making pottery. At best, such examples should be kept in reserve, in case subsequently better evidence comes to light. They ought not to appear in a standard lexicon without some indication of their uncertainty.

9   I have no doubt that further research will disclose many more examples of the uses demonstrated above. I have checked out numerous other references without finding anything which could not be explained by the scheme of meanings given above. For convenience, I set forth here the complete scheme:

1   *without plan, anyhow, at random.*
2   *without thought for the consequences, heedlessly, recklessly.*
3   (with verbs of believing) *without good cause.*
4   *to no purpose, in vain.*
5   *as is likely, reasonably, probably.*

ἐκτός

1   LSJ divides this into three sections: **I** as preposition; **II** absolutely; **III** with verbs of motion. The first section is further divided into four senses: 1 *out of, far from, beyond*; *free from, exempt from.* 2 of time *beyond.* 3 *except, besides, apart from* (with an odd example used absolutely, which should have been in **II**). 4 *without the consent of.* It is difficult in such a case to decide whether construction or sense should have priority, especially as both prepositional and absolute uses occur in Homer (a fact concealed by LSJ). But it can hardly be doubted that historically ἐκτός was first an adverb, which came to be used with an ablatival genitive, so becoming a preposition. Since both usages remain common throughout antiquity, it would seem easier to make the principal classification semantic, and to subordinate construction to this. It is obvious that *out of* and *exempt from* belong to different senses, and further nuances will appear when we study the examples. It has here been necessary to supplement the material given by LSJ, and references preceded by an asterisk are not listed there.

2   We may start with the physical examples referring to situation *on the outside* as opposed to inside an area, building, etc.:

ὡς δὲ ἴδεν νεῦρόν τε καὶ ὄγκους ἐκτὸς ἐόντας. 'on seeing the thread and barbs (of the arrow) were outside (the wound)'.

*Il. 4. 151.

ἐκτὸς μὲν δὴ λέξο 'outside the tent or hut'.   *Il. 24. 650.

Similarly:

οἱ μὲν ἄρ' ἐκτὸς ἄμαξαν ἐΰτροχον ἡμιονείην
ὅπλεον.   *Od. 6. 72.

πῶς ἔλεγον αἵδε ...
ὡς ἐκτὸς εἴης. 'away from home'.   E. IT 1310.

οὐκ ὥρων οἱ ἐντὸς τοὺς ἐκτὸς ὅ τι ἔπρησσον.   *Hdt. 6. 79. 2.

ἀνιὼν ἐκ Πειραιῶς ὑπὸ τὸ βόρειον τεῖχος ἐκτός.

*Pl. R. 439e.

The 1968 Supplement adds an example of ἡ ἐκτός, sc. γῆ:

ἐκ τῆς ἐκτός.   Didyma 25A 9, B 21 (ii BC).

3   We can place next the adverbial usage with expressions implying motion, *to the outside, out*:

ἐκτὸς οὖσ' ἀγαλμάτων
εὔχου 'go away from the statues and pray'. A. Th. 265.

οὔκουν μ' ἐάσεις κἀκτὸς εἶ;—πορεύσομαι.   S. OT 676.

σὺ δ' ἐκτὸς ᾖξας πρὸς τί;   S. El. 1402.

ἔρριψεν ἐκτὸς αὐτόν.   S. Tr. 269.

χώρει δέ, θύγατερ, ἐκτός.   E. IA 1117.

τὸν δὲ Ἀρδιαῖον ... εἷλκον παρὰ τὴν ὁδὸν ἐκτὸς ἐπ' ἀσπαλάθων
κνάμπτοντες. 'They dragged A. off the road mangling him on
thorns.'   Pl. R. 616a.

4   The prepositional use with genitive means therefore *on the outside of, out of* a designated area, building, etc. It may stand before
or after the substantive.

παρὰ τάφρον ὀρυκτὴν τείχεος ἐκτός.   *Il. 9. 67; 21. 608.

στῆ δ' ἐκτὸς κλισίης.   Il. 14. 13.

ἔχε μώνυχας ἵππους
ἐκτὸς ὁδοῦ.   *Il. 23. 424.

αὐλῆς ἐκτὸς ἐών.   *Od. 4. 678; *23. 178.

καπνοῦ καὶ κύματος ἐκτὸς ἔεργε
νῆα.   Od. 12. 219.

τῶν δὲ ἐκτὸς τούτων (sc. ὅρων) οἰκημένων.   *Hdt. 8. 47.

This too is used with expressions implying motion:

Ἥρη δ' Ἀπόλλωνα καλέσσατο δώματος ἐκτός.   *Il. 15. 143.

οὐδέ μιν ἐκτὸς ἀταρπιτοῦ ἐστυφέλιξεν.   *Od. 17. 234.

(LSJ does not admit any Homeric use in the section on motion.)

καί σ' ἐκτὸς αὐλείων πυλῶν
τοῦδ' οὕνεκ' ἐξέπεμπον.   S. Ant. 18.

οὐκ εἶ πατρῴας ἐκτὸς ὡς τάχιστα γῆς.   *E. Hipp. 1065.

μή σ' ὁ θυμὸς ἁρπάσας
ἐκτὸς οἴσει τῶν ἐλαῶν.   Ar. Ra. 995.

5   The spatial sense may be used in a figurative phrase, thus
opening the way for the development of transferred senses. The
phrase ἐκτὸς ἔχειν πόδα means *keep one's foot away,* as we should
say, *keep clear:*

καλὰ γινώσκοντ' ἀνάγκᾳ
ἐκτὸς ἔχειν πόδα.   Pi. P. 4.289.

With genitive:

ἴσως ἂν ἐκτὸς κλαυμάτων ἔχοις πόδα.   S. Ph. 1260.

6   The fully developed transference occurs when the reference is
no longer simply to space, but includes the attendant circumstances, *outside, away from* a situation:

εἰ δ' ἐκτὸς ἔλθοις, πημονὰς εὔχου λαβεῖν.   S. Tr. 1189.

The reference here is to transgressing an oath.

θεοῦ δὲ νόμον
οὐ παραβαίνομεν.
ἃ δ' ἐκτός, ὄμμα τέρψει ...   E. Ion 231.

τῶν δ' ἐκτὸς οὐδὲν περισκεπτομένη 'taking no notice of the
circumstances.'   Plb. 2. 4. 8.

With genitive:

καὶ γὰρ ἂν τὸν ἄριστον ἄνδρα ... ἐκτὸς τῶν ἐωθότων
νοημάτων στήσειε.   *Hdt. 3. 80. 3.

ὃς δ᾽ ἂν ἐκτὸς βαίνῃ τούτων (sc. τῶν νόμων). *Pl. Prt. 326d.

ἐκτὸς τῶν νῦν ἠθῶν ... θρέψονται. *Pl. R. 541a.

7 Slightly different is the case where membership of a group is concerned, *not belonging, outside* a group or category:

ὃς ... οὐκέτι συντρόφοις
ὀργαῖς ἔμπεδος, ἀλλ᾽ ἐκτὸς ὁμιλεῖ. S. Aj. 640.

πρὸς τοὺς ἐκτός τε καὶ ἀλλοφύλους 'with regard to strangers and aliens'. Pl. Lg. 629d.

πολλά ... καὶ λέγειν καὶ ποιεῖν πρὸς τοὺς ἐκτός.
Plb. 2. 47. 10.

Here οἱ ἐκτός means 'those not in the immediate circle,' 'the general public'. In LXX Si. prol. 4 the same phrase means 'those who are not Jews'. With genitive, *apart from, not counting*:

ὅπλα δὲ οὐ νομίζουσι ἔχειν ... ἐκτὸς ἐγχειριδίου (v.l. ἔξω ἐγχειριδίων). *Hdt. 7. 85. 1.

ταὐτὰ ἐσθίοντι καὶ πίνοντι βοΐ τε καὶ ἵππῳ καὶ πᾶσιν ἐκτὸς ἀνθρώπου. *Hp.VM 3 (p. 576 L.)

ἀπέκτειναν ἅπαντας τοὺς ἐκ Μιλήτου ἐκτὸς ὀλίγων.
X. HG 1. 2. 3.

ἔχεις τι ἐκτὸς τούτων λέγειν ... ; Pl. Grg. 474d.

καὶ ἐάν τις ἐκτὸς ὢν τῶν ὀλίγων συμβουλεύῃ. Pl. Prt. 322e.

πάντας τοὺς ἐκτὸς τῶν ἀρχόντων. *Pl. R. 552d.

8 As a sub-sense we can add here *going beyond, exceeding*, with genitive:

ἐκτὸς ἐλπίδος γνώμης τ᾽ ἐμῆς
σωθείς. S. Ant. 330.

Cf. without genitive:

ἀλλ᾽ ἡ γὰρ ἐκτὸς καὶ παρ᾽ ἐλπίδας χαρά
ἔοικεν ἄλλη μῆκος οὐδὲν ἡδονῇ. S. Ant. 392.

δοκημάτων ἐκτὸς ἦλθεν ἐλπίς. E. HF 771.

ἐπείτε δὲ κατέστη θόρυβος καὶ ἐκτὸς πέντε ἡμερέων ἐγένετο 'when the uproar died down and more than five days had passed'. Hdt. 3. 80. 1.

LSJ gives this a special sense to itself 'of time'; but though true,

the category of time is indicated by the reference to days, and it
would be very surprising to find, e.g., ἐκτὸς ὄρθρου meaning 'after
dawn'.

9   Next we can place the sense, with genitive, *having no share or
part in, exempt from, untouched by*:

> σώφρονα θυμὸν ἔχων ἐκτὸς ἀτασθαλίης.   Thgn. 754; cf. 744.

> ἐκτὸς αἰτίας κυρεῖς.   A. *Pr*. 330.

> ἐκτὸς μὲν ἔσεσθε πρὸς ἐκείνου αἰτίης, ἐκτὸς δὲ πρὸς ἡμέων.
> Hdt. 4. 133. 3.

> ἐκτὸς ἄτας.   S. *Ant*. 614.

> ἐκτὸς ὄντα πημάτων.   S. *Ph*. 504; *fr*. 724.

> ἐκτὸς ὤν γε συμφορᾶς.   *E. *HF* 1249.

> οἰκεῖν ἐν πάσῃ εὐδαιμονίᾳ ἐκτὸς κακῶν.
> Pl. *Grg*. 523b; *R*. 498c.

> ἐκτὸς εἶ τοῦ μέλλειν ἀποθνήσκειν αὔριον.   Pl. *Cri*. 46e.

> ἐκτὸς ἐὼν πάσης ἀδικίης ἑκουσίης καὶ φθορίης.   *Hp. *Jusj*.

10   Slightly different is the use, with genitive, to mean *not subject
to, beyond the reach of*:

> πόλεις ... ὅσαι ἦσαν ἐκτὸς τῆς ἑαυτῶν δυνάμεως.
> *Th. 2. 7. 1.

So in the phrase ἐκτὸς ἑαυτοῦ *out of one's own control, beside oneself*:

> καὶ ἐκτὸς ἑωυτοῦ ἐγένετο.   Hp. *Epid*. 7. 46; 7. 90.

11   A curious absolute use occurs with εἰ μή in later Greek, to
mean *except in the case that, unless*:

> γνωρίζω δὲ ὑμῖν ... τὸ εὐαγγέλιον ... τίνι λόγῳ εὐηγγελισάμην
> ὑμῖν, εἰ κατέχετε, ἐκτὸς εἰ μὴ εἰκῇ ἐπιστεύσατε.
> *1 Ep. Cor*. 15. 2.

(This passage is also discussed in the note on εἰκῇ.)

> ἐκτὸς εἰ μὴ κατὰ τὸν Θάμυριν ... εἴη τὴν φύσιν 'unless he
> resembles Thamyris in nature'.   Luc. *Pisc*. 6.

Similarly ἐκτὸς ὅτι means *apart from the fact that*:

> ἐκτὸς γὰρ ὅτι φοίνικές τε ὑπερμήκεις ...   Hld. 10. 5.

12   The senses might be re-arranged as follows:

1   *on the outside* (2); with expressions implying motion, *to the outside, out* (3).
2   w. gen. *on the outside of, out of* (4).
3   ἐκτὸς ἔχειν πόδα, (fig.) *keep one's foot away, keep clear* (5).
4   *outside, away from* a situation (6).
5   *not belonging, outside* a group or category (7).
6   w.gen. *apart from, not counting* (7). **b** *going beyond, exceeding* (8).
7   *having no share or part in, exempt from, untouched by* (9).
8   *not subject to, beyond the reach of* (10).
9   ἐκτὸς εἰ μή, *except in the case that, unless;* ἐκτὸς ὅτι, *apart from the fact that* (11).

ἐλύς

1   The 1968 Supplement had an entry for this word which must be quoted in full:

ἐλύς, ύ, dub. sens., οἰκόπεδον ἐλὺ [κ]αὶ χέρ[σον] *SEG* 10. 238. 51 (Athens, v B.C.); cf. εἰλύ, ἕλος, ἐλεόθρεπτος (Suppl.)

It has been removed from the New Supplement. There is a gloss in Hesychius, quoted by LSJ: εἰλύ· μέλαν, and an entry εἰλύς = ἰλύς *mud, slime.* Ἕλος is of course the normal word for a piece of wetland or marsh, and this occurs in the compound ἐλεόθρεπτος, an epithet of σέλινον parsley (Il. 2. 776). This is changed by the Supplement to read ἐλεο-, which agrees with the modern OCT. Since the aspirate in Homer is quite clearly the product of the tradition, East Ionic being a psilotic dialect, it is immaterial which breathing is used. The three words compared in this entry are therefore an adjective meaning *black* or *dark,* a substantive meaning *marsh* and a derivative of this. No wonder the Editor regarded the sense as doubtful. If he had included ἰλύς, this too would point in the direction of wet ground; but if εἰλύ is associated with ἰλύς, this excludes the connexion with ἕλος, a quite unrelated word. ΕΛΥ in an Old Attic inscription can stand for εἰλ- or ἠλ- as well as ἐλ- ; but it should not be interpreted ἐλ- , etc., since this would be written *ΗΕΛΥ*. The temptation to emend it to ἐδύ must also be resisted, not only for this reason, but because in the Old Attic alphabet *Λ* cannot be a misreading of *Δ*.

2 The context is which the word occurs is a lengthy inscription recording details of confiscated property. The relevant section is quoted by B. D. Merritt, *Hesperia*, 8 (1939) 93 thus:

[ο]ἰκό[πε]δ̣ον ἐλὺ [κ]αὶ χέρ[ρον]

and since this is reproduced by *SEG*, the quotation by the Supplement is inexact. There is of course no reason to replace Attic χέρρον with χέρσον. Merritt's commentary reads: 'The traditional reading of this line is [ο]ἰκό[πεδ]ον ἐ Λυσαρχε—. In the curious word Λυσαρχε— there is no trace of a sigma and the "rho" is certainly an iota. The reading should be [κ]αὶ and not ϛαρ, and this leaves the adjectives ἐλύ and χέρ[ρον] as descriptive epithets of the οἰκόπεδον. The word χέρρον means fallow or uncultivated, and raises no problem; the word ἐλύ is known only from Hesychius (where it is written εἰλύ) and supposedly means the same as μέλαν (cf. εἰλύ in Liddell & Scott).'

3 Against this it can be argued that οἰκόπεδον does not mean simply a piece of land, but specifically a piece intended for the construction of a building, what we term a building-plot. It is difficult therefore to reconcile the sense of *barren*, much less *fallow*, with this word. If ἐλύ means dark, this too is an inappropriate detail to record in this context. Of course a *dry* plot would be a commendation, and this may well be right; but it will then be necessary to give ἐλύ some other meaning.

4 I hesitate to differ from a noted epigraphist such as Merritt, and without autopsy I cannot comment on the actual reading of the stone. But I think there is good enough reason to question his restoration, given that the details are so uncertain. But there is a stronger argument which must be used. How probable is it that there existed in the Attic dialect of v BC a word which has left only one example in either literature or inscriptions and reappears only as a gloss, which may well be corrupt, in a late lexicographer? If the word had a plausible meaning and etymology, we might accept it; but so long as it remains isolated, I beg to suggest that it should

be banished to the growing limbo of dubious forms awaiting either rehabilitation or consignment to the dustbin.

ἐνδαής

Hesychius has the entry ενδαγει· εμμανει, which Latte suggested emending to ἐνδαμεῖ· ἐμμένει. An easier emendation would be to suppose that Hesychius (or his source or his tradition) has confused, as often, Γ and Ϝ. If we read this as ἐνδαϜεῖ, it can be explained as the dative of an adjective compounded of ἐν and δάος 'torch', which is well known to have lost a digamma; cf. δαβελός· δαλός. Λάκωνες. 'Fired with a torch' by a simple extension of sense can be used for 'frenzied', and the gloss ἐμμανεῖ may therefore be accurate.

ἑξῆς, ἑξείης

1 The etymology of this word is not entirely clear, but it is generally agreed to be a case-form of a substantive formed on the root of ἔχω, but with the sense of 'cling' associated with ἔχομαι. The aspirate will be the consequence of a suffix -σ-, as in future ἕξω. The compound ἐφεξῆς strongly suggests a substantive in the genitive, meaning *row*, *series*, or the like. All words which denote some aspect of the concept of order are capable of a tripartite division of senses: with reference to space, time, and sequence as an abstract. For instance, if we say A comes before B, this might be realised in space in a written alphabet, or in time if it is recited; but the order exists irrespective of its realisation in time or space. We should certainly expect to find this principle underlying the arrangement of senses in the Lexicon. Curiously LSJ mentions 'of time, *thereafter, next*' only in **I 4**, and 'of place' then appears as **4 b**. So how do we understand the meaning *in a row* placed and exemplified in **I 1**? It is evident that the article needs to be completely rewritten.

2 Another problem concerns adverbs which are constructed with substantives so as to become prepositions or quasi-prepositions. Should the article be divided into **A** *adverb* and **B** *preposition*? Or

is it more convenient to keep the semantic division as the leading discriminator and subordinate construction to it? In a short article like this, I would suggest that meaning is more important, and the **A/B** arrangement will involve unnecessary duplication.

3   I should therefore begin with *contiguity in space*. But at once it becomes evident that ἑξῆς covers two different ideas. We can define the first as *in proximity, close by, near*:

> ἔνθα σ' ἐγὼν ἀγαγοῦσα ἅμ' ἠοῖ φαινομένηφιν
> εὐνάσω ἑξείης.   Od. 4. 408.

Menelaus is recounting an exploit of Odysseus, when Eidothee told him how to overcome Proteus, and volunteered to introduce him among the seals, so that he would be near enough to grip Proteus before he was fully awake.

> Ἀτθίδας δ' ἄγων
> ἑξήκοντα ναῦς ὁ Θησέως
> παῖς ἑξῆς ἐναυλόχει.   E. *IA* 249.

With dative:

> ἀγοράσω τ' ἐν τοῖς ὅπλοις ἑξῆς Ἀριστογείτονι.   Ar. *Lys.* 633.
> Λάχητί τ' οἰκήσαιμι τὴν ἑξῆς θύραν.   Ephipp. 16.4.

and with elliptical genitive:

> σίτησιν αὐτὸν ἐν πρυτανείῳ λαμβάνειν
> θρόνον τε τοῦ Πλούτωνος ἑξῆς.   Ar. *Ra.* 765.

4   But there is another spatial sense where the idea of contiguity refers to plural subjects, i.e. *next to one another, in a row*:

> φῶκαι δ' ἐξ ἁλὸς ἦλθον ἀολλέες. αἱ μὲν ἔπειτα
> ἑξῆς εὐνάζοντο παρὰ ῥηγμῖνι θαλάσσης.   Od. 4. 449.

> ἑξῆς δ' ἑζόμενοι πολιὴν ἅλα τύπτον ἐρετμοῖς.   Od. 4. 580.

LSJ begins the article with these examples, but unfortunately not all the others placed here belong to this sense. Th. 7. 29. 4 will be found in 7 below.

5   We can now proceed to proximity in time: *next in time, immediately following*:

τὸν ἑξῆς χρόνον. Pl. *Plt.* 271b.

ἐγένετο δὲ ἐν τῇ ἑξῆς ἡμέρᾳ. *Ev. Luc.* 9. 37; cf. 7. 11.

εἰς τὸ ἑξῆς. *P. Oxy.* 474. 28 (ii AD).

This too can be used prepositionally with dative:

ὅτι τὸ ἑξῆς ἔργον τοῖς Μαραθῶνι διεπράξαντο. Pl. *Mx.* 241a.

Also, with genitive:

βούλομαι τοίνυν ἐπανελθεῖν ἐφ' ἃ τούτων ἑξῆς ἐπολιτευόμην.
D. 18. 102.

6   It is not always easy to distinguish between proximity in time and proximity in sequence, but we can see a difference in the following examples, where we can use the definition *next in sequence*:

τὸν ἑξῆς λόγον οὐδένες ... ἀποδοῖεν. Pl. *Ti.* 20b.

This is not the next argument in time, but that which follows logically from what has gone before. So, I think, (notice the use of the present imperative):

λέγε μόνον ἑξῆς   Pl. *Plt.* 286c.

ἐὰν ὦσιν ὁσοιδηποτοῦν ἀριθμοὶ ἑξῆς ἀνάλογον. Euc. 8. 1.

καὶ τὰ ἑξῆς 'and what follows'.   Longin. 23. 4

With dative:

δοκεῖ τούτοις ἑξῆς εἶναί τι χρῆμα. Pl. *Cra.* 399d.

οὐκ ὀρθῶς τὸ ἑξῆς ἐλάβομεν τῇ γεωμετρίᾳ.
Pl. *R.* 528a.; cf. Longin. 9. 14.

With genitive:

τὰ τούτων ἑξῆς 'the following lines (in a poem)'.   Pl. *R.* 390a.

τούτων τοίνυν ἑξῆς ὀψόμεθα ἐάν ...   Pl. *Phlb.* 42c.

7   This also has a relative sense, similar to the spatial one described in 4 above, *in close succession, without intermission, one after another*. Here too it is sometimes difficult to distinguish between succession in time and in sequence.

ὁ δ' ἔπειτα θεοῖς εὔχεσθαι ἀνώγει
πάσας ἑξείης. Il. 6. 241.

τοὺς ἀνθρώπους ἐφόνευον φειδόμενοι οὔτε πρεσβυτέρας οὔτε
νεωτέρας ἡλικίας, ἀλλὰ πάντας ἑξῆς. Th. 7. 29. 4.

ὅστις δὲ πάσας συντιθεὶς ψέγει λόγῳ
γυναῖκας ἑξῆς, σκαιός ἐστι κοὐ σοφός. E. fr. 672.

This can also be used with the singular of πᾶς, since this is a
virtual plural ('every' = 'all'):

οὐκοῦν ἄγξουσ' εὖ καὶ χρηστῶς ἑξῆς τὸν πάντα γέροντα
διὰ τὴν ἄγνοιαν, ἐπεὶ καὶ νῦν γιγνώσκοντες πατέρ' ὄντα.
                                                              Ar. Ec. 638.

8   I believe the structure proposed is adequate to accommodate
all uses of this word, though it would obviously be impossible to
make a categoric statement without assembling and analysing all
the examples to be recovered from the whole of Greek literature.
But some remarks are necessary on items which appear in LSJ
and not here. **I b** is 'Math. ἑ. ἀνάλογον in continued proportion',
quoted from Euclid with similar examples from other mathemati-
cal works. The Euclid example has been given above in 6, and I
can see no reason why this should be accorded a special sense.

9   LSJ alleges the existence of a sense '*in a regular, consequential
manner*'. On its own admission ὁ ἑξῆς λόγος, which is placed here,
means 'the following argument', and this falls plainly under my
definition. But it is just possible that in some of the examples
quoted from Plato it means *as a logical consequence*. If certainly
established, this would require a new sense. But although it is
possible, it does not appear to me to be strictly necessary.

10   In grammar τὸ ἑξῆς is alleged to mean '*grammatical sequence*'
as opposed to ὑπερβατόν (**I 3**). This is clearly another special
application of the sense defined under 6 above.

11   In **II** LSJ inserts under the prepositional use with the dative
two curious examples:

οὐ γὰρ παρὰ τὸ ἑξῆς τῷ νοερῷ ζῴῳ (ὁ θάνατος) οὐδὲ παρὰ
τὸν λόγον τῆς κατασκευῆς. M. Ant. 4. 5.

This is translated '*that which befits ...*', which is possible sense. But
I do not see why in this case τῷ νοερῷ ζῴῳ is not placed between

τό and ἑξῆς. I should translate 'death is not for a thinking animal contrary to what comes next', i.e. if we think about the human condition, we shall recognise that death follows life in inevitable sequence. I think this is at least as acceptable as Farquharson's 'for it is not contrary to what is conformable to a reasonable creature', or C. R. Haines's 'for it is not out of keeping with an intellectual creature'. The other example is from a papyrus of i AD, which is a memorial to a magistrate complaining that the writer's wife has left him and taken away some of his property. The relevant part runs:

κα[ὶ ἐ]γὼ μὲν οὖν ἐπεχορήγησα αὐτῇ τὰ ἑξῆς καὶ ὑπὲρ δύναμιν. ἡ δὲ ἀλλότρια φρονήσασα τῆς κοινῆς συμβιώ[σεως] κατὰ πέρ[α]ς ἐξῆ[λθε] καὶ ἀπηνέ⟨γ⟩καντο τὰ ἡμέτερα ὧν τὸ καθ᾽ ἕν ὑπόκειται. 'And I went so far as to make her a gift of the following, even beyond my means. But she was so estranged from the life we shared together that she went further and they carried off our property, the details of which are recorded below.'   *P. Oxy.* 282. 7.

At the end, which is largely missing, there was a list of the property claimed. It seems obvious that τὰ ἑξῆς has its normal sense of *the following*. However LSJ translates this example 'made *suitable* provision for her'. I beg to suggest this sense is totally illusory.

ἐσχάρα

1 I discussed the semantic history of this word in an article contributed to Ernst Risch's Festschrift (*O-o-pe-ro-si,* ed. A. Etter (Berlin, 1986) 515–23). In this I demonstrated that of the six main sections into which the article in LSJ is divided, five were already so defined in ancient lexica, and the sixth is an illusory sense which needs to be redefined. I do not propose here to repeat all the discussion, but shall confine myself to suggesting the pattern which is needed to disclose the original meaning and the lines of its semantic development. The New Supplement has largely followed my suggestions.

2 The earliest use was probably that of a place in which a fire can be made:

ὅσσαι μὲν Τρώων πυρὸς ἐσχάραι.   Il. 10. 418.

LSJ assign the meaning *watch-fire* to this example, but the addition of πυρός is against this, though in the context it is the reason for the fires. So in the Odyssey the word is used of the domestic *hearth*:

πῦρ μὲν ἐπ' ἐσχαρόφιν μέγα καίετο.   Od. 5. 59; cf. 20. 123.

In the other examples it is the *hearth* as a place by which people sit:

ἡ δ' ἧσται ἐπ' ἐσχάρῃ ἐν κονίῃσι
πὰρ πυρί.   Od. 7. 153.

Clearly there is here an overlap with ἑστία, from which ἐσχάρα was later distinguished. LSJ claim as a special sense *sacrificial hearth* quoting:

οἱ δ' ὗν εἰσῆγον μάλα πίονα, πενταέτηρον.
τὸν μὲν ἔπειτ' ἔστησαν ἐπ' ἐσχάρῃ, οὐ δὲ συβώτης
λήθετ' ἄρ' ἀθανάτων, φρεσὶ γὰρ κέχρητ' ἀγαθῇσιν.
ἀλλ' ὅ γ' ἀπαρχόμενος κεφαλῆς τρίχας ἐν πυρὶ βάλλεν
ἀγριόδοντος ὑός ...   Od. 14. 420.

Again the purpose of the action was a sacrificial ritual, but the place where it was conducted was the ordinary domestic hearth. After Homer this sense is rare and uncertain:

ὑψηλῆς δρυός
κόρμους πλατείας ἐσχάρας βαλὼν ἔπι.   E. Cyc. 384.

This describes the Cyclops making a fire in his cave, and the epithet πλατείας supports the idea that it means simply a *fire-place*. Otherwise it seems only to occur in much later Greek, at a time when revivals of obsolete words and meanings were fashionable:

ἐν ταῖς ἐσχάραις ἔγραφε σχήματα τῶν γεωμετρικῶν.
Plu. Marc. 17. 11.

This clearly means in the ashes left by a fire on a hearth.

2   The normal classical sense is *a portable container for a fire, brazier*. A drawing of such an object in bronze is reproduced in my article. This was a small example suitable only for a charcoal fire, but larger ones clearly existed consisting of a metal basket with

ventilation to ensure a good draught for the fire. Such braziers were in use for cooking, and probably also for space-heating:

δμῶες ἐξενέγκατε
τὴν ἐσχάραν μοι δεῦρο καὶ τὴν ῥιπίδα. Ar. *Ach.* 888.

In a list of kitchen utensils:

δοίδυκα τυρόκνηστιν ἐσχάραν χύτραν. Ar. *V.* 938.

A papyrus mentions:

ἐσχάρα σιδηρᾶ ἀρτοπτρίς αʹ. *P. Cair. Zen.* 692.

Specifically for space-heating, for which it was inadequate:

ἐν χειμῶνι καὶ ψύχει τῶν φίλων τινὸς ἐστιῶντος αὐτόν,
ἐσχάραν δὲ μικρὰν καὶ πῦρ ὀλίγον ἐσενέγκαντος, ἢ ξύλα ἢ
λιβανωτὸν ἐσενεγκεῖν ἐκέλευσεν. Plu. 2. 180e.

3 As the last example implies, these utensils were also employed in religious rituals, especially to burn incense:

καὶ νυκτίσεμνα δεῖπν' ἐπ' ἐσχάρᾳ πυρός
ἔθυον. A. *Eu.* 108.

In this use it is distinguished from βωμός (= Latin *ara*), the solid table or pillar on which the ἐσχάρα (= Latin *altare*) is placed:

βωμοὶ γὰρ ἡμῖν ἐσχάραι τε παντελεῖς
πλήρεις ὑπ' οἰωνῶν τε καὶ κυνῶν βορᾶς. S. *Ant.* 1016.

βώμιοι γὰρ ἐσχάραι
πέλας πάρεισι, κοὐκ ἔρημα δώματα. E. *Ph.* 274.

LSJ translates the second example as 'structured altars'; but it surely means altars with braziers placed on top of them.

4 As a natural development from this we find ἐσχάρα used in the sense of *altar*:

... ὅτι ... ἐπὶ τῆς ἐσχάρας τῆς ἐν τῇ αὐλῇ Ἐλευσῖνι ... ἱερεῖον
θύσειεν. [D.] 59. 116.

These are often associated with the name of a god:

πρὸς ἐσχάραν
Φοίβου. A. *Pers.* 205.
Πυθικὴν πρὸς ἐσχάραν. E. *Andr.* 1240.

Such altars might be portable, and again the implication is that they were metal artefacts:

καὶ πῦρ ὄπισθεν αὐτοῦ ἐπ' ἐσχάρας μεγάλης ἄνδρες εἵποντο φέροντες. Χ. *Cyr.* 8. 3. 12.

5   It is now possible to see the meaning of this word in Mycenaean Greek, where it appears in the spelling *e-ka-ra* in a list of objects apparently stored in a treasury. This can only be the portable metal object, so that although the Homeric sense of *fire-place* is logically anterior, the earliest attestation (xiii BC) has the value *brazier*.

6   From both these two fundamental meanings transferred senses developed. From the appearance of a place where a fire is regularly made, the word is used of the scab or cicatrice formed on wounds, especially those in which an area of the skin and underlying tissue is destroyed making a depressed scar. The Suda actually calls them κοῖλα ἕλκη. The medical writers have preserved the term 'eschar' in English, especially when due to cauterisation, and given the basic meaning this may have been an original restriction:

καῦσον τὴν κεφαλὴν ἐσχάρας ὀκτώ.   Hp. *Morb.* 2. (12(1.) 6).

ταῦτα καίειν δεῖ, ὅπως ἡ ἐσχάρα ἐκεῖ πέσῃ.   Arist. *Pr.* 863ª12.

7   Secondly, the word is understandably used for the hollow piece of wood in which a drill is rotated to make a fire.

δεῖ δὲ τὴν ἐσχάραν (πυρείου) ἐκ τούτων (*sc. kinds of wood*) ποιεῖν, τὸ δὲ τρύπανον ἐκ δάφνης.   Thph. *HP* 5. 9. 7.

This is the example loosely and misleadingly translated by LSJ as *fire-stick*.

8   Thirdly, the word is used of the external female genitals:

καὶ μολύνων τὴν ὑπήνην καὶ κυκῶν τὰς ἐσχάρας.
Ar. *Eq.* 1286.

This is the point of the parody in Aristophanes of Euripides:

ὦ χρόνιος ἐλθὼν σῆς δάμαρτος ἐς χέρας.   E. *Hel.* 566.

Aristophanes repeats this line (*Th.* 912) with the last three

syllables changed to ἐσχάρας. The *double entendre* of course
depends on ἐσχάρα also having the meaning *hearth*.

9   The other line of development begins from the sense of *brazier*
as a construction of basket type, so that it can be applied to anything made of a lattice of criss-crossing members. This is shown
plainly by the epithet δικτυωτῷ in the following example:

> καὶ ποιήσεις αὐτῷ (*sc.* θυσιαστηρίῳ) ἐσχάραν ἔργῳ δικτυωτῷ
> χαλκῆν. LXX *Ex*. 27. 4.

Thus it could be used for the framework on which a ballista was
mounted; Vitruvius (10. 11. 9) calls it *basis, quae appellatur
eschara*. There is a Greek example of the diminutive form in
Polybius:

> προσχωννύντες τὰς ἀνωμαλίας τῶν τόπων ἐπὶ τῇ τῶν
> ἐσχαρίων ἐφόδῳ. Plb. 9. 41. 4.

This form is also used of the 'cradle' used for launching ships.

ἔτυς

1   The 1968 Supplement has the following entry, which has been
omitted from the new version:

> 'ˣἔτυς, prob. *one year old*, ἔτυν δέλλιν *SEG* 2. 710. 13
> (Pednelissus, i B.C.).'

Reference to LSJ discloses two words written δέλλις: one with
genitive -ῑθος meaning a kind of *wasp*, the other with accusative
δέλλιν = δέλφαξ quoted from an earlier publication of the same
inscription. The reference there was corrected in the Supplement
to agree with this. My immediate reaction was one of disbelief.
Simple adjectives in -υς are almost all oxytone, so why assume a
paroxytone accent? And is it likely that such an inherited adjective
corresponding to ἔτος would exist without being attested by more
than one example and that a late one?

2   Further investigation revealed that this inscription contains a
number of unusual features, and was regarded by the Editor of
SEG 2 as a specimen of the Greek used in Pisidia. But although

apparently written in standard κοινή and otherwise correctly spelled, it has a number of otherwise unknown words and at least one common word used in a totally unknown and unlikely sense. Most of the ἅπαξ εἰρημένα vaguely resemble known words, and it was not difficult to guess their meaning. But there are no features which suggest the influence of a strange dialect, and I suspect another explanation is possible. During my years on the teaching staff of the Faculty of Classics at Cambridge I was never provided with the services of a shorthand-typist, except for a brief period when I was discharging an administrative office. At that time the faculty secretary was a lady who had long been resident in England, but was not a native English-speaker. She was quite well able to take dictation, provided it was for routine correspondence; but whenever the subject was unfamiliar or involved technical expressions, she found herself unable to read back her shorthand, so she adopted two strategies. Either she would substitute for the unreadable word another word somewhat resembling it, sometimes emending the context to make it sound a little more plausible; or she would make a rough phonetic transcription of her note, and assure me that was what I had said. As a result, after wasting a good deal of time solving these puzzles, I decided it was quicker and safer to type such letters myself.

3   Reluctant as I am to believe unlikely hypotheses, I cannot help thinking that this Pednelissus inscription was dictated to a secretary whose Greek education was limited to routine matters, and whenever he heard something unfamiliar he did not know how to transcribe it. For some reason, such as absence abroad or even death, the author never checked the written version until it had been inscribed. The more suspicious elements are as follows:

> ἕως ὅσου = ἕως ὅτου 'until' (cf. *Ev. Luc.* 13. 8, an idiom which survives into Modern Greek)
>
> ἐπηρασίαν = ἐπήρειαν
>
> *HAN* = ἐάν
>
> *ETYN* = ἔτειον
>
> *ΔΕΛΛΙΝ* = δελφάκιον
>
> *ΕΜΗ* apparently = εἵματα

The last is perhaps the most remarkable; the priestesses are commanded μέλανα *EMH* περιβαλλέσθωσαν, to put on dark clothes. But there is no such word as ἔμος or ἔμος from the root of ἔννυμι, and it is hard to see how there could be, since the μ of εἷμα, etc. is part of the termination. I suspect therefore that εἵματα was sufficiently unfamiliar for the secretary to have written down EM and then made up a word to match it. Set in this context *ETYN ΔΕΛΛΙΝ* can be plausibly reconstructed as ἔτειον δελφάκιον 'a one-year-old piglet.' Thus the new adjective ἔτυς can be consigned to the rubbish-bin.

4   But before leaving this subject I am inclined to speculate about the word which is used in what I have no doubt now is the wrong sense. We find among the offerings to be made:

πυρῶν ἱππέα καὶ ἀμυγδάλων ἱππεῖς δ΄.

As the Editor saw, the word needed here is ἑκτεῖς. But how could this have been misheard, by however barbarous a scribe, as ἱππεῖς? Perhaps he consulted a better educated friend, who thought without knowing the context that the word he heard was the Latin *equites* and he explained this in Greek by ἱππεῖς, which the scribe therefore introduced into the text. We shall never know. But all the items specified in this note ought to be kept in limbo, until such time as their existence is confirmed by at least one other example.

Ϝάγανον

1   This word, which has caused quite unnecessary perplexity, occurs in a Boeotian inscription from Thespiae, dated to early iv BC. It is quoted by C. D. Buck, *Greek Dialects*[3], No. 39 (p. 228); see *SEG* 24. 361, N. Platon-Feyel, *BCH* 62 (1938), 149–66, J. Tailardat, P. Roesch, *Rev. de Phil.* 40 (1966), 70–87. It is a simple catalogue of the public property of the people of Thespiae contained in the Heraeum. Each item is specified, followed by a numeral (unless this is one), with notes of the material as appropriate. Many of the entries are vessels of various types:

ὑδρίαι hένδεκα
10   στάμνοι χάλκιωι τρῖς
      φιάλα

But it goes on to list cooking utensils of other types, such as meat-hooks (κρεάγραι) and cheese-graters (τυροκνασστίδες). Immediately after this we have the entries:

  ϝαγάνω δύο
  πούραμα
20 φρυνοποπεῖον

2 İt is obvious that ϝαγάνω is a dual, which might therefore be from a masculine singular in -ος or a neuter in -ον. It has been dismissed as a new word 'of unknown meaning' (Buck). But this should never have given any trouble, for the word is already in LSJ if you know where to look for it. It must mean some item of kitchen equipment. The initial ϝ- can be discarded, since it will not appear in most dialects, and is in any case ignored by LSJ for alphabetical purposes. Since we do not know the quantity of either α, for the corresponding Attic–Ionic form there will be four possibilities: ἀγαν-, ἠγαν-, ἀγην-, ἠγην-. The first of these leads us to ἀγανός, a poetic adjective of unsuitable meaning. The third and fourth produce nothing, but the second gives a highly satisfactory result. LSJ has the entry:

  ἤγανον, τό, Ion. for τήγανον, Anacr. 26.

τήγανον is a well-known word for a *frying-pan,* a sense wholly appropriate to the context. Thus we can mark the quantities as ϝᾱγᾰνω.

3 This, however, is not the end of the story. The more common name for a *frying-pan* was τάγηνον, of which τήγανον has been regarded as a variant; but the details of its formation are obscure. Ἤγανον could therefore have arisen by misdivision of τήγανον as τ' ἤγανον, exactly the reverse of τανηλεγέος from τ' ἀνηλεγέος, ἔχε νήδυμος from ἔχεν ἤδυμος, etc. (see Schwyzer, *Gram.* i. 413; M. Leumann, *Homerische Wörter,* 45). But the reality of ἤγανον, however derived, is confirmed by a gloss in Hesychius: ἠγάνεα· πέμματα τὰ ἀπὸ τηγάνου.

4 In view of the Boeotian form, which plainly demands a different etymology, one might now propose a different history. If there were two words of similar meaning ϝάγανον > ἤγανον and τάγηνον, contamination could have been responsible for τήγανον

combining the initial τ- with the metric pattern of ἤγανον. Thus τήγανον will have replaced both the original forms, and it is this which in the diminutive τηγάνι survives into Modern Greek.

ζῆλος

1 LSJ's treatment of this word is more than usually confusing. The article is arranged thus:

> I *jealousy; eager rivalry, emulation.* 2 c. gen. pers. *zeal for, emulation of;* absol. *passion.* 3 c. gen. rei, *rivalry, emulous desire for;* pl. *ambitions.* 4 *fervour, zeal.* 5 personified. II *pride, honour, glory.* III *spirit;* pl. *tastes, interests.* 2 *style.*

Part of the difficulty with this word is that it refers to both welcome and unwelcome emotions, which suggests that its original meaning may have been any outburst of emotion, though in fact this sense only appears in later Greek. If the examples in II are defined as *the state of being admired, success,* it becomes easier to see how it arose. But III is a dubious collection of examples, which will need discussion below.

2 I should begin then with the positive emotion, *strong admiration, or enthusiasm;* with genitive, *enthusiasm for.*

> ταῦτα ... ἃ ζῆλον πολὺν εἶχε καὶ φιλοτιμίαν ὑμῖν, ἠφάνισται.
> D. 22. 73.

> ἐν σκότει καὶ πολλῇ δυσκλείᾳ πᾶς ὁ πρὸ τοῦ ζῆλος τῶν Ἑλλήνων γέγονεν. [D.] 60. 24.

> ἐναντίον γὰρ ζήλῳ καταφρόνησίς ἐστι. Arist. *Rh.* 1388ᵇ22.

> τοὺς πατρίους νόμους οἳ πᾶσιν ἀνθρώποις εἰς ζῆλον ἥκουσιν
> 'which have excited the admiration of all mankind'.
> J. *BJ* 7. 358.

With genitive:

> οὐδείς ποτ᾽ αὐτοὺς τῶν ἐμῶν ἂν ἐμπέσοι
> ζῆλος ξυναίμων, ὥστ᾽ ἐμοῦ τρέφειν βίᾳ.
> 'No amount of admiration for my blood-relations would induce them to harbour them in my despite.' S. *OC* 943.

> ἔπειτ᾽ ἐθρέφθην ἐλπίδων καλῶν ὕπο
> βασιλεῦσι νύμφη, ζῆλον οὐ σμικρὸν γάμων

ἔχουσ', ὅτου δῶμ' ἑστίαν τ' ἀφίξομαι.
'Then again I was brought up with high hopes of being a king's
bride, with no small enthusiasm for getting married, (to see) to
whose home and hearth I should come.' E. *Hec.* 352.

This seems to me a much more likely explanation than LSJ's
'causing *rivalry* for my hand'; ἔχω does not ordinarily mean 'to
cause'. It is closely paralleled by the first of these examples:

> ἵνα μὴ Διόνυσος ἀκούσας
> τῶν Ἀριαδνείων ζῆλον ἔχοι λεχέων. *AP* 5. 228. 5.
> διὰ ζῆλον τῶν γεγενημένων καὶ φθόνον τῶν πεπραγμένων.
> Lys. 2. 48.

LSJ treats ζῆλος as a synonym for φθόνος, but it is surely more
likely that a fine distinction is drawn between them, as here,
'admiration for past events and envy of their achievements'.

> ζήλῳ τῶν ἀρίστων καὶ φυγῇ τῶν χειρόνων. Luc. *Ind.* 17.

Similarly with περί:

> τοῦ δὲ περὶ τὰ στρατιωτικὰ ζῆλον τά τε ὄχανα ποιοῦνται
> τεκμήρια καὶ τὰ ἐπίσημα. Str. 14. 2. 27.

With πρός:

> τὸν πρὸς αὐτὴν ζῆλον. Phld. *Rh.* 2. 53. S.

3 A special development from this is where it is regarded from
the point of view of the admired rather than the admirer; we might
define this as *the state of being admired, success, good fortune.*

> ἴδετε τὴν ὁμευνέτιν
> Αἴαντος, ὃς μέγιστον ἴσχυσε στρατοῦ,
> οἵας λατρείας ἀνθ' ὅσου ζήλου τρέφει. S. *Aj.* 503.

Probably also:

> οὐ ζήλῳ πολιτῶν καὶ τύχαις ἐπιβλέπων. S. *OT* 1526.

if this means ' not envying the success and good fortune of the
citizens.' (The attribution of this line to Sophocles is insecure.)

> τῷ μὲν στεφανουμένῳ τὸν αὐτὸν ἔχει ζῆλον ὁ στέφανος, ὅπου
> ἂν ἀναρρηθῇ. D. 18. 120.

ὅτε ταῦτ' ἐπράττετο καὶ ζήλου καὶ χαρᾶς καὶ ἐπαίνων ἡ πόλις
ἦν μεστή ... D. 18. 217; cf. 273.

ἃ καὶ ζῆλόν τινα καὶ τιμὴν φέρει τῇ πόλει ῥηθέντα. D. 23. 64.

ὁ ἐν τῷ ὑμετέρῳ θεάτρῳ χρύσεος στέφανος ἐπιτεθεὶς ζήλου
πρὸς τὸ ἄκρον ἦγεν. [Hp.] 9. 420. 19.

ἐν ὧι ποτε Παμφίλη ἥδε
ζῆλον ἔχōσ' ὤικει τὸμ μακαριστότατον.
IG 2. 4054 (Athens, iv BC).

ζήλου δὲ αὐτῷ γέμοντι ἐπὶ τούτοις τὸ δαιμόνιον ἐνεμέσησε
τοῦ ζήλου, καὶ ὁ στρατὸς ἐστασίασεν. App. BC 5. 128.

Possibly we should place here the personification of Ζῆλος in
Hesiod, in view of the nouns with which it is associated:

Στὺξ δ' ἔτεκ' Ὠκεανοῦ θυγάτηρ Πάλλαντι μιγεῖσα
Ζῆλον καὶ Νίκην καλλίσφυρον ἐν μεγάροισι
καὶ Κράτος ἠδὲ Βίην. Hes. Th. 384.

4 A different line of development, seen again from the point of
view of another, is where admiration turns to envy. We might
define this as *distress or anger provoked by another's success, envy*.
LSJ translates this '*jealousy* (= φθόνος)'; but since it is often
coupled with φθόνος, it is surely more likely that a distinction is
intended, such as we can make between envy and jealousy.

ζῆλος δ' ἀνθρώποισιν ὀιζυροῖσιν ἅπασι
δυσκέλαδος κακόχαρτος ὁμαρτήσει στυγερώπης.
Hes. Op. 195.

The uncomplimentary epithets leave no doubt of the sense here.

ἄλλος ἄλλον ὁρῶν καὶ εἰς ζῆλον ἰὼν τὸ πλῆθος τοιοῦτον
αὐτῶν ἀπηργάσατο. Pl. R. 550e.

εἰ γάρ ἐστι ζῆλος λύπη τις ἐπὶ φαινομένῃ παρουσίᾳ ἀγαθῶν
ἐντίμων. Arist. Rh. 1388ᵃ32.

ὦ μέλεαι ζήλοιό τ' ἐπισμυγερῶς ἀκόρητοι. A. R. 1. 616.

Οἰνώνη δὲ χόλῳ ζέεν, ἔζεε πικρῷ
ζήλῳ θυμὸν ἔδουσα. AP 2. 1. 216.

παυσαμένη ζήλου Διὸς ἂν φάτο σύγγαμος Ἥρη. AP 9. 248. 5.

ζῆλος ἐπεὶ μανίης μεῖζον κακόν. AP 9. 345. 3.

μέλλω μαίνεσθαι· ζῆλος γάρ μ' ἔχει καὶ κατακάομαι.
P. Grenf. 1. 1. 13 (ii BC).

Distinguished from φθόνος, though the distinction is perhaps sometimes artificial:

ὃ δὴ φιλεῖ ἐκ τῶν ἀνθρώπων εὖ πράττουσι προσπίπτειν, πρῶτον μὲν ζῆλος, ἀπὸ δὲ ζήλου φθόνος. Pl. *Mx.* 242a.

οὔτε γὰρ ὕβρις οὔτ᾽ ἀδικία, ζῆλοί τε αὖ καὶ φθόνοι οὐκ ἐγγίγνονται. Pl. *Lg.* 679c.

5   In later Greek, for I have found no early example which must be so taken, there develops the sense of *emulation, rivalry*:

κολοιὸς δὲ τοῦτον (*sc.* τὸν ἀετὸν) θεασάμενος διὰ ζῆλον μιμήσασθαι ἤθελε. Aesop. 2. 2.

πρὸς ἃ μιμητικὸς οὐ γίνεται ζῆλος. Plu. *Per.* 2.

κατὰ ζῆλον Ἡρακλέους. Plu. *Thes.* 25. 5.

ὡρμημένου δὲ αὐτοῦ καὶ ἐς τὴν Βρεταννίαν κατὰ τὸν τοῦ πατρὸς ζῆλον στρατεῦσαι. D. C. 49. 38. 2.

κατὰ ζῆλον τὸν πρὸς Κορινθίους. Luc. *Demon.* 57.

6   Another late use is perhaps due to an etymological association with ζέω, as appears in the collocation of the words in *AP* 2. 1. 216 quoted in 4 above. Here it seems to mean an *outburst of strong emotion*, a sense which was taken over into Latin and so reached English as *zeal*.

κῦμα τὸ πικρὸν Ἔρωτος ἀκοίμητοί τε πνέοντες
    ζῆλοι καὶ κώμων χειμέριον πέλαγος,
ποῖ φέρομαι; *AP* 5. 190. 2.

Commonly in the Septuagint:

ὁ ζῆλος Κυρίου τῶν δυνάμεων ποιήσει τοῦτο. LXX *4 Ki.* 19. 31.

ἕως πότε, κύριε ... ἐκκαυθήσεται ὡς πῦρ ὁ ζῆλός σου. LXX *Ps.* 78. 5.

οἳ καὶ ἐζήλωσαν τὸν ζῆλόν σου καὶ ἐβδελύξαντο μίασμα αἵματος αὐτῶν 'who were fired with zeal for your cause and abominated their pollution with blood'. LXX *Ju.* 9. 4.

Hence in the New Testament:

πυρὸς ζῆλος ἐσθίειν μέλλοντος τοὺς ὑπεναντίους.
    Ep. Hebr. 10. 27.

7   Finally, we can perhaps attach here the use in which it refers
to a style of oratory. LSJ defines it as 'esp. in Lit. Crit., *style*', but
the only two examples quoted both refer to the Ἀσιανὸς ζῆλος, so
perhaps it means rather the *forceful style* of oratory:

> Ἡγησίας ὁ ῥήτωρ, ὃς ἦρξε μάλιστα τοῦ Ἀσιανοῦ λεγομένου
> ζήλου. Str. 14. 1. 41.

> τῷ καλουμένῳ μὲν Ἀσιανῷ ζήλῳ τῶν λόγων. Plu. *Ant.* 2. 8.

8   This leaves unaccounted for two curious uses given by LSJ in
III 1. The first is:

> ἀμφοτέροις τοίνυν ὁ ζῆλος οὗτος τῆς πολιτείας αἴτιος κατέστη
> τῶν μεγίστων συμπτωμάτων. Plb. 4. 27. 8.

According to LSJ it here means *spirit,* but much depends upon the
meaning attached to πολιτείας. It may refer to an excessive zeal in
pursuing a policy, in which case it might be placed under 6 above.
However LSJ may perhaps be right in suggesting a general sense
of *style;* if so, it would fit there. The other example is:

> ὅταν γὰρ τοῖς ἀπὸ διαφόρων ἐπιτηδευμάτων βίων ζήλων
> ἡλικιῶν λόγων ἔν τι … ἅπασι δοκεῖ. Longin. 7. 4.

Here D. A. F. Russell in his edition takes ζῆλοι to mean *tastes,*
ἡλικίαι *periods of life,* and speculates whether λόγων is corrupt.
There seems to be no good reason why ζῆλοι should not mean
something like *enthusiasms,* in which case it could be assigned to 2
above. At least I can see no justification here for the general sense
given by LSJ as **III 1**, and we should await better examples before
assuming this new development.

ἤ, ἦ

1   It is a fairly safe generalisation to assume that no one will look
up these words in a major lexicon to find out their meaning.
Beginners will very soon learn that ἤ is to be translated as *or* or
than, and readers of Homer will not get far without discovering the
two main uses of ἦ. It follows that the function of the articles on
such words must be to provide detailed evidence of their usage,
especially any restrictions in terms of date, genre, etc. The
majority of what is said in these articles in LSJ is unexceptionable;

but there are questions left unanswered and an important fact is concealed by its method of treatment. The present note is not an attempt to rewrite these entries, but to discuss some of the important points LSJ ignores.

2   The first problem is to decide how many words there are which are spelt H in classical Greek. The excellent discussion of ἦ by J. D. Denniston (*The Greek Particles*², 279–88) assumes that it is always distinguishable from ἤ, and is thus of limited use for the purpose of this enquiry. There are plenty of pairs of words which are distinguished only by their accent; some are etymologically different, such as ἀραιός/ἀραιός, δῆμος/δημός, others are separate uses of what is etymologically one word, such as τίς/τις, νῦν/νυν, ἄλλα/ἀλλά. The conventional view is that η as a disjunctive or comparative particle is ἤ (or rather ἤ, since the oxytone form can only occur before an enclitic), the affirmative or interrogative is ἦ. This is plainly stated by Hesychius:

> η ψιλούμενον καὶ βαρυνόμενον δηλοῖ διαζευκτικόν, καὶ συναπτικὸν ⟨ἴσον⟩ τῷ εἰ. η ψιλούμενον καὶ περισπώμενον σύνδεσμον δηλοῖ παραπληρωματικὸν ἴσον τῷ δή, καὶ ἀντὶ ἀπορηματικοῦ τοῦ ἆρα. 'η with smooth breathing and barytone accent signifies a disjunctive and a hypothetical conjunction equivalent to εἰ. η with smooth breathing and perispomenon accent signifies an expletive conjunction equivalent to δή, and instead of ἆρα as marking doubt.'

The remark that it can have the force of εἰ is significant in view of the absence of this sense from LSJ, except in Cypriot (ἤ (c) 1). The four main uses can be tabulated thus:

A disjunctive; translation *or*; traditional accent ἤ; epic variant ἠέ.

B comparative; translation *than*; accent ἤ; epic ἠέ.

C affirmative; translation *truly*; accent ἦ; no variant.

D interrogative; translation *is it that...?*; accent usually ἦ; no variant.

The restriction of ἠέ to types **A** and **B** implies that either this is a suffixed form or that ἤ is a contracted form of ἠέ and therefore a different word from ἦ. In view of the differing views on accentuation of grammarians and manuscripts, not to mention modern editors, especially in Homer, I have decided in this note to ignore

the distinction and to print η (or ηε) without even a breathing, to
indicate that I am not prejudging the issue until the classification
can be established by other means.

3 The accepted etymology of ἠέ is from η + ϝε, an enclitic particle
found also in Latin -ue, Sanskrit va (which is rare except in
compounds, being replaced by vā). This would imply that it is
properly confined to the 'alternative' sense, a term I prefer to the
grammarians' 'disjunctive' = διαζευκτικός. It is certainly frequent
in Homer in that use, where it is freely used for metric reasons as
a variant of η. But it is also used in the comparative sense, though
curiously LSJ quotes no example; e.g.

αἰδομένων ἀνδρῶν πλέονες σόοι ηε πέφανται. Il. 5. 531.

It is more often reinforced with περ:

ἤδη γάρ ποτ' ἐγὼ καὶ ἀρείοσιν ηε περ ὑμῖν
ἀνδράσιν ὡμίλησα. Il. 1. 260; cf. 16. 688.

The restriction to types A and B appears to be observed by other
epic authors (as Hesiod, Homeric hymns) and by their Hellenistic
imitators (Apollonius Rhodius, Callimachus). Now if ηε had been
felt to be merely a metrical 'distraction' of η, it is unlikely that the
later authors would have restricted its use, so this is an argument
in favour of regarding the two forms distinguished by accent, that
is, pronunciation, as having been originally separate words.

4 This raises the interesting possibility that wherever η of types
A and B occurs, it represents a contraction of ηε, with of course an
adjustment of the accent due to its proclitic usage. We can compare the generation of ἀλλά from ἄλλα. Until an example can be
found in a dialect which retains intervocalic digamma, there is no
way of checking this theory. But it is worth remarking that the
Cypriot inscription known as the Idalian bronze (Schwyzer, 679.
10-1), which normally preserves ϝ, has the form e- in e-to-se
ka-si-ke-ne-to-se e-to-se pa-i-ta-se = ἒ τὸς κασιγνέτος ἒ τὸς παῖδας.
On the other hand in Homer it has been observed that η is more
often placed before a vowel than a consonant, so that in these cases
it might represent ηϝ'. There are thus indications pointing in
either direction, but as will appear later, the theory which
separates the two forms is more likely to be correct.

5   Another accentual problem should be mentioned here, the
treatment of the phrase ἀλλ᾽ ἤ. Conventionally our texts print ἀλλ᾽,
thus implying that the elided word is ἀλλά. But when written
divisim or with words intervening before ἤ, we have always, so far
as I can discover, ἄλλο: e.g.

> οἵ τε γὰρ Λακεδαιμόνιοι ... ἄλλο οὐδὲν ἢ ἐκ γῆς ἐναυμάχουν.
> 'The Lacedaimonians were engaged in what was really a sea-
> fight conducted from the shore.'   Th. 4. 14. 3.

The phrase is thus quasi-adverbial, and this applies also to the
phrase ἢ ἄλλο τι (Pl. *Alc.* 1. 116d, *Phdr.* 258a). This is further evidence that the traditional accentuation cannot be wholly trusted,
though no doubt it is not far from the truth.

6   Another problem concerns the grammatical definition of ἤ as a
part of speech. LSJ classifies types **A** and **B** as a conjunction, **C** and
D as an adverb. The facts however, are more complicated, since
conjunctions may be co-ordinating or subordinating, and there is
good reason to believe that ἤ developed from one to the other. But
unlike many adverbs, ἤ never developed to a preposition, since a
substantive following it is in apposition to the preceding one, e.g.

> οἱ δ᾽ ἐπὶ γαίῃ
> κείατο, γύπεσσιν πολὺ φίλτεροι ἢ ἀλόχοισιν.
> 'They lay on the ground, much more welcome to
> vultures than to their wives.'   Il. 11. 162.

This is familiar from the use of Latin *quam* or English *than;* and
modern Greek παρά, which has taken over this sense, behaves in
the same way. The closest parallel in Greek is with ὡς, which
shows the same tendency to combine with enclitics (ὥς περ like ἤ
περ, ὥς τε, etc.).

7   The co-ordinating use of alternative ἤ (type **A**) is too familiar
to require comment. Where the first of a pair or series of alterna-
tives is introduced with ἤ, it needs to be translated in English by
either; but that this is not really a separate use is shown by the
similar use of Latin *aut ... aut, uel ... uel*. The elements so introduced may be complete sentences, and this raises the question
whether the first may sometimes be felt to be interrogative (type
D), and it is often accented ἦ. But since the second part of a

double question is introduced by what is plainly alternative η, it is hard to separate this from the cases where the first part of the question too is introduced by this particle. Examples with other types of question:

> ἔπος τί κε μυθησαίμην,
> η αὐτὸς κεύθω;   Od. 21. 194.

> τίνες αὐτῷ
> κοῦροι ἔποντ᾽; Ἰθάκης ἐξαίρετοι, η ἑοὶ αὐτοῦ
> θῆτές τε δμῶές τε;   Od. 4. 643.

> ἤκουσας η οὐκ ἤκουσας, η κωφῇ λέγω;   A. Th. 202.

> τίνα ταύτην; η τὸ πλοῖον ἀφῖκται ἐκ Δήλου ... ;   Pl. Cri. 43c.

With the leading question introduced by η:

> ηε τι Μυρμιδόνεσσι πιφαύσκεαι, η ἐμοὶ αὐτῷ,
> ηε τιν᾽ ἀγγελίην Φθίης ἒξ ἔκλυες οἶος;   Il. 16. 11–12.

> πόθεν πλεῖθ᾽ ὑγρὰ κέλευθα;
> η τι κατὰ πρῆξιν η μαψιδίως ἀλάλησθε
> οἷά τε ληϊστῆρες ... ;   Od. 3. 72.

> η τις ἁμετέρας χθονὸς
> δυσμενὴς ὄρι᾽ ἀμφιβάλλει
> στραταγέτας ἀνήρ;
> η λησταὶ κακομήχανοι
> ποιμένων ἀέκατι μήλων
> σεύοντ᾽ ἀγέλας βίᾳ;   B. 18. 5, 8.

The use of ηε in Il. 16. 11-12 proves that in these cases this is not the interrogative η, which is never found in this sense. But the accentuation of such passages has caused much confusion. In Homer we usually find printed ἤ (ἠέ) followed by ἦ (ἦε); but in the Bacchylides passage it is printed ἦ ... ἤ. Whatever the tradition or the grammarians assert, it seems clear that in these cases we are dealing with the alternative η, and both should be accented ἤ. The position is further complicated when η occurs introducing an indirect question; but we shall postpone consideration of this development until later (14).

8   There is an interesting idiom where η introduces a conse-quence of rejection rather than a genuine alternative. Here it may be translated *or if this is not so, or else*. LSJ quotes this (ἤ A **I 3**) from only one classical author:

εἰδέναι δεῖ περὶ οὗ ἂν ᾖ ἡ βουλή, ἢ παντὸς ἁμαρτάνειν ἀνάγκη.

Pl. *Phdr.* 237c.

An even better example given by LSJ is:

μή με λυπεῖτε,
ἢ φεύξομ᾽ ἐκ τῆς οἰκίας.   Herod. 5. 74.

I find it hard to believe there are not other classical examples; here are two from Aristophanes:

ὑπερβαλεῖσθαι σ᾽ οἴομαι τούτοισιν, ἢ μάτην γ᾽ ἂν
ἀπομαγδαλιὰς σιτούμενος τοσοῦτος ἐκτραφείην.   Ar. *Eq.* 413.

ἐγὼ νόθος; τί λέγεις; σὺ μέντοι νὴ Δία
ὢν γε ξένης γυναικός. ἢ πῶς ἄν ποτε
ἐπίκληρον εἶναι τὴν Ἀθηναίαν δοκεῖς
οὖσαν θυγατέρ᾽, ὄντων ἀδελφῶν γνησίων;   Ar. *Av.* 1652.

9   The presence of ηε in epic strongly suggests that the comparative use (type **B**) developed from the alternative. It is not impossible to derive *as compared with* from *as an alternative*, or perhaps a vaguer origin can be constructed for both. The first thing to note here is that there is no real difference between its use with the comparative and with expressions indicating difference or preference. If we define it as meaning *the point of reference being, as compared with*, this should be obvious. But LSJ does not sufficiently distinguish the examples where the point of reference is a point *in time*. In this sense it will often translate *before* or *after*.

Ἐλπῆνορ, πῶς ἦλθες ὑπὸ ζόφον ἠερόεντα;
ἔφθης πεζὸς ἰὼν ἢ ἐγὼ σὺν νηΐ μελαίνῃ.
'You got here on foot before I did with a ship.'   Od. 11. 58.

So too with πρόσθεν:

ἦν ἂν ὑμῖν ἐν δόμοις
τὰ δρώμεν᾽ ὑμῶν πρόσθεν ἢ τὰ σώματα.   S. *El.* 1333.

Meaning *after*:

τῇ ὑστεραίᾳ ᾗ ᾗ τὰ ἐπινίκια ἔθυεν.   Pl. *Smp.* 173a.

Not surprisingly there are variant readings in the manuscripts, and ᾗ is omitted by some, which would change the analysis of η to the use discussed in 12 below.

10 Both the affirmative and the interrogative uses of η (types **C** and **D**) can be explained as developing from the exclamatory η, which is little more than a noise made to attract attention; see ἦ (B) in LSJ. The affirmative may be translated *truly*, *indeed*, or the like, but the force of the word is perhaps weaker than these expressions suggest. It should be observed that this η normally stands first in a sentence, though it may be preceded by a vocative:

> ὄλβιε Λαέρταο πάϊ, πολυμήχαν' Ὀδυσσεῦ,
> ἦ ἄρα σὺν μεγάλῃ ἀρετῇ ἐκτήσω ἄκοιτιν.   Od. 24. 193.

Common in epic and and copied by the Hellenistic imitators, it is also found in Attic tragedy, but rarely in prose. However it is probably not absent from the colloquial language, if we can judge by Aristophanes. It usually serves to emphasise the following word:

> η μέγ' ἐνορῶ βούλευμ' ἐν ὀρνίθων γένει.   Ar. *Av.* 162, cf. 13.

> νὴ τὸν Δί' η 'γώ σου καταπαύσω τὰς πνοάς. '*I'll* put a stop.'
>   Ar. *Av.* 1397.

Another idiom to be found in Aristophanes is the use of ἀλλ' η to mean *to be sure*:

> ἀλλ' η τὸ πέος τόδ' Ἡρακλῆς ξενίζεται.   Ar. *Lys.* 928.

> οὐκ ἔσθ' ὅπως ὁ δακτύλιός ἐσθ' οὑτοσὶ
> οὑμός· τὸ γοῦν σημεῖον ἕτερον φαίνεται,
> ἀλλ' η οὐ καθορῶ.   Ar. *Eq.* 953.

This cannot mean 'I do not make out anything else' because of the preceding words 'the mark looks different'. Another passage where η is sometimes regarded as interrogative is:

> —ἀλλ' η τριχόβρωτες τοὺς λόφους που κατέφαγον.
> —ἀλλ' η πρὸ δείπνου τὴν μίμαρκυν κατέδομαι.
>   Ar. *Ach.* 1111–12.

11 The interrogative use (type **D**) is common in Homer. It may be translated *Is it that...?*, but in many cases it corresponds to nothing but the ¿ which precedes a question in Spanish. In tragedy:

> πῶς φῄς; ...
> —Τροίαν Ἀχαιῶν οὖσαν· η τόρως λέγω;   A. *Ag.* 269.

This does not mean 'am I to speak plainly?' but 'am I making myself plain?'

τί δῆτα χρῄζεις; ἢ με γῆς ἔξω βαλεῖν;   S. OT 622.

It seems to be rare in Attic prose; a possible example is:

ἀλλὰ τίς σοι διηγεῖτο; ἢ αὐτὸς Σωκράτης;   Pl. Smp. 173a.

But here we might have the alternative η, and it is printed ἤ in the
Oxford Text. If so, the implication is: 'the question is unnecessary
if, as an alternative, it was Socrates himself.' But it is found in
Aristophanes:

οὔκ, ἀλλὰ βραχέα σου πυθέσθαι βούλομαι.
ἢ μνημονικὸς εἶ;   Ar. Nu. 483.

There is also the colloquial idiom η γάρ, which is printed ἦ, e.g.

οὐκοῦν ... οὗτος δήπου ποιεῖ ἃ δοκεῖ αὐτῷ· η γάρ; —ναί.
Pl. Grg. 468d, cf. 449d, Tht. 160e.

Here the use of γάρ implies that there is an ellipse of some kind,
perhaps therefore as in the case of η οὐ, which implies η οὐ σοὶ
δοκεῖ; In both of these expressions there is no reason to regard η as
interrogative, since it is an alternative question. I therefore think
that η γάρ too is more likely to be alternative than interrogative, I
am asking, for you may have an alternative.

12   There is no section in LSJ for η as a subordinating conjunction, i.e. followed by a subordinate clause. We saw above (9) that
the suppression of ἦ would in some passages have the effect of
bringing about this change. Where the sense is temporal, η will
then mean *from the point in time when,* and may be translated *after*
or *before.* There are examples from West Greek dialects, which are
perfectly clear:

ē̄ κ' ἀποθάνēι ἀνὲρ ē̄ γυνά, αἰ μέν κ' ἐ̄ι τέκνα ... , τούτος ἔκε[ν]
τὰ κρέ̄ματα. 'After the death of a man or woman, if there are
children ..., they are to have the property.' *Leg. Gort.* 5. 9.

αἰ δέ κα κοσ[μ]ίōν ἄγēι ē̄ κοσμίοντος ἄλλος, ē̄ κ' ἀποστᾶι,
μōλὲ̄ν 'to bring it to trial after he has resigned from office'.
Leg. Gort. 1. 51.

ἐν ταῖς τριάκοντα ē̄ κα Ϝείποντι 'in the thirty (days) after their
declaration'. *Leg. Gort.* 8. 18.

αἴ κα μὴ περαιṓσει η κα πρίαται ἐν ταῖς τριάκοντ' ἀμέραις 'if
he does not complete the transaction in thirty days from the
time of the purchase'.   Schwyzer 181. 7. 15.

ἐν τῶι πέμπτωι καὶ δεκάτωι Ϝέτει ἀπὸ τῶ ποτεχεῖ Ϝέτεος η
Ἀριστίων ἐφορεύει 'in the fifteenth year from that succeeding
the year when Aristion is ephor'.   Tab. Heracl. 1. 121.

It is also found in Arcadian:

ἰν τῶι ὕστερον Ϝέτ[ε]ι η Νικῆς ἐδαμιόργη 'in the last year when
N. was damiorgos'.   SEG 37. 340. 23 (Mantinea, iv BC).

εἰ δέ τι ἐκ τῶν ἔμπροσθε χρόνων η οἱ Ὀρχομένιοι Ἀχαιοὶ
ἐγέ[νον]το Νεάρχ[ω]ι ἔγκλημα γέγονεν ...
                    Schwyzer 428. 13 (Orchomenos, iii BC).

13 Except for the last examples these are all from West Greek
dialects, so that it may perhaps have been a specific development
of that region, and the Arcadian usage is under their influence. But
before we come to that conclusion, we need to consider carefully
the use of the phrases πρὶν η, πρόσθεν η, etc. I do not think there
can be any doubt that πρίν was originally an adverb, which
developed into a conjunction by the addition of a clause. But in the
case of πρὶν η, although from a synchronic point of view it can be
treated as an indivisible phrase, which LSJ does, η must here
be the conjunction, just as much as in the examples at the end of
section 12. Thus the preference of πρίν for an infinitival construction, which is plainly a noun clause, can be seen as the starting-
point for the development of the construction with a finite verb. A
good example where πρίν is separated from η in Homer:

            ἀτὰρ οὐ μὲν σφῶϊ γ' ὀίω
πρίν γ' ἀποπαύσεσθαι, πρίν γ' η ἕτερόν γε πεσόντα
αἵματος ἆσαι Ἄρηα.   Il. 5. 288.

Later:

        ἐλαύνειν ὡς δύναιτο τάχιστα ἐπὶ τὰς Σάρδις, πρὶν η τὸ
    δεύτερον ἁλισθῆναι τῶν Λυδῶν τὴν δύναμιν.   Hdt. 1. 79. 1.

With indicative:

        καὶ οὐ πρόσθεν ἔστησαν πρὶν η πρὸς τοῖς πεζοῖς ... ἐγένοντο.
                            X. Cyr. 1. 4. 23.

With πρόσθεν:

    σχεδόν τι πρόσθεν η σὺ τῆσδ' ἔχων χθονὸς
    ἀρχὴν ἐφαίνου τοῦτ' ἐκηρύχθη πόλει.   S. OT 736.

With subjunctive:

τοῖσι δὲ ἡ Πυθίη ... οὐκ ἔφη χρήσειν, πρὶν ἢ τὸν νηὸν ...
ἀνορθώσωσι. Hdt. 1. 19. 3.

There is no reason to doubt that this is correctly accented ἤ.

14 There are also examples of the subordinating use which seem
rather to belong to the interrogative type, i.e. η introduces an
indirect question and can be translated *whether*.

ὄφρα δαῶμεν
η ἐτεὸν Κάλχας μαντεύεται, ηε καὶ οὐκί. Il. 2. 300.

μερμήριξεν
η ὅ γε φάσγανον ὀξὺ ἐρυσσάμενος παρὰ μηροῦ
τοὺς μὲν ἀναστήσειεν, ὁ δ᾽ Ἀτρείδην ἐναρίζοι,
ηε χόλον παύσειεν ἐρητύσειέ τε θυμόν. Il. 1. 190.

ἀλλ᾽ ἄγε μοι τόδε εἰπὲ καὶ ἀτρεκέως κατάλεξον,
η καὶ Λαέρτῃ αὐτὴν ὁδὸν ἄγγελος ἔλθω
δυσμόρῳ ... Od. 16. 138.

In many cases the manuscripts vary between εἰ and η, and the
former is for obvious reasons preferred by editors:

ὄφρα καὶ Ἕκτωρ
εἴσεται εἰ καὶ ἐμὸν δόρυ μαίνεται ἐν παλάμῃσιν. Il. 8. 111.

So also Od. 13. 415, etc. This usage is found in West Greek:

τὼς δὲ πολιανόμως ... ἀμφίστασθαι, η κα πεφυτεύκαντι πάντα
κὰτ τὰν συνθήκαν. 'The city-commissioners are to decide
whether they have performed the planting in accordance with
the contract.' *Tab. Heracl.* 1. 125.

διαψαφίξασθαι κατὰ τὸν νόμον, η δοκεῖ αὐτὸν στεφανῶσαι
θαλλοῦ στεφάνωι. *IG* 12(3). 170. 12 (Astypalaea).

I am indebted to Professor A.-P. Christides for some further
examples from the lead tablets found at Dodona, on which questions were submitted to the oracle. There are examples where η
introduces a direct question, e.g.

τύχα ἀγαθά. η τυγχάνοιμί κα ἐμπορευόμενος ...
Schwyzer 309.

Hence it is obvious that the use in indirect questions follows the
same principle:

ἐπερώτη Ἀσκλαπιάδας τὸν Δία τὸν Ναὸν καὶ [Δ]ιώναν η
λώιον καὶ ἄμεινον ἀπολυομένῳ παῖδα. M 83 (iv BC).

Εὐηΐδας ἀνερώτη τὸν θεὸν η τυγχάνοι κα ποιῶν [M 188.

ἐπερωτῶντ[ι Δ]ωδωναῖοι τὸν θεὸν η ἀσφαλέως ἐστὶ μένειν.
                                                        M 846.

15   A puzzling usage occurs in two identical passages of the
Gortyn Law Code, where the meaning appears to be *where*, or
more likely *in the way in which, as*:

μōλὲν ὀπê κ' ἐπιβάλλει, πὰρ τōι δικαστᾶι ê ϝεκάστō
ἔγρατται. 'to take action at law where may be appropriate,
before the judge as prescribed in each case'.

                                              Leg. Gort. 6. 31; 9. 23.

It is difficult to judge where this usage needs to be attached, but it
is clearly an example of the subordinating use of η. If genuine, this
sense might offer an alternative explanation of the obscure early
Laconian inscription from Gythium:

μēδένα ἀποστρύθεσται· αἰ δὲ ἀποστρύ[θ]ēται, ἀϝατᾶται ê ho
δōλος. Schwyzer 51.

No one knows the meaning of the verb which is the subject of this
prohibition. But ἀϝατᾶται is a dialect form from ἀτάομαι used in the
sense of 'suffers punishment'. It is generally assumed that the last
three words stand for ἢ αὐτὸς ἢ ὁ δοῦλος, but it would be remarkable if an offender were able to send his slave to suffer the punishment vicariously. If however η can here mean *as*, it would imply
that the offender is to be punished as, i.e. in the same way as a
slave, a much more drastic penalty. The article then will be in its
generalising sense.

16   There is also a case where η appears to mean *if* introducing a
conditional clause. It needs first to be observed that this is normal
in Boeotian, where η is the regular spelling for αι, and these
examples do not belong here. But it is found in Cypriot in the
Idalian Bronze:

e-ke si-se o-na-si-lo-ne e-to-se ka-si-ke-ne-to-se ... e-xe o-ru-xe ...
pe-i-se-i-o-na-si-lo-i ... (i.e. ê κέ σις Ὀνάσιλον ê τὸς κασιγνέτος
... ἐξ ὀρύξê ... πείσει Ὀνασίλōι ...) 'if anyone expels Onasilos
or his brothers, he shall pay to Onasilos ...'

                                              Schwyzer 679. 10.

ἡμέτερος

A papyrus of iii AD, *P. Oxy. Hels.* 49. 12 has the form ἐμέτερος for ἡμέτερος. This is an interesting anticipation of the process by which ἡμεῖς appears in modern Greek as εμείς. Once ἡμεῖς and ὑμεῖς had become homophones, it was necessary to change them to maintain the distinction. ἡμεῖς therefore became ἐμεῖς after ἐμέ, and ὑμεῖς could then be remodelled as ἐσεῖς after σέ (or perhaps already ἐσέ). ἐμέτερος shows an early stage in the process, though of course it is probably a 'learned' form, since the adjective was very early abandoned in favour of the genitive of the pronoun.

ἡμιεκτάνιον, ἡμιοκτάνιον

1 This is an addition to the Greek vocabulary, found in an inscription written in the North Ionic of v BC on a lead sheet found at Pech-Maho in the Aude department of France (J. Pouilloux, M. Lejeune, *CRAI* (1988), 526–35). The expression τρίτον ἡμιεκτάνιον or ἡμιοκτάνιον (the inscription is presumably psilotic) occurs three times in this text, and it is common ground that in each case it denotes a sum of money. But beyond that point agreement breaks down, and my suggestion (*ZPE* 82 (1990), 161–6) that the two spellings are variants of the same word has not met with general acceptance. It is therefore appropriate to re-examine here the use of these spellings with a view to further elucidating their meaning.

2 The complete text runs as follows:

ἀκάτι[ον] ἐπρίατο [?Κύ]πρι[ος παρὰ τῶν]
Ἐμποριτέων· ἐπρίατο τε[   ]
3 ἐμοὶ μετέδωκε τῶμισυ τ[ρίτ]ō ἠ[μι]οκταν-
ίō· τρίτον ἡμιεκτάνιον ἔδωκα ἀριθμῶ-
ι καὶ ἐγγυητήριον τρίτην αὐτός. καὶ κε-
6 ῖν' ἔλαβεν ἐν τῶι ποταμῶι· τὸν ἀρραβῶν' ἀνέδωκα ὅκō τἀκάτια ὁρμίζεται.
μάρτυρ(ες)· Βασιγερρος καὶ Βλερυας καὶ
9 Γολο[.]βιυρ καὶ Σεδεγων. ο[ὗ]τοι μάρτ-
υρες εὖτε τὸν ἀρραβῶν' ἀνέδωκα,
εὖτε δὲ ἀπέδωκα τὸ χρῆμα τρίτον
12 [ἡμ]ιοκτάνι[ο]ν [.]αναρυας Ναλβ[..]ν.

My proposed translation would read: *Kyprios(?) bought a boat [from the] Emporitans. He also bought [   ] He passed over to me a half share at the price of 2½ hektai (each). I paid 2½ hektai in cash, and two days later personally gave a guarantee. The former he received on the river. The pledge I handed over where the boats are moored. Witness(es): Basigerros and Bleruas and Golo.biur and Sedegon; these (were) witnesses when I handed over the pledge. But when I paid the money, the 2½ hektai, .auaras, Nalb..n.*

3   The question whether ἡμιεκτάνιον and ἡμιοκτάνιον are two separate words or variant spellings of the same word cannot be answered directly. The assumption must be that different spellings represent different words, until they can be proved to have the same meaning, so the onus of proof lies on those who claim identity. There are cases in all languages of two long words which differ by only one letter, like English *dissimilation* and *dissimulation*. But it will be found that, like homophones, they are not likely to be used in the same context. In particular, numerals are always carefully distinguished for obvious reasons. In languages known to me I can think of very few instances where any pair of numerals between one and ten is distinguished by only a single phoneme (French *six/dix*, Japanese *ichi/shichi* = 1/7). Indeed radiotelephony demands greater than normal discrimination, and *nine* is now replaced for this purpose by *niner* to avoid the vowel of *five*, German *zwei* by *zwo* to avoid confusion with *drei*. This observation is significant if the syllables εκτ and οκτ represent different numerals.

4   But the particular arguments applicable to this case are more telling than any general ones. It is agreed that both expressions refer to a sum of money. But if the words are different, we have to explain the extraordinary coincidence that both are used in the same idiom, compounded with ἡμι- and accompanied by an ordinal numeral. This idiom is known from Herodotus: an ordinal numeral followed by the name of the unit compounded with ἡμι- is equivalent to $n - \frac{1}{2}$ times the unit. Thus τρίτον ἡμιεκτάνιον means 2½ *ektania*. What is even more extraordinary is that the ordinal numeral is the same in all three cases. Is it really likely that one document will refer to, let us say, two-and-a-half pounds and two-and-a-half pence?

5   But the case is even more peculiar, if the syllables εκτ and οκτ are interpreted as meaning *six* and *eight*. We are apparently faced with the proposition that one sum is specified as $2\frac{1}{2} \times 6a$, the other as $2\frac{1}{2} \times 8a$. This is an incredible way of saying $15a$ and $20a$.

6   But this is not the end of the surprises in store for those who separate these words. The syllable εκτ can only refer to *six* if it is an ordinal numeral (ἔκτος); in multiplicative compounds *six* is represented by ἑξα- (as ἑξακόσιοι, ἑξάγωνος, ἑξάπολις, etc.) But οκτ can only refer to the cardinal numeral ὀκτώ, since the ordinal is (for whatever reason) ὄγδοος. It follows that the relation between the units must be $\frac{1}{6}a : 8a :: 1a : 48a$. Thus the numbers indicated in the text must be $2\frac{1}{2} \times \frac{1}{6} = \frac{5}{12}\, a$ and $2\frac{1}{2} \times 8 = 20a$. This difficulty is ignored by the French editors, but I still find it quite incredible.

7   These difficulties are at once solved, if we accept the two spellings as variants of the same word. But there still remains the problem of what is the unit designated by ἐ/ὀκτάνιον. Nothing of the kind seems to have been recorded, but there was a coin of Phocaea, the mother city of Massilia and therefore of the trading stations such as this on the coasts of France and Spain, known as ἕκτη *one sixth,* that is, of a stater. It is hard to separate this from the unit here mentioned, and I therefore proposed that the form -εκτάνιον was the 'correct' spelling, and -οκτάνιον was a spelling variant. It is true that ε and ο do not ordinarily alternate in this way, but it is perhaps possible that the effect of the preceding ι was to dissimilate ε to a sound written hesitantly as ο.

8   The effect of reading the two forms as variants is of course to cast doubt on the interpretation proposed by the first editors and accepted by H. van Effenterre and J. Vélissaropoulos-Karakostas (*Revue historique de droit français et étranger,* 69 (1991), 217–26) and R. A. Santiago (*Faventia,* 11 (1991), 163–79). I ventured to suggest a different interpretation in my article in *ZPE* (loc. cit.). In *Revue archéologique narbonnaise,* 21 (1988) 19–59 Lejeune proposed to remedy the objection made in 6 above by emending ἡμιεκτάνιον to ἡμιε⟨ξ⟩άνιον, surely a desperate remedy.

9   A final point concerns the ending of this word. No one seems to have commented on the formation -ανιον, yet I am unable to find

any satisfactory parallel. The α must either be short, or a lengthened ᾱ arising after the Ionic shift of ᾱ to η. In the latter case ᾱ
might be due to loss of ϝ after ν (cf. Ionic φθάνω, Attic φθάνω <
*φθάνϝω). But this does not appear to offer any solution. Perhaps
then it is a simple -άνιον ending devised to denote a coin with the
value of a ἕκτη, though it remains unparalleled.

ἧρυς

1 I have discussed this word in an article entitled 'ΗΡΥΣ—A
Greek Ghost-word' in B. Broganyi and R. Lipp (eds.), *Historical
Philology* (Amsterdam, 1992), 99–102. It owes its existence to
P. Kretschmer, who in *Glotta*, 15 (1927), 306–7 published some
Greek funerary inscriptions from Marsala in Sicily. He attributed
them to ii BC, but this date is almost certainly too early. In the case
of males the formula ἧρως ἀγαθός is used, but in two cases where
females are recorded this is inflected as ἧρυς ἀγαθά. The presence
of ἀγαθά rather than ἀγαθή shows that this is not standard κοινή,
and Kretschmer added the feminine ἧρυς (or ἡρύς) as a dialect
form. He assumed that ἧρως was the product of *ἧρωυς, the genitive being *ἧρωϝος, and a reduced grade in the feminine could well
appear as ἡρῦς. Unfortunately we now know from Mycenaean,
which has ἧρως in the compound *ti-ri-se-ro-e* = *tris-hērōei* (dative)
that this stem lacks the υ element presumed by this etymology.

2 V. Pisani, *Ist. Lomb.* 73 (1939–40), 490, questioned the existence of this feminine, suggesting that it was merely an ignorant
spelling of the normal ἡρωΐς. He supported this by a presumed
phonological development of ωϊ to ωι diphthong and so to οι,
which in late inscriptions is often written υ. I suggested rather
that ἡρωΐς was an unfamiliar word at least in its spoken form, so
that written ΗΡΩΙΣ might have been read as containing a long
diphthong, and once this distinction was lost -οις could have been
written -υς. In either case the existence of a separate feminine form
of this type must remain dubious, and this word too needs to be
consigned to limbo until better evidence for its existence is forth-
coming.

θάλασσα

1   There are three small points to be added to the record of this
word. One is due to a reference culled from the New Supplement,
which quotes a Laconian inscription of v BC containing the clause:

hόπνι κα Λα[κεδαιμόνιο]ι hαγίōνται καὶ κα[τὰ γᾶν κ]αὶ
καθάλαθαν. SEG 26. 461. 7.

The last word is plainly to be read as κὰ(θ) θάλα(θ)θαν, geminate
letters not being written. At first sight the form may not appear
remarkable, especially as θάλαθθα is already recorded as a late
Cretan dialect form (Schwyzer 186. 9, ii BC). But Cretan differs
from Laconian in its treatment of words containing -σσ- of Ionic,
and there is no reason to expect anything but -σσ- in this word in
Laconian.

2   However, from iv BC Laconian inscriptions show the graph Σ
replacing Θ, e.g. ΑΝΕΣΗΚΕ, and the same spellings are found in
earlier literary sources, such as Alcman, Aristophanes' Lysistrata
and the Spartan treaties in Thucydides (5. 77, 79). But it is
possible that in literary texts these spellings were introduced by a
later editor, who knew the current practice in Laconia at his own
date. This feature of the dialect was particularly resistant to
change, and it survived into the modern Tsakonian dialect of the
region. It is generally agreed that Σ here indicates some kind of
spirant pronunciation, and the obvious conclusion is that the
development of t^h to a spirant [θ], which became general in later
Greek, was anticipated by Laconian. But, as I have pointed out
before, it is unlikely that this change coincided with the introduction of the standard alphabet. Thus the letter Θ presumably
already had the value of a spirant in v BC, and this seems to be what
this spelling of θάλασσα proves. Whether the initial θ had the same
value as the medial one may be doubted; there is after all a range
of phonetic possibilities, and modern Greek makes do with a
single graph Σ to represent both [s] and [ʃ] in loan-words. At least
we can now offer proof that the examples of Σ in non-Spartan
literary sources in v BC are not anachronistic.

3   The form θάλασσα, in fact [θ]άλασ[σαν] but the restoration is
certain, has been quoted as Attic by L. Threatte (Grammar of Attic

Inscriptions i. 538). It occurs in an inscription from the Acropolis of Athens (*IG* 2² 236) which contains the text of the oath which Philip II required of all Greeks after the battle of Chaeroneia in 338 BC. It can hardly be distinguished in its dialect from normal Attic, except for this use of -σσ- which is confirmed by the similar [Θεσ]σαλῶν. But it is hardly likely that in prescribing the exact wording of the oath Philip would have left each city free to adapt it to the local dialect, so it is much more likely to be a specimen of the Macedonian chancery's official language. This was based upon literary Attic, no doubt propagated by Athenian school-teachers, and popularised by the performance of Attic tragedies in Macedonia. It thus became the basis of the κοινή. Confirmation of this early use by Macedonians comes from an inscription from Teos containing a letter of Antigonus I of about 303 BC (D. F. McCabe *et al.*, *Teos Inscriptions*, 59). I have discussed this in a note published in *Palaeographica et Mycenaea Antonino Bartoněk oblata* (Brno, 1991), 13–16.

4   The last point is a semantic one. It has escaped the notice of LSJ that the specific sense of the word to mean a particular stretch of land-locked water is extended, possibly under Hebrew influence, in the Septuagint and the New Testament to include relatively small freshwater lakes. The obvious example is Lake Tiberias, known as the Sea of Galilee:

πέραν τῆς θαλάσσης τῆς Γαλιλαίας τῆς Τιβεριάδος.
Ev. Jo. 6. 1.

It now becomes plain why the same Hebrew term was applied to a small artificial pool in the Temple complex constructed by Solomon, and this was translated by θάλασσα in the Septuagint:

καὶ ἐποίησε τὴν θάλασσαν δέκα ἐν πήχει ἀπὸ τοῦ χείλους ἕως τοῦ χείλους αὐτῆς στρογγύλον κύκλῳ τὸ αὐτό· πέντε ἐν πήχει τὸ ὕψος αὐτῆς.   LXX 3 Ki. 7. 23; cf. 2 Ki. 8. 8.

In the second reference we are told that it was of bronze, though it is not clear whether it was a free-standing vessel or partially sunk into the ground and lined with bronze plates. If raised above ground it would have required an immensely heavy substructure to support the weight of water in it. LSJ translated this as *laver,* giving the second reference only. There is, however, another example:

140   θάλος, θάλεα

καὶ ἐποίησε θάλασσαν χωροῦσαν δύο μετρητὰς σπέρματος
κυκλόθεν τοῦ θυσιαστηρίου ... καὶ διεπορεύετο τὸ ὕδωρ κύκλῳ
τοῦ θυσιαστηρίου, καὶ τὴν θάλασσαν ἔπλησαν ὕδατος.
                                            LXX 3 Ki. 18. 32, 35.

This was given a separate meaning, *channel*, by LSJ. In one way
this is correct; the altar was surrounded by a channel full of water
as a kind of moat. But the name θάλασσα was applied because the
ring of water could also be seen as a circular pool with the altar on
an island in the middle. So both of these usages can be brought
together under a definition 'used of small artificial lakes, *pool*'.

θάλος, θάλεα

1 LSJ has two separate entries for these words, while admitting
somewhat reluctantly that θάλεα is 'in form and accent pl. of θάλος.'
It is not unheard-of for a noun to have a meaning in the plural
which differs from that of the singular; and sometimes a new
plural is formed for a particular meaning. Ἷνες is a good example,
for it seems in origin to be nothing but a plural to ἴς, but it has been
specialised in the sense of 'sinews'. But if the two numbers are
admitted to be inflexional variants of the same word, then they are
better treated in one article as separate senses restricted to
singular and plural.

2 The neuter θάλος is the 'abstract' substantive corresponding to
an adjective *θαλύς, which is used only in the feminine θάλεια. The
masculine and neuter are supplied by θαλερός (cf. γλυκύς, γλυκερός)
and there is also some evidence for θάλειος (θαλείοις στέφεσι Emp.
112. 6), probably a back-formation from the feminine. The root
also appears in θαλία, θαλλός, and θάλλω. This shows that it denotes
the growth of a healthy plant, and it is extended from that to other
things, much like *flourish* in English.

3 It would therefore be expected that a neuter θάλος would mean
flourishing condition, well-being, prosperity, and this sense has been
noted only in the following examples:

    εὐάμπυκες
[ἀέ]ξετ' ἔτι, Μοῖσαι, θάλος ἀοιδᾶν. Pi. *fr.* 70a. 14.

ἀλλά, Τύχα, τέκ[ν]οις μὲν ἀεὶ θάλος, ἀνδρὶ δὲ βουλὰν
σώφρονα, ματρὶ δ' ἐμᾷ κοῦφα πόροις δάκρυα.
Epigram in *BCH* 85. 849 (Imperial date).

The plural, however, is used in this sense from Homer onwards,
though it is only poetic and in restricted use:

εὕδεσκ' ἐν λέκτροισιν, ἐν ἀγκαλίδεσσι τιθήνης,
εὐνῇ ἐν μαλακῇ, θαλέων ἐμπλησάμενος κῆρ.   Il. 22. 504.
καὶ κῆνος ἐν σάλεσσι πολλοῖς ἥμενος μάκαρς ἀνήρ.
Alcm. 15 P.
τὼ μὲν ἐγὼ θαλέεσσιν ἀνέτρεφον.   Call. *fr.* 337 Pf.

The two examples of the singular are enough to destroy the logic
of LSJ's arrangement.

4   As frequently, a word denoting an abstract idea can be used in
a concrete sense to mean 'an instance of this', i.e. the product of
flourishing, the young shoot. In practice it seems to be used only
of sons and daughters, but the idea of a *flourishing* offspring is
always present. English *scion* is an adequate translation:

οὔ σ' ἔτ' ἔγωγε
κλαύσομαι ἐν λεχέεσσι, φίλον θάλος, ὃν τέκον αὐτή.
Il. 22. 87.

λευσσόντων τοιόνδε θάλος χόρον εἰσοιχνεῦσαν.   Od. 6. 157.

κούρην τὴν ἔτεκον γλυκερὸν θάλος.   *h. Cer.* 66; also 187.

τὸν μὲν ἐπὴν δὴ πρῶτον ἴδης θάλος ὀφθαλμοῖσι,
γηθήσεις ὁρόων.   *h. Ven.* 278.

There are several examples in Pindar and other lyric poets, but
apparently none in tragedy:

Ἀδραστιδᾶν θάλος ἀρωγὸν δόμοις.   Pi. *O.* 2.45
σεμνὸν θάλος Ἀλκαϊδᾶν.   Pi. *O.* 6. 68; also *N.* 1. 2; *I.* 7. 24.
Εὐρύαλε γλαυκέων Χαρίτων θάλος.   Ibyc. 7 P.
χαριτόφωνε θάλος (cj.) Ἐρώτων.   Philox. 8 P.
κάπρος ἡνίχ' ὁ μαινόλης ...
Κυπρίδος θάλος ὤλεσεν.   *Lyr. Adesp.* 111 P.

θᾶς

1   This addition to the vocabulary was recorded by the new
Supplement, since it now occurs twice in papyri of Alcaeus, having been emended to ἇς when first found.

> δαπτέτω πόλιν ὡς καὶ πεδὰ Μυρσι[λ]ω[
> θᾶς κ' ἄμμε βόλλητ' Ἄρευς ἐπιτ[Alc. 70. 8 (L–P).

> ...]ξη δὲ θᾶς κε Ζεῦς [
> καὶ] μοῖρα ...   Alc. 206. 6 (L–P).

In both examples it is followed by κε, the verb, where it is preserved, is in the subjunctive, and the meaning is clearly *until*. The
only problem is to explain the form; E.-M. Hamm, *Grammatik zu
Sappho und Alkaios* (Berlin, 1957) 112, says simply 'θ- ungeklärt
ist.' Ionic ἕως represents the normal phonetic development of
*ἇϝος, cf. Skt. *yāvat* (with a different final consonant). This would
contract, following the loss of intervocalic ϝ in West Greek and
Aeolic to ἇς. The problem therefore is to explain the initial θ-.

2   Ionic and Attic τέως, the demonstrative correlate of ἕως, is
occasionally used as a conjunction to mean *until*; see LSJ **I 2**, e.g.

> καὶ τέως μὲν ἂν παῖδες ὦσιν ... φιλοῦσι τοὺς ἄνδρας.
>   Pl. *Smp.* 191e.

The original form can be reconstructed as *τᾶϝος, cf. Skt. *tāvat*, so
the Aeolic descendant should have the form *τᾶς. The simplest
explanation, that θᾶς owes its aspirate to the correlative ἇς, will
hardly serve, since Lesbian is a psilotic dialect, and our text of
Alcaeus shows the absence of aspiration when a stop is exposed by
elision: κατισδάνει, ἐπ' ἄλμυρον. I can only suggest that on the loss
of ϝ it became transformed into an aspirate before disappearing
entirely, just as initial ϝ- sometimes yields an aspirate, even where
it is not the product of *sw-, e.g. ἑσπέρα and occasionally ἕτος for
ἔτος. The contraction of *τᾶhος, with this secondary aspirate,
might perhaps have resulted in its transfer to initial position, as in
τὸ ἱμάτιον becoming θοἰμάτιον. Even so, it is a remarkable phenomenon in a securely psilotic dialect.

θυμός

1 Whether or not LSJ is right in approving Plato's etymology for this word (*Cra.* 419e) as derived from θύω (B) is still disputed. Chantraine (*DELG*) is inclined to support it, Frisk (*GEW*) is persuaded, probably rightly, that θύω (A) and θύω (B) were in origin a single word, later distinguished by two diverging lines of development. This can be explained if its original meaning was *be in violent movement, seethe, billow*, and the transitive sense *make a fire offering* and hence *sacrifice* arose from that. Anything, whether flesh or incense, thrown on an open fire will produce billowing smoke. It is interesting that θύος is found in Myceneaean (*tu-wo*, also plural *tu-we-a*) apparently meaning an aromatic substance. If so, θυμός may have started by meaning *smoke* or *vapour*, the sense preserved by its cognates in other languages (Sanskrit *dhūmá-*, Latin *fumus* and similar forms in Balto-Slavonic). Of this there is no direct trace in Greek, where its place is taken by καπνός, except for a few cases where it appears to mean *breath* (see 3 below); but this will provide a useful starting-point for our investigation.

2 Another feature of LSJ's treatment is the preponderance of quotations from the Iliad; no fewer than 54 references are given, out of a total of 434 in this work, but many of these of course are in repeated lines and formulas. Against this there are 13 references to tragedy, 5 to early lyric, and 23 to prose authors. At least a larger selection of prose would show that the word continued down to a late date in normal prose use, and in the sense of *anger* survives into modern Greek (together with the verb θυμοῦμαι).

3 The sense nearest to the presumed original meaning is that of *breath*, which is visible emerging from the body in cold weather, and can thus have arisen from the postulated sense of *smoke* or *vapour*. It is remarkable, however, that even in Homer it is only used in this physical sense in one, or more likely two ways. The first is *breath as the characteristic of the living body* (whether human or animal), and it may thus be translated *life*:

ἧς ὑπεροπλίῃσι τάχ᾽ ἄν ποτε θυμὸν ὀλέσσῃ. Il. 1. 205.
κάππεσεν ἐν Λήμνῳ, ὀλίγος δ᾽ ἔτι θυμὸς ἐνῆεν. Il. 1. 593.

καὶ τοὺς μὲν (ἄρνας) κατέθηκεν ἐπὶ χθονὸς ἀσπαίροντας,
θυμοῦ δευομένους.   Il. 3. 294.

ἄμφω θυμὸν ἀπηύρα.   Il. 6. 17.

θυμοῦ καὶ ψυχῆς κεκαδών.   Il. 11. 334.

λίπε δ' ὀστέα θυμός.   Il. 12. 386.

After Homer this seems to be very rare:

οὗτω τὸν αὐτοῦ θυμὸν ὁρμαίνει πεσών.   A. *Ag.* 1388.

This depends on the sense given to ὁρμαίνει, which Denniston and Page regard as corrupt; but at least θυμόν is here likely to mean 'the breath of life'.

4   The other case where θυμός may have preserved its earliest sense of breath is more problematical. There are two passages in Homer where it is the subject of the verb πάτασσε.

Ἕκτορί τ' αὐτῷ θυμὸς ἐνὶ στήθεσσι πάτασσεν.   Il. 7. 216.

This describes Hector's reaction on realising he has to fight Ajax.

τοὶ δ' ἐλατῆρες
ἕστασαν ἐν δίφροισι, πάτασσε δὲ θυμὸς ἑκάστου
νίκης ἱεμένων.   Il. 23. 370.

This describes the charioteers taking part in an exciting race. So in both cases we may be sure that this event is the result of intense excitement. But what does πάτασσε mean? LSJ says 'each man's heart beat high', which might pass as a poetic translation; but there is nothing to suggest that θυμός can mean *heart* in the physical sense, and 'high' implies rather the θυμός as the seat of the emotions, see 8 below. πατάσσω according to LSJ is used intransitively only in these two passages and a further Homeric example and one from late prose:

ἐν δέ τέ οἱ κραδίη μεγάλα στέρνοισι πατάσσει.   Il. 13. 282.

ἐκπλαγῆναι ἀνάγκη καὶ πατάσσειν αὐτῷ τὴν καρδίαν.
Arr. *Cyn.* 15.

Elsewhere it is used transitively to mean '*strike, smite*' (LSJ). Since Il. 13. 282 must mean 'his heart beats hard', it is tempting to suppose that θυμός also means the heart, and this may be how LSJ arrived at its translation. But excitement, provoking an increase in the secretion of adrenalin, not only raises the rate of the the heart-beat, but also the rate of respiration, so that breath is drawn in noisy gulps and expelled violently. This might therefore be the sense of πάτασσε; the word is very likely connected with πάταγος (despite the -γ-, cf. πράσσω and πρᾶγος) and thus refers to the knocking noise made.

5   If this interpretation is accepted, it may receive some support from another passage:

> οὐδέ οἱ ἀτρέμας ἦσθαι ἐρητύετ᾽ ἐν φρεσὶ θυμός 'nor was his θυμός checked so as to rest quietly in his φρένες'.   Il. 13. 280.

If, as generally accepted, φρένες denotes the diaphragm and the surrounding area of the body, then θυμός can hardly mean anything but *breath*. But both of these words are often used in trans-ferred senses, in which case this example can be assigned to the sense discussed in 7 below.

6   It is a little surprising to find that θυμός is also used as the *seat of consciousness*. This is very likely the explanation of the use of φρήν or φρένες as meaning the mind. The *diaphragm*, if that is the correct anatomical identification of φρήν, is closely associated with the lungs and respiration; and there is good evidence that the ancients attributed consciousness (φρόνησις) to the presence of air in the body, since its absence certainly causes unconsciousness. This is neatly shown by Hippocrates:

> ὁ δ᾽ ἐς τὸν πλεύμονά τε καὶ τὰς φλέβας ἀὴρ συμβάλλεται ἐς τὰς κοιλίας ἐσιὼν καὶ ἐς τὸν ἐγκέφαλον, καὶ οὕτω τὴν φρόνησιν καὶ τὴν κίνησιν τοῖσι μέλεσι παρέχει. 'Air entering the lungs and tubes is distributed into the cavities [i.e. lungs] and the brain, and thus causes consciousness and the motor action of the limbs.'   Hp. *Morb. Sacr.* 10.

Further confirmation can be found in the derivatives such as λιπο-θυμία, which continued in medical use down to recent times as the technical name for a faint. We can define θυμός in this sense as *the conscious mind, attention*:

> ᾔδεε γὰρ κατὰ θυμὸν ἀδελφεὸν ὡς ἐπονεῖτο.   Il. 2. 409.
>
> εὖ γὰρ ἐγὼ τόδε οἶδα κατὰ φρένα καὶ κατὰ θυμόν.   Il. 4. 163.

As we have seen above (5), Homer regarded the φρένες as the seat of the θυμός, so it is not surprising to find them coupled. Likewise:

φράζετο θυμῷ. Il. 16. 646.

where φράζομαι may be etymologically related to φρήν.

σώφρονές τ' ἐγένοντο πινυτοί τε θυμόν. Pi. I. 8. 28.

This is commonly used in expressions with βάλλω and similar verbs meaning *pay attention to, mark*:

ἐν θυμῷ δ' ἐβάλοντο ἔπος. Il. 15. 566.

τοὺς ἐμοὺς λόγους
θυμῷ βαλ'. A. Pr. 706.

μή νυν ἔτ' αὐτῶν μηδὲν ἐς θυμὸν βάλῃς. S. OT 975.

—οὐχὶ ξυνίης;—οὐδέ γ' ἐς θυμὸν φέρω. S. El. 1347.

ἰδὼν ... τῶν τινα Λυδῶν ... καταβάντα ... ἐφράσθη καὶ ἐς θυμὸν ἐβάλετο. Hdt. 1. 84. 4; also 7. 51. 3; 8. 68. γ.

7 Much more often θυμός comes to mean *strength of mind, determination, spirit*. We might sometimes translate in English by *heart*, but this is of course ambiguous.

ὡς δὲ ἴδεν νεῦρόν τε καὶ ὄγκους ἐκτὸς ἐόντας
ἄψορρόν οἱ θυμὸς ἐνὶ στήθεσσιν ἀγέρθη. Il. 4. 152.

It is clear that this does not mean 'he recovered consciousness', but when he realised that the wound was superficial his spirits rose again.

οἶσθα καὶ αὐτή,
οἷον κείνου θυμὸς ὑπερφίαλος καὶ ἀπηνής. Il. 15. 94.

τάρβησαν, πᾶσιν δὲ παραὶ ποσὶ κάππεσε θυμός. Il. 15. 280.

As we might say, their hearts were in their boots. If Il. 13. 280 does not belong with the examples in 4 (see 5 above), it must be placed here.

τείρετο δ' ἀνδρῶν θυμὸς ὑπ' ἐρεσίης ἀλεγεινῆς. Od. 10. 78.

πίνετε οἶνον
εἰς ὅ κεν αὖτις θυμὸν ἐνὶ στήθεσσι λάβητε. Od. 10. 461.

μή μ' ἄσαισι μηδ' ὀνίαισι δάμνα,
πότνια, θῦμον. Sapph. 1. 4.

κεῖνος αἰνεῖν καὶ τὸν ἐχθρόν
παντὶ θυμῷ σύν τε δίκᾳ καλὰ ῥέζοντ' ἔννεπεν.   Pi. P. 9. 96.

ὥσπερ γὰρ ἵππος εὐγενής, κἂν ᾖ γέρων,
ἐν τοῖσι δεινοῖς θυμὸν οὐκ ἀπώλεσεν.   S. El. 26.

θάρσει τε τούτου εἵνεκα καὶ θυμὸν ἔχε ἀγαθόν.
Hdt. 1. 120. 3; 3. 85. 2; 7. 52. 2.

ἑσσωμένοι ἦσαν τῷ θυμῷ 'they had been disheartened'.
Hdt. 8. 130. 3.

θυμῷ καὶ ῥώμῃ τὸ πλέον ἐναυμάχουν ἢ ἐπιστήμῃ 'they conducted the seafight with more spirit and brute force than skill'.
Th. 1. 49. 3.

οὐ γὰρ οὐδεὶς πώποτ' αὐτῶν τοὺς ἐναντίους ἰδὼν
ἠρίθμησεν, ἀλλ' ὁ θυμὸς εὐθὺς ἦν Ἀμυνίας.   Ar. Eq. 570.

ἐστὶ θυμὸς ἵππῳ ὅπερ ὀργὴ ἀνθρώπῳ.   X. Eq. 9.2.

In the plural, of people in general:

θωπείας κολακικάς, αἳ ... τοὺς θυμοὺς ποιοῦσιν κηρίνους.
Pl. Lg. 633d.

8   We can place next the sense of θυμός as the *seat of the emotions*,
where pleasure, grief, fear, anger, etc. are felt. LSJ places the seat
of anger in the same section as *anger* itself, which is misleading. It
clearly belongs here. The obvious English translation is again
heart, but *mind* is also possible.

χωόμενον κατὰ θυμόν.   Il. 1. 429.

ἐπεί μιν ἄχος κραδίην καὶ θυμὸν ἵκανεν.   Il. 2. 171.

ἐμῷ κεχαρισμένε θυμῷ.   Il. 5. 243.

δεῖσε δ' ὅ γ' ἐν θυμῷ.   Il. 8. 138.

θυμὸς ἐνὶ στήθεσσι γεγήθει.   Il. 9. 343.

εὔνοον
θῦμον σκέθοντες.   Alc. 129.10 (L-P).

γυνὰ ...
ἐκ θυμοῦ στέργοισα κασίγνητόν τε πόσιν τε.   Theoc. 17. 130.

9   This needs to be distinguished from the *mind as the spring of
action, will*. This is used by Plato to provide an etymology for
ἐπιθυμία:

οὐδ' "ἐπιθυμία" χαλεπόν· τῇ γὰρ ἐπὶ τὸν θυμὸν ἰούσῃ δυνάμει δῆλον ὅτι τοῦτο ἐκλήθη τὸ ὄνομα. Pl. *Cra.* 419d.

Otherwise this use seems to be mainly confined to verse:

φεῦγε μάλ', εἴ τοι θυμὸς ἐπέσσυται. Il. 1. 173.

πιέειν ὅτε θυμὸς ἀνώγοι. Il. 4. 263.

βαλέειν δέ ἑ ἵετο θυμός. Il. 8. 301.

ἔτι δ' ἤθελε θυμῷ
εἰσιδέειν ... φύλοπιν αἰνήν. Il. 16. 255.

τὸν Ϝὸν θυμὸν αἰτιάμενος. Alc. 358 (L–P).

κῶττι μοι μάλιστα θέλω γένεσθαι
μαινόλᾳ θύμῳ. Sapph. 1. 18 (L–P).

δὴ τότ' ἐς γαῖαν πορεύεν θυμὸς ὦρμα
Ἰστρίαν νιν. Pi. *O.* 3. 25.

τὰ θυμῷ βουλόμενοι αὐτοὶ ἂν ἔχοιτε. 'if you really want them, you can have them.' Hdt. 5. 49. 4.

Μήδεια ...
ἔρωτι θυμὸν ἐκπλαγεῖσ' Ἰάσονος. E. *Med.* 8.

διέφαινεν ἡ κατήφεια τὸν θυμὸν οὐ τεταπεινωμένον. Plu. *Mar.* 41.6.

10 This needs to be distinguished from a particular impulse of the will, *desire, appetite, wish*:

ἕνα θυμὸν ἔχοντες. Il. 15. 710; cf. 22. 263.

ἕτερος δέ με θυμὸς ἔρυκεν. Od. 9. 302.

So later θυμός ἐστί μοι and similar phrases meaning *I have a wish to*:

σὲ γάρ μοι
θῦμος ὕμνην. Alc. 308. 2(b) (L–P).

ἄρχ' αὐτὸς ὥς σοι θυμός. S. *El.* 1319.

ὠνέεσθαι τῶν φορτίων τῶν σφι ἦν θυμὸς μάλιστα.
Hdt. 1. 1. 4.

ἢ ἄλλως σφι θυμὸς ἐγενέετο θεήσασθαι τὸν πόλεμον.
Hdt. 8. 116. 2.

βῆξαί τε θυμὸς αὐτοῖς ἐγγίνεται. Hp. *Prog.* 8.

ἀπελαύνετε ὅποι ὑμῖν θυμός. X. *Cyr.* 3. 1. 37.

So with prepositions, ἀπὸ θυμοῦ, πρὸς θυμόν, *as one might wish*:

> ἀλλ' ἀπὸ θυμοῦ
> μᾶλλον ἐμοὶ ἔσεαι. Il. 1. 562.

> κήνων ὁ φύσγων οὐ διελέξατο
> πρὸς θῦμον. Alc. 129. 22 (L–P).

11   In 8 above we have assembled the examples where θυμός means the seat of the emotions. From this it naturally extends to mean the emotion itself; but in practice it is not any emotion, but specifically *anger, passion*. LSJ, as noted above, confuses this with **II 4** '*the seat of anger*'. The sense of *anger* is the predominant one in prose writers, and survives into modern Greek.

> ἦε χόλον παύσειεν ἐρητύσειέ τε θυμόν. Il. 1. 193.

> θυμὸς δὲ μέγας ἐστὶ διοτρεφέων βασιλήων. Il. 2. 196.

> ἀλλ', Ἀχιλεῦ, δάμασον θυμὸν μέγαν· οὐδέ τί σε χρὴ
> νηλεὲς ἦτορ ἔχειν. Il. 9. 496.

> εἴξας ᾧ θυμῷ.
> Il. 9. 598; cf. S. *Ant.* 718 (whether θυμοῦ or θυμῷ is read).

> μὴ πάντα ἡλικίῃ καὶ θυμῷ ἐπίτρεπε, ἀλλ' ἴσχε καὶ κατα-
> λάμβανε σεωυτόν. Hdt. 3. 36. 1.

> ὀνείδεα κατιόντα ἀνθρώπῳ φιλέει ἐπανάγειν τὸν θυμόν.
> Hdt. 7. 160. 1.

> εἰσὶ χἀτέροις γοναὶ κακαὶ
> καὶ θυμὸς ὀξύς, ἀλλὰ νουθετούμενοι
> φίλων ἐπῳδαῖς ἐξεπᾴδονται φύσιν. S. *OC* 1193.

> οἱ λογισμῷ ἐλάχιστα χρώμενοι θυμῷ πλεῖστα ἐς ἔργον
> καθίστανται. Th. 2. 11. 7; cf. Plu. *Publ.* 9. 4.

> θυμὸς δὲ κρείσσων τῶν ἐμῶν βουλευμάτων. E. *Med.* 1079.

> τὸν θυμὸν δακών. Ar. *Nu.* 1369; *V.* 567.

> οἱ τῷ θυμῷ πραχθέντες φόνοι 'murders committed in anger'.
> Pl. *Lg.* 867b.

> σβέσαντες τὸν θυμόν. Pl. *Lg.* 888a.

> πλεύσαντες ἐπὶ τὴν Λακωνικὴν ... ἐκτεῖναι τὸν θυμόν, ἀρχὴν
> πολλῶν κακῶν. And. 3. 31.

> ἐπλήσθησαν πάντες θυμοῦ ... ἀκούοντες ταῦτα. *Ev. Luc.* 4.28.

πίεται ἐκ τοῦ οἴνου τοῦ θυμοῦ τοῦ θεοῦ. *Apoc.* 14. 10.

ὁ μὲν Ῥωμύλου θυμὸς εἰς ἔργον ἐξέπεσε.
Plu. *Rom. Thes.* 3. 2.

The phrase ἀποπιμπλάναι or πληροῦν τὸν θυμόν means to *satisfy* or *appease anger*:

τά τε ἄλλα γάρ μιν κρίνειν εὖ καὶ δὴ καὶ τῷ ἐπιμεμφομένῳ ἐκ τῆς δίκης παρ' ἑωυτοῦ διδόντα ἄλλα ἀποπιμπλάναι αὐτοῦ τὸν θυμόν. 'that he was in other respects a fair judge and in particular satisfied the anger of one who complained about his judgment by giving him other things out of his own property'.
Hdt. 2. 129. 2.

θυμουμένοις τε οὖν ὑπείκειν δεῖ καὶ ἀποπιμπλᾶσι τὸν θυμὸν ... συγγιγνώσκοντα. Pl. *Lg.* 717d.

πληρῶν τὸν θυμόν. Pl. *R.* 465a.

In the plural it will mean *instances of anger*:

περὶ φόβων τε καὶ θυμῶν καὶ πάντων τῶν τοιούτων.
Pl. *Phlb.* 40e.

ἐπὶ τούτοις που οἵ τε θυμοὶ γίγνονται καὶ αἱ κολάσεις.
Pl. *Prt.* 323e.

καὶ οἱ θυμοὶ ὀξεῖς μὲν ἀσθενεῖς δέ εἰσιν. Arist. *Rh.* 1390ᵃ11.

ἱερός

1 It is not easy to see the pattern which underlies the various meanings of this word, and the haphazard arrangement adopted by LSJ is unhelpful. English *sacred* clearly covers many of the senses, but this needs to be more closely defined. I have chosen to start with the value which is most nearly 'concrete', where it is applied to property *belonging to the gods*. This has the advantage of being also the earliest proven value, since the Mycenaean texts have the expression

e-ne-ka ku-ru-so-jo i-je-ro-jo = ἕνεκα χρυσοῖο ἱεροῖο
Pylos Ae 303.

This must refer to gold in the ownership of a deity. This also seems to be the best starting-point from which to demonstrate the development of the known senses, and preferable to a metaphysical concept such as *holy*, since the general tendency of language is always to extend physical or concrete meanings to include mental or metaphysical concepts. However, it cannot be excluded that a word of this type may have started in the metaphysical sphere and been later extended to more mundane objects.

2   It is believed that ἱερός developed a generalised sense of *mighty, powerful,* etc. I hope to be able to show that although possible, this is not by any means necessary, and I shall therefore endeavour to explain all the examples known to me by reference to the starting-point I have indicated. The diversity of meaning has caused the etymologists to speculate about the possibility that the word as we know it is in origin a conflation of two or even three separate words. Chantraine (*DELG*) has an excellent account of the question, to which I wish only to add that if I can show that it is unnecessary to suppose plural origins, some at least of this speculation can be set aside. But it is worth remarking that the dialectal diversity the word displays may well have resulted from this source. The form ἱερός is found in Mycenaean, Attic, Arcadian, and Cypriot; ἱαρός in West Greek (not merely North-West Greek, where the change of ερ to αρ is regular); ἱρός in Aeolic and some Ionic dialects. There is evidence that psilotic forms were in use where psilosis was not general; these may have been the result of **iharos* not yet having shifted the aspirate to the initial position. There are also cases where the initial vowel is long, even though there is no obvious reason for metrical lengthening in a word of this shape. Sanskrit *iṣirá-* may correspond exactly to ἱαρός, but cannot to ἱερός. It is clear that in this case the etymological approach must be subordinated to the contextual.

3   Apart from Mycenaean the sense *belonging to a deity, in divine ownership* is attested by some of the earliest alphabetic inscriptions, frequently found on objects dedicated in a temple. It may be followed by the name of the owner in the genitive case.

> hιαρὸν Ἀπόλ(λ)ōνος Καρυκε̄ϝίο.
> *LSAG* pl. 7. 5 (Boeotia, vii BC).
>
> τō̄νναλίō̄ ἱαρά.   *LSAG* pl. 26. 2 (Argos, vii BC).

So in Homer and later literature:

καὶ κλυτὸν ἄλσος ἵκοντο

ἱρὸν Ἀθηναίης. Od. 6. 322.

ἱερὰς ἀνὰ βήσσας

Κίρκης. Od. 10. 275.

ἱεροῖς ἐν δώμασι Κίρκης. Od. 10. 426.

ἄντρον ... ἱρὸν νυμφάων. Od. 13. 104.

ἐς ὀλιγωρίαν ἐτράποντο καὶ ἱερῶν καὶ ὁσίων ὁμοίως.
Th. 2. 52. 3 (cf. note on ὅσιος); X. Vect. 5. 4.

ἐάν τε ἱερὰ χρήματα ᾖ ἐν τῇ πόλει, ταῦτα ἀναλώσει.
Pl. R. 568d.

χῆνες ἱεροί (on the Capitol at Rome). Plu. 2. 325c.

So of persons, i.e. ἱερόδουλοι:

ἱερὸν τὸ σῶμα τῷ θεῷ δίδωμ' ἔχειν. E. Ion 1285.

καὶ τῶν ἱερῶν σωμάτων ἐκλέλοιπε τὸ πλῆθος. Str. 6. 2. 6.

Humorously:

ἐγὼ δὲ καὶ αὐτὸς ἡγοῦμαι ὁμόδουλός τε εἶναι τῶν κύκνων καὶ
ἱερὸς τοῦ αὐτοῦ θεοῦ. Pl. Phd. 85b.

4   An obvious development from the sense 'owned by a god' is to
the more general one of *associated with religious cult, religious*:

ἄγειν δ' ἱερὴν ἑκατόμβην. Il. 1. 99; 1. 431.

ἱεροὺς κατὰ βωμούς 'at the altars of the gods'. Il. 2. 305.

θύρας ἱεροῖο δόμοιο 'the doors of the temple'. Il. 6. 89.

ἄλλων τ' ἀθανάτων ἱερὸν γένος αἰὲν ἐόντων.
Hes. Th. 21; 57; 93.

διφασίοισι δὲ γράμμασι χρέονται (οἱ Αἰγύπτιοι), καὶ τὰ μὲν
αὐτῶν ἱρά, τὰ δὲ δημοτικὰ καλέεται. Hdt. 2. 36. 4.

ἔστι δὲ περὶ αὐτῶν (sc. ἐρινέων εἱμάτων) ἱρὸς λόγος λεγόμενος.
Hdt. 2. 81. 2; cf. Pl. Ep. 335a.

δαιμόνων
ἀγάλμαθ' ἱερά. S. OT 1379.

ἐκλέλοιπ' ἤδη τὸν ἱερὸν τρίποδα καὶ χρηστήριον
Ξοῦθος ... ; E. Ion 512.

τὴν ἱερὰν ... τριήρη i.e. sent to Delos for the festival. D. 4. 34.

ἔθεσθ' ἱερὸν νόμον αὐτῷ τῷ θεῷ περὶ τῆς ἱερομηνίας.
D. 21. 35.

ὅτι ἀπὸ βρέφους ἱερὰ γράμματα οἶδας. 2 Ep. Tim. 3. 15.

The connexion with religion is sometimes remote:

Λακεδαιμόνιοι δὲ μετὰ ταῦτα τὸν ἱερὸν καλούμενον πόλεμον
ἐστράτευσαν. Th. 1. 112. 5; Ar. Av. 556.

5 A special sense is where the word is applied to towns and other
places which are regarded as *under divine protection*, and thus
sacred, holy:

Ἴλιον ἱρήν.   Il. 5. 648; Alc. 424 (L–P).

ὄφρ' οἷοι Τροίης ἱερὰ κρήδεμνα λύωμεν.   Il. 16. 100.

Σούνιον ἱρόν.   Od. 3. 278.

ἐς γουνὸν Ἀθηνάων ἱεράων.
Od. 11. 323; Pi. fr. 75. 5; S. Aj. 1221.

Πύλου ἱερῆς.   Od. 21. 108.

Θήβας ἐξ ἱερᾶς.   Sapph. 44. 6 (L–P).

ὦ πολιοῦχε Παλλάς, ὦ
τῆς ἱερωτάτης ...
μεδέουσα χώρας.   Ar. Eq. 582.

With a curious adaptation of the Homeric formula discussed in 9
below:

Ἀρτέμιδος χρυσαόρου ἱερὸν ἀκτήν 'the holy shore of Artemis
of the golden sword'.   Oracle in Hdt. 8. 77. 1.

Used as part of a proper name:

ἐξ ὄρεος ἱροῦ.   Hdt. 1. 80. 1.

τὰς δὲ ἄλλας (νήσους) ... Διδύμην καὶ Στρογγύλην καὶ Ἱεράν.
Th. 3. 88. 2; Plb. 1. 60.3.

Ἱερὰ ἄκρα καὶ αἱ Χελιδόνιαι.   Str. 14. 3. 8.

ἰόντες ... τὴν ἱρὴν ὁδὸν διὰ Φωκέων τε καὶ Βοιωτῶν ἤισαν.
Hdt. 6. 34. 2.

ἰοῦσι δὲ ἐπ' Ἐλευσῖνα ἐξ Ἀθηνῶν ἣν Ἀθηναῖοι καλοῦσιν ὁδὸν
ἱεράν.   Paus. 1. 36. 3.

6 An easy step from this is the development to mean more generally *placed under divine protection, dedicated*:

ὡς δ᾽ ἄνεμος ἄχνας φορέει ἱερὰς κατ᾽ ἀλωὰς
ἀνδρῶν λικμώντων. Il. 5. 499.

It is a little surprising to find this epithet applied to anything as humdrum as a threshing-floor; but it is perhaps associated with the application to crops (see 9), and harvesting is often accompanied by religious rituals. Boundary marks are often inscribed ἱερός, possibly because they are all under the protection of Ζεὺς Ὅριος, but so far as I know this word is only used when the adjacent land is the property of or otherwise consecrated to a deity. They are sometimes further defined as ἄσυλος; e.g.

ὄρος ἱερὸς ἄσυλος Ἀρτέμιδος Σαρδιανῆς.

See P. Hermann, *Chiron* 19 (1989) 133, and further L. Robert, *Hellenica* 6. 33ff. Even in modern times the *Book of Common Prayer* (1662) contains in the Commination Service for Ash Wednesday the imprecation 'Cursed is he that removeth his neighbour's land-mark'.

ὄρϝος hιαρὸς τᾶς Ἀκρίας (*sc.* Ἥρας).
    Schwyzer 135. 2 (Corcyra, v BC).

τοὺς μὲν (ὅρως) ... ἐπιγεγραμμένως hιαρὼς Διονύσω χώρων.
    Tab. Heracl. 1. 74.

So we have Xenophon quoting a stele erected outside a temple:

ἱερὸς ὁ χῶρος τῆς Ἀρτέμιδος. X. *An.* 5. 3. 13.

In the examples quoted the boundary mark is delimiting the property of a deity, but it is possible that it may be used also where the area is placed under divine protection without legally being the property of a deity.

7 A proverbial expression describes advice (συμβουλή) as ἱερὸν χρῆμα Pl. *Thg.* 122b. This may be, as LSJ suggests, because it was regarded as a *sacred duty*. It is more likely that it was felt to be *under divine protection,* because, as a speaker reported by Xenophon said, advice was given under oath with the same rewards, if honestly, and penalties, if not honestly, given.

ἐπευξάμενος εἶπεν ὧδε· Εἰ μὲν ξυμβουλεύοιμι ἃ βέλτιστά μοι
δοκεῖ, πολλά μοι καὶ ἀγαθὰ γένοιτο· εἰ δὲ μὴ, τἀναντία. αὕτη
γὰρ ἡ ἱερὰ ξυμβουλὴ λεγομένη εἶναι δοκεῖ μοι παρεῖναι· νῦν
γὰρ δὴ ἂν μὲν εὖ ξυμβουλεύσας φανῶ, πολλοὶ ἔσονται οἱ
ἐπαινοῦντές με, ἂν δὲ κακῶς, πολλοὶ ἔσεσθε οἱ καταρώμενοι.
                                      X. An. 5. 6. 4.

Other references are Ar. *fr*. 33 (37 Bl, 104 D, 39 B); Pl. *Ep*. 321c;
Luc. *Rh. Pr*. 1.

8   It is well known that the Greeks regarded most natural objects
and phenomena as manifestations of divine power. Hence the term
ἱερός was freely applied in early Greek to water in its various
forms, possibly as being essential for life, so frequently of streams
and rivers, which were regarded as minor deities; but also of the
sea, presumably because this was the domain of Poseidon. We may
thus define its sense here as *numinous*.

ἱερὸν ῥόον Ἀλφειοῖο.   Il. 11. 236.

ἐκ θ᾽ ἱερῶν ποταμῶν.   Od. 10. 351.

σὰν λιπὼν ἱερὰν λιβάδ᾽.   S. *Ph*. 1215.

        ἱρὰς ἐξ ἀειρύτου χοὰς
κρήνης ἐνεγκοῦ.   S. *OC* 469.

ἄνω ποταμῶν ἱερῶν χωροῦσι παγαί.   E. *Med*. 410.

Of rain:

                      τὸ μήτε γῇ
μήτ᾽ ὄμβρος ἱερὸς μήτε φῶς προσδέξεται.   S. *OT* 1428.

ἵνα δρόσοι τέγγουσ᾽ ἱεραί.   E. *Ion* 117.

Of the sea:

Ἐρυθρᾶς ἱερὸν
χεῦμα Θαλάσσης.   A. *fr*. 323 M.

μὰ τὴν Καλυψὼ τάς τε Νηρέως κόρας,
τά θ᾽ ἱερὰ κύματ᾽ ἰχθύων τε πᾶν γένος.
            E. *Cyc*. 265; *Hipp*. 1206.

9   The idea of immanent divinity was extended to other natural
products and phenomena. In a famous, if obscure, Homeric
formula it is used of grain. Partly because of its scansion, it has
been supposed that this is a different word; but the idea of the

crops as the gift of a deity has always been potent and is by no means dead today. Modern Greek poets have used the term 'blessed' of wheat (το βλογημένο στάρι).

> ἠδὲ μέλι χλωρόν, παρὰ δ' ἀλφίτου ἱεροῦ ἀκτήν.   Il. 11. 631.

This was modified, perhaps ignorantly, by Hesiod to:

> Δημήτερος ἱερὸν ἀκτήν.   Hes. Op. 597; 805.

as if ἱερός could be used with two terminations only; for a further variant on this theme see 5 above. Likewise an olive-tree, as sacred to Athena:

> ἱερῆς παρὰ πυθμέν' ἐλαίας.   Od. 13. 372.

Of a sea-bird:

> ἱαρὸς ὄρνις.   Alcm. 26 P.

Rather different is its use of natural phenomena such as as day and night:

> ὄφρα μὲν ἠὼς ἦν καὶ ἀέξετο ἱερὸν ἦμαρ.   Il. 8. 66.
> ὅτ' ἂν φάος ἱερὸν ἔλθῃ.   Hes. Op. 339.
> ἐπὶ κνέφας ἱερὸν ἔλθῃ.   Il. 11. 194.

Note that in the last three examples the ῑ is again long.

10   Another Homeric phrase which has spilled a sea of ink is the ἱερὸς ἰχθύς; but it needs to be observed that the context is that of fishing. The fish is given to mankind as food by Poseidon, and this is enough to justify the use of this term:

> ἕλκε δὲ δουρὸς ἑλὼν ὑπὲρ ἄντυγος, ὡς ὅτε τις φὼς
> πέτρῃ ἔπι προβλῆτι καθήμενος ἱερὸν ἰχθὺν
> ἐκ πόντοιο θύραζε λίνῳ καὶ ἤνοπι χαλκῷ.   Il. 16. 407.

The ancients thought that ἱερός here indicated a particular species of fish and offered various guesses:

> ὅπου δ' ἂν ἀνθίας ᾖ οὐκ ἔστι θηρίον· ᾧ καὶ σημείῳ χρώμενοι
> κατακολυμβῶσιν οἱ σπογγεῖς, καὶ καλοῦσιν ἱεροὺς ἰχθῦς
> τούτους. 'Where the *anthias* is, no savage creature is found; so
> using this as a sign, sponge-fishers dive and call these sacred
> fish.'   Arist. *HA* 620ᵇ35.

For more guesses on this subject see Ath. 7. 282e, Plu. 2. 981d, and Call. *fr.* 394 Pf.

11   It now becomes clear how ἱερός developed the sense *not to be used for profane purposes, inviolable, untouchable, sacred*. For instance, the chariot driven by Automedon is so called because the horses that pulled it were divine, and it was able to cut through the battle unscathed, though the driver alone could not also hurl a spear:

> οὐ γάρ πως ἦν οἶον ἐόνθ' ἱερῷ ἐνὶ δίφρῳ
> ἔγχει ἐφορμᾶσθαι καὶ ἐπίσχειν ὠκέας ἵππους.   Il. 17. 464.

> τὰς δὲ θηλέας (βοῦς) οὔ σφι ἔξεστι θύειν, ἀλλ' ἱραί εἰσι τῆς
> Ἴσιος.   Hdt. 2. 41. 1; 2. 42. 5.

> ἱερὸς γὰρ οὗτος τῶν κατὰ χθονὸς θεῶν
> ὅτου τοδ' ἔγχος κρατὸς ἁγνίσῃ τρίχα.   (*Mors loquitur*)
>   E. *Alc.* 75.

> —δὸς σύ μοι τὸ τριβώνιον ...
> —μὴ δῆθ'·   ἱερὸν γάρ ἐστι τοῦ Πλούτου πάλαι.   Ar. *Pl.* 937.

> γῆ μὲν οὖν ἑστία τε οἰκήσεως ἱερὰ πᾶσι πάντων θεῶν.
>   Pl. *Lg.* 955e.

> ἐκ παντὸς ἱεροῦ καὶ βεβήλου τόπου.   D. H. 7. 8. 4.

This sense can be used of persons who are protected by their office, such as kings, princes, heralds, etc.

> οἱ δὲ γέροντες
> ἥατ' ἐπὶ ξεστοῖσι λίθοις ἱερῷ ἐνὶ κύκλῳ,
> σκῆπτρα δὲ κηρύκων ἐν χέρσ' ἔχον ἠεροφώνων.   Il. 18. 504.

> βασιλέες ἱεροί.   Pi. *P.* 5. 97.

So perhaps:

> ἥκω γὰρ ἱερὸς εὐσεβής τε καὶ φέρων
> ὄνησιν ἀστοῖς τοῖσδ'.   S. *OC* 287.

This will now produce an explanation for the formulae with ἴς and μένος as a periphrasis for the person found in the Odyssey, since the three persons to whom they are applied are Telemachus, Alcinous, and Antinous.

> ἱερὴ ἴς Τηλεμάχοιο.   Od. 2. 409 (and six other examples).

> ἱερὸν μένος Ἀλκινόοιο.   Od. 8. 2 (five other examples).

ἱερὸν μένος Ἀντινόοιο. Od. 18. 34.

The formula was then extended by a later poet to the sun:

ἱερὸν μένος ἠελίοιο. h. Ap. 371.

Later still ἱερός was used to denote persons given special status as sacred:

Γναθίō τō σφυχ[έ] (= ψυχή) ὄλετ᾽ ἐ[ν δαΐ]· hιερός εἰμι
τō Hερōιάδō. IG 1². 920.

hιαρὸς Χαροπ[ί]νος. Schwyzer 66 (Messenia, iv BC).

ὁ γραμματεὺς τῶν συνέδρων τοὺς γενηθέντας ἱεροὺς ὁρκιξάτω
παραχρῆμα. Schwyzer 74. 1 (Andania, i BC).

This too will perhaps explain the dialogue in the *Frogs* between Aeacus and the slave Xanthias, when Aeacus is testing his alleged divinity by beating him:

—τί τάτταται;
μῶν ὠδυνήθης; —οὐ μὰ Δί᾽ ἀλλ᾽ ἐφρόντισα
ὁπόθ᾽ Ἡράκλεια τὰν Διομείοις γίγνεται.
—ἄνθρωπος ἱερός. δεῦρο πάλιν βαδιστέον. Ar. Ra. 652.

This might of course mean *pious,* but in the absence of any evidence to support this, it would seem preferable to make it mean 'under divine protection'. Significantly the translators of the *Res Gestae Divi Augusti* chose ἱερός to translate Latin *sacrosanctus.*

ἵνα ἱερὸς ὦ [καὶ] δ[ιὰ βίου] τὴν δημαρχικὴν ἔχω ἐξουσίαν.
Mon. Anc. Gr. 5. 17.

So too:

ἔφη γὰρ ἱερὸν τὸν δήμαρχον εἶναι καὶ ἄσυλον. Plu. TG 15. 2.

In imperial times the superlative was used as an honorific title, being applied to imperial officials and institutions as well as the emperor himself.

τῷ ἱερωτάτῳ τοῦ κρατίστου ἡγέμονος Γαίου Σεπτιμίου
Οὐεγέθου βήματι. P. Hambr. 4. 8. (i AD).

ἐπὶ τοῦ ἱερωτάτου σου ταμείου ὠφελείᾳ. SIG 888. 10 (iii AD).

12 It is not at first sight easy to distinguish the last sense from that which now follows. The criterion is whether the inviolability described is of a genuinely religious or purely human nature. It is

twice used in Homer of sentries, where commentators have been inclined to take it as meaning merely *strong*; but the sense of *inviolable* or at least *which ought not to be violated* fits better.

αἴ κ' ἐθέλῃσιν
ἐλθεῖν ἐς φυλάκων ἱερὸν τέλος ἠδ' ἐπιτεῖλαι.   Il. 10. 56.

ὅπως Πρίαμον βασιλῆα
νηῶν ἐκπέμψειε λαθὼν ἱεροὺς πυλαωρούς.   Il. 24. 681.

Perhaps the same idea lies behind the description of the army at the funeral of Achilles in the last book of the Odyssey:

μέγαν καὶ ἀμύμονα τύμβον
χεύαμεν Ἀργείων ἱερὸς στρατὸς αἰχμητάων.   Od. 24. 81.

Again in a military context we find Plato using the superlative:

τοὺς νομοφύλακας συλλέξαντες εἰς χωρίον ὡς ἱερώτατόν τε καὶ ἱκανώτατον καθίσαι, χωρὶς μὲν τοὺς ὁπλίτας, χωρὶς δὲ τους ἱππέας ...   Pl. *Lg.* 755e.

In contexts which seem to exclude religious dedication:

παρακαταθήκην εἶναι μεγίστην ἡγούμενοι καὶ ἱερωτάτην.
Pl. *Lg.* 927c.

ἢ δέ τί κα πάθει Ἀθανοδώρα, παρμενεῖ Ἀνδρικὸς τὸν περιττὸν χρόνον πὰρ Δωΐλον, ἔπιτα ἰαρὸς ἔστω μεὶ ποθίκων μειθενὶ μειθέν. 'If anything happens to Athanodora, Andricus is to remain for the remaining period with Doïlus, and then let him be inviolate, in no wise belonging to anyone.'
Schwyzer, 509. 19 (Lebadea, iii BC); cf. 511. 2.

For a possible development of this sense, see the note on γερός.

13   In later Greek we find the expression ἱερὰ ἄγκυρα as the name of the reserve anchor carried by a ship, and therefore used only in a dire emergency.

ἄγκυρα ἱερά, ᾗ χωρὶς ἀνάγκης οὐ χρῶνται.   Poll. 1. 93.

This is clearly an extension of the sense *inviolable, untouchable*. It is, however, most often used figuratively, of something which is the *last resort*.

τὴν ἐπίπονον καὶ μοχθηρὰν ὄντως ὥσπερ τινὰ ἱερὰν ἄγκυραν εἰς ἅπαντα πάθη διαρκῆ παραληψόμεθα λιμοκτονίαν.
Gal. 11. 182.

ἄκουσον ἤδη τὴν ἱερὰν, φασίν, ἄγκυραν καὶ ἦν οὐδεμίᾳ μηχανῇ
ἀπορρήξεις. Luc. *J. Tr.* 51; *Fug.* 13.

So with σκεῦος instead of ἄγκυρα:

μηδ᾽ ὥσπερ ἐν πλοίῳ σκεῦος ἱερὸν ἀποκεῖσθαι τὰς ἐσχάτας
περιμένοντα χρείας τῆς πόλεως καὶ τύχας.

Plu. 2. 812c; cf. 815d.

14 Rather similar is ἱερὸν ὀστοῦν = *os sacrum*, the lowest of the
vertebrae making up the spine. Many fanciful explanations have
been offered of this name in both ancient and modern times. I
rather like that attributed to Alex. Monro in 1732: 'from being
offered as a dainty bit in sacrifice'. But it is clearly a special sense
of *untouchable*, seeing that it is an essential part of the skeleton, so
it belongs with the anchor.

ἀπὸ μὲν τοῦ ἱεροῦ ὀστέου ἄχρι τοῦ μεγάλου σπονδύλου.

Hp. *Art.* 45.

Likewise the spinal canal:

ἡ μέντοι διὰ τῶν σφονδύλων πορεία, δι᾽ ἣν ὁ μύελος τέταται,
σωλὴν καλεῖται, καὶ ἱερὰ σῦριγξ. Poll. 2. 180.

15 In games and sports we can trace also the same sense of *last
resort*, which we see in anchors. It appears in a list of throws of
dice, Eub. 57. 1. The feminine ἱερά (*sc.* γραμμή) was the name of a
line on the gaming board, presumably that from which pieces were
only moved by necessity. This at least is Eustathius' explanation
of a fragment of Alcaeus:

κινήσαις τὸν ἀπ᾽ ἴρας †πυκινὸν† λίθον. Alc. 351 (L–P).

In a figurative phrase:

ἡ βουλὴ (*sc. the Roman senate*), καθάπερ ἐν χειμῶνι πολλῷ καὶ
κλύδωνι τῆς πόλεως, ἄρασα τὴν ἀφ᾽ ἱερᾶς ἀφῆκεν.

Plu. *Cor.* 32.

Likewise of victories or crowns, *unattainable* because of a dead
heat:

ἀνδριάντα ... ἐπιγραφὴν ἔχοντα τήν τε τῶν ἄλλων ἀγώνων
μαρτυρίαν καὶ δηλοῦσαν ὑπὲρ τῆς ἱερᾶς, ἣν μόνος ἀπ᾽ αἰῶνος
ἀνδρῶν ἐποίησεν. *SIG* 1073. 48.

ἀλλ' ὡς ἂν ἀπαθῶς κἀήττητοί τινες ἄνδρες, ἱερὸν ἐποίησαν τὸν
στέφανον. Plb. 1. 58. 5; 29. 8. 9.

16 I have left to last the famous ἱερὰ νόσος, because it is evident
that the ancients themselves were uncertain how the disease
acquired its name. It is well known that it was a popular name for
epilepsy, but it does not seem in origin to have been restricted to
that.

τήν τε οἴησιν ἱερὰν νόσον ἔλεγε (Ἡράκλειτος) καὶ τὴν ὄρασιν
ψεύδεσθαι. Heracl. fr. 46.

Here οἴησις is said to mean 'self-conceit'; Diehl translates *Eigen-
dünkel*. But by the time of Herodotus the name was being used for
epilepsy.

καὶ γάρ τινα καὶ ἐκ γενεῆς νοῦσον μεγάλην λέγεται ἔχειν ὁ
Καμβύσης, τὴν ἱρὴν ὀνομάζουσί τινες. Hdt. 3. 33.

This was then adopted as the title of a famous Hippocratic work
περὶ ἱερῆς νούσου. But its author makes it plain that the name was
not given because it was a divine visitation:

αὕτη δὲ ἡ νοῦσος ἡ ἱερὴ καλουμένη ἀπὸ τῶν αὐτῶν προφασίων
γίνεται ἀφ' ὧν καὶ αἱ λοιπαί. Hp. *Morb. Sacr.* 21.

It would therefore appear that it was more likely named as being
untouchable, i.e. *incurable,* and then popularly misinterpreted as
meaning 'sent by the gods'. At all events *epilepsy* became its
normal sense; e.g. Thphr. *HP* 9. 11. 3; Call. *fr.* 75 Pf.

17 To sum up, the need for any sense not related to *sacred* has
not been proved, though it is hardly possible to be sure now what
exactly Homer meant in some of his formulae; he may not have
known himself. I would suggest that this re-arrangement of the
senses allows us to see coherent lines of development, and to
understand better the way the uses came into existence.

ἰπνός

1 It is obvious that this word is associated with the domestic use
of fire, but we must not fall into the trap of supposing that it meant
the same thing to all Greeks at all periods. The earliest use is on a

Mycenaean clay tablet of xiii (?xiv) BC at Knossos (Uc 160.v), where the spelling *i-po-no* is followed by a schematic representation of a shallow bowl:

i-po-no  14

The most probable interpretation of this is of a coarse earthenware vessel which can be placed on a hearth inverted and covered in hot embers in order to bake its contents. This is the object known in later Greek as *κρίβανος* or *κλίβανος*; the variation in form may point to a foreign origin for the word. But evidence that it could in later times too be made of earthenware comes from the compound *ἰπνοπλάθος* Pl. *Tht.* 147a. However, that passage distinguishes three types of clay, that used by potters, makers of *ἰπνοί*, and brickmakers (*πλινθουργοί*), so this is something larger than an ordinary domestic utensil (see further 4 below). A passage of Hippocrates which refers to *ἰπνοῦ ὄστρακα* (Hp. *Morb.* 2. 47, p. 68L) may perhaps be used to support this, but here again the reference is probably to a *kiln*.

2 It would be expected that with the development of kitchen-technology the simple 'Dutch oven' described above would be replaced by a larger structure, built into the kitchen and offering a safe place for lighting a fire and a closed area in which food could be placed for baking. The exact sense cannot be deduced from this passage:

> *μαρτύριον δέ οἱ εἶναι ὡς ἀληθέα ταῦτα λέγει, ὅτι ἐπὶ ψυχρὸν τὸν ἰπνὸν Περίανδρος τοὺς ἄρτους ἐπέβαλε.* 'Periander had put his loaves into a cold oven.' Hdt. 5. 92. *η*. 2.

Nor am I sure what to infer from a curious comic fragment:

> *ὁρῶν μὲν ἄρτους λευκοσωμάτους ἰπνὸν*
> *καταμπέχοντας ἐν πυκναῖς διεξόδοις,*
> *ὁρῶν δὲ μορφὴν κριβάνοις ἠλλαγμένους ...*
> Antiphanes 176. 4 (= 174 K–A).

Similarly the following tell us only that it was used for cooking:

> *ὁμῶς κροκόδειλον ἂν ὀπτὸν*
> *δασσαίμην ἀπ' ἰπνοῦ, τερπνὸν παίδεσσιν Ἰώνων.*
> Archestratus *fr.* 46. 4 (Ath. 7. 319d).

> *τὰ δ(ὲ κάρυα) ἐν τοῖς ἰπνοῖς φρυγόμενα ὀλιγότροφα.*
> Diphilus Siphnius (Ath. 2. 54a).

There are also references which make it plain that it contained some sort of stove or furnace, and I am indebted to Professor L. A. Moritz for the suggestion that the essential feature of a classical ἰπνός was that it contained its own source of heat. This is clear from the reference to soot (ἀσβόλη):

οὔτε πρὸς ἰπνὸν ἀσβόλην ἀλευμένη
ἴζοιτ'.   Semon. 7. 61.

Likewise:

καὶ αἰθάλην ἀπὸ τοῦ ἰπνοῦ τρίψασα.
                          Hp. Mul. 1. 91 (8. 220. 4 L)

Used for heating:

προσιόντες εἶδον αὐτὸν θερόμενον πρὸς τῷ ἰπνῷ.
                          Arist. PA 1. 5. 645ᵃ20.

For heating water:

ὑπεράνω τῶν ἰπνῶν τῶν βαλανείων.   Dsc. 5. 88. 4.

3   A further collection of references suggests that an ἰπνός was a structure large enough for a person to get inside; but the complication here is that the word may also have been used for the room in a house containing the heating or cooking stove, i.e. it is equivalent to ἰπνών. This certainly seems to be the meaning in the following:

οὐ γὰρ ὁ Λάβης ἀρτίως
ὁ κύων παράξας ἐς τὸν ἰπνὸν ὑφαρπάσας
τροφαλίδα τυροῦ Σικελικὴν κατεδήδοκεν;   Ar. V. 837.

Cheese would hardly be kept in an oven, but it could have been stored in the stove-room to mature.

ἀδελφοὶ δὲ δύο ... ἐκρύπτοντο ὑπὸ ἰπνῷ.   App. BC 4. 4. 22.

ἄγε δὴ σὺ καὶ σὺ τὴν πανοπλίαν μὲν πάλιν
ταύτην λαβόντε κρεμάσατον τυχἀγαθῇ
ἐς τὸν ἰπνὸν εἴσω πλησίον τοὐπιστάτου.   Ar. Av. 437.

The ἐπίστατον will be the stand or base on which the stove rests. This sense is supported by numerous references in the later lexicographers; a particularly interesting example is:

Ἡράκλειτος ὁ Ἐφέσιος καθήμενος ἐντός ποτε τοῦ ἰπνοῦ (ἰπνὸς
δέ ἐστιν οἷον οἰκίδιον ἐν ᾧ τοὺς ἄρτους ἔψομεν ...)
                          Mich. in PA 1. 4 (3. 22 Hayduck).

Likewise:

> Λυκοῦργος ... μέρος τι τῆς οἰκίας οὕτω καλεῖται, τό
> λεγόμενον παρ' ἡμῖν μαγειρεῖον.   Harp. (s.v. ἰπνός).

4   Clear evidence for the use of an ἰπνός as a *kiln* to fire pottery
comes from the Hippocratic Corpus:

> ὁ ἀπὸ τοῦ κεραμέου ἰπνοῦ καταπεσών.
> Hp. *Epid.* 4. 20 (p. 160 L).

I suspect therefore the ὄστρακα mentioned in 1 above may be
sherds from a kiln.

5   Apparently in conflict with what we have seen so far are some
examples where an ἰπνός is used as a source of light, and is thus
misleadingly translated *lantern*. In the ancient world lighting out
of doors was always a problem. Pine-torches were often used,
especially in processions, but these produced also a good deal of
smoke and smell. Oil lamps were obviously impracticable if
exposed to the wind, and glass technology was hardly far enough
advanced to make the design of satisfactory lanterns possible, or at
least cheap enough for ordinary use. The solution adoped was to
make a portable version of the ἰπνός, a vessel enclosing a pan of
charcoal embers, which would glow the more brightly the stronger
the wind. The clearest example is in Aristophanes' description of
guests returning from a smart dinner party each carying an ἰπνός,
so that they look from a distance like stars:

> ἀπὸ δείπνου τινὲς
> τῶν πλουσίων οὗτοι βαδίζουσ' ἀστέρων
> ἰπνοὺς ἔχοντες, ἐν δὲ τοῖς ἰπνοῖσι πῦρ.   Ar. *Pax* 841.

Probably also:

> ὁ δ' ἰπνὸς γέγον' ἡμῖν ἐξαπίνης ἐλεφάντινος.   Ar. *Pl.* 815.

So in a list of offerings to be made:

> καὶ μέλιτος τέτορες κοτυλ[έ]αι, καὶ τυροὶ ὄιεοι δυώδεκα, καὶ
> ἰπνὸς καινός ...
>   *SIG* 1027. 13 (= Paton and Hicks 39. 13, Cos, iv/iii BC).

Made of bronze:

> ἴπνου [*sic*] χαλκείοιο θοὸν σέλας.   Opp. *H.* 5. 430.

Used in fishing at night:

> γαλήνην εἶναι χρή, καὶ εἰ ταῦθ᾽ οὕτως ἔχει, τῆς πρῴρας
> τῶν ἀκατίων κοίλας τινὰς ἐξαρτῶσιν ἐσχαρίδας πυρὸς
> ἐνακμάζοντος· καὶ εἰσὶ διαφανεῖς, ὡς καὶ στέγειν τὸ πῦρ καὶ
> μὴ κρύπτειν τὸ φῶς· ἰπνοὺς καλοῦσιν αὐτάς.   Ael. NA 2. 8.

6   This accounts for all the usable material for the word known to
me, but LSJ offers another sense: '= κοπρών, *dunghill, privy*, Ar.
Fr. 353, Hsch.' This is based upon the following passage of
Hesychius; it should be observed that there is only one piece of
evidence, and its meaning depends upon an unreliable source:

> ἰπνός ... Ἀριστοφάνης δὲ ἐν Κωκάλῳ καὶ τὸν κοπρῶνα οὕτως
> εἶπεν.

Without any context it is impossible to judge this, but it seems
prima facie unlikely. The adjective ἴπνιος is quoted by Suidas from
Callimachus:

> λέγει δὲ τὴν κόπρον τῶν ζῴων Καλλίμαχος
> σὺν δ᾽ ἄμυδις φορυτόν τε καὶ ἴπνια λύματ᾽ ἄειρεν.
> 'and altogether took the rubbish and the **** dirt'.
>
> (Call. *Hec*. 295).

But there is no reason to suppose on the basis of this quotation that
this means 'animal dung'. This sense should at least be kept in
limbo pending further evidence.

ἰσχυρός

1   If you belong to the school of thought that believes one English
word is all that is needed to translate a Greek one, you may be
content with LSJ's treatment of this word. The four senses distinguished are given as: *strong*; *powerful*; *forcible*; *vigorous* of literary
style. The first begins with physical strength of persons, and
moves on rapidly to 'things'; but the thing quoted is an arrow, so
it here means *powerful* or *forceful*, and the quite common sense of
things which are *strongly made* or *robust* is totally missing. The
whole article is a strange congeries of different meanings, with
little effort made to separate them out, and very incomplete coverage of standard authors. A minimum of research was enough to

add a number of useful examples, often much better quotations than those actually given. This also confirmed that the word is absent from early epic and Pindar; it seems to be first recorded in Alcaeus. New examples are marked with an asterisk.

2   It is obvious that the article should begin, as LSJ does, with physical strength. But LSJ quotes only two examples for the meaning *possessing physical strength, powerful, vigorous*:

ὡς ἄνδρ' ἑλών μ' ἰσχυρὸν ἐκ βίας ἄγει. S. *Ph.* 945.

ἀεὶ γὰρ ἄνδρα σκαιὸν ἰσχυρὸν φύσει
ἧσσον δέδοικα τἀσθενοῦς τε καὶ σοφοῦ. E. *fr.* 290 (N).

εἰ δ' ἰσχυρὸς εἶ
τί μ' οὐκ ἀπεψώλησας; *Ar. *Ach.* 591.

Σώφιλον τὸν παγκρατιαστήν (ἰσχυρός τις ἦν, μέλας, εὖ οἶδ'
ὅτι γιγνώσκουσίν τινες ὑμῶν ὃν λέγω). *D. 21. 71.

εἰ τὸν εἰδότα ὅτι μικρός τε καὶ αἰσχρὸς καὶ ἀσθενής ἐστιν
ἐπαινοίη λέγων ὅτι καλός τε καὶ μέγας καὶ ἰσχυρός ἐστιν.
*X. *Mem.* 2. 6. 12; *3. 9. 1.

It is also used of plants:

τάχυ ἂν καὶ ἰσχυρὸν τὸ φυτὸν ἡγοῦμαι βλαστάνειν.
*X. *Oec.* 19. 10.

3   In military contexts ἰσχυρός means *strong in fighting power*. It is not always easy to distinguish this from the next sense (see 4 below), as for instance in the passages of Demosthenes quoted here.

ὁρῶντες οὐδὲν ἰσχυρὸν ἀπὸ τῶν Λεσβίων. Th. 3. 6. 1; 5. 111.

τὴν ἀκμὴν τοῦ ναυτικοῦ αὐτῶν ἀφείλετο γενομένην καὶ πάνυ
ἰσχυράν. *Th. 8. 46. 5.

ὠφελεῖν Ἀθηναίους Λακεδαιμονίους τρόπῳ ὁποίῳ ἂν δύνωνται
ἰσχυροτάτῳ. Treaty in Th. 5. 23. 1.

οὐκ ἔστιν ἰσχυροτέρα φάλαγξ ἢ ὅταν ἐκ φίλων συμμάχων
ἠθροισμένη ᾖ. X. *Cyr.* 7. 1. 30; *HG 6. 5. 18.

χαλεπωτέρῳ καὶ ἰσχυροτέρῳ χρησόμεθ' ἐχθρῷ.
*D. 8. 50; *3. 28.

4   In a more general sense ἰσχυρός means *imposing compliance, powerful, mighty;* this may be used of gods or of men.

τί δῆτα πρὸς ταῦτ' ἄλοχος ἰσχυρὰ Διός; A. *Supp.* 302.

τοῦτον τὸν ἰσχυρὸν θεὸν
ἐγὼ ποιήσω τήμερον δοῦναι δίκην. Ar. *Pl.* 946.

ὁ δὲ ὀπίσω μου ἐρχόμενος ἰσχυρότερός μού ἐστιν.
Ev. *Matt.* 3. 11.

τὸ πολλὸν δ' ἥγέαται ἰσχυρὸν εἶναι. 'They believe strength lies in numbers.' Hdt. 1. 136. 1.

πῶς οὖν ἔτ' ἂν γένοιτ' ἂν ἰσχυρὰ πόλις ... ; E. *Supp.* 447.

πολλοὶ παρ' ὑμῖν ἐπὶ καιρῶν γεγόνασιν ἰσχυροί. *D. 19. 297.

ἔστι Θηβαίους ταπεινοὺς ποιεῖν ἄνευ τοῦ Λακεδαιμονίους ἰσχυροὺς καθιστάναι. 'It is possible to humble the Thebans without making the Lacedaemonians powerful.' *D. 16. 24.

LSJ quotes also a dubious reading in [X.] *Ath.* 1. 14, where most editors emend ἰσχυροί to χρηστοί; but if the manuscript reading is correct, it belongs here. It is also used with the infinitive to mean *capable of, strong enough to.*

πρὸς ὀργὴν καὶ πρὸς ἔχθραν ἰσχυρότατος ἦν ὑπὲρ τῶν δικαίων ἀντιστῆναι. *Plu. *Arist.* 4. 1.

5   Physical objects may also exhibit powerful effects, so we find a sense *effective, potent*:

τῷ μὲν οἴνῳ, ἔφην, ἔγωγε νομίζω τῷ ἰσχυροτάτῳ πλέον ἐπιχεῖν ὕδωρ. *X. *Oec.* 17. 9; Luc. *Nigr.* 5.

So of foods:

ἀφροδισίων τε ἀπέχεσθαι βρωμάτων τε λιπαρῶν καὶ κερχνωδέων, καὶ ἰσχυρῶν πάντων 'to abstain from sexual intercourse and fatty foods and those productive of hoarseness, and everything potent'. Hp. *Art.* 50.

LSJ translated the word in this passage as *indigestible*, which is clearly a possibility; the 1968 Supplement changed this to *heavy*. I am not sure what 'heavy' means in this context; but it seems much more likely that what is meant is everything that might have an intense effect. It is also used of plants, apparently meaning *having a strong taste*:

γένη ... τοῖς χυλοῖς δριμύτερα καὶ ἰσχυρότερα.
Thphr. *HP* 7. 6. 1.

6 A different class of things may be described as effective, such
as *binding* contracts or oaths, *compelling* proofs or evidence. It is
possible that a law might also be so described, but the examples
seem rather to belong in the sense discussed in 10 below. The
second example plays upon these two meanings, and the instance
I classify here is underlined.

> ἰσχυρότερος ἐς πειθὼ λόγος πολλαχῇ γίνεται χρυσοῦ.
>
>   Democr. 51.

> ἄνευ γὰρ ἀναγκαίης <u>ἰσχυρῆς</u> συμβάσιες ἰσχυραὶ οὐκ ἐθέλουσιν
> συμμένειν. 'Strict agreements do not usually last except under
> the compulsion of necessity.' Hdt. 1. 74. 4.

> ἡγούμενος οὕτως ἂν τὸν ἔλεγχον ἰσχυρότερον γενέσθαι τῶν
> τούτου λόγων. *Lys. 7. 34.

> τἀληθὲς ἰσχυρόν. *D. 19. 208.

> μὴ τοῖς ἰσχυροτέραν νομίζουσι τῶν νόμων τὴν αὑτῶν
> βδελυρίαν εἶναι. *D. 42. 15.

> ὅρκους ἰσχυροὺς ὠμόσαμεν ἀλλήλοις. *D. 48. 9.

> δέον σε διομόσασθαι ὅρκον τὸν μέγιστον καὶ ἰσχυρότατον.
>
>   Antipho 5. 11.

> τοῦτο ἰσχυρὸν ἦν ἂν τούτῳ πρὸς ὑμᾶς τεκμήριον ὅτι ...
>   *D. 49. 58; *SIG* 685. 84.

>   τοῦτο γὰρ
> ἰσχυρὸν οἴεταί τι πρὸς τὸ πρᾶγμ' ἔχειν. Men. *Epit.* 347.

7 In all the previous uses the sense of ἰσχυρός is active, *exerting
force*. These can be distinguished from a second group which
are passive, i.e. where the term describes passive strength or
resistivity. In a purely physical sense we find *resistant to breakage,
strongly made or constructed.*

> ἰσχυρόν ἐστιν (τὸ ἀγγεῖον) ὦγάθ', ὥστ'
> οὐκ ἂν καταγείη ποτ'. *Ar. *Ach.* 943.

> διὰ τί οὔτ' ἰσχυροτέρους οὔτε πολυτελεστέρους τῶν ἄλλων
> ποιῶν τοὺς θώρακας πλείονος πωλεῖς; *X. *Mem.* 3. 10. 10.

> ὥσπερ γὰρ οἰκίας, οἶμαι, καὶ πλοίου ... τὰ κάτωθεν
> ἰσχυρότατ' εἶναι δεῖ. *D. 2. 10.

> ὡς εἶδε τὸ κέρας (τοῦ κριοῦ) ἰσχυρὸν καὶ στερεὸν ἐκ μέσου τοῦ
> μετώπου πεφυκός. *Plu. *Per.* 6. 2.

Used metaphorically with reference to literary style:

οὐκέτι λείας συλλαβὰς ἀλλ᾽ ἰσχυρὰς καὶ ἀντιτύπους θήσει.

D. H. *Comp.* 16. 10.

ταῦθ᾽ ὅτι μέν ἐστιν ἰσχυρὰ καὶ στιβαρὰ καὶ ἀξιωματικά.

D. H. *Comp.* 22. 12.

In a figurative phrase:

στάσεις λαμβάνειν ἰσχυρὰς 'take up firm positions'.

D. H. *Comp.* 22. 1.

8 To this we can now attach a further military sense, of positions, fortifications, etc., meaning *hard* for an enemy *to penetrate, defensible*. The neuter is often used as a substantive to mean a *stronghold*.

ἡ δὲ Πτερίη ἐστὶ τῆς χώρης ταύτης τὸ ἰσχυρότατον κατὰ Σινώπην πόλιν. Hdt. 1. 76.

τεῖχος ἐπὶ λόφου ἰσχυρόν. *Th. 3. 105. 1.

πρὸς ἰσχυρὰ χωρία καὶ ἀνθρώπους παρεσκευασμένους μάχεσθαι. X. *An.* 4. 6. 11.

οὐκ ἰσχυρὸν ἐτείχιζον. Th. 4. 9. 3.

οἱ ... ἀποδόμενοι ... τὰ τῆς πόλεως ἰσχυρά.

Aeschin. 3. 66; X. *Eq. Mag.* 8. 24.

In a rather more general sense:

ἤλπιζον ... ἤδη σφῶν ἰσχυρὰ τὰ πράγματα γίγνεσθαι 'they were hopeful that their situation was already becoming more secure'. *Th. 4. 24. 4.

9 Applied to a wide range of substantives ἰσχυρός denotes *intense, extreme, severe*:

σιτοδείην ἰσχυρήν. Hdt. 1. 94. 3.

λιμὸς ἰσχυρός. *Th. 3. 85. 2; *Ev. Luc.* 15. 14.

ἐν δὲ τοῖσι ἰσχυροῖσι ψύχεσι. Hdt. 4. 29.

τῷ ἰσχυρῷ χειμῶνι. *X. *An.* 5. 8. 14.

τῆς κεφαλῆς θέρμαι ἰσχυραί ... μετὰ βηχὸς ἰσχυροῦ.

Th. 2. 49. 2, 3.

ἢν μὴ μέγα καὶ ἰσχυρὸν τὸ νόσημα ᾖ. Hp. *Acut. (Sp.)* 4.

γενομένης δ᾽ ἰσχυρᾶς τῆς ναυμαχίας. *Th. 7. 72. 1.

ἐδίωκε καὶ ἰσχυρὰν τὴν φυγὴν τοῖς πολεμίοις κατέχων ἐποίει.

*X. *Cyr.* 1. 4. 22.

Of mental states:

> τὴν ἰσχυρὰν ἐπιθυμίαν ἔρωτα καλοῦσιν. *X. Mem. 3. 9. 7.
>
> ἰσχυρὰν ἔχθραν ἀναιρούμενος. Pl. Phdr. 233c.
>
> ἰσχυρᾶς παρὰ τῷ δήμῳ ὀργῆς ἐτύγχανεν. *D. 24. 133.
>
> ἰσχυρὰ καὶ ἄκρατος ἀπάθεια πρὸς γαμετήν.
> *Plu. Comp. Lyc. Num. 3. 2.

10 This needs to be distinguished from a sense where the substantive so qualified is not simply in an extreme state, but is *applied rigorously, strict, severe*; e.g. of laws, decisions, decrees, etc.

> ἀρετὴ δὲ ἔπακτός ἐστι ἀπό τε σοφίης κατεργασμένη καὶ νόμου ἰσχυροῦ. Hdt. 7. 102. 1.
>
> Μαρδονίου δὲ (γνώμη) ἰσχυροτέρη τε καὶ ἀγνωμονεστέρη καὶ οὐδαμῶς συγγινωσκομένη. Hdt. 9. 41. 4.
>
> εἴ τῳ δοκεῖ μεγάλη ἡ ζημία καὶ λίαν ἰσχυρὸς ὁ νόμος.
> Lys. 15. 9.
>
> ἴστε ... ὅτι τὸ Καννωνοῦ ψήφισμά ἐστιν ἰσχυρότατον.
> *X. HG 1. 7. 20.

Of vengeance or punishments:

> ὡς ἄρα ἀνθρώποισι αἱ λίην ἰσχυραὶ τιμωρίαι πρὸς θεῶν ἐπίφθονοι γίνονται. Hdt. 4. 205; *Lys. 1. 31.

Of restraint:

> ἐπεὶ δὲ ἔγνωσαν ἑαλωκότες ἰσχυρὰν καὶ ἄφυκτον ἅλωσιν.
> *Plu. Num. 15. 4.

καρχήσιον

1 This is defined in LSJ as **I** '*drinking-cup* narrower in the middle than at top and bottom; **II** *mast-head of a ship*, through which the halyards worked; **III** *triangular instrument used in carpentry;* **IV** *cage* or *chamber* in a torsion engine; **V** *crane* for unloading ships.' It is very hard to envisage how a word for a drinking-cup could have come to possess the nautical meaning of sense **II**. Now the distinguishing feature of the cup called καρχήσιον is its hour-glass shape, a practical feature since it allows

the vessel to stand firmly without great risk of being knocked over, and one which in a more evolved form is still used in wine-glasses. The nautical καρχήσιον must therefore be an object of similar shape. The Latin loan *carchesium* reproduces the same meanings.

2   From the references in the lexicographers it is evident that to them the καρχήσιον was not the mast-head itself, since it might be surmounted by the θωράκιον, a kind of top or crow's nest, but was a device secured near the mast-head in order to allow the yard carrying the sail to be raised or lowered. This device is well known, for all sailing vessels need one; its technical name in English is *truck,* and this should appear as the equivalent in any lexicon; it now appears in the New Supplement. The examples quoted below can all be so understood, though of course the actual form of the device may have changed with time, due to technological improvements in ship-design. Presumably the name was given because in its primitive form it resembled a cup of hour-glass shape. I find it hard to imagine a structure of this kind surmounting the mast, since unless it were made of metal it would be hard to make it sufficiently strong or firmly secured to take the strain imposed by the yard. Perhaps therefore the καρχήσιον was originally a short wooden spar tapering from either end towards a narrower waist, which could be lashed transversely to the mast. If a shallow notch were cut in the mast to fit its smaller dimension, it could easily be made secure, and no metal would be required. The broad ends projecting either side of the mast could then be pierced to allow the halyards to be reeved through them. This crude device would serve well enough for small ships, though it was no doubt much improved later; but the name once given would automatically be transferred to any device serving the same purpose.

3   LSJ's first example of the sense *mast-head* is:

ἀνὰ δ' ἱστία τεῖνον
πρὸς ζυγὸν καρχασίου. Pi. N. 5. 51.

This expression for 'set sail' must be literally 'stretch the sails up to the yoke of the καρχήσιον.' Clearly the sense here is the *mast-head bracket,* and the resemblance to a yoke should be noted. The second is in a Hippocratic passage describing a treatment for

curvature of the spine due to injury. The patient is strapped to a
ladder set up against a tower or mast.

> ἀπὸ μέντοι τύρσιος ἀφιεὶς ἢ ἀπὸ ἱστοῦ καταπεπηγότος
> καρχήσιον ἔχοντος ἔτι κάλλιον ἄν τις σκευάσαιτο, ὥστε ἀπὸ
> τροχιλίης τὰ χαλώμενα εἶναι ὅπλα ἢ ἀπὸ ὄνου 'When it is let
> down from a tower, or from a mast fixed in the ground and
> provided with a truck, it is a still better arrangement to have a
> lowering tackle from a pulley or wheel and axle'
>   (E. T. Withington, Loeb).   Hp. *Art*. 43.

Further examples are:

> ἤ τιν' ἄλλον ἐκ μηχανῆς θεὸν ἐπὶ τῷ καρχησίῳ καθεζόμενον.
>   Luc. *Merc. Cond*. 1.

> τὸ δὲ πρὸς τῷ τέλει (τοῦ ἱστοῦ καλεῖται) καρχήσιον. ἔχει δὲ
> τοῦτο κεραίας ἄνωθεν νευούσας ἐφ' ἑκάτερα τὰ μέρη, καὶ
> ἐπίκειται τὸ λεγόμενον αὐτῷ θωράκιον.
>   Asclep. Myrl. ap. Ath. 11. 474f.
>   κευθὺ τοῦ καρχησίου
> ἄνελκε τὴν γραῦν.   Epicr. 9 (K–A).

In the plural:

> ἀλλ' οὐ τάχ', ἡνίκ' ἄν σε ποντία νότις
> —μῶν ναυστολήσῃ γῆς ὅρους Ἑλληνίδος;
> —κρύψῃ μὲν οὖν πεσοῦσαν ἐκ καρχησίων.   E. *Hec*. 1261.

> γλαῦκα δ' ὀφθῆναι διαπετομένην ἀπὸ δεξιᾶς τῶν νεῶν καὶ τοῖς
> καρχησίοις ἐπικαθίζουσαν.   Plu. *Them*. 12. 1.

4   In the other mechanical senses it would appear to be applied to
a kind of universal joint; see F. Walbank on Polybius 8. 5. 10,
quoting Hero *Bel*. 88. 5 – 89. 9 (Wescher). But in most cases it can
refer to a drum on a winch or windlass, where again the resemblance to the drinking-vessel would be obvious.

καταλαμβάνω

1   The 1968 Supplement has under **V 1** 'after "Pass." insert "*to be
covered*, χρυσίῳ LXX 2 *Ch*. 9. 20."' Sense **V** in LSJ is '*hold down,
cover*, τῇ χειρὶ τὸν ὀφθαλμόν ... etc.' so it is obvious that this new
sense is only connected by the use of the English word *cover*, the
action described being very different. The passage reads in full:

καὶ πάντα τὰ σκεύη τοῦ βασιλέως Σαλαμὼν χρυσίου, καὶ πάντα τὰ σκεύη οἴκου δρυμοῦ τοῦ Λιβάνου χρυσίῳ κατειλημμένα. LXX 2 Ch. 9. 20.

The sense is evident: one lot of vessels was of gold, the other covered with gold. But this would be a most unusual sense for καταλαμβάνω. It would, however, be a normal sense of κατειλέω, and the correction to κατειλημένα is extremely easy; but it is not even an emendation, since it is in fact the reading of one manuscript.

2 The examples quoted by LSJ make it clear that in later Greek κατειλέω was regularly used to mean *wrap up, cover*. The first (X. *Eq.* 10. 7) is doubtful and the passage has been emended. But there are clear examples of the perfect passive participle, as here:

ταινίαις κατειλημένος τὴν κεφαλήν. Luc. *Symp.* 47.

ἄγαλμα ... τελαμῶνι προφυρῷ τὸν μηρὸν κατειλημένον.
Paus. 8. 28. 6.

ἕκαστον ἄγκιστρον δέλεαρ φέρει Λακαίνης πορφύρας κατειλημένον. Ael. *NA* 15. 10.

The Septuagint passage is thus by far the earliest example of this use; but that is much more probable than the implausible sense attributed in 1968 to καταλαμβάνω, and now withdrawn by the New Supplement.

καταχαρίζομαι

1 The basic meaning is quite clear: *make a present of, give away* something *as a favour*. Three applications of this can be distinguished, and it is really the second which is badly handled by LSJ. First, in the literal sense:

αἰτιάσεται δὲ Πολύευκτον καὶ τὴν γυναῖκ' αὐτοῦ, καὶ φήσει πάντα ταῦθ' ὑφ' ἐμοῦ πεισθέντας καταχαρίσασθαι.
D. 41. 12.

φαίνονται δὲ καὶ καταδωροδοκούμενοι καὶ καταχαριζόμενοι πολλὰ τῶν κοινῶν. Arist. *Pol.* 1271ᵃ3.

τῶν τοῦ πολέμου λαφύρων οὐδεμίαν μοῖραν εἰς τὸ δημόσιον ἀήνεγκεν, ἀλλ' οἷς αὐτὸς ἐβούλετο κατεχαρίσατο.
D. H. 6. 30. 2; 7. 63. 3.

2 Secondly, this is naturally extended to immaterial objects such as justice, truth, if these are conferred as corrupt favours. LSJ defines this meaning as *surrender corruptly,* which might do as a translation in some cases; but the basic meaning is still to give away as a favour:

> οὐ γὰρ ἐπὶ τούτῳ κάθηται ὁ δικαστής, ἐπὶ τῷ καταχαρίζεσθαι τὰ δίκαια, ἀλλ' ἐπὶ τῷ κρίνειν αὐτά. Pl. *Ap.* 35c.

> οὐ προδιδοὺς ὑμᾶς οὐδὲ τὸν ἀγῶνα καταχαριζόμενος. Aeschin. 3. 53.

> κατεγορήκαμεν ἡμεῖς ⟨οὐδὲν⟩ οὐδενὶ καταχαρισάμενοι τῶν κοινῶν δικαίων. Din. 1. 105; cf. J. *AJ* 4. 8. 14; Ael. *VH* 11. 9.

> ἐπαινεῖν χρὴ τὴν πόλιν μὴ καταχαριζομένην τἀληθὲς τοῖς πολίταις. Ael. *VH* 14. 5.

Similarly with persons as objects:

> οἴεται δεῖν καταχαρίζεσθαι ταῖς γυναιξὶ τοὺς προδότας καὶ πολεμίους τῆς πατρίδος 'he thought it necessary to make a present of the traitors and enemies of the state to their wives (i.e. by granting a pardon)'. Plu. *Publ.* 7.

3 Thirdly, used intransitively with the dative, *show favour (to):*

> ἀδύνατον δὲ καὶ ὑμῖν ἐστι, περὶ τοιούτου πράγματος φέρουσι τὴν ψῆφον, ἢ κατελεῆσαι ἢ καταχαρίσασθαι Ἀνδοκίδῃ. Lys. 6. 3.

> μᾶλλον τοῖς ἐναντιουμένοις ταῖς ὑμετέραις γνώμαις προσέχειν τὸν νοῦν ἢ τοῖς καταχαριζομένοις. Isoc. 8. 10.

Also with no dative:

> μὴ καταχαριζόμενον ἀλλὰ διαμαχόμενον. Pl. *Grg.* 513d.

> τὰ μὲν καταχαρίζεται, τὰ δὲ ψεύδεται. Ael. *VH* 1. 23.

καταχράομαι

1 This compound with κατα- can have two basic meanings, depending on whether the force of the prepositional element is intensive or pejorative. There are also differences in construction, which are less important than the semantic ones, and a special use of the active. In such cases it might appear more tidy to begin with

the active; but since the predominant use is in the medio-passive, it is preferable to keep the arrangement of LSJ in this respect. The following is a sketch of how I should like to see the article rearranged, but makes no claim to completeness.

2 If we start with the intensive value of κατα-, we can follow LSJ in placing first the sense *make good use of, exploit,* but this needs to separated from *apply* (see below).

κενῇ προφάσει ταύτῃ κατεχρῶ καὶ ψευδεῖ. D. 18. 150.

ἆρ' ἂν οἴεσθε Λάκριτον ... τοὺς αὐτοὺς λόγους λέγειν οἷσπερ νυνὶ κατακέχρηται ... ; D. 35. 44.

3 With expressions of purpose it may lack any intensive force and mean simply *use* (for a stated purpose):

ἵνα καταχρῆται αὐτὸς αὐτοῖς ἐπὶ τὸν σύνδεσμον τῆς πόλεως.
Pl. *R.* 520a.

διὸ φαίνεταί μοι τούτῳ (*sc.* τῷ ρῶ) πρὸς ταῦτα καταχρῆσθαι.
Pl. *Cra.* 426e.

μάρτυσι καταχρῶμαι πρὸς τὸ τινὰς ἡδονὰς εἶναι δοκούσας, οὔσας δ' οὐδαμῶς. Pl. *Phlb.* 51a.

With accusative:

οὐκ ἐξῆν ἄλλο εἰς ἄλλο καταχρῆσθαι μέλους εἶδος.
Pl. *Lg.* 700c.

ἀποκειμένας παρ' αὐτῷ τετταράκοντα μνᾶς λαβὼν κατεχρήσατο. Lys. 19. 22.

διηγήσασθαι ὑμῖν, τά τε ὀφειλόμενα, καὶ εἰς ὅ τι ἕκαστον αὐτῶν κατεχρήσατο. [D.] 49. 4.

τὸ οὖν ἀργύριον τὸ πεπορισμένον τῷ Θεοφήμῳ ἀποδοῦναι ἐνταῦθα κατεχρησάμην. [D.] 47. 50.

In the passive:

ἀνάγκη γὰρ τὰ μὲν μέγιστ' αὐτῶν ἤδη κατακεχρῆσθαι, μικρὰ δ' ἔτι παραλελεῖφθαι. 'The most important topics must have already been exhausted.' Isoc. 4. 74.

μόχλοι ... κατεχρήσθησαν εἰς σφῆνας.
IG 2². 1672. 304 (iv BC).

4 In a pejorative sense a distinction needs to be made between persons and things, thus, *apply to a wrong purpose, misuse* a thing.

μάλιστα δ' ἂν νικώμεθα καὶ ὑμεῖς νικῷητε, εἰ παρα-
σκευάσαισθε τῇ τῶν προγόνων δόξῃ μὴ καταχρησόμενοι μηδ'
ἀναλώσοντες αὐτήν. Pl. Mx. 247b.

οὐδὲ τὸ πιστευθῆναι προλαβόντα παρ' ὑμῶν εἰς τὸ μείζω
δύνασθαι κακουργεῖν καταχρῆσθαι. D. 19. 277.

Ἀναξαγόρας δὲ καταχρῆται τῷ ὀνόματι τούτῳ οὐ καλῶς·
ὀνομάζει γὰρ αἰθέρα ἀντὶ πυρός. Arist. Cael. 270ᵇ24.

οὕτω δὲ τετράπλευρον μᾶλλον ἢ τρίπλευρον φαίη τις ἂν τὸ
σχῆμα, τρίγωνον δ' οὐδοπωσοῦν, πλὴν εἰ καταχρώμενος.
Str. 5. 1. 2.

εἴ τὰς θυσίας τὰς προγεγραμμένας εἴ τῶν τοῦ κοινοῦ τι
κακῶσαι ἢ διελέσθαι ἢ τοῦ ἀρχαίου τι καταχρήσασθαι.
Test. Epict. 8. 8.

5   With an object-clause, *declare falsely, allege (that)*:

οἵτινες κατεχρῶντο ὡς τῷ Πολέμωνι ... οὐδεμία γένοιτο
ἀδελφή. [D.] 43. 39.

κατεχρήσατο πρὸς τοὺς δικαστὰς ὅτι ἐγὼ τὴν οἰκίαν ...
μεμισθωμένος εἴην παρ' αὐτοῦ. [D.] 48. 44.

6   With persons as object it means *maltreat*, and is sometimes
used as a euphemism for *put to death, kill*. LSJ made a special
sense for the first example, to which the new Supplement has
added a further, precisely similar one.

οὐδ' ἥκω παραιτησόμενος ὑμᾶς, ἀλλὰ καταχρήσασθέ μοι, εἰ
δοκῶ τοιοῦτος εἶναι. Aeschin. 1. 122; 2. 70.

As a euphemism:

τὸν δὲ ἕνα λέγουσι ... αὐτοῦ μιν ἐν τῇσι Θυρέῃσι καταχρήσασθαι ἑωυτόν. (i.e. committed suicide). Hdt. 1. 82. 8.

τέῳ δὴ μόρῳ τὸν παῖδα κατεχρήσαο;
Hdt. 1. 117. 2; 4. 146. 3.

ἐπεὶ δὲ κατεχρήσαντο μὲν ἀσεβῶς τοὺς αἰχμαλώτους, τροφῇ
ταύτῃ χρώμενοι, κατεχρήσαντο δὲ τὰ δουλικὰ τῶν σωμάτων.
Plb. 1. 85. 1.

In the passive:

οἱ γὰρ Ἐλαιούσιοι τῷ Πρωτεσίλεω τιμωρέοντες ἐδέοντό μιν
καταχρησθῆναι 'requested that he should be put to death'.
Hdt. 9. 120. 4.

κεφαλή

1   I have already mentioned the treatment of this word by LSJ
in the article I contributed to F. Létoublon (ed.), *La Langue et les
Textes en grec ancien* (Amsterdam, 1992), 281–8. Here I shall
attempt a brief sketch of the kind of article I should expect to find.
The starting-point is very clear: *the highest or anterior part of a
person or animal, which contains the brain and carries the principal
sense organs*. I cannot see how to avoid a long-winded definition
which would serve equally for English *head*. But the details given
are needed to explain some of the developed senses which will be
discussed. It is hardly necessary to quote examples for the basic
meaning, but since LSJ has dispersed them, one or two may be
useful.

> Ἐρύλαον ἐπεσσύμενον βάλε πέτρῳ
> μέσσην κὰκ κεφαλήν. Il. 16. 412.

LSJ places this, correctly on its own principles, under **I 1 b**, the
phrase κατὰ κεφαλήν. But there is here no special meaning attached
to the phrase, as the epithet μέσσην shows.

> σφάξαντες δὲ (τὸ κτῆνος) ἀποτάμνουσι τὴν κεφαλήν.
> Hdt. 2. 39. 1.

2   What is more interesting is where the head is mentioned for
one of its characteristic features. Thus, *the head as the highest part
of the body*. As a measure of height:

> ἤτοι μὲν κεφαλῇ καὶ μείζονες ἄλλοι ἔασι. Il. 3. 168.
> μείων μὲν κεφαλῇ Ἀγαμέμνονος. Il. 3. 193.

More generally:

> ἐκάλυψε νέκυν μεγάθυμος Ἀχιλλεὺς
> ἐς πόδας ἐκ κεφαλῆς. Il. 23. 169.

The fact that the body is lying down does not invalidate this
classification; head and feet are chosen to represent the two
extremities (cf. 10 below). So the phrase κατὰ (κὰκ) κεφαλῆς means
'down upon the head, over the head'.

> ἑλὼν κόνιν αἰθαλόεσσαν
> χεύατο κὰκ κεφαλῆς. Il. 18. 24.

πορφύρεον μέγα φᾶρος ἑλὼν χερσὶ στιβαρῇσι
κὰκ κεφαλῆς εἴρυσσε. Od. 8. 85.

ἔγχεε κέρναις ἕνα καὶ δύο
πλήαις κὰκ κεφάλας. Alc. 346. 5.

Similarly κατὰ κεφαλήν *overhead*:

κατὰ κεφαλὴν τὸ τεῖχος τῆς ἀκροπόλεως διώρυττον.
X. *HG* 7. 2. 8.

ὅταν … μὴ γένηται τὸ κατὰ κεφαλὴν ὕδωρ 'when there is no rainfall'. Thph. *HP* 4. 10. 7.

In a reference to trimming stone for masonry, *on top* (cf. with 11 below):

[ἐπικόπτων τὰ λιθολογήματα ὀρ]θὰ κα[ὶ κ]α[τ]ὰ κεφαλήν.
IG 2² 463. 42; 44.

Also ὑπὲρ κεφαλῆς:

τὸν ὑπὲρ κεφαλῆς
αἰθέρ' ἰδέσθαι σπεύδω. E. *fr.* 308.

Likewise ἐπὶ κεφαλήν means *on one's head*, i.e. *head first, headlong*.

Περσέων … δυώδεκα … ἑλὼν ζῶντας ἐπὶ κεφαλὴν κατώρυξε.
Hdt. 3. 35. 5; 7. 136. 1.

Figuratively:

μὴ εὐθὺς ἐπὶ κεφαλὴν εἰς τὸ δικαστήριον βαδίζειν. D. 42. 12.

ἐκ τῆς δ' οἰκίας
ἐπὶ κεφαλὴν ἐς κόρακας ὦσον τὴν καλὴν
Σαμίαν. Men. *Sam.* 353.

And in a more general sense, *precipitately, in a hurry*.

οὐ βουλόμενος πολίτας ἄνδρας ἐπὶ κεφαλὴν εἰσπράττειν τὸν μισθόν. Hyp. *Lyc.* 17.

In the plural ἐπὶ ταῖς κεφαλαῖς means literally *over their heads*, but the English idiom would be *shoulder-high*.

ὥστε μόνον οὐκ ἐπὶ ταῖς κεφαλαῖς περιφέρουσιν αὐτοὺς οἱ ἑταῖροι. Pl. *R.* 600d.

3   A more significant development is where the head is used to mean the *vital part of the body*, hence damage inflicted on it is

liable to be fatal. LSJ goes so far as define this sense as *life*; but although in some contexts this might do as a translation, κεφαλή has still here the sense of the *head as a vital organ*.

εἴ περ γάρ τε καὶ αὐτίκ' Ὀλύμπιος οὐκ ἐτέλεσσεν,
ἔκ τε καὶ ὀψὲ τελεῖ, σύν τε μεγάλῳ ἀπέτεισαν,
σὺν σφῇσιν κεφαλῇσι γυναιξί τε καὶ τεκέεσσιν. Il. 4. 162.

οὔ τι τόσον νέκυος περιδείδια Πατρόκλοιο ...
ὅσσον ἐμῇ κεφαλῇ περιδείδια, μή τι πάθῃσι,
καὶ σῇ. Il. 17. 242.

σφὰς γὰρ παρθέμενοί κεφαλὰς κατέδουσι βιαίως
οἶκον Ὀδυσσῆος 'risking their own heads'. Od. 2. 237.

ἀποβαλέεις τὴν κεφαλὴν, καί σε οὔτε ἐγὼ δυνήσομαι ῥύσασθαι
οὔτ' ἄλλος. Hdt. 8. 65. 5.

4 To this may be attached the special use of the head as the part which is exposed to punishment or injury, especially in imprecations and wishes. The parallel use of *head* in English may be the result of its appearance in the New Testament.

τὰ μὲν γὰρ πρότερον ἐγώ τε ἔπρηξα καὶ ἐγὼ κεφαλῇ
ἀναμάξας φέρω 'what I did formerly and is now imposed as a burden on my head'. Hdt. 1. 155. 3.

πολυπραγμοσύνη νυν ἐς κεφαλὴν τράποιτ' ἐμοί.
Ar. *Ach.* 833; *Nu.* 40.

λέγεις ἃ σοὶ ... οἱ θεοὶ τρέψειαν εἰς κεφαλήν.
D. 18. 290; 294.

Often with an ellipse of the verb:

ἐς κεφαλὴν σοί. Ar. *Pax* 1063; *Pl.* 526.

σοὶ εἰς κεφαλήν. Pl. *Euthd.* 283e.

τὸ αἷμα ὑμῶν ἐπὶ τὴν κεφαλὴν ὑμῶν. *Act. Ap.* 18. 6.

5 Since the head carries the distinguishing features, it can be used to identify a person; hence it comes to be used to mean something like *person, individual*. In some contexts it can be translated *self*.

τὸν ἐγὼ περὶ πάντων τῖον ἑταίρων,
ἶσον ἐμῇ κεφαλῇ. Il. 18. 82.

πολλὰς ἰφθίμους κεφαλὰς Ἄϊδι προϊάψειν. Il. 11. 55.

ὄφρα φιλῆς κεφαλῆς ὀλετῆρα κιχείω.   Il. 18. ί14.

τοίην γὰρ κεφαλὴν ποθέω μεμνημένη αἰεί.   Od. 1. 343.

ἑᾷ κεφαλᾷ
ἐξοπίσω γέρας ἔσσεσθαι.   Pi. O. 7. 67.

καὶ ταῦτ' ἔλεγ' ἡ μιαρὰ καὶ ἀναιδὴς αὕτη κεφαλή.
D. 21. 117.

6   This sense may also be used with a suitable epithet in addressing a person.

Τεῦκρε, φίλη κεφαλή.   Il. 8. 281; 23. 94.

ὦ κακαὶ κεφαλαί.   Hdt. 3. 29. 2.

Ἄπολλον, ὦ δία κεφαλά.   E. Rh. 226.

Φαῖδρε, φίλη κεφαλή.   Pl. Phdr. 264a.

7   A special use in this sense is in counting, either with a numeral or in the phrase κατὰ κεφαλήν per head.

πεντακοσίας κεφαλὰς τῶν Ξέρξεω πολεμίων λυσάμενοι.
Hdt. 9. 99. 2.

κατὰ κεφαλὴν ἕκαστος εἰσφέρει τὸ τεταγμένον 'each pays the allotted poll-tax'.   Arist. Pol. 1272ª14; LXX Ex. 16. 16.

8   Two more special uses are found referring to an artificial head of some kind. A κεφαλὴ περίθετος is apparently some kind of head-dress.

ἠδὶ μὲν οὖν
κεφαλὴ περίθετος, ἣν ἐγὼ νύκτωρ φέρω.   Ar. Th. 258.

And by a natural transference a head of Homer is used to mean a representation of a head, i.e. a portrait-bust.

οὐ φαυλῶς ἔστησα κατ' ὀφθαλμούς σε, Μένανδρε,
τῆσδέ γ' Ὁμηρείης, φίλτατέ μοι, κεφαλῆς.   IG 14. 1183. 10.

9   Proceeding now to the transferred senses, where κεφαλή means something resembling a head, we can classify these by the feature which is picked out as the point of resemblance. First, the bulbous root of a plant:

φάρμακον
καταπλαστὸν ἐνεχείρησε τρίβειν, ἐμβαλὼν
σκορόδων κεφαλὰς τρεῖς Τηνίων.   Ar. Pl. 718; Plb. 12. 6. 4.

ῥίζαν μεγάλην, κεφαλὰς ἔχουσαν πλείονας, στρογγύλας.

Dsc. 3. 120.

The head formed by the seed-pod (cf. 11 below):

ἔστι δὲ ὁ ὀπισμὸς ἀπὸ τῶν καυλῶν ... ἢ ἀπὸ τῶν ῥιζῶν ἢ τρίτον ἀπὸ τῆς κεφαλῆς, ὥσπερ τοῦ μήκωνος.

Thphr. HP 9. 8. 2.

Of parts of the body:

μέχρι τῆς κεφαλῆς ἑκατέρου τοῦ ὄρχεως.

Arist. HA 510ª14; Gal. 4. 565.

χιτῶνα, τὸν περικάρδιον ὀνομαζόμενον, ὃς ἐκ τῆς κεφαλῆς αὐτῆς ἐκφυόμενος ... τελευτᾷ καὶ αὐτὸς εἴς τινα κώνου κορυφήν. Gal. UP 6. 16 (=3. 488); UP 7. 14 (=3. 568).

Of bones:

τὰς κεφαλὰς τῆς κάτω γνάθου. Hp. Art. 30; Poll. 2. 186.

10   In a less obvious transference, κεφαλή can mean simply *either extremity of a linear object*. LSJ gets into difficulties with rivers, since in one case it refers to the sources:

Τεάρου ποταμοῦ κεφαλαὶ ὕδωρ ἄριστον ... παρέχονται.

Hdt. 4. 91. 2,

in another to the mouth:

οἶδα Γέλα ποταμοῦ κεφαλῇ ἐπικείμενον ἄστυ.

Call. *fr.* 43. 46 Pf.

A similar problem arose in dealing with ἀρχή, where in one case it appeared to mean not beginning but end; in English a rope has two ends, in Greek two ἀρχαί. Other examples of this usage are quoted by LSJ from papyri.

11   But this must be distinguished from the examples where the point of the resemblance is the head as the highest point, hence meaning *summit, top*.

ἑστηκότες ἐπὶ τῆς κεφαλῆς τῆς τάφρου 'at the top or lip of the trench'. X. *Cyr.* 3. 3. 66.

αἶγα,
ἅτις ὑπὲρ κεφαλᾶς αἰεὶ τὸν ἀμολγέα πληροῖ.

Theoc. 8. 87 (see Gow on 7. 147)

ἐπὶ τὰς κεφαλὰς τῶν στύλων.   LXX *3 Ki.* 7. 16; Poll. 7. 121.

καὶ τοὺς κείονας μετὰ τῶν βωμο[σ]πειρῶν καὶ κεφαλῶν
κατ[ε]σκευακότα.   *CIG* 2782. 31.

The last two examples are translated *capital* of a column by LSJ,
but they do not prove that κεφαλή here had such a specialised
meaning.

12   Closely allied to this is the use where it means the *leading
part*. This occurs in military contexts, where the right wing of a
phalanx is called κεφαλή and the left οὐρά.

τὸ μὲν ἥμισυ τὸ ἐν δεξιᾷ, δεξιὸν καλεῖται κέρας καὶ κεφαλή,
τὸ δ' ἐν ἀριστερᾷ, εὐώνυμον κέρας καὶ οὐρά.   Arr. *Tact.* 8. 3.

This may reflect the natural tendency of spearmen to move
towards the right, the hand holding the spear. LSJ places together
with this the following passage, but translates *band* of men. However, the context suggests that it is a moving column which is
meant, and a three-pronged attack is so described.

οἱ ἱππεῖς ἐποίησαν ἡμῖν κεφαλὰς τρεῖς καὶ ἐκύκλωσαν τὰς
καμήλους.   LXX *Jb.* 1. 17.

13   Finally moving from material to abstract objects, a distinction
LSJ fails to make, κεφαλή means either *end* of a process, period or
like, and has further developments from this. We can see the
beginning of the process in a figurative use of the phrase ἐκ ποδῶν
εἰς κεφαλήν *from one end to the other*.

ὡς ἐγὼ τὰ πράγματα
ἐκ τῶν ποδῶν ἐς τὴν κεφαλήν σοι πάντ' ἐρῶ.   Ar. *Pl.* 650.

The fully developed sense, *consummation, conclusion* appears first
in Plato.

ὥσπερ κεφαλὴν ἀποδοῦναι τοῖς εἰρημένοις.
Pl. *Phlb.* 66d; *Grg.* 505d; *Ti.* 69b.

ὅταν ἁπασῶν τῶν ὀκτὼ περιόδων τὰ ... τάχη σχῇ κεφαλήν.
Pl. *Ti.* 39d.

ὥσπερ κεφαλὴν ἔχουσα ἐπιστήμη τῶν τιμιωτάτων.
Arist. *EN* 1141ᵃ19.

τὸ τοιοῦτον γὰρ ἀεί πως μέρος
ἐπιπαίζεται, κεφαλὴ δὲ δείπνου γίγνεται.   Alexis 178 (K–A).

14 A special use of this is to mean the *sum* or *total* of a number of figures, a concept more often expressed by the derivative κεφαλαῖον.

κεφαλὰ πάσας ἐρρηγείας χίλιαι ἡενενήκοντα πέντε σχοῖνοι 'the total of all the arable 1095 *skhoinoi*'.

> *Tab. Heracl.* 1.36; *IG* 12(9). 7. 4.

15 On the same principle as the rivers, it may also mean the *starting-point*.

Ζεὺς κεφαλή, Ζεὺς μέσσα, Διὸς δ' ἐκ πάντα τελεῖται.

> Orph. *fr.* 21a.

οἱ δ' ἐν τῇ λεγομένῃ κεφαλῇ τοῦ Κρόνου· αὕτη δ' ἐστὶ τῶν ἑπτὰ πλανητῶν. *Placit.* 2. 32. 2.

κινέω

1 This is one of the cases where there is an obvious English equivalent, which has some of the same developed senses. But the diversity of usage presented in LSJ is alarmingly confused, with similar examples separated and differing ones juxtaposed, sometimes merely because the same translation could be used. This is an attempt to sort the more important examples into a more intelligible pattern.

2 The basic meaning is clearly *set in motion, stir*. This can be movement from one place to another or self-contained, i.e. vibratory, motion; the distinction is not really worth making, but can be exemplified by the first two of the following passages:

ὡς δ' ὅτε κινήσῃ Ζέφυρος βαθὺ λήϊον ἐλθών. Il. 2. 147.

τῇ (sc. ῥάβδῳ) ῥ' ἄγε κινήσας, ταὶ δὲ (ψυχαὶ) τρίζουσαι ἕποντο. Od. 24. 5.

καὶ λύσσα καὶ μάταιος ἐκ νυκτῶν φόβος
κινεῖ ταράσσει καὶ διωκάθει πόλεως
χαλκηλάτῳ πλάστιγγι λυμανθὲν δέμας. A. Ch. 289.

This last is assigned by LSJ to sense **II** *disturb*, but this is conveyed by ταράσσει, so κινεῖ must be taken literally.

ἀκτὶς ἀελίου ... φῶτα ...
φυγάδα πρόδρομον ὀξυτόρῳ
κινήσασα χαλινῷ. S. *Ant.* 109.

κινεῦντα μηδὲ κάρφος i.e. keeping absolutely still.
Herod. 3. 67; 1. 55; so probably 3. 49.

ὅτε δὲ κλαίοι (τὸ παιδίον), τῇ προβοσκίδι τὴν σκάφην ἐκίνει
(ἡ ἐλέφας). Phylarch. 36 (J) = Müller *FHG* 1. 343.

χορδαὶ ἐν λύρᾳ συμπαθῶς κινηθεῖσαι. Plot. 4. 4. 8.

3 Special uses are, first, with parts of the body as object.

κινήσας δὲ κάρη προτὶ ὃν μυθήσατο θυμόν 'shaking his head'.
Il. 17. 442.

οὐδέ τι κινῆσαι μελέων ἦν οὐδ' ἀναεῖραι. Od. 8. 298.

This is of Ares and Aphrodite caught in Hephaistos' trap.

κινεῖ γὰρ ἀνὴρ ὄμμα κἀνάγει κάρα. S. *Ph.* 866.

This is evidence that he is awake.

ὥστ' οὐκέτ' ἀρκεῖ τἀμά σοι σκέλεα κινεῖν. Herod. 5. 2.

This is, as LSJ rightly observes, *sensu obscoeno* ; but it is not at all
the same sense as in the other examples in this section (**II**; see 8
below). Of a plant used medicinally, *move* the bowels.

κινεῖ κοιλίαν. Dsc. 2. 6.

A very strange figure belongs here, where a ship is said to 'stir its
returning foot' meaning 'begin a homeward voyage'.

ἐπεὶ νόστιμον
ναῦς ἐκίνησεν πόδα καί μ' ἀπὸ γᾶς
ὥρισεν Ἰλιάδος. E. *Hec.* 940.

5 The passive is used in a reflexive sense, *move oneself,* with the
same possibilities as in 2 above. The military sense *move forward*
proposed by LSJ is illusory.

ἔκλαγξαν δ' ἄρ' ὀϊστοὶ ἐπ' ὤμων χωομένοιο
αὐτοῦ κινηθέντος.
'The arrows rattled on his shoulders as he moved, so angry he
was.' Il. 1. 47.

κινήθη δ' ἀγορὴ φὴ κύματα μακρὰ θαλάσσης. 'A ripple ran
through the assembly.' Il. 2. 144; so probably Il. 16. 280.

εἴπερ οἵδε κινοῦνται λόχοι
πρὸς ἄστυ Θήβης. S. *OC* 1371; E. *Ph.* 107.

ποντία
θύελλα κινηθεῖσα. S. *OC* 1660.

τί κεκίνηται; E. *Andr.* 1226.

It proves to be the goddess Thetis.

προειπεῖν ὡς μηδεὶς κινήσοιτο ἐκ τῆς τάξεως.
X. *HG* 2. 1. 22.

So of suffering an earthquake, where we might think of the island being moved, but the Greeks probably thought of it as moving itself.

Δῆλος ἐκινήθη ... καὶ πρῶτα καὶ ὕστατα μέχρι ἐμοῦ σεισθεῖσα. Hdt. 6. 98. 1; Th. 2. 8. 3.

Here too we may place, without giving it a special section as in LSJ:

αἰσχύνονται μὲν κινεῖσθαι τῷ σώματι τὰ τοιαῦτα 'to perform such bodily movements', a description of dancing.
Pl. *Lg.* 656a.

In later Greek we find the active used intransitively in this sense.

καὶ ἐκίνησεν ἐκεῖθεν Ἀβραὰμ εἰς γῆν πρὸς Λίβα.
LXX *Ge.* 20. 1.

αὖθις ἐκ ποδὸς ἐκίνει ποιούμενος τὴν πορείαν ὡς ἐπ' Ἀρκαδίας. Plb. 2. 54. 2.

6   Another special sense is to *move* a thing *from its place, remove.* The first example refers to moving a counter in a game.

κινήσαις τὸν ἀπ' ἴρας †πύκινον λίθον. Alc. 351.

τὸν ἱρέα ἀπέκτεινε ἀπαγορεύοντα μὴ κινέειν τὸν ἀνδριάντα.
Hdt. 1. 183. 3.

κινήσαντά τι τῶν ἀκινήτων. Hdt. 6. 134. 2.

μὴ κινείτω γῆς ὅρια μηδείς. Pl. *Lg.* 842e.

καὶ διώκειν καὶ κινεῖν τὸ στρατόπεδον νυκτὸς οὐκ ἀσφαλὲς ἐδόκει εἶναι. X. *An.* 6. 4. 27.

In two special senses:

κινήσας δὲ θύρην προσέφη τροφὸν Εὐρύκλειαν. i.e. partly opening the door. Od. 22. 394.

σκληρὰ ... ἡ γῆ ἔσται κινεῖν τῷ ζεύγει. X. *Oec.* 16. 11.

As LSJ rightly says, this refers to ploughing, but the sense of κινέω is more general.

7 With persons (or animals) as object, *rouse to action, excite, stir up*. The reaction provoked may be physical or emotional.

τοὺς (*sc.* σφῆκας) δ᾽ εἴ περ παρά τίς τε κιὼν ἄνθρωπος ὁδίτης
κινήσῃ ἀκέων. Il. 16. 264.

μὴ κίνει Καμάριναν, ἀκίνητος γὰρ ἀμείνων.
Orac. ap. St. Byz.

ἐγερτὶ κινῶν ἄνδρ᾽ ἀνὴρ ἐπιρρόθοις
κακοῖσιν. S. *Ant.* 413.

πειράσατ᾽ ἀλλ᾽ ὑμεῖς γε κινῆσαι πατρὸς
τὸ δυσπρόσοιστον κἀπροσήγορον στόμα. S. *OC* 1276.

ἐξ ὕπνου κινεῖν δέμας. E. *Ba.* 690.

τί ... κινεῖς στρατιάν ... ; E. *Rh.* 18.

καὶ ἐγὼ ... βουλόμενος ἔτι λέγειν αὐτὸν ἐκίνουν καὶ εἶπον ...
Pl. *R.* 329e.

This last is translated by LSJ *incite* or *stir* one *up* to speak, but it is obvious that λέγειν is governed by βουλόμενος.

ὁ Σωκράτης βουλόμενος κινεῖν τὸν Εὐθύδημον ... ἔφη ...
X. *Mem.* 4. 2. 2.

ἐάν με κινῇς καὶ ποιήσῃς τὴν χολὴν
ἅπασαν ... ζέσαι ... Anaxipp. 2 (K–A); Pherecr. 75. 5 (K–A).

ὥστε κινήσαντος τοῦ Δίωνος δρόμῳ χωρεῖν. Plu. *Dio* 27.

κεινεῖσθαι (*sic*) παθητικῶς. Phld. *Rh.* 1. 193 (S).

The perfect participle passive has the usual aspectual force of denoting a present condition of arousal. By itself it can mean 'having one's passions aroused'.

ὡς πρὸ τοῦ κεκινημένου τὸν σώφρονα δεῖ προαιρεῖσθαι φίλον.
Pl. *Phdr.* 245b.

Ζεὺς, Ἄρης, Ἑρμῆς πρακτικοὺς, θερμοὺς, κεκινημένους
ἀποτελοῦσιν. Vett. Val. 44. 22 (P) = 1. 20. 18.

This may be further restricted with a prepositional phrase.

ἐξ ὧν μάντεις τε κατασκευάζονται πολλοὶ καὶ περὶ πᾶσαν τὴν
μαγγανείαν κεκινημένοι 'as a result of which many are turned

out as soothsayers and people deeply involved in all kinds of magic'. Pl. *Lg.* 908d.

The Loeb edition (R. G. Bury) here emends unnecessarily to γεγενημένοι.

ἐκ τούτων αὐτὴν κεκινημένην μᾶλλον πρὸς τὴν ἐπιμέλειαν
'that she is rather more concerned about taking care'.

X. *Oec.* 8. 1.

8 This verb is sometimes used of sexual stimulation, but it probably began as a polite substitute for the rhyming word βινέω (q.v.).

γυναῖκ' ἐκίνουν. Eup. 247. 3 (K–A); *AP* 11. 7.

It is found as variant reading in Aristophanes (*Ach.* 1052) and may well be correct there. Also in an obscene sense:

ἐγὼ δὲ κινήσω γέ σου τὸν πρωκτόν. Ar. *Eq.* 364.

So probably in the passive:

ὦ κινούμενοι,
πρὸς τῶν θεῶν δέξασθέ μου
θοἰμάτιον. Ar. *Nu.* 1103.

9 To *bring into operation, set going, provoke* (an action or a result).

πᾶν χρῆμα ἐκίνεε 'he was trying everything.' Hdt. 5. 96. 1.

ἡλίου σέλας
ἐῷα κινεῖ φθέγματ' ὀρνίθων σαφῆ. S. *El.* 18.

μὴ κινήσῃς
ἀγρίαν ὀδύνην πατρός. S. *Tr.* 974.

ὅπλα μὲν μήπω κινεῖν (i.e. take warlike action). Th. 1. 82. 1.

τὸν ἐκεῖ πόλεμον κινεῖν. Th. 6. 34. 3; Pl. *R.* 566e.

μὴ κινεῖν δόρυ. E. *Andr.* 607.

μήτηρ
κινεῖ κραδίαν, κινεῖ δὲ χόλον. E. *Med.* 99.

ἡ δὲ ῥίζα ... ποθεῖσα οὔρησιν κινεῖ. Dsc. 2. 109. 2; 2. 127.

ὁ κινῶν αὐτὰ (sc. τὰ φαινόμενα) λόγος. S. E. *M.* 8. 360.

Ἐμπεδοκλέα μὲν γὰρ ὁ Ἀριστοτέλης φησὶ πρῶτον ῥητορικὴν κεκινηκέναι. S. E. *adv. dogmat.* 1. 6. (p. 191 B)

This last is quoted by LSJ as Arist. *fr.* 65, but the expression is more likely that of Sextus. In the middle:

τάχ' ἂν στρατὸς
κινοῖτ' ἀκούσας νυκτέρους ἐκκλησίας.   E. *Rh.* 139.

10   To *raise the question of, bring up, put forward* (a subject, argument, etc.).

οὐδ' ἐπαισχύνεσθε γῆς
οὕτω νοσοῦσαν ἴδια κινοῦντες κακά;   S. *OT* 636.

ἐπεὶ δὲ κινεῖς μῦθον ...   E. *El.* 302.

τούτου χάριν τὰ πολλὰ καὶ ἄτοπα ταῦτα ἐκινήσαμεν.
Pl. *Tht.* 163a.

πάντα κινεῖ λόγον.   Pl. *Phlb.* 15e; *R.* 450a.

11   To *make a change in, interfere with, upset, disturb*. The implication is that change is always for the worse.

νόμαιά τε κινέει πάτρια καὶ βιᾶται γυναῖκας.   Hdt. 3. 80. 5.

τὸ κινεῖν τοὺς πατρίους νόμους.
Arist. *Pol.* 1268ᵇ28; *Cael.* 271ᵇ11.

ἐπὶ γοῦν τῶν ἄλλων ἐπιστημῶν τοῦτο συνενήνοχεν, οἷον
ἰατρικὴ κινηθεῖσα παρὰ τὰ πάτρια καὶ γυμναστική.
Arist. *Pol.* 1268ᵇ35.

τὸ μὲν οὖν τὴν γραφὴν κινεῖν ἐκ τοσούτων ἐτῶν
εὐδοκιμήσασαν περιττὸν ἴσως 'to change the formula'.
Str. 7. 3. 4.

τὰ μέντοι ῥήματα, οὐκ ὄντα δεκτικὰ πτώσεως ἢ μόνης
εὐθείας, ἀκωλύτως τὸ τέλος ἐκίνει ἐν προσώποις, ἐπεὶ οὐκέτι
τὰ τῆς πτώσεως ἀμφήριστα.   A.D. *Pron.* 104. 15.

With a clause as object:

μὴ κινοίη τις τὸ τὰ ἄκρα τῆς Ἰνδικῆς ... ἀνταίρειν τοῖς κατὰ
Μερόην.   Str. 2. 1. 12.

κινήσομεν τὸ πᾶν ζῷον ἐκ πάντων τὴν σύστασιν ἔχειν.
Plot. 2. 1. 6.

Absolutely:

ἐν Αἰγύπτῳ μετὰ τὴν τετραήμερον κινεῖν ἔξεστι τοῖς ἰατροῖς.
Arist. *Pol.* 1268ᵇ35.

μένος

1 Any attempt to determine the meaning of this word is liable to be influenced by the Indo-Iranian parallels. Not only is Vedic *mánas-*, Avestan *manah-* formally identical, but the parallel extends to the compound adjectives, δυσμενής = Av. *dušmanah-*, Skt. *durmanas-*, εὐμενής ≈ Skt. *sumánas*, and the presence of the same element is attested in proper names. But although we can trace a common semantic element, the Indo-Iranian words seem to have developed in a different direction from the Greek. The Sanskrit word is thus defined by Monier-Williams's Dictionary: 'mind (in its widest sense as applied to all the mental powers), intellect, intelligence, understanding, perception, sense, conscience, will.' This meaning appears to be totally absent from the Greek usage. Only later does Monier-Williams mention *mood, temper, spirit,* which come closer to the meaning in Greek. Readers may be puzzled to find that the meaning *strength,* often used by translators, does not appear as the basic sense. The semantic investigation should begin without any preconceived notion of the word's meaning, and judgment should be postponed until the whole article has been read.

2 I should begin with μένος regarded as a permanent characteristic, and it is evident that it refers to a mental, not a physical, state. It may be defined as *determination to impose one's own will, resolve, spirit.*

> Τρωσίν, τῶν μένος αἰὲν ἀτάσθαλον, οὐδὲ δύνανται
> φυλόπιδος κορέσασθαι ὁμοιΐου πτολέμοιο. Il. 13. 634.
>
> μένος ἄσχετοι υἷες Ἀχαιῶν. Od. 3. 104.
>
> Ἀμφιτρύωνος υἱὸς μένος αἰὲν ἀτειρής. Od. 11. 270.
>
> σχέτλιος εἶς, Ὀδυσεῦ, περί τοι μένος οὐδέ τι γυῖα
> κάμνεις. Od. 12. 279.

Of a goddess:

> μητρός τοι μένος ἐστὶν ἀάσχετον, οὐκ ἐπιεικτόν,
> Ἥρης. Il. 5. 892.
>
> Τριτογένειαν
> ἶσον ἔχουσαν πατρὶ μένος καὶ ἐπίφρονα βουλήν.
> Hes. *Th.* 896.

As a characteristic of wild animals and monsters, *fierceness, fury*.

οὔτ᾽ οὖν παρδάλιος τόσσον μένος οὔτε λέοντος
οὔτε συὸς κάπρου. Il. 17. 20.

ἤματι τῷ ὅτε μοι μένος ἄσχετος ἤσθιε Κύκλωψ
ἰφθίμους ἑτάρους. Od. 20. 19.

ταύρου ἐριβρύχεω μένος ἀσχέτου. Hes. *Th.* 832.

οὐ γάρ τοι ταύρων σχήσει μένος οὐδὲ λέοντος
ἀντιβίην. Orac. ap. Hdt. 7. 220. 4.

Of Cassandra compared to a newly captured animal:

ἥτις λιποῦσα μὲν πόλιν νεαίρετον
ἥκει, χαλινὸν δ᾽ οὐκ ἐπίσταται φέρειν
πρὶν αἱματηρὸν ἐξαφρίζεσθαι μένος. A. *Ag.* 1067.

3   As a temporary state of mind, *aggressiveness, reckless courage, temper*.

μένεος δὲ μέγα φρένας ἀμφὶ μέλαιναι
πίμπλαντ᾽, ὄσσε δέ οἱ πυρὶ λαμπετόωντι ἐΐκτην. Il. 1. 103.

ἦ, καὶ σκηπανίῳ γαιήοχος ἐννοσίγαιος
ἀμφοτέρω κεκοπὼν πλῆσεν μένεος κρατεροῖο. Il. 13. 60.

ὁρμήθη δ᾽ Ἀχιλεύς, μένεος δ᾽ ἐμπλήσατο θυμὸν
ἀγρίου. Il. 22. 312.

εἶθαρ μὲν μένεος πλῆντο φρένες. Hes. *Th.* 688; *Sc.* 429.

This idiom reappears in later Greek, possibly as a distant echo of Homer.

ξυσταλεὶς εὔτακτος ὀργῆς καὶ μένους ἐμπλήμενος.
Ar. *V.* 424.

μένους μὲν τὴν ψυχὴν πληρουμένην.
Alcid. ap. Arist. *Rh.* 1406ᵃ2.

οἷον πληρωθεὶς μένους. Plot. 5. 5. 8.

This last is translated 'spiritual exaltation' by LSJ, but this ignores the effect of οἷον 'as if'. In other contexts:

ἔνθ᾽ αὖ Τυδεΐδῃ Διομήδεϊ Παλλὰς Ἀθήνη
δῶκε μένος καὶ θάρσος. Il. 5. 2; Od. 1. 321.

ὣς εἰπὼν ὄτρυνε μένος καὶ θυμὸν ἑκάστου. Il. 5. 470.

In later Greek:

> ὑπὸ δὲ προθυμίας καὶ μένους καὶ τοῦ σπεύδειν συμμεῖξαι
> δρόμου τινὲς ἦρξαν. X. *Cyr.* 3. 3. 61.

> οὕτω πολὺ μένος καὶ θάρρος τοῖς στρατιώταις φασὶν ἐμπεσεῖν.
> X. *HG* 7. 1. 31.

> ὅτε ζέσειεν τὸ τοῦ θυμοῦ μένος. Pl. *Ti.* 70b.

It is also thought of as distinguished by heavy breathing, hence
people are said to breathe μένος.

> μένεα πνείοντες Ἄβαντες. Il. 2. 536; Od. 22. 203.

This will explain a curious passage which has puzzled commentators, of Odysseus' anger on finding Laertes reduced to the condition of a peasant farmer.

> τοῦ δ᾽ ὠρίνετο θυμός, ἀνὰ ῥῖνας δέ οἱ ἤδη
> δριμὺ μένος προὔτυψε φίλον πατέρ᾽ εἰορόωντι. Od. 24. 319.

4   Of animals:

> ὣς εἰπὼν ἵπποισιν ἐνέπνευσεν μένος ἠΰ. Il. 17. 456; 17. 476.

> αἱ δ᾽ (ἵπποι) ἐξηρώησαν, ἐπεὶ μένος ἔλλαβε θυμόν. Il. 23. 468.

> μένει δ᾽ ἐχάρασσον ὀδόντες
> ἄγρια δερκομένω (δράκοντε). Hes. *Sc.* 235.

> αἱ (κύνες) δ᾽ ὑπὸ χαρᾶς καὶ μένους προΐασιν. X. *Cyn.* 6. 15.

5   Similarly, the loss of μένος is the result of injury or defeat, or it
may become milder if calmed down.

> μή μ᾽ ἀπογυιώσῃς μένεος, ἀλκῆς τε λάθωμαι. Il. 6. 265.

There is a variant reading μή μ᾽ ἀπογυιώσῃς, μένεος δ᾽ ἀλκῆς τε
λάθωμαι, but in either case μένος is distinguished from ἀλκή.

> σχέτλιος, αἰὲν ἀλιτρός, ἐμῶν μενέων ἀπερωεύς. Il. 8. 361.

> ὀξεῖαι δ᾽ ὀδύναι δῦνον μένος Ἀτρεΐδαο. Il. 11. 268.

> αὐτὰρ ἐπεὶ Ξάνθοιο δάμη μένος. Il. 21. 383.

> ἔρχεο Περσεφόνη παρὰ μητέρα κυανόπεπλον
> ἤπιον ἐν στήθεσσι μένος καὶ θυμὸν ἔχουσα.
> h. *Cer.* 361; cf. 368.

6   When the loss of μένος is in the context of death, it means little
more than the force which keeps a person or animal alive, *life-
force*.

ἀπὸ γὰρ μένος (ἀρνῶν) εἵλετο χαλκός.   Il. 3. 294.

τοῦ δ' αὖθι λύθη ψυχή τε μένος τε.   Il. 5. 296.

καὶ μὲν τῶν ὑπέλυσε μένος καὶ φαίδιμα γυῖα.   Il. 6. 27.

λῦσεν δὲ βοὸς μένος.   Od. 3. 450.

ἄξεις δ' ἐξ Ἀΐδαο καταφθιμένου μένος ἀνδρός.   Emp. 111. 9.

ἔτι γὰρ θερμαὶ
σύριγγες ἄνω φυσῶσι μέλαν
μένος.   S. *Aj.* 1412.

7   The sense of aggressiveness is sometimes realised as actual
hostile activity, aggression, fighting.

οὐ γὰρ παυσωλή γε μετέσσεται, οὐδ' ἠβαιόν,
εἰ μὴ νὺξ ἐλθοῦσα διακρινέει μένος ἀνδρῶν.
                                    Il. 2. 387; Od. 16. 269.

σύν ῥ' ἔβαλον ῥινούς, σὺν δ' ἔγχεα καὶ μένε' ἀνδρῶν
χαλκεοθωρήκων.   Il. 4. 447.

οἱ δὲ μένος χειρῶν ἰθὺς φέρον.   Il. 5. 506; 16. 602.

προφυγόντα μένος καὶ χεῖρας Ἀχαιῶν.   Il. 6. 502; Od. 9. 457.

                          οὕς τε Κρονίων
θυμοβόρου ἔριδος μένεϊ ξυνέηκε μάχεσθαι.   Il. 7. 210.

                          ὅθι περ Τρῶες καὶ Ἀχαιοὶ
ἐν μέσῳ ἀμφότεροι μένος Ἄρηος δατέονται.   Il. 18. 264.

τῶν ἄμυδις μίχθη μένος, ὦρτο δ' ἀϋτή.   Il. 20. 374.

τῷ κέ τεῳ στύξαιμι μένος καὶ χεῖρας ἀάπτους. 'I would make
him dread my attack and invincible hands.'   Od. 11. 502.

8   *Μένος* with the genitive of a personal name is used as a
periphrasis for the person, but with the implication that he is a
person who commands respect for his forcefulness.

ὡς ἔπεσ' Ἕκτορος ὦκα χαμαὶ μένος ἐν κονίῃσι.   Il. 14. 418.

τὴν μὲν Ἐχεκλῆος κρατερὸν μένος Ἀκτορίδαο
ἠγάγετο πρὸς δώματ', ἐπεὶ πόρε μυρία ἕδνα.
          Il. 16. 189; 23. 837; Hes. *fr.* 252. 6.

ὡς εἰπὼν δεσμὸν ἀνίει μένος Ἡφαίστοιο.   Od. 8. 359.

The masculine participle here is particularly noteworthy, though if the original text read *ΕΙΠΟΝ* it is possible that εἰπών is a later interpretation.

ἱερὸν μένος Ἀντινόοιο.   Od. 18. 34.

On the last see the note on ἱερός, section 11. In view of the differing sense of both noun and epithet, the equation of this phrase with Vedic *iṣiréṇa mánasā* seems even more questionable, but a proper investigation of this must await a similar appraisal of the sense of the Vedic words.

9   The traditional view that μένος means *physical strength, might* is not unjustified, although as demonstrated most examples refer to mental qualities, or at least may do so. But there are a small number where the physical sense is, if not strictly necessary, sufficiently plausible for this to be admitted as a possibility. One example relates to a spear-thrust which had lost its impetus, described as Ares losing his μένος, but it is clear from the context that this is not the god, but simply martial spirit.

ἔνθα δ᾽ ἔπειτ᾽ ἀφίει μένος ὄβριμος Ἄρης.   Il. 13. 444.

More persuasively, it is used to describe the effect of food and drink; this might have an effect on morale, but its obvious result is to give strength.

ἀλλὰ πάσασθαι ἄνωχθι θοῆς ἐπὶ νηυσὶν Ἀχαιοὺς
σίτου καὶ οἴνοιο· τὸ γὰρ μένος ἐστὶ καὶ ἀλκή.   Il. 19. 161.

This suggests a similar meaning where it is coupled with provisions.

καί νύ κεν ἤια πάντα κατέφθιτο καὶ μένε᾽ ἀνδρῶν,
εἰ μή τίς με θεῶν ὀλοφύρατο.   Od. 4. 363.

Even clearer is its application to mules, where their stubbornness is hardly the point at issue.

κούρην δὲ προτὶ ἄστυ φέρεν μένος ἡμιόνοιϊν.   Od. 7. 2.

So after Homer:

καρπαλίμως δ᾽ ἄρ᾽ ἔπειτα μένος καὶ φαίδιμα γυῖα
ηὔξετο τοῖο ἄνακτος.   Hes. *Th.* 492.

παντὶ μένει σπεύδων.   Hes. *Sc.* 364.

And perhaps:

λογισμὸς μὲν ὦν ὁ κρατέων τᾶς γνώσιος, θυμὸς δὲ ὁ κρατέων
τῶ μένεος.   Theages ap. Stob. 3. 1. 117.

10   In Homer and early and classical Greek verse a number of
natural phenomena are described as possessing μένος. This may be
because *strength* or *power* can be attributed to them. But to the
primitive mind these phenomena can be regarded as having a will
of their own and being capable of inflicting harm, so that they are
to some extent personified. Thus rivers (cf. Xanthos in Il. 21. 383,
section 5 above):

ποταμῶν μένος εἰσαγαγόντες.   Il. 12. 18.
     ἔνθα ποταμὸς ἐκφυσᾷ μένος
κροτάφων ἀπ᾽ αὐτῶν.   A. *Pr.* 720.

Wind or storm:

     ὄφρ᾽ εὕδῃσι μένος Βορέαο καὶ ἄλλων
ζαχρειῶν ἀνέμων.   Il. 5. 524.
οὔτ᾽ ἀνέμων διάη μένος ὑγρὸν ἀέντων.   Od. 5. 478.
παύσεις δ᾽ ἀκαμάτων ἀνέμων μένος.   Emp. 11. 3.
χειμῶνος ἐκφυγόντες ἄγριον μένος.   E. *Heracl.* 428.

Of fire:
           Χίμαιρα,
δεινὸν ἀποπνείουσα πυρὸς μένος αἰθομένοιο.   Il. 6. 182.
πρῶτον μὲν κατὰ πυρκαϊὴν σβέσατ᾽ αἴθοπι οἴνῳ
πᾶσαν, ὁπόσσον ἐπέσχε πυρὸς μένος.   Il. 23. 238; 24. 792;
Od. 11. 220.
δεῦρο Μοῦσ᾽ ἐλθὲ φλεγυρὰ πυρὸς ἔχουσα μένος.   Ar. *Ach.* 665.

The sun or other heavenly bodies:

     μὴ πρὶν μένος ἠελίοιο
σκήλει᾽ ἀμφὶ χρόα ἴνεσιν ἠδὲ μέλεσσιν.   Il. 23. 190.
     ὁ μὲν ποταμόνδε κατήϊεν ἐκ νομοῦ ὕλης
πιόμενος· δὴ γάρ μιν ἔχεν μένος ἠελίοιο.
     Od. 10. 160; *h. Ap.* 371; Hes. *Op.* 414.
ἄστρων θερμὸν μένος.   Parm. 11. 3.
αἰθέριον μὲν γάρ σφε μένος πόντονδε διώκει.   Emp. 115. 9.

This is then extended to an abstract concept by Aeschylus:

ποῖ καταλήξει
μετακομισθὲν μένος ἄτης;   A. Ch. 1076.

11   From these cases it became extended to other things regarded
as active forces, usually with the implication of being dangerous.
The first is a difficult example, where we may suspect that personification is implied.

ἔνθ᾽ οὔτ᾽ ἠελίοιο διείδεται ὠκέα γυῖα
οὐδὲ μὲν οὐδ᾽ αἴης λάσιον μένος οὐδὲ θάλασσα.   Emp. 27. 2.

This plainly means where neither the sun nor the earth nor the sea
can be discerned. The ὠκέα γυῖα of the sun obviously imply personification, and since λάσιος properly means 'covered with hair'
and only acquires by transference the sense of 'densely wooded', it
is likely that the earth here is thought of as resembling a shaggy
monster. If so, this passage should not be quoted by LSJ as evidence for the meaning 'overgrown'. There is in any case a further
extension of the sense in the phrase λάσιαι φρένες quoted by LSJ,
so that the sense of 'dangerous, menacing' may be present here
too.

12   A clearer case for the meaning *effectiveness, powerful force*
emerges from the following examples:

ὕδωρ μεταποτέον ὀλίγον· ἧσσον γὰρ ἂν οὕτω τὸ ἀπὸ τοῦ οἴνου
μένος ἅπτοιτο κεφαλῆς καὶ γνώμης.   Hp. Acut. 63.

τὸ γὰρ τοῦ λιμοῦ μένος δύναται ἰσχυρῶς ἐν τῇ φύσει τοῦ
ἀνθρώπου.   Hp. VM 9.

Aeschylus twice uses μένος to mean the controlling force of a
bridle:

ἵππος χαλινῶν ὣς κατασθμαίνων μένει.   A. Th. 393.
βίᾳ χαλινῶν τ᾽ ἀναύδῳ μένει.   A. Ag. 238.

μέξ, μές

1   The form μές is now listed by the New Supplement. It occurs
in two Thessalian inscriptions of ii BC from Larissa:

γυμνασιαρχέντουν μὲς μὲν τᾶς πετράδος τοῖ Ὁμολουίοι μεινvὸς
Νικασίμμοι ... κτλ.   SEG 31. 577.

Since this is contrasted with ἆτ τᾶς μὰ πέμπτας (= ἀπὸ τῆς δέ πέμπτης) it is clear that it means 'up to the fourth of the month'. Similarly:

γυμνασιαρχέντουν μὲς τᾶς πέμπ[τ]ας [τ]οῖ Ὁμολουίοι
BCH 109. 163. B. 8.

In both these cases we can assume a sense *as far as, up to* (here a point in time). The same element is well known to occur in compounds in Thessalian μέσποδι, a conjunction meaning 'until', and epic μέσφα (preposition with genitive or accusative and conjunction); μέσφ' ἐς occurs in Callimachus (fr. Del. 47), later epic also μέσφι, West Greek μέστα, Arcadian μέστε (conjunction).

2   There is now a Thessalian inscription from Scotoussa of ii BC, recently published by V. Messailidou-Despotidou, *ABSA* 88 (1993), 187–217, which contains several times the form μὲς πότ followed by an accusative and once μέξ ἐμ ποταμόν. In each case μές or μέξ is immediately followed by a preposition expressing motion, and it seems preferable to read them as independent words μές and μέξ. There can be no doubt that they both mean 'as far as', 'up to', in this case a point in space. The form μέξ is new, and opens up the possibility that μές is the preconsonantal form of μέξ. It is significant that apart from epic, where it may be of Aeolic origin, this word appears only in dialects which also show ἐς as the preconsonantal form of ἐξ, viz. Thessalian, Arcadian, and Cretan.

3   The various endings attached to this element do not show any consistent pattern. The new examples show it preceding a normal preposition (πότ = ποτί, ἐν + accusative). The conjunction μέσποωῶ δι has been analysed as containing the reflex of a neuter relative *kʷod (cf. εἰς ὅ κε) and a deictic -ι. The new form suggests that a corruption of μεσ-πότι is also a possibility, but there is no way of verifying this. The elements -φα, -φι (if not really -σφα, -σφι) are obscure, since although -φι might be a case form, -φα cannot. The forms μέστα and μέστε answer to Aeolic ὄτα and Arcadian ὄτε, with a dental and not a labio-velar suffix, since *o-te* is also Mycenaean.

4   There is, however, evidence for a Cretan form spelt *MET* in an inscription of v BC from Lyttos (H. and M. van Effenterre, *BCH* 109 (1985), 163). This has been plausibly taken by the editors as

representing μέτ(τ)' since in both examples a vowel follows. The clearer one is:

ἆι ἀ ὁδὸς ὑπανπέτιν μετ(τ)' ἐς Πυτ[B 8 'following the ascending road as far as Pyt[.'

The last word is presumably a place-name; the other is similar:

ἆι ἀ ὁδὸς ἀ εἰθεῖα μέτ[τ]' Ἀμαρτει[. .]ε B 5 'following the straight road as far as'.

Here the editors tentatively suggest restoring the place name as Ἀρματεί[αζ]ε 'jusque vers (le lieu-dit) Les Fautes'. It is certainly hard to separate the examples with ἐς from μέξ ἐν and μέσφ' ἐς. But there does not seem to be any way of reconciling these with the form μέττ(α). Cretan assimilates σθ to θθ, but not στ to ττ. It would only be possible to bring these forms together by reconstructing *μέκ-τα, which would be liable to develop to μέττα; cf. Λύττος < Λύκτος.

5 Another form of the same meaning is the familiar μέχρι, with its variant ἄχρι. It has been doubted whether α- really represents the zero-grade with *ṃ; but the parallel of ἄλευρον and Mycenaean me-re-u-ro = meleuron is some confirmation that this falls into the same pattern as μέγα-/ἀγα-. The possibility therefore arises that μέχρι is the product of *meks-ri, though the termination is again obscure.

6 But what could μέξ represent? It is tempting to associate it with μέγας, itself a problematic word. Merely as a suggestion I should speculate on the existence of an abstract neuter noun *μέγας, exactly paralleled by Sanskrit mahah, meaning 'size', of which μέξ might be a reduced or syncopated form. (For my views on the effect of the Thessalian accent see Glotta 70 (1992), 2–14.) This would allow the explanation of its absence from later Greek as due to transference to the category of adjective (cf. Latin adjective uetus from a substantive = Greek ἔτος). It is surely significant that the only inflected forms are accusative μέγαν and neuter μέγα, the rest of the inflexion being supplied by the suffix -λος. This would seem to be easier than the proposal to derive μέγας from μέγα.

7 There remains the alleged Armenian cognate merj meaning 'near'; on this see now J. Clackson, *The Linguistic Relationship*

between Armenian and Greek, (Oxford: Blackwell, 1994), 152. Since it is not precisely parallel in sense, it might be related without giving any useful information about the precise form of this root. In view of the many uncertainties, all that is safe to say is that the etymology of this group of words needs to be revised in the light of the new evidence for a form μέξ.

νέμω

1   LSJ divides its article into two major parts: A *deal out, dispense*; B *pasture, graze*. At first sight it is hard to discern any semantic link between these two senses, yet unless we have here a conflation of two different lexical items, there must at some stage have been an archetypal sense which can be reconstructed as the starting-point for all later developments. Both logic and experience dictate that archetypal senses are not vague and abstract, but specific and concrete. I believe therefore that a satisfactory starting-point can be found in the notion of *providing with food, feeding*. It is very easy to see that providing domesticated animals with food is normally achieved by driving them out to pasture, and the verb thus becomes a general expression for tending animals, a notion which will be constantly needed in an agricultural community. The other main sense is a little harder to explain, but may begin from the operation of feeding a human community, where the person in charge has to divide the food into portions and see that it is fairly distributed. The English words *lord* and *lady* likewise disclose a preoccupation with food, since both contain the Old English *hlāf* 'loaf', bread. It is then possible to see the sense of *assign, distribute* arising naturally from the process of doling out food.

2   For this reason a lexical treatment ought to begin with the 'pastoral' senses. Their arrangement is complicated by two factors: senses may be classified by the type of object with which the verb is used; and in certain senses the middle voice is employed. Thus I would place first *pasture, graze* a domesticated animal.

> ἐθήτευον ... ὁ μὲν ἵππους νέμων, ὁ δὲ βοῦς, ὁ δὲ νεώτατος ...
> τὰ λεπτὰ τῶν προβάτων.   Hdt. 8. 137. 2.

παῖδες μὲν οὖν μοι κλιτύων ἐν ἐσχάτοις
νέμουσι μῆλα νέα νέοι πεφυκότες. E. *Cyc*. 28.

τὸν ἱιερὲν πέντε καὶ εἴκοσι οἷς νέμεν καὶ ζεῦγος καὶ αἶγα.
'The priest may pasture 25 sheep, a yoke (of oxen) and a goat.'
Schwyzer 654. 1 (Tegea, iv BC).

καθάπερ ποιμένες κτήνη πλήγῃ νέμοντες. Pl. *Criti*. 109c.

In the passive:

πᾶν γὰρ ἑρπετὸν πλήγῃ νέμεται. Heraclit. 11.

ἔφασαν (ἵππους) νεμομένας ἁρπασθῆναι ὑπὸ τῶν ἄνω Θρηίκων
'they claimed the mares had been rustled while out to pasture'.
Hdt. 8. 115. 4.

There seems to be no Homeric example of this transitive use, but
it occurs used absolutely, *tend animals*.

μένομεν τέ μιν ἔνδον
ἥμενοι, ἧος ἐπῆλθε νέμων. Od. 9. 233.

ἰν Ἀλέαι μὲ νέμεν μέτε ξένον μέτε ϝαστόν, εἰ μὲ ἐπὶ θοίναν
ἵκοντα. 'Neither stranger nor citizen may pasture his animals
in Alea, unless attending a festival.' Schwyzer 654. 11.

εἰ μέλλομεν ἱκανὴν (χώραν) ἕξειν νέμειν τε καὶ ἀροῦν.
Pl. *R*. 373d.

3 A natural development from this is where the object is not the
animals, but the land on which they are pastured. We may define
this sense as *range over with animals, use* land *as pasture*.

ἡ μὲν γὰρ (χώρη) πρὸς τὴν ἠῶ τῆς Λιβύης, τὴν οἱ νομάδες
νέμουσι, ἐστὶ ταπεινή τε καὶ ψαμμώδης. Hdt. 4. 191. 3.

μηδετέρους οἰκεῖν τὸ χωρίον, ἀλλὰ κοινῇ νέμειν 'neither party
to settle the area, but to share the pasturage'. Th. 5. 42. 1.

τί δ' ὑμεῖς ... ἐπεὶ ὄρη ἀγαθὰ ἔχετε, ἐθέλοιτ' ἂν ἐᾶν νέμειν
ταῦτα τοὺς Ἀρμενίους ... ; X. *Cyr*. 3. 2. 20.

In the passive, with the dative of the animals:

οὐκ ἄβατόν ἐστι τὸ ὄρος, ἀλλὰ νέμεται αἰξὶ καὶ βουσίν.
X. *An*. 4. 6. 17.

The same sense is conveyed by the middle, i.e. *use for oneself as
pasture*.

τὸ δὲ πρὸς τὴν ἠῶ ... νομάδες ἤδη Σκύθαι νέμονται, οὔτε τι
σπείροντες οὐδὲν οὔτε ἀροῦντες. Hdt. 4. 19.

4   By a transference this sense is used to mean *range over* with fire.

> πυρὶ δὲ καὶ ταύτας (*sc.* χώρας) νείμαντας.   Hdt. 6. 33. 2.

In the passive:

> ὡς εἴ τε πυρὶ χθὼν πᾶσα νέμοιτο.   Il. 2. 780.

> ἔδοξε γὰρ πυρὶ νέμεσθαι πολλῷ τὴν Μακεδόνων φάλαγγα.
>   Plu. *Alex.* 18. 4.

5   This leads naturally to the use of the middle of animals *graze*, either absolutely or with an accusative of the pasture.

> αἵ (βόες) ῥά τ' ἐν εἰαμένῃ ἕλεος μεγάλοιο νέμονται.
>   Il. 15. 631.

> αἱ δὲ (σύες) νέμονται
> πὰρ Κόρακος πέτρῃ ἐπί τε κρήνῃ Ἀρεθούσῃ
> ἔσθουσαι βάλανον.   Od. 13. 407.

> φανέντων δὲ αὐτῶν (*sc.* ὀφίων) οἱ ἵπποι, μετιέντες τὰς νομὰς νέμεσθαι, φοιτῶντες κατήσθιον.   Hdt. 1. 78. 1.

> κραγέται δὲ κολοιοὶ ταπεινὰ νέμονται.   Pi. *N.* 3. 82.

> ὀρεία τις ὡς λέαιν' ὀργάδων
> δρύοχα νεμομένα τάδε κατήνυσεν.   E. *El.* 1163.

6   By a transference from this it may be similarly used of other things which *spread* or *extend*.

> ἐπὶ τοῦ μαστοῦ ἔφυ φῦμα, μετὰ δὲ ἐκραγὲν ἐνέμετο πρόσω.
>   Hdt. 3. 133. 1.

> πρὸς τὰ νεμόμενα ἕλκη.
>   Thphr. *HP* 9. 9. 5; Philum. *Ven.* 17. 1.

With accusative:

> τοῦτο τὸ ψεῦδος ἰὸν ἔχει, νέμεται τὴν ψυχήν.   Plu. 2. 165a.

—unless the sense is 'devour', see 12 below.

7   It is not always clear whether pasturage or more general occupancy is intended. But we can certainly see examples where the middle is used to mean *occupy as living space*, *live on*.

> οἵ θ' Ὑρίην ἐνέμοντο καὶ Αὐλίδα πετρήεσσαν.   Il. 2. 496.

> οἱ περὶ Δωδώνην δυσχείμερον οἰκί' ἔθεντο,
> οἵ τ' ἀμφ' ἱμερτὸν Τιταρησσὸν ἔργ' ἐνέμοντο.   Il. 2. 751.

If ἔργα means 'worked land', this example belongs here; but it might also be assigned to the sense *exploit* (see 8 below). So too:

οἵ δ᾽ ἐθελημοὶ
ἥσυχοι ἔργ᾽ ἐνέμοντο σὺν ἐσθλοῖσιν πολέεσσιν.   Hes. *Op.* 119.

καὶ τέμενος νεμόμεσθα μέγα Ξάνθοιο παρ᾽ ὄχθας.
   Il. 12. 313; Od. 11. 185.

οἳ νεμόμεσθ᾽ Ἰθάκην εὐδείελον.   Od. 2. 167.

ὄφρα σὺ μὲν χαίρων πατρώϊα πάντα νέμηαι
ἔσθων καὶ πίνων.   Od. 20. 336.

   ἀγρούς τε πάντας, τοὺς ἀπούρας
ἀμετέρων τοκέων νέμεαι.   Pi. *P.* 4. 150.

ἡ δὲ εἶχε αὐτὴ τοῦ παιδὸς τὰ γέρεα ἐν Κυρήνῃ καὶ τἆλλα
νεμομένη.   Hdt. 4. 165. 1.

πόλιες μὲν αὗται αἳ τὸν Ἄθων νέμονται.
   Hdt. 7. 23. 1; 7. 123. 1.

νεμόμενοί τε τὰ αὑτῶν ἕκαστοι ὅσον ἀποζῆν.   Th. 1. 2. 2.

This may well imply pasturage, but probably includes other forms of agriculture.

8   In examples which are plainly not agricultural we may establish the sense *occupy for profit, exploit, enjoy*. This sense survives into modern Greek.

ὄρος ... ἐν τῷ χρύσεά τε καὶ ἀργύρεα ἔνι μέταλλα, τὰ
νέμονται Πίερες.   Hdt. 7. 112; Th. 1. 100. 2.

καὶ μέχρ[ι] τ[οῦ] νῦν νέμομα[ι π]ροσόδους.
   BGU 256. 9 (ii AD).

So also in the active:

Γᾶ ... ἃ τὸν μέγαν Πακτωλὸν εὔχρυσον νέμεις.   S. *Ph.* 393.

The examples with ἔργα mentioned in 7 above may belong here.

9   In both middle and active the verb can be used to mean *live* in specified circumstances.

   ἀλλὰ παρὰ μὲν τιμίοις θεῶν ...
      ἄδακρυν νέμονται
αἰῶνα.   Pi. *O.* 2. 66.
ἡσυχᾷ τε νεμόμενος.   Pi. *P.* 11. 55.

μεταμειβόμενοι δ' ἐναλλὰξ ἀμέραν τὰν
μὲν παρὰ πατρὶ φίλῳ
Δὶ νέμονται.   Pi. N. 10. 56.

Two of these examples are quoted by LSJ as examples of *spend,
pass* time, as if αἰῶνα and ἀμέραν were direct objects. In the active:

ὃς Συρακόσσαισι νέμει βασιλεύς.   Pi. P. 3. 70.

10   To *direct, guide, wield* a physical object.

ἀσπίδ' εὔκυκλον νέμων (*var. lect.* εὐκήλως ἔχων)
πάγχαλκον.   A. Th. 590.

γλῶσσαν ἐν τύχᾳ νέμων 'using his tongue at random'.
                                                    A. Ag. 685.

οὐδ' εὖ πραπίδων οἴακα νέμων   A. Ag. 802.

Describing the bandaging of the head:

ἄγομεν τὴν ἐπείλησιν ... ἐπικάρσιον ... κατὰ τοῦ βρέγματος
... καὶ παρὰ τὰς ἑτέρας λεγομένας μετωπιαίας ἄνω νέμομεν.
                                                    Sor. Fasc. 4.

In the middle:

ἐπὶ τὸ ἄνω νεμέσθω (τὸ ὀθόνιον) ἐπιδέων.   Hp. Fract. 4; 16.

11   From the notion of taking animals to pasture arises that of
controlling generally; hence a meaning *be in charge of, control, rule*.

ἀλλ' ὦ Κρόνιε παῖ Ῥέας, ἕδος Ὀλύμπου νέμων.   Pi. O. 2. 12.

This example might also be taken as meaning *live in* (7 above).
More clearly:

τόνδε λαὸν ἀβλαβῆ νέμων.   Pi. O. 13. 27.

Perhaps:

εἰ δέ τις ἔνδον νέμει πλοῦτον κρυφαῖον.   Pi. I. 1. 67.

ὁ πάντα νέμων ... Ζεύς.   A. Pr. 526.

ἐπί τε τοῖσι κατεστῶσι ἔνεμε τὴν πόλιν κοσμέων καλῶς τε καὶ
εὖ.   Hdt. 1. 59. 6; 5. 29. 2.

οἵ περ ἔνεμον τότε τὰς Ἀθήνας.   Hdt. 5. 71. 2.

                          ὡς τὰ σὰ
κράτη θανόντος καὶ δόμους νέμοιμι σούς.   S. Aj. 1016.

τοῖς τὴν σύνοδον νέμουσιν.   OGI 50. 3 (Ptolemais, iii BC).

In the passive:

τό τε κατ' ὑμέας, τάδε πάντα ὑπὸ βαρβάροισι νέμεται 'and as
far as you are concerned all this might be subject to barbarians'.
                                               Hdt. 7. 158. 2.

καὶ μέχρι τοῦδε πολλὰ τῆς Ἑλλάδος τῷ παλαιῷ τρόπῳ
νέμεται.   Th. 1. 5. 3; 1. 6. 2.

12   As a different line of development the middle may be used of
living creatures, *have as food, feed on*; cf. Latin *uescor*.

τοῖσιν δ' (ἵπποις) ἀμβροσίην Σιμόεις ἀνέτελλε νέμεσθαι.
                                                   Il. 5. 777.

Polyphemos addressing his ram:

οὔ τι πάρος γε λελειμμένος ἔρχεαι οἰῶν,
ἀλλὰ πολὺ πρῶτος νέμεαι τέρεν' ἄνθεα ποίης.   Od. 9. 449.

οὐ φορβὰν ἱερᾶς γᾶς σπόρον, οὐκ ἄλλων
αἴρων τῶν νεμόμεσθ' ἀνέρες ἀλφησταί
'taking as food not the seed of holy earth, not of other things
that we men feed on'.   S. *Ph.* 709.

                αἳ δὲ νεμομέναις χλόην
μόσχοις ἐπῆλθον.   E. *Ba.* 735.

νεμόμεσθα δ' ἐν κήποις τὰ λευκὰ σήσαμα.   Ar. *Av.* 159.

As a metaphor from this we find νέμομαι used of fire, to *devour* (in
the first example absolutely; cf. 4 above).

ἐν δὲ πυρὸς μένος ἧκε σιδήρεον, ὄφρα νέμοιτο.   Il. 23. 177.

τὰ περιέσχατα νεμομένου τοῦ πυρός.   Hdt. 5. 101. 2.

13   A quite different line of development starts from the action of
dividing up and distributing food and drink. Literally to *distribute,
dispense* food and drink:

Πάτροκλος μὲν σῖτον ἑλὼν ἐπένειμε τραπέζῃ
καλοῖς ἐν κανέοισιν, ἀτὰρ κρέα νεῖμεν Ἀχιλλεύς.   Il. 9. 217.

οἱ δ' ἤδη μοίρας τ' ἔνεμον κερόωντό τε οἶνον.   Od. 8. 470.

           κρητῆρα κερασσάμενος μέθυ νεῖμον
πᾶσιν ἀνὰ μέγαρον.   Od. 7. 179.

ἡ δὲ τρίτη κρητῆρι μελίφρονα οἶνον ἐκίρνα
ἡδὺν ἐν ἀργυρέῳ, νέμε δὲ χρύσεια κύπελλα.   Od. 10. 357.

ν[έ]μ[ε]ν Ἐρυθραῖον [τ]ο[ῖ]s παρôσι[ν τὸν κρεὸν τ]ὸs
hιεροπο(ι)ὸs δρ[αχ]μὲν [hεκ]ά[σ]τôι. IG 1². 10. 3.

14 Then later it is used generally to mean *distribute, allot*.

γεôνόμôs δὲ hελέσθ[αι] ... hοûτοι δὲ νεμάντ[ôν τὲν γὲν].
IG 1². 45. 7.

οὐκ ἔστιν ὅτῳ
μείζονα μοῖραν νείμαιμ' ἢ σοί. A. *Pr.* 292.

Λύκῳ
τὸν ἀντίπλευρον κῆπον Εὐβοίας νέμει. S. *fr.* 24.

τρίτον μέρος νείμαντες τῶν σκύλων τοῖς Ἀθηναίοις.
Th. 3. 114. 1.

In the perfect passive, with retained accusative, *be divided* or
distributed:

λέγοντες ὡς πλεῖστα μέρη ἡ οὐσία νενεμημένη εἴη.
Pl. *Prm.* 144d.

τρίποδες ... κρεῶν μεστοὶ νενεμημένων. X. *An.* 7. 3. 21.

ἐκ δὲ φυλῆς ἑκάστης ἦσαν νενεμημέναι τρίττυες μὲν τρεῖς ...
Arist. *Ath.* 8. 3; 63. 4.

So in the middle, *conduct the distribution of property*.

πρὸς τὸν ἀδελφὸν δ' οὕτως ἐνειμάμην ὥστ' ἐκεῖνον πλέον
ὁμολογεῖν ἔχειν ἐμοῦ τῶν πατρῴων. Lys. 16. 10; 19. 46.

ἔμ' οἴεσθ' ὑμῖν εἰσοίσειν, ὑμεῖς δὲ νέμεσθαι; D. 21. 203.

15 This is then naturally extended to abstract objects, *confer,
assign, devote*. This sense is very common and only a few of the
examples are quoted here.

Ζεὺς δ' αὐτὸς νέμει ὄλβον Ὀλύμπιος ἀνθρώποισιν.
Od. 6. 188.

νέμων εἰκότως
ἄδικα μὲν κακοῖς, ὅσια δ' ἐννόμοις. A. *Supp.* 403.

Ζεὺς τά τε καὶ τὰ νέμει. Pi. *I.* 5. 52; *P.* 5. 55.

τὸν πατρὸς φόνον
πράξαντα μητρὸς μηδαμῶς τιμὰς νέμειν. A. *Eu.* 624; 747.

θεῶν τὰ ἴσα νεμόντων 'if the gods are even-handed'.
Hdt. 6. 11. 3; 6. 109. 5.

εἰ νέμοι τις αἴρεσιν 'if anyone gave you the choice'.
S. *Aj.* 265; *Tr.* 57.

ἦ καὶ τὸ πιστὸν τῆς ἀληθείας νεμεῖς; 'will you also guarantee the truth of this?' S. *Tr.* 398.

τήνδ᾽ οὖν ἐκείνῳ πᾶς τις αἰτίαν νέμει. S. *Aj.* 28.

μήτε οἴκτῳ πλέον νείμαντες μήτ᾽ ἐπιεικείᾳ 'making greater concessions neither to pity nor to fairness'. Th. 3. 48. 1.

τῷ τ᾽ ὄχλῳ πλέον νέμεις. E. *Hec.* 868.

   ἵν᾽ ὁ ποντο-
μέδων πορφυρέας λίμνας
ναύταις οὐκέθ᾽ ὁδὸν νέμει. E. *Hipp.* 745.

κἀμοὶ δεῖ νέμειν ὑμᾶς χάριν. Ar. *Av.* 384; cf. Gal. 6. 753.

ὅτι πενίᾳ καὶ πλούτῳ ... διαφέρουσαν οὐδ᾽ ἡντινοῦν τιμὴν καὶ τροφὴν νέμετε. Pl. *Lg.* 696a.

The use of τροφή here recalls the origin of this sense.

ἔλασσον ἔνειμαν ἂν τῷ τεθνηκότι τῶν ἐν τῷ νόμῳ κειμένων 'they would have paid less respect to the dead man than is laid down in the law'. Antipho 5. 10.

16   Used with a predicate it acquires the sense *assign to a category, rank as*.

καὶ τὸ μὲν ἀπ᾽ ἡμέων οὕτω ἀκίβδηλον νέμεται ἐπὶ τοὺς Ἕλληνας. Hdt. 9. 7. a. 2.

σὲ δ᾽ ἔγωγε νέμω θεόν. S. *El.* 150; 598.

φίλον σ᾽ ἐγὼ μέγιστον Ἀργείων νέμω. S. *Aj.* 1331.

ἥμαρτον, εἴ τι τήνδ᾽ ἁμαρτίαν νέμεις. S. *Tr.* 483.

νομοθέτῃ κολαστὴν τῶν ἁμαρτημάτων θάνατον ἀνάγκη νέμειν.
                                                    Pl. *Lg.* 863a.

καὶ τοὺς μὲν μετοίκους τοιούτους εἶναι νομίζομεν, οἵους περ ἂν τοὺς προστάτας νέμωσιν 'we judge the character of metics by the kind of people they adopt as patrons'.
                     Isoc. 8. 53; Hyp. *fr.* 21; Arist. *Pol.* 1275ᵃ12.

17   It is easy then to see how this develops to mean *assign to a list, register*.

σὺ δ᾽ ἐν θρόνοισι γραμμάτων πτυχὰς ἔχων
νέμ᾽ εἴ τις οὐ πάρεστιν ὃς ξυνώμοσεν.
'Note down if any of the conspirators are not present.'
                                                    S. *fr.* 144.

νεῖμαι δὲ καὶ τοὺς ἄλλους πρὸς τὴν λῆξιν ἑκάστην 'and to register the others as eligible for each selection by lot'.

Arist. *Ath.* 30. 3; 31. 3.

τὰς γυναῖκάς φασιν ἐν καλῷ τίθεσθαι ὅτι πλείστους νέμειν ἄνδρας 'they say that the women account it honourable to list as many husbands as possible.'   Str. 11. 13. 11.

In the passive with adverb:

οὐδέ μοι ἐμμελέως τὸ Πιττάκειον
νέμεται.
'Nor in my opinion is this properly assigned to the sayings of Pittakos.'   Simon. 5. 9 (= 37. 12).

ἄχρι τε͂[ς] ηοδο͂ τε͂σδε τὸ ἄστυ τε͂ιδε νενέμε͂ται 'the city is recorded as extending here up to this road'.   *IG* ι². 893.

The perfect participle passive thus means *duly listed, entered on the register.*

οὐδὲ ... τούς γε μὴ νενεμημένους ... παρίεμεν εἰς τοὺς ἀθλητικοὺς ἀγῶνας.   Plb. 6. 47. 8.

18   I am well aware that this analysis of the pattern of development of this verb is at variance with the general opinion held on this subject. See for example the study by E. Laroche, *Histoire de la racine *nem- en grec ancien* (Paris, 1949). It is assumed that νέμω and νόμος are from the same base, and must therefore be given matching senses. There can be no doubt that νομός, νομή, νομεύς, νομάς, νωμάω all belong to the root of νέμω. But the question must be asked, how does νόμος with its derivatives such as νομίζω fit into this picture? The absence of both these words from Homer suggests that they may be of rather later origin, and could thus have arisen from one or more of the transferred senses of νέμω. It is just possible to regard νόμος as that which is meted out, a legal decision, and thus what is acceptable to society; cf. θέμιστες. This would explain the sense of νόμος meaning 'custom', which is alleged to occur in Hesiod. There is in fact room to dispute the earliest recorded sense of νόμος. In Hesiod's description of the Muses we read:

ἐρατὴν δὲ διὰ στόμα ὄσσαν ἱεῖσαι
μέλπονται πάντων τε νόμους καὶ ἤθεα κεδνὰ
ἀθανάτων κλείουσι.   Hes. *Th.* 66.

It is not impossible here to give νόμους the regular musical sense of 'melody'. Likewise in a Homeric hymn:

πάντη γάρ τοι, Φοῖβε, νόμος βεβλήατ' ἀοιδῆς.   h. Ap. 20.

the peculiarity of having to make βεβλήαται singular has inspired the emendation to νόμοι; in any case the association with ἀοιδή speaks in favour of music. Then again we have Alcman, clearly using the musical sense:

Ϝοῖδα δ' ὀρνίχων νόμως
πάντων.   Alcm. 40. 1.

But by the time of Alcaeus and Pindar the sense of 'customary usage', 'rule of law' seems to be firmly established.

ἔνθα νόμος ...   Alc. 72. 6.

οὐ κὰν νόμον ...   Alc. 129 .25.

νόμος ὁ πάντων βασιλεύς.   Pi. fr. 169.1 (=152. 1 B).

To sum up, it is certainly worth considering whether νόμος has not been wrongly associated with νέμω; and even if the connexion is proved, more research is needed on the history of the noun.

19   A conspectus of senses may be useful. The numbers in parentheses refer to the paragraphs above.

  1 *pasture, graze* animals; absolutely, *tend animals* (2).

  2 *range over with animals, use as pasture* (3). **b** *range over* with fire (4).

  3 mid. of animals, *graze*, absolutely or with pasture as object (5). **b** transf., *spread, extend* (6)

  4 mid., *occupy as living space, live on* (7).

  5 mid., also act., *occupy for profit, exploit, enjoy* (8).

  6 mid. and act., *live* in specified circumstances (9).

  7 *direct, guide, wield* a physical object (10).

  8 *be in charge of, control, rule* (11).

  9 mid., *have as food, feed on*; metaph., *devour* (12).

  10 *distribute, dispense* food and drink (13).

  11 generally, *distribute, allot* (14).

  12 *confer, assign, devote* abstract objects (15).

  13 *assign to a category, rank as* (16). **b** *assign to a list, register* (17).

ὄβδη

The only evidence for this word appears to be a single fragment of Callimachus, which reads:

Μούσῃ γὰρ ἦλθον εἰς ὄβδην.   Call. *fr*. 218 Pf.

The word is variously cited by grammarians, and also given as εἰσόβδην or ἐσόβδην. It is fairly obvious that the meaning is *into view*, and it has been correctly assigned to the group of ὄψις, ὄπωπα, etc. But the existence of such a substantive must be doubtful, and a much more plausible analysis is to regard the whole phrase as one word, an adverb of the same type as συλλήβδην, with the common ending -δην (see Schwyzer, *Gram*. i. 626). For adverbial compounds with εἰσ- cf. εἰσάπαξ, εἰσαῦθις. It would thus appear that, *pace* Pfeiffer, the entry ὄβδη can be banished from our lexica, and the adverb εἰσόβδην entered instead.

ὅδε

1   Every student of Greek knows that when the demonstratives ὅδε, οὗτος, and ἐκεῖνος are used as adjectives, in prose the article must be inserted before the substantive. This may be more a matter for grammars than dictionaries; but it is curious to find no mention of the fact in LSJ's article on ὅδε. Verse always retained the freedom to omit the article, and this also occurs occasionally in Herodotus. It would be interesting to know how much more widespread this usage was.

2   The New Supplement reports a sense which does not appear in LSJ, where ὅδε is used as a substitute for a name or specification which the speaker leaves the hearer to fill in as appropriate. The nearest English equivalent is *this or that, such-and-such*. It can be quoted from two passages of Plato, where, however, other interpretations might be possible:

οἱ μὲν οὖν τοιοίδε ὑπὸ τῶν τοιῶνδε λόγων διὰ τήνδε τὴν αἰτίαν
εἰς τὰ τοιάδε εὐπειθεῖς, οἱ δὲ τοιοίδε διὰ τάδε δυσπειθεῖς.
Pl. *Phdr*. 272a.

C. J. Rowe translates: 'So people of one kind are easily persuaded for this reason by one kind of speech to hold one kind of opinion, while people of another kind are for these reasons difficult to persuade.' But the point is that the αἰτία in question has not been specified, and it should surely be taken to mean 'for such-and-such a reason'. It would be clumsy and confusing to have written διὰ τοιάνδε αἰτίαν. In another sentence just below we find:

ἢ προσοιστέον τούσδε ὧδε τοὺς λόγους ἐπὶ τὴν τῶνδε πειθώ.

272a.

Here again the reference is not to specific arguments or people, but those to whom the hearer may choose to apply it. An even better example is quoted from the *New Testament*.

ἄγε νῦν οἱ λέγοντες, Σήμερον ἢ αὔριον πορευσόμεθα εἰς τήνδε τὴν πόλιν καὶ ποιήσομεν ἐκεῖ ἐνιαυτόν. *Ep. Jac.* 4. 13.

Here too no specific town is meant; it is for the recipient of the letter to fill in any name he chooses. Another example is:

ὁπόσων δ' ἂν προσδέῃ, οἵδε ᾑρημένοι νομοθέται ὑπὸ τῆς βουλῆς ἀναγράφοντες ἐν σανίσιν ἐκτιθέντων πρὸς τοὺς ἐπωνύμους σκοπεῖν τῷ βουλομένῳ, καὶ παραδιδόντων ταῖς ἀρχαῖς ἐν τῷδε τῷ μηνί. Decree in And. 1. 83.

It would seem inevitable that there are many more such examples waiting to be discovered, but I can think of no easy method of locating them. Perhaps once the usage has been pointed out, others will be able to contribute examples.

3   This suggests that there is a possible new explanation of the expression ὁ δεῖνα, etc. It is clear that when used indeclinably the form is always δεῖνα, but it is also declined as a nasal stem, δεῖνος, δεῖνι, and similarly in the plural. These forms are all based on the assumption that δεῖνα is either the accusative singular or neuter plural of a consonant stem. It has been suggested that it began in the neuter plural *ταδεῖνα contracted from τάδε *ἕνα, the second element being that assumed to be that required by the etymology of (ἐ)κεῖνος. But this is of course an o-stem, and neuter plural *τὰ δεῖνα appears to be one of the few forms that do not occur. It would surely be more likely that this expression started from a locution involving a nasal stem. Thus I would suggest the accusative singular τόνδε ἕνα, which would have the effect of making τόνδε less specific. The indefinite use of εἷς is familiar in εἷς τις, so it would

mean 'such-and-such a one.' This explanation will hold good for
the other inflected forms, but with a plausible shift of accent to
agree with the accusative (τοῦ δεῖνος < *τοῦδε ἑνός, τῷ δεῖνι < *τῷδε
ἑνί).

ὀλερός

1 Galen believed that he had found a new word in the
Hippocratic Corpus:

> ὀλερόν· δυσῶδες ἢ μέλαν, ἀπὸ τοῦ τῶν σηπιῶν ὅλου.
>
> Gal. 19. 126.

There is no such word in our *Hippocratic Corpus,* but it sounds
like a description of urine. This is quite often described as dark or
foul-smelling; the two words δύσωδεα and μέλανα occur together at
Prognostic 12. But the term which is often used of urine is θολερός
'turbid'.

> οὖρα ... θολερὰ δὲ καὶ οὐδὲν καθιστάμενα, οὐδ' ὑφιστάμενα.
>
> Hp. *Epid.* 1. 7.

This bears such a close resemblance to the alleged ὀλερός that one
must ask whether it was not just a corruption in Galen's text, and
in some such passage the θ was omitted. (The substantive θολός is
used of 'the ink of the cuttle-fish' in Hippocrates and Aristotle.)
The New Supplement adds a reference to Str. 1. 2. 21, where it is
a conjecture, τοῦ λοιποῦ Νότου ὀλεροῦ πως ὄντος for ὅλου Εὔρου.

2 However, it is perfectly possible for an adjective in -ρός to have
been created on the basis of a substantive ὀλός, just as θολερός is
built on θολός. So we must enquire into the credentials of ὀλός.
It is quoted by LSJ meaning 'the ink of the cuttle-fish' in one
passage of the *Hippocratic Corpus.*

> τοῖσι πάνυ χολώδεσιν, ἐν πυρετοῖσι μάλιστα, ὀλῷ ἰκέλη (ὅλως
> ἐπὶ σκέλεα Littré) ἡ κάθαρσις. Hp. *Epid.* 4.20.

and 'prob. read by Gal. in Hp. *Morb.* 2. 73', where Littré reads ὅτε
δὲ πολύπου θολόν. There are also two references to lexicographers,
Phryn. *PS* p. 19 B and Phot. (ὀλός· θόλος) neither of which is en-
lightening. There is thus some reason to think that this is another

ghost-word, generated by the loss of θ-. LSJ also gives a second
sense 'metaph. *blood*' quoting from an acrostic

Ὁλὸς οὔ με λιβρὸς ἱρῶν
Λιβάδεσσιν οἷα κάλχη
Ὑποφοινίῃσι τέγγει.   *AP* 15. 25. 1.

3   There is no easy solution to this problem, but the improbability of the existence of two words with such a specialised meaning differing in only one letter surely demands a high standard of
proof. It is evident that the onus of proof is on those who believe
that ὀλός and ὀλερός were so used; but I think we ought to suspend
judgment and banish these forms to limbo, until such time as
better evidence can be adduced for them.

ὀξύς

1   The general sense of the word is so close to English *sharp,* that
it might seem unnecessary to devote a note to a detailed investigation. However, on some points I disagree with the analysis of LSJ,
so I have drafted an outline of the way I should revise the article,
though without claiming to have covered it exhaustively.

2   The basic sense is clearly that of physical objects which are
unpleasant to the touch, *having a cutting edge, pointed, sharp*.

ὀξὺ ... βέλος.   Il. 4. 185.

ὀξὺν ἄκοντα.   Il. 10. 335.

ὕπερθεν δὲ σκολόπεσσιν
ὀξέσι ἠρήρει, τοὺς ἵστασαν υἷες Ἀχαιῶν.   Il. 12. 56; 64.

βάλε δ' Ἕκτορος ἡνιοχῆα
... μετώπιον ὀξέϊ λᾶϊ.   Il. 16. 739.

Πηλεΐδης δ' ἄορ ὀξὺ ἐρυσσάμενος παρὰ μηροῦ.
Il. 21. 173; Hes. *Sc.* 457.

ἔκτοσθεν μὲν γὰρ πάγοι ὀξέες.   Od. 5. 411.

μόχλον ... ὀξὺν ἐπ' ἄκρῳ.   Od. 9. 382.

οἱ δὲ δύω σκόπελοι, ὁ μὲν οὐρανὸν εὐρὺν ἱκάνει
ὀξείῃ κορυφῇ.   Od. 12. 74.

λίθος ὀξὺς πεποιημένος (used as the tip of an arrow)
Hdt. 7. 69. 1; 3. 8. 1.

In a figurative phrase:

ἀκτὶς ἀελίου ...
... ὀξυτέρῳ
κινήσασα χαλινῷ. S. *Ant.* 108.

I find it hard to see how LSJ can be right in putting this under *swift*; but a better reading is ὀξυτόρῳ. The neuter is used as a substantive to mean *a sharp end, point.*

τοῦ Δέλτα δὲ τούτου κατὰ τὸ ὀξὺ περιρρήγνυται ὁ Νεῖλος.
Hdt. 2. 16. 2.

δύο ὄρεα ἐς ὀξὺ τὰς κορυφὰς ἀπηγμένα. Hdt. 2. 28. 2.

κυρβασίας (*a kind of headgear*) ἐς ὀξὺ ἀπηγμένας ὀρθὰς εἶχον πεπηγυίας. Hdt. 7. 64. 2.

τὸ ὀξὺ τοῦ ᾠοῦ. Arist. *GA* 752b8.

ἐνταῦθ' ἡ καρδία τὸ ὀξὺ ἔχει. Arist. *Resp.* 478b5.

The feminine ὀξεῖα occurs in a list of surgical instruments, presumably a fine point of some kind (*Hermes* 38. 282).

3 As a subsection I should add here the use in geometry of angles, *acute.*

ὀξεῖα δὲ (γωνία) ἡ ἐλάσσων ὀρθῆς.
Euc. 1. *Def.* 12; Arist. *Top.* 107a16; Archim. *Spir.* 16.

4 From sharp-edged objects the word can be extended to other physical phenomena, which have a similarly unpleasant effect on the senses. Of light, *painfully intense, blinding, dazzling.*

οὐδ' ἂν νῶϊ διαδράκοι Ἥλιός περ,
οὗ τε καὶ ὀξύτατον πέλεται φάος εἰσοράασθαι. Il. 14. 345.

πέπτατο δ' αὐγὴ
ἠελίου ὀξεῖα. Il. 17. 372.

ἕλωρ μένος ὀξέος Ἠελίοιο. h. *Ap.* 374.

Σείριος ... ὀξὺς ἐλλάμπων. Archil. 63 D.

ξειᾶν ὁ γενέθλιος ἀκτίνων πατήρ. Pi. O. 7. 70.

So of white or coloured objects, *bright, brilliant.*

Αἴτνα, πανέτης
χιόνος ὀξείας τιθήνα. Pi. P. 1. 20.

(This example is understood differently by LSJ, but it is hard to say precisely how.)

τρεῖς λόφους ἔχοντα καὶ φοινικίδ᾽ ὀξεῖαν πάνυ.
    Ar. *Pax* 1173; cf. Plu. *Cat. Mi.* 6. 3; Ael. *NA* 4. 46.

αἱ μὲν οὖν χροιαὶ σημαίνουσιν αἱ μὲν ὀξεῖαι θερμὸν καὶ
ὕφαιμον. Arist. *Phgn.* 806^{b}4.

5   It can also be applied to things which have similar effects on the other senses; of hearing, *shrill, piercing.*

                  ὦρτο δ᾽ αὐτὴ
ὀξεῖ᾽ ἀμφοτέρωθεν. Il. 15. 313.

τελευταῖαι δ᾽ ἐπηλάλαξαν
Ἀραὶ τὸν ὀξὺν νόμον. A. *Th.* 954.

ἡ παῖς ὁρᾶται κἀνακωκύει πικρᾶς
ὄρνιθος ὀξὺν φθόγγον. S. *Ant.* 424.

ἡνίκ᾽ ἂν ὁ θεσπέσιος ὀξὺ μέλος ἀχέτας (*sc. the cicada*)
θάλπεσι μεσημβρινοῖς ἡλιομανὴς βοᾷ. Ar. *Av.* 1095.

Contrasted with the basic sense (2 above):

οἷον τῷ ὀξεῖ ἐν φωνῇ μὲν ἐναντίον τὸ βαρύ, ἐν ὄγκῳ δὲ τὸ
ἀμβλύ. Arist. *Top.* 106^{a}13.

This is frequently used in the neuter, singular or plural, adverbially.

    βῆ δὲ ...
ὀξέα κεκληγώς, φλογὶ εἴκελος Ἡφαίστοιο
ἀσβέστῳ· οὐδ᾽ υἱὸν λάθεν Ἀτρέος ὀξὺ βοήσας.
                Il. 17. 88–9; 18. 71; 22. 141.

        ἰάχεσκε σάκος μεγάλῳ ὀρυμαγδῷ
ὀξέα καὶ λιγέως. Hes. *Sc.* 233; 348.

        ὀξέα κλάζων
αἰετός. S. *Ant.* 112.

6   As a subsection we can attach here the special use to refer to musical sounds or the human voice, meaning *high-pitched*:

τοὺς τόνους τῆς φωνῆς ποιούμενον, ὀξύ, βαρύ, μικρόν, μέγα.
                        X. *Cyn.* 6.20.

ἐπισταμένους ὡς οἷόν τε ὀξυτάτην καὶ βαρυτάτην χορδὴν
ποιεῖν. Pl. *Phdr.* 268d.

214 ὀξύς

ὅσοι φθόγγοι ταχεῖς τε καὶ βραδεῖς ὀξεῖς τε καὶ βαρεῖς
φαίνονται. Pl. *Ti*. 80a; Arist. *Rh*. 1403ᵇ29.

This is then used as the name of the rise in pitch indicated by the
acute accent:

προσῳδίας ... ὀξεῖαν βαρεῖαν περισπωμένην.
S. E. *M*. 1. 113; D. T. 674b. 3; 14.

7   Likewise it is used of taste and smell, *pungent*.

ὄψα ... ὅσα ἐστὶν ὀξέα καὶ δριμέα καὶ ἁλμυρά.
X. *Cyr*. 6. 2. 31; Pl. *Ti*. 74c.

ἔστιν ἔνδον ὄξος ὀξύ σοι;   Diph. 18. 1 K–A.

καὶ δριμεῖα καὶ αὐστηρὰ καὶ ὀξεῖα καὶ λιπαρά ἐστιν ὀσμή.
Arist. *de An*. 421ᵃ30.

Adverbially:

ὄζουσι χαῦται πρεσβέων ἐς τὰς πόλεις
ὀξύτατον.   Ar. *Ach*. 193.

8   So of feelings of pain, whether bodily or mental, *intensely dis-
tressing, fierce, keen*:

ὡς δ' ὅτ' ἂν ὠδινοῦσαν ἔχῃ βέλος ὀξὺ γυναῖκα ...
ὣς ὀξεῖ' ὀδύναι δῦνον μένος Ἀτρεΐδαο.   Il. 11. 268, 272 (note
that LSJ quotes from line 272, but gives the reference as 268).

ἄχος ὀξύ.   Il. 19. 125.

ὀξεῖαι μελεδῶναι.   Od. 19. 517.

ὀξεῖαν ἐπιμομφάν.   Pi. *O*. 10. 9.

ὀξείαισι ... πάθαις.   Pi. *P*. 3. 97.

Then of other phenomena, *intense, severe*.

μάχη ὀξέα περὶ τοῦ νεκροῦ γίνεται.   Hdt. 9. 23. 1.

ἔστι δὲ ἡ φλὸξ ὀξυτέρα τούτων.   Thphr. *HP* 5. 9. 3.

τούτοις ὀξύτατος ὁ πυρετὸς ἐκλάμπει.
Hp. *VM* 16; Gal. 9. 887.

ὀξείας δὲ νόσους ἀπαλάλκοι.   Pi. *O*. 8. 85.

ἀπροσίκτων δ' ἐρώτων ὀξύτεραι μανίαι.   Pi. *N*. 11. 48.

9   As applied to persons or animals, *having keen sense perceptions*.

This again can be divided according to the organ of sense involved. Of sight or the eye, *keen, sharp*:

κείνου γὰρ (sc. Λυγκέως) ἐπιχθονίων παν-
των γένετ᾽ ὀξύτατον
ὄμμα. Pi. N. 10. 62.

ὄψις γὰρ ἡμῖν ὀξυτάτη τῶν διὰ τοῦ σώματος ἔρχεται
αἰσθήσεων. Pl. Phdr. 250d.

This is most frequent in the adverbial use:

ἀετός, ὃν ῥά τέ φασιν
ὀξύτατον δέρκεσθαι ὑπουρανίων πετεηνῶν. Il. 17. 675.

ὁ δ᾽ ἄρα σχεδὸν εἴσιδε γαῖαν
ὀξὺ μάλα προϊδών, μεγάλου ὑπὸ κύματος ἀρθείς. Od. 5. 393.

βλέποντ᾽ ἀποδείξω σ᾽ ὀξύτερον τοῦ Λυγκέως.
Ar. Pl. 210; 1048; Lys. 1202.

τῷ ὀξύτατα καθορῶντι τὰ παριόντα. Pl. R. 516c.

10   When applied to living creatures, it means *quick in movement, lively, active*:

ὄφρα κε θᾶσσον ἐγείρομεν ὀξὺν Ἄρηα. Il. 2. 440.

There does not seem to be any reason for preferring a sense of *quick to anger, passionate* (LSJ).

θυμοῦ τ᾽ αὖ μένος ὀξὺ κατισχέμεν. h. Hom. 8. 14; cf.

εἰσὶ χἀτέροις γοναὶ κακαὶ
καὶ θυμὸς ὀξύς. S. OC 1193.

ζευγνυμένους δὲ (τοὺς ἵππους) ὑπ᾽ ἄρματα εἶναι ὀξυτάτους
(s.v.l.) Hdt. 5. 9. 2.

διάφοροι γὰρ πλεῖστον ὄντες τὸν τρόπον, οἱ μὲν ὀξεῖς, οἱ δὲ
βραδεῖς. Th. 8. 96. 5; Pl. Ap. 39b.

ὑπερβολῇ δ᾽ εἰσὶν οἱ ἀκρόχολοι ὀξεῖς.
Arist. EN 1126ᵃ18; EE 1240ᵃ2.

From this it is extended to actions and other things:

κἀκφυσιῶν ὀξεῖαν αἵματος σφαγήν. A. Ag. 1389; cf.

καὶ φυσιῶν ὀξεῖαν ἐκβάλλει ῥοὴν
λευκῇ παρείᾳ φοινίου σταλάγματος. S. Ant. 1238.

λαμπρᾶς γὰρ ἄτερ στεροπᾶς
ᾄξας ὀξὺς νότος ὣς λήγει. S. Aj. 258.

ὀξεῖα γάρ σου βάξις ὡς θεοῦ τινος
διῆλθ᾽ Ἀχαιούς. S. Aj. 998.

Here too belongs a late use, of a military command:

ἵνα ... ὑπ᾽ ὀξὺ παράγγελμα πάντες ὦσιν ἐν τάξει.
Onosander 10. 2.

Equally the use to mean the *express* post (*P. Oxy.* 900.7; 2115. 6,
iv AD). When associated with the action of the verb, we might
translate *quick to*.

ὡς ἥδε μοι
ὀξεῖα φοιτᾷ καὶ ταχεῖ᾽ ἀπέρχεται. S. Ph. 808.

This example seems to me to be wrongly placed with diseases by
LSJ (see 8 above); but the implication is surely that what is quick
to come is also quick to depart.

οἱ δ᾽ ἂν εἴξωσιν αὐτοῖς, κατὰ πόδας τὸ εὔψυχον ἐν τῷ ἀσφαλεῖ
ὀξεῖς ἐνδείκνυνται. 'They are quick to display their courage in
pursuit, when it is safe to do so.' Th. 4. 126. 6.

I believe the following adverbial use would be better placed here,
though it is also possible to regard this as meaning simply 'high-
pitched', 'shrill'.

ὡς ὀξὺ πρὸς τὰς ἰσχάδας κεκράγατε. Ar. Ach. 804.

The situation is that the Megarian is trying to sell off his
daughters as piglets, and when the Athenian offers them chick-
peas (ἐρεβίνθους), they respond, perhaps after being prodded, with
a squeal (κοΐ κοΐ). But then when offered dried figs (and of course
with a *double entendre*), they squeal again, and the Athenian says
'How quick you are to cry out at the mention of figs'.

11 A further development is the use of opportunities as meaning
short-lived, fleeting.

ὁ βίος βραχύς, ἡ δὲ τέχνη μακρή, ὁ δὲ καιρὸς ὀξύς, ἡ δὲ πεῖρα
σφαλερή. Hp. Aph. 1. 1.
ἵνα μὴ ἐν ὀξεῖ καιρῷ θορυβούμενοι ... μηδὲν ... ἀνύσωσι.
Onosander 6. 1.
τότ᾽ ἡνίκ᾽ ἂν ὀξὺς ὁ καιρὸς ὢν διαμέλλειν τῷ γράφοντι μὴ
διδῷ. Longin. 27. 2.

12 Finally we may place *quick in perception, perceptive, keen, sharp*:

δειλῶν τοι τελέθει καρδίη ὀξυτέρη.   Thgn. 366; 1030.

σὺ δὲ
ὀξεῖαν ἀκοὴν τοῖς ἐμοῖς λόγοις δίδους ... S. *El.* 30

οἵ τε φύσει λογιστικοὶ εἰς πάντα τὰ μαθήματα ὡς ἔπος εἰπεῖν
ὀξεῖς φύονται.   Pl. *R.* 526b.

Πῶλος δὲ ὅδε νέος ἐστὶ καὶ ὀξύς.   Pl. *Grg.* 463e.

τὰς ἐνθυμήσεις ὀξύν.   Luc. *Salt.* 81.

Adverbially:

εἰ μὴ ἄρ' ὀξὺ νόησε Διὸς θυγάτηρ Ἀφροδίτη 'if she had not
been quick to notice'.   Il. 3. 374.

ὡς ἔφατ', ὀξὺ δ' ἄκουσεν Ὀϊλῆος ταχὺς Αἴας.   Il. 17. 256.

καὶ τὰ περὶ ταῦτα ὀξὺ μὲν ἀκούουσιν βλέπουσίν τε ὀξύ.
                                                    Pl. *Lg.* 927b.

With infinitive:

οἱ μέν γε νεωτεροποιοὶ καὶ ἐπινοῆσαι ὀξεῖς καὶ ἐπιτελέσαι
ἔργῳ ἃ ἂν γνῶσιν.   Th. 1. 70. 2.

καὶ γνῶναι πάντων ὑμεῖς ὀξύτατοι τὰ ῥηθέντα.   D. 3. 15.

ὀργάω

This is a favourite word in the Hippocratic Corpus, which has
caused difficulty to translators, myself included. As LSJ indicates,
it is used of wounds, ulcers, etc. which can be compared to fully
ripe fruits, ready to burst open. It is also used with the infinitive
to mean to *be keen or anxious to*.

οὐδ' ὀργᾷ τοῦτο δρᾶν.   Hp. *Mul.* 1. 57 (8. 114 L).

But the impersonal use seems to have been overlooked, though one
example is given as a reference only.

πέπονα φαρμακεύειν καὶ κινεῖν, μὴ ὠμά, μηδ' ἐν ἀρχῇσιν, ἢν
μὴ ὀργᾷ· τὰ δὲ πλεῖστα οὐκ ὀργᾷ.   Hp. *Aph.* 1. 22.

This is repeated in slightly different forms elsewhere in the

Corpus. It is of course possible to understand πέπονα as the subject of ὀργᾷ, which seems to be LSJ's interpretation. But this would be little more than a tautology, and there are other examples of the same phrase which make it clear that the verb is here impersonal, e.g.

τὰς κυούσας φαρμακεύειν, ἢν ὀργᾷ, τετράμηνα καὶ ἀχρὶ ἑπτὰ μηνῶν, ἧσσον δὲ ταύτας. 'Pregnant women can be purged, if ..., at four months and up to seven, but less in the latter case.'

Hp. *Aph.* 4. 1.

φαρμακεύειν ἐν τοῖσι λίην ὀξέσιν, ἢν ὀργᾷ, αὐθημερόν· χρονίζειν γὰρ ἐν τοῖσι τοιουτέοισι κακόν. 'Purge in extremely acute cases, if ..., the same day; for delay is bad in such cases.'

Hp. *Aph.* 4. 10.

ὅταν ὧδε ἔχῃ, διδόναι κοῦφα σιτία· κἢν ὀργᾷ, φάρμακον πῖσαι κάτω. 'In such cases give a light diet; and if ..., administer a purgative draught for the bowels.'

Hp. *Mul.* 1. 37 (8. 90 L).

In all these passages the sense which fills the gap is 'if the need is pressing'. So in the first example we should translate: 'Purge and shift what is ripe, not what is unripe, nor at its beginning, unless the need is pressing; and it most cases it is not.'

ὀρχηστής

1 Reluctant as I am to add to the voluminous literature on the subject of the Dipylon Vase (*IG* 1 Suppl. 492a = Schwyzer App. I.a = *LSAG* pl. 1. 1), I feel obliged as a lexicographer to put on record the reasons why I cannot share the current opinion about this inscription. Being possibly the earliest alphabetic Greek text known, it is difficult to judge in comparison with other similar texts, and it is always possible that it is as unique in subject-matter as it is in date. For my purpose the exact date is unimportant, but I accept the opinion of experts that *c.*725 BC is a good estimate. It is worth commenting that it is in the Attic, not Ionic dialect. This is proved by the contracted genitive plural ὀρχε̄στο̂ν, where Ionic would have had -έων or -ήο̄ν, even if scanned as one syllable; cf. Naxian ἀλ(λ)ήο̄ν scanned as a spondee in the famous Nicandre inscription (Schwyzer 758).

2 The reading of the first line presents no difficulties:

ἡὸς νῦν ὀρχε̄στὸν πάντο̄ν ἀταλο̄́τατα παίζει ...

It is the remaining twelve letters which cause the trouble. The reading most widely accepted is: ΤΟΤΟΔΕΚΑΔΜΙΝ. Three explanations of the first six letters have been proposed: (1) τὸτο δέ (= τοῦτο δέ); (2) τὸτο̄ δέ (= τούτου δή); (3) τὸ τόδε (= τοῦ τόδε). Both the first two interpretations are wrecked on the rock of the true diphthong in the first syllable of οὗτος, which cannot therefore be written ο except by error. There is in fact one example of this error: SEG 31. 2. C. 46 has ἕκαστον τοτο[ν = τούτων, but the same inscription has also (A. 42) [τ]ούτο̄ν τὸν πόλεο̄ν. It is true that Mycenaean, which carefully writes true diphthongs with u, has the form to-to ; but it is far from certain that this is a form of τοῦτο and not a reduplication of τό, for even if it goes back to *τοδ-τοδ, this would yield *τοστο, which is also possible as an interpretation of the spelling. On the whole the simplest explanation is undoubtedly the third.

3 The next question raised by the second line is its length. It is not long enough to make even a hemistich up to the caesura, unless we adopt the second interpretation, which offers two and a half feet, but at the expense of a rather gratuitous δή. I know of no completely preserved archaic metrical inscription which follows a complete line with only two feet at most of a second. We have very many instances of metrical inscriptions running to two or more lines; but nowhere do we find anything like the fragmentary lines of the Aeneid. I can only infer that the inscription is incomplete because the writer left his work unfinished. If so, we should be able to suggest some kind of supplement which would restore sense to the whole. Since no elegiacs are known of such archaic date, the line was most probably a hexameter. Now the most likely reason for abandoning an inscription scratched on a fired jar is the consciousness of a mistake. I should therefore propose the smallest correction possible, the change of a poorly written Δ into a N. (For the reading ΚΑΔΜΙΝ see M. Guarducci, Rendiconti dell' Accademia Nazionale dei Lincei, 4:3 (1993), 349–59.) This will give ΚΑΝΜΙΝ, i.e. κἄν μιν ..., as the beginning of the final clause. Purely exempli gratia I might suggest:

τὸ τόδε, κἄν μιν [ἔχε̄ι τεθνεότα δο̂μ' Ἀΐδαο.]

It is all too easily forgotten that the vase was found in a cemetery, and must have been used in the funeral rites, not just buried with the ashes. I am not alone in taking the text as unfinished; see for instance most recently Y. Duhoux, *Kadmos,* 30 (1991) 165.

4 We can now revert to line 1. The first point I want to make is that it is a statement of fact, not a potential. Although *ΠΑΙΖΕΙ* might theoretically be subjunctive, the absence of ἄν or any other particle ensures that the reader would take it for an indicative. It is thus clearly to be distinguished from such an apparent parallel as the Ischia cup (for a bibliography see A. Heubeck, 'Die Schrift', in *Archaeologia Homerica,* X 199–200):

> hòs δ' ἄν τόδε πίϵσι ποτϵρί[ō] 'whoever drinks from this cup ...'

I propose to translate into Latin rather than English or any other modern language because this allows us to keep closer to a word-for-word version.

> *Qui nunc saltatorum omnium delicatissime ludit, ejus hoc, quamuis eum [teneat mortuum domus Ditis.]*

The temporal word νῦν (which cannot be read νυν for metrical reasons) must go closely with ὀρχϵστόν; i.e. the equivalent in prose would be τῶν νῦν ὀρχηστῶν 'the dancers of the present day'. Ἀταλός, probably an artificial back-formation from ταλάφρων, has very much the semantic range of Latin *delicatus.* Παίζει must not be translated 'performs'; it is quite specifically 'sports', and its connexion with παῖς is never far from the mind. I submit therefore that such language can only be used by a lover to describe his youthful partner.

5 It is now clear that ὀρχηστής in such a context cannot refer to the victor in some dancing competition. In fact, the idea of presenting the victor with a previously inscribed cup is a familiar one to us, but has no parallels in antiquity. We have countless dedications by victors of their prize; but without exception these record the name of the dedicator and usually the deity to whom it is offered. Thus we must ask whether ὀρχηστής might refer to sexual activity; and the answer is provided by the series of archaic graffiti from Thera, e.g.

Βάρβακς ὀρκḡστά[ς] τε ἀγαθός ...   IG 12(3). 536ff.

(Schwyzer 214).

Ἐνπεδοκλῆς ἐνεϨόπτετο τάδε Ϩώρκêτο μὰ τὸν Ἀπό(λ)λω.

IG 12(3). 536.

Εὔμηλος ἄριστος ὀρκḡστά[ς]   Ibid. 540. II, cf. 546.

There is also in these graffiti a strange word κονίαλος, which must be a form of κονίσαλος, glossed by Hesychius as meaning an obscene dance. The repeated presence of ὀρχηστής in these contexts creates a strong case for assuming a similar meaning was intended by the author of the inscription on the Dipylon Vase.

ὅσιος

1   Many users of LSJ must have been puzzled to find that a word which is translated *holy* can in certain contexts bear the meaning *profane*. It is therefore a prime candidate for more detailed investigation, for although a word can in the course of time come to mean its opposite, this is hardly likely to occur contemporaneously.

2   A preliminary point concerns the relationship of ὅσιος to the substantive ὁσία. It is simple to say with Frisk (*GEW*, accepted by Chantraine, *DELG*) that ὁσία stands for *ὁσι-ία, but this does not explain why the substantive antedates the adjective by several centuries. Ὁσία, more often in its Ionic form ὁσίη, is in the Odyssey and Attic tragedy, but is rare in prose; an example in Iamblichus is not likely to come from the normal language of the time. Ὅσιος does not seem to be attested before vi BC (Theognis), but it remains in good prose use for centuries. Possibly ὁσία and ὅσιος are both derivatives of a stem which has been lost, very likely as the result of becoming a homophone of ὅσος, like ἐλευθερία and ἐλευθέριος from ἐλεύθερος. This might account for the fact that ὁσία does not mean exactly 'the quality of being ὅσιος'. It will therefore be convenient to start with an analysis of the substantive.

3   The Homeric sense is clearly *conduct pleasing to the gods, propriety, right*:

οὐδ' ὁσίη κακὰ ῥάπτειν ἀλλήλοισιν.   Od. 16. 423.

οὐχ ὁσίη κταμένοισιν ἐπ' ἀνδράσιν εὐχετάασθαι.   Od. 22. 412.

φιλεῖ δέ σε μητίετα Ζεὺς
ἐκ πάσης ὁσίης 'as is wholly proper'.   h. Merc. 470.

In later epic:

σύ γ' ἀείσῃ καὶ τά περ οὐχ ὁσίη.   Call. Aet. 31. 5 (= 75. 7).

Elsewhere:

ὁσία κλυτὰν χέρα οἱ προσενεγκεῖν
ἦρα καὶ ἐκ λεχέων κεῖραι μελιαδέα ποίαν;   Pi. P. 9. 36.

καὶ ταύτης (τελετῆς) μοι πέρι εὔστομα κείσθω, πλὴν ὅσον
ὁσίη ἐστὶ λέγειν.   Hdt. 2. 171. 2.

τοῖσι γὰρ οὐδὲ κτήνεα ὁσίη θύειν ἐστί.   Hdt. 2. 45. 2.

ὁσίας ἕκατι θεά θ' ὅπως τιμὰς ἔχῃ.   E. IT 1461.

A similar expression, ὁσίας ἕνεκα, is found in a comic fragment
variously attributed (Eub. 110 = 109 K–A, Ephipp. 15. 4; LSJ
quotes these references as if they were separate examples).

καὶ οὔτε θεοὺς οὔθ' ὁσίαν οὔτ' ἄλλ' οὐδὲν ἐποιήσατ' ἐμποδὼν
τοιούτῳ λόγῳ, οὔθ' ὤκηνσεν.   D. 21. 104.

Humorously:

κἀγὼ νομίσας πολλὴν ὁσίαν τοῦ πράγματος.   Ar. Pl. 682.

To this we may attach two examples in Euripides where ὁσία is
personified:

Ὁσία πότνα θεῶν,
Ὁσία δ' ἃ κατὰ γᾶν
χρυσέαν πτέρυγα φέρεις
τάδε Πενθέως ἀίεις;   E. Ba. 370.

ἀπέπτυσ'· Ὁσίᾳ γὰρ δίδωμ' ἔπος τόδε.   E. IT 1161.

4   It is easy to see how this general sense was then particularised
to mean a specific religious rite or observance:

ὡς γὰρ τὰ πρώτισθ' ὁσίη γένεθ', οἱ δὲ ἄνακτι
εὔχονται.   h. Ap. 237.

ἔνθ' ὁσίης κρεάων ἠράσσατο κύδιμος Ἑρμῆς.
h. Merc. 130; also 173.

καὶ λιτῇ προσγελάσαις ὁσίῃ 'and may you smile upon our
frugal rite.'   AP 9. 91.

παρέμεινέ τε ἄχρι τῆς τελευτῆς αὐτῷ καὶ τὴν ὁσίαν
ἀπεπλήρωσε. Iamb. *VP* 30. 184.

There is no need to follow LSJ in giving the last example a special
sense *funeral rites;* it is obvious from the context what rite is
meant.

5 With this introduction we can now turn to the adjective ὅσιος.
Its primary sense is clearly of persons to mean *observing the
religious code, showing reverence for divine order*. It is thus close
to Latin *pius,* but English *pious* is rather misleading; perhaps
righteous is the English word which comes nearest to its sense, and
this will also cover the cases where it is applied to deities. The
earliest example applied to persons seems to be in a Law of Solon
about justifiable homicide quoted by Andocides:

ὁ δὲ ἀποκτείνας τὸν τοιαῦτα ποιήσαντα καὶ ὁ συμβουλεύσας
ὅσιος ἔστω καὶ εὐαγής. And. 1. 96.

It is probably wrong to give this the legal sense of *justified;* as
εὐαγής implies, it refers to freedom from religious guilt. In verse:

καὶ Ζεὺς σωτὴρ τρίτος, οἰκοφύλαξ
ὁσίων ἀνδρῶν. A. *Supp.* 27.

φιλόξενοι δὲ χὤσιοι περὶ ξένους; E. *Cyc.* 125.

          Παλλάδος
ὁσίαν ἥξεις πόλιν. E. *El.* 1320.

Ζεὺς ἐξ ἐμοῦ μὲν οὐκ ἀκούσεται κακῶς·
εἰ δ' ἐστὶν ὅσιος αὐτὸς οἶδεν εἰς ἐμέ. E. *Heracl.* 719.

ἐγὦδ', ἀνόσιός εἰμι μητέρα κτανών,
ὅσιος δέ γ' ἕτερον ὄνομα, τιμωρῶν πατρί. E. *Or.* 547.

ὁσίους ἐς θιασώτας. Ar. *Ra.* 327.

By a natural extension it can be used of hands or mouths:

πρῶτον μὲν ἱρὰς ἐξ ἀειρύτου χοὰς
κρήνης ἐνεγκοῦ, δι' ὁσίων χειρῶν θιγών. S. *OC* 470.

ἐκ δ' ὁσίων στομάτων καθαρὴν ὀχετεύσατε πηγήν.
                                        Emp. 3. 7.
In prose:

σεμνοὶ μὲν πρὸς τοὺς θεοὺς τῷ δικαίῳ, ὅσιοι δὲ πρὸς τοὺς
τοκέας τῇ θεραπείᾳ, δίκαιοι δὲ πρὸς τοὺς ἀστοὺς τῷ ἴσῳ,
εὐσεβεῖς δὲ πρὸς τοὺς φίλους τῇ πίστει. Gorg. 6.

This shows clearly the idea of *pietas*, here expressed in reverence for parents.

ὅτι ὅσιοι πρὸς οὐ δικαίους ἱστάμεθα. Th. 5. 104.

The idea is that 'we have the gods on our side'.

καὶ ὅσους μὲν αἰσθάνοιτο ἐπιόρκους καὶ ἀδίκους ὡς εὖ ὡπλισμένους ἐφοβεῖτο, τοῖς δὲ ὁσίοις καὶ ἀλήθειαν ἀσκοῦσιν ὡς ἀνάνδροις ἐπειρᾶτο χρῆσθαι. X. *An.* 2. 6. 25.

As the title of some priests at Delphi:

ὁσιωτῆρα μὲν καλοῦσι τὸν θυόμενον ἱερεῖον, ὅταν ὅσιος ἀποδειχθῇ. πέντε δ' εἰσὶν ὅσιοι διὰ βίου ...

Plu. 2. 292d; 365a.

There does not seem to be any reason to regard the meaning as specialised in the following example, though LSJ translates it 'the saints':

ψάλατε τῷ Κυρίῳ οἱ ὅσιοι αὐτοῦ. LXX *Ps.* 29(30). 4.

With a genitive, presumably meaning *observant (of)*:

ἱερῶν πατρῴων δ' ὅσιος ὢν μομφῆς ἄτερ τέθνηκεν. A. *Th.* 1010.

6   From this it is naturally extended to actions and things used in actions:

οἶσ' ὁσίη, Κύρνε, μέμηλε δίκη. Thgn. 132.

τρίποδ' ἀμφίπυρον λουτρῶν ὁσίων θέσθ' ἐπίκαιρον. S. *Aj.* 1405.

ἐν ὄρεσσι βακχεύων ὁσίοις καθαρμοῖσιν. E. *Ba.* 77.

δεῖ με δεύτερον μέλος χέρνιβι θεοσεβὲς ὅσιον ἐπιβοᾶν. Ar. *Av.* 898.

Neuter as substantive:

ἀποδίδοντες ποιέετε ὅσια. Hdt. 6. 86. a. 1.

ὅσια μὲν ποιεῖν, ὅσια δὲ καὶ λέγειν. Hdt. 9. 79. 2.

ὅσιά τε φωνεῖς ἔστι τ', ὦ τέκνον, θέμις. S. *Ph.* 662.

ἢ τοὺς τεκόντας ὅσια δρᾶν δίκαιος ὤν. E. *Hipp.* 1081.

θεοὺς ὅσιόν τι δράσας. E. *Supp.* 40.

τῶν δίκαια καὶ ὅσια πρασσόντων.   Antipho 2. 2. 2.

As an abstract:

οὐ ταὐτόν ἐστιν ἐν πάσῃ πράξει τὸ ὅσιον αὐτὸ αὑτῷ ... ;
Pl. *Euthphr.* 5d; 12d.

Ὅσιόν ἐστι + infinitive:
οὐ γάρ σοι θέμις
οὐδ' ὅσιον ἐχθρᾶς ἀπὸ γυναικὸς ἱστάναι
κτερίσματ'.   S. *El.* 432.

θιγεῖν γὰρ ὅσιόν ἐστ' ἐμοὶ μόνῃ.   E. *IT* 1045.

οὐ γὰρ ἂν νόμιμον οὐδ' ὅσιον ἂν εἴη.   Pl. *Lg.* 861d.

In the comparative:

καὶ γὰρ ⟨ἂν⟩ δικαιότερον καὶ ὁσιώτερον καὶ πρὸς θεῶν καὶ
πρὸς ἀνθρώπων γίγνοιτ' ὑμῖν.   Antipho 1. 25.

With negative, οὐχ ὅσιος is an alternative to ἀνόσιος = *impious,
wicked*:

αἱ ταφαὶ τοῦ οὐκ ὅσιον ποιοῦμαι ... ἐξαγορεύειν τοὔνομα.
Hdt. 2. 170. 1.

ἀίεις οὐχ ὁσίαν
ὕβριν ἐς τὸν Βρόμιον.   E. *Ba.* 374.

οὐχ ὁσίων ἐρώτων.   E. *Hipp.* 764.

δέξαι θυσίας,
ἃς ὁ παρ' ἡμῖν νόμος οὐχ ὁσίας
ἀναφαίνει.   E. *IT* 465.

καὶ πρὸς ἅπαντας ἀγαθῷ εἶναι οὐχ ὅσιον ἡγοῦμαι.
D. *Ep.* 5. 3.

7   By a further natural extension the adjective may be applied to
anything which is *sanctioned by divine law, due*:

μηδ' ἐλινύσαιμι θεοὺς ὁσίαις
θοίναις ποτινισομένα
'May I not cease approaching the gods with due banquets.'
A. *Pr.* 529.

ὦ πότνι' Εἰλείθυι' ἐπίσχες τοῦ τόκου,
ἕως ἂν εἰς ὅσιον μόλω 'γὼ χώριον.   Ar. *Lys.* 743.

It is often used of money due for religious reasons:

ἀργυρίō hοσίō [κεφάλαιο]ν.   *IG* 1². 186.

εἰς δὲ τὸ ἀνάλωμα τὸν ταμίαν τῶν ὁσίων ὑ[πηρετῆ]σαι.
SEG 1. 366. 58 (Samos, iii BC).

In the neuter ὅσια can have a more general sense of *religious dues*:

hόπō ξένον ὅσια λανχάνειν καὶ θύειν ἐξεῖμεν ἐπιτυχόντα. 'If he happens to be present he is to be permitted to receive religious dues and to sacrifice as a stranger.'
Schwyzer 362. 2 (Oeanthea, v BC).

οὐδὲ ὅσια τὴν ἐκείνου κτῆσιν τῇ τοῦ θνητοῦ χρυσοῦ κτήσει συμμείγνυντας μιαίνειν. Pl. R. 416e.

There is often a reference to payments made for religious reasons, and thus a contrast between ὅσια *religious revenues,* and ἱερά *religious possessions*:

ἐς ὀλιγωρίαν ἐτράποντο καὶ ἱερῶν καὶ ὁσίων ὁμοίως 'they became equally contemptuous of the gods' property and their dues'. Th. 2. 52. 3.

τυραννίς, ἢ ... τἀλλότρια ... ἀφαιρεῖται, καὶ ἱερὰ καὶ ὅσια καὶ ἴδια καὶ δημόσια. Pl. R. 344a; cf. Lg. 857b.

τὴν μὲν δημοκρατίαν οὕτω κοσμήσασαν τὴν πόλιν καὶ τοῖς ἱεροῖς καὶ τοῖς ὁσίοις. Isoc. 7. 66.

The only example where there might be a contrast between *sacred* and *profane,* as alleged by LSJ, is:

τὸν νόμον, δι' οὗ τῶν ἱερῶν μὲν χρημάτων τοὺς θεούς, τῶν ὁσίων δὲ τὴν πόλιν ἀποστερεῖ. D. 24. 9.

But the contrast is rhetorical rather than real. 'By this law he will deprive the gods of their property and the city of its religious dues.' He is probably thinking of profits such as the banking charges levied by Athena for holding the treasury. The meaning *profane* may thus be safely banished from our lexica.

παρθένος

1 LSJ begins its article with '*maiden, girl*', adding later '*virgin,* opp. γυνή'. This leads to sense 2 'of unmarried women who are not virgins'. One can almost feel the implied disapproval of the Victorian clerics. It was of course no different in antiquity, but women in epic times faced the additional hazard of being seduced

by a god, so it is strange LSJ did not attempt to mitigate their disgrace by making a separate section for virgins who gave birth to the children of gods; there is no lack of material. But a close reading of the passages where the word is used in early or classical times reveals that it is a *social* and not a *biological* term. Once correctly defined, the physical condition of the girl can be seen to be irrelevant.

2   I propose therefore a rather long-winded definition, but one I believe to be necessary to account for the observed facts: *a female who has reached the age of puberty but remains a member of her father's household*. The old-fashioned word *spinster* is perhaps the nearest English equivalent. For practical purposes the translation *girl* is usually adequate, but it must be observed that it cannot be used of younger children, as the English word can. The time of her marriage was the fundamental turning-point in a Greek woman's life; as the saying went

> δύ' ἡμέραι γυναικός εἰσιν ἥδισται·
> ὅταν γάμῃ τις, κἀκφέρῃ τεθνηκυῖαν.   Hippon. 68 M.

At this point she left her father's house for her husband's, and was henceforth known by his name, since the given name of a respectable woman was never used in public. These two facts express the difference between a παρθένος and a γυνή, and this is neatly stated by Sophocles:

> ἕως τις ἀντὶ παρθένου γυνὴ
> κληθῇ, λάβῃ τ' ἐν νυκτὶ φροντίδων μέρος,
> ἤτοι πρὸς ἀνδρὸς ἢ τέκνων φοβουμένη.   S. *Tr.* 148.

3   The case of what we used call 'unmarried mothers'—probably an unacceptable term in these enlightened days—is of course covered by this definition. So Homer giving the genealogy of Askalaphos and Ialmenos:

> οὓς τέκεν Ἀστυόχη δόμῳ Ἄκτορος Ἀζείδαο,
> παρθένος αἰδοίη, ὑπερώϊον εἰσαναβᾶσα,
> Ἄρηι κρατερῷ.   Il. 2. 514.

She is respected (αἰδοίη) for being the choice of a god. So too Herakles in the *Trachiniae* commends his old flame Iole to his son Hyllos as παρθένος:

—τὴν Εὐρυτείαν οἶσθα δῆτα παρθένον;
—Ἰόλην ἔλεξας, ὥς γ᾽ ἐπεικάζειν ἐμέ. S. Tr. 1219.

Disapproval in classical times is evident:

τὰς παρθένους οὐ φυλάσσουσι, ἀλλ᾽ ἐῶσι τοῖσι αὐταὶ
βούλονται ἀνδράσι μίσγεσθαι· τὰς γυναῖκας ἰσχυρῶς
φυλάσσουσι. Hdt. 5. 6. 1.

Here too belongs a humorous use by Aristophanes, comparing
himself on his début as a playwright to a παρθένος who has left her
child to be fostered by another.

κἀγώ, παρθένος γὰρ ἔτ᾽ ἦν, κοὐκ ἐξῆν πώ μοι τεκεῖν,
ἐξέθηκα, παῖς δ᾽ ἑτέρα τις λαβοῦσ᾽ ἀνείλετο. Ar. Nu. 530.

4 The age at which a girl became παρθένος is clearly defined for
us by Hippocrates, for in his case-notes he records that a girl had
her first menstruation during the course of her illness, adding the
explanation:

παρθένος γὰρ ἦν. Hp. Epid. 3. 17. 12.

The end of the period is defined by marriage, as among the
Sarmatians:

οὐ γαμέεται παρθένος οὐδεμία πρὶν τῶν πολεμίων ἄνδρα
ἀποκτείνῃ. Hdt. 4. 117; cf. Hp. Aër. 17.

τῷ βασιλέϊ μοῦνοι τὰς παρθένους μελλούσας συνοικέειν
ἐπιδεικνύουσι· ἡ δὲ ἂν τῷ βασιλέϊ ἀρεστὴ γένηται, ὑπὸ τούτου
διαπαρθενεύεται. Hdt. 4. 168. 2.

If she remained unmarried, the term παρθένος could continue to be
used.

ἡ παρθένος ἡ καλὴ ἡ τοῦ Νερίου ἦν μὲν εἰκοσαέτης, ὑπὸ δὲ
γυναίου φίλης παιζούσης ... ἐπλήγη. Hp. Epid. 5. 50.

5 I have been unable to discover any passage in classical Greek
where παρθένος must have the biological sense of virgin, familiar as
this is, both from the adjectival use (see LSJ II) and in compounds. The only example I have located is from Daphnis and
Chloe, though I suspect a thorough search would produce more.

τὸν δὲ Δάφνιν ὁ Διονυσιφάντης ἀναστήσας μόνον ἀνέκρινεν εἰ
παρθένος ἐστί. Long. 4. 31.

Where this sense is required in earlier Greek, an epithet must be added.

ὡς ἥ γ' ἀμφιπόλοισι μετέπρεπε παρθένος ἀδμής.
Od. 6. 109; 228.

παρθένῳ ἀδμήτῃ μέγεθος καὶ εἶδος ὁμοίη.   h. Ven. 82.

νέαι παλαιαὶ παρθένοι τ' ἔτ' ἄζυγες.   E. Ba. 694.

6   It hardly needs to be added that the virginity of the mother of Jesus Christ does not depend upon her description as παρθένος, which here bears its normal sense; the misunderstanding has been attributed to a Greek Bible used by Matthew (1. 22) which translated the Hebrew word for 'young woman' as παρθένος (A. Richardson, *An Introduction to the Theology of the New Testament* (London, 1958), 173). In fact the translation is perfectly correct. But we have the express statement in Luke's Gospel.

πῶς ἔσται τοῦτο, ἐπεὶ ἄνδρα οὐ γινώσκω;   Ev. Luc. 1. 34.

She was of course taken as a wife by Joseph before giving birth, so that at this time she was no longer παρθένος but γυνή.

πάσχω

1   The basic sense of this verb is easy enough to grasp, but in view of its passive meaning is not easy to define accurately. It can perhaps best be regarded as meaning *be the recipient of* an experience, *have* something *happen to one, undergo, experience*. It does not matter whether the experience is pleasant or unpleasant, but the nature of human life perhaps ensures that the latter type predominates, and this is the starting-point for a development of the sense (see 5 below). LSJ (**I, II**) attempts a distinction between '*have* something *done to one*' and '*have* something *happen to one*'; but this is an unreal distinction, since it appears to separate events which are due to known causes from those which are the result of chance. There may be a difference of construction in that the first type may have an agent expressed, but the effect on the subject of the verb is no different. On the other hand there is a real difference between the transitive uses, where the experience is indicated as the object of the verb and the intransitive one where it is construed with an adverb. LSJ confuses these in **III**. I propose to quote only

a few examples of the more important usages, since the full coverage can be supplied from LSJ and other sources.

2 First then the basic sense as defined above:

πήματ' ἔπασχον. Il. 5. 886.

ἀλλὰ τίη νῦν οὗτος ἀναίτιος ἄλγεα πάσχει ...; Il. 20. 297.

καὶ κήδεά περ πεπαθυίη. Od. 17. 555.

οὐ πάθοντες οὐδάμα πῶσλον οὐ[δέ]ν. Alc. 69. 5; cf. Pi. P. 9. 89.

τάλαν γένος. —τάλανα παθόν. A. Th. 983.

ἴδεσθέ μ', οἷα πρὸς θεῶν πάσχω θεός. A. Pr. 92.

ἐπ' αὐτὸν (sc. ὗν) ἐξελθόντες ποιέεσκον μὲν κακὸν οὐδέν, ἔπασχον δὲ πρὸς αὐτοῦ. Hdt. 1. 36. 1.

τερπνὸν εἴ τι που πάθοι. S. Aj. 521.

ὅπερ νῦν ὑμεῖς ... ἐς Λακεδαιμονίους πεπόνθατε. Th. 6. 11. 5.

τί χρῆμα πάσχεις ὦ πάτερ; Ar. Nu. 816.

πολλὰ γὰρ φιλικὰ ἔπαθον ὑπ' ἐκείνου. X. Cyr. 4. 6. 6.

καί τι ἔφη αὐτόθι γελοῖον παθεῖν. Pl. Smp. 174e.

3 There are two uses of the phrase τί πάθω; One is that which might be expected, namely, 'what am I to undergo?' or as we should say 'what is to become of me?'

ὤ μοι ἐγώ, τί πάθω; Il. 11. 404.

τί γὰρ πάθωμεν μὴ βουλομένων ὑμέων τιμωρέειν;
　　　　　　　　　　　　　　　　　Hdt. 4. 118. 3.

τί γὰρ πάθω; σκάπτειν γὰρ οὐκ ἐπίσταμαι. Ar. Av. 1432.

But it is also used to mean 'what else am I to undergo?' or as we should say 'what else can I do?'

ὡς παῖδα ...
λούσω προθῶμαί θ'—ὡς μὲν ἀξία, πόθεν;
οὐκ ἂν δυναίμην· ὡς δ' ἔχω—τί γὰρ πάθω—
κόσμον τ' ἀγείρασ' αἰμαλωτίδων πάρα ... E. Hec. 614.

ἢ οὐ σοὺς ὡμολόγηκας αὐτοὺς εἶναι; —ὡμολόγηκα, ἔφην· τί γὰρ πάθω; Pl. Euthd. 302d.

4 Intransitively with adverbs, be treated in a specified manner.

κακῶς πάσχοντος ἐμεῖο. Od. 16. 275.

ἥτις ἐκ Διὸς πάσχω κακῶς.   A. *Pr.* 759.

εὖ δρῶσαν, εὖ πάσχουσαν, εὖ τιμωμένην.   A. *Eu.* 868.

ἀνθ' ὧν ἔπασχον εὖ τελεσφόρον χάριν
δοῦναί σφιν.   S. *OC* 1489.

οὐ γὰρ πάσχοντες εὖ, ἀλλὰ δρῶντες κτώμεθα τοὺς φίλους.
Th. 2. 40. 4.

However, εὖ πάσχειν is also used with a genitive to mean *have the enjoyment of*:

τῶν αὐτοῦ κτεάνων εὖ πασχέμεν.   Thgn. 1009.

ἐόντων εὖ τε παθεῖν καὶ ἀκοῦσαι φίλοις ἐξαρκέων.   Pi. *N.* 1. 32.

5   As indicated above, the verb develops the extended sense of *undergo something unpleasant, suffer*:

πόλλ' ἔπαθες καὶ πόλλ' ἐμόγησας.   Il. 23. 607.

παθὼν δέ τε νήπιος ἔγνω.   Hes. *Op.* 218.

ὑπὲρ δὲ τῆς αὐτῶν πλεονεξίας ἑτοίμοις οὖσιν ὁτιοῦν πάσχειν.
Isoc. 12. 133.

εἰκός τι πάσχειν. 'There must be something the matter with him.'   Men. *Kith.* 49.

This is frequently used in a judicial context to mean *incur a penalty*:

ὁ γροφεὺς ταὐτά κα πάσκοι, [αἴ τ]ιν' [ἀζ]ικέο[ι]. 'The scribe is to incur the same penalty, if he wrongs anyone.'
Schwyzer 409. 8 (Elis, v BC).

ἐν ᾗ (δίκῃ) αὐτὸν ἔδει κριθῆναι ὅ τι δεῖ παθεῖν ἢ ἀποτεῖσαι.
X. *Mem.* 2. 9. 5; Pl. *Plt.* 299a.

Under this head we may classify the expression ἤν τι πάθω and similar forms, where τι is understood to mean something unpleasant, and this is used as a euphemism for dying, exactly like Latin *si quid mihi acciderit* and English *if anything happens to me*. It does not of course *mean* 'if I suffer death'; the whole point of the expression is that it avoids any specific mention of death.

Μαρδονίου δέ, ἤν τι πάθῃ, λόγος οὐδεὶς γίνεται.
Hdt. 8. 102. 3.

εἰ ... ἔπαθέ τι πρὶν καταπλεῦσαι δεῦρο.   Lys. 19. 51; D. 4. 11.

οὐδ᾽ εἴ τι πάθοις.   Theoc. 8. 10.

This can even be used of things, i.e. *suffer damage, be lost*:

ἐὰν δέ τι πάσχō, μελεδαίνēν με, ὃ Σιγειές (*monumentum loquitur*).   Schwyzer 731. B. 7 (Attic, vi BC).

ἤν τι ναῦς πάθῃ.   E. *IT* 755; Syngr. ap. [D.] 35. 13.

A similar meaning seems likely in the following passage, though the New Supplement appears to differ:

καλὸς ἑαυτῷ φανεὶς καὶ παθών τι πρὸς τὴν ὄψιν 'suffering damage to his face'.   Plu. 2. 682b.

6   There remain, however, some examples where the object of the verb is not so much an experience as a state of mind. It is natural that this should be the case where the perfect aspect is employed, but other tenses are also found in this sense. It is not always easy to identify these, but the following may serve as specimens.

τοιαῦτα δὲ ὁ Εὔφημος εἶπεν. οἱ δὲ Καμαριναῖοι ἐπεπόνθεσαν τοιόνδε· τοῖς μὲν Ἀθηναίοις εὖνοι ἦσαν ... 'the effect on the Camarinaeans was as follows'.   Th. 6. 88. 1.

ὅ τι μὲν ὑμεῖς ... πεπόνθατε ὑπὸ τῶν ἐμῶν κατηγόρων, οὐκ οἶδα. 'I do not know what effect my accusers have had on you.'
Pl. *Ap.* 17a; *Phd.* 98c.

In the present or aorist systems:

ὑμεῖς τὰ αὐτὰ πρὸς ἐμὲ πάσχετε οἷάπερ ἐγὼ πρὸς τὸν ἐμοὶ δοκοῦντα καλὸν εἶναι. 'you receive the same sort of impression from me as I do from one who appears to me to be beautiful'.
X. *Smp.* 4. 11.

ἀλλ᾽ ἀδίδακτος ἂν εἰσῆλθεν ὁ χορὸς καὶ πράγματ᾽ αἴσχιστ᾽ ἂν ἐπάθομεν 'we should have received a most disgraceful impression'.   D. 21. 17.

Absolutely ὁ πάσχων means 'one who receives impressions, one who feels'.

ὁ μὲν γὰρ σώφρων ὁ μὴ πάσχων, ὁ δὲ ἐγκρατὴς ὁ πάσχων καὶ τούτων κρατῶν ἢ οἷός τε ὢν πάσχειν.   Arist. *MM* 1203ᵇ21.

7   Homer has an idiom with the participle, τί παθών, meaning 'how does it happen that ...'

Τυδεΐδη, τί παθόντε λελάσμεθα θουρίδος ἀλκῆς; 'what has happened to make us forget ...?' Il. 11. 313.

Ἀμφίμεδον, τί παθόντες ἐρεμνὴν γαῖαν ἔδυτε
πάντες κεκριμένοι καὶ ὁμήλικες; Od. 24. 106.

8 It is also used where the subject is in no way concerned in the action of the verb, so that it can be used of things as well as people. This may be defined as *have* something *happen in one's case*, though we should naturally employ a different idiom in English.

πεπόνθασι δὲ οὔτι μοῦναι αἱ Ἰώνων ὁρταὶ τοῦτο, ἀλλὰ καὶ Ἑλλήνων πάντων ὁμοίως πᾶσαι ἐς τωὐτὸ γράμμα τελευτῶσι 'it is by no means only the Ionians' festivals of which this is true'. Hdt. 1. 148. 2.

εἰ ἐτησίαι αἴτιοι ἦσαν, χρῆν καὶ τοὺς ἄλλους ποταμούς ... ὁμοίως πάσχειν καὶ κατὰ ταὐτὰ τῷ Νείλῳ. Hdt. 2. 20. 3.

πάσχει δὲ ταὐτὸ τοῦτο καὶ τὰ κάρδαμα. 'The very same happens in the case of watercress.' Ar. *Nu.* 234.

ὅπερ γὰρ οἱ τὰς ἐγχέλεις θηρώμενοι πέπονθας.
                Ar. *Eq.* 864; *V.* 946, 947.

ὅτι υἱκὸν αὐτῷ δοκοίη πάσχειν ὁ Κριτίας. X. *Mem.* 1. 2. 30.

σχεδὸν οἷον τὰ γράμματα πεπονθότ' ἂν εἴη. Pl. *Sph.* 253a.

ὁρᾶτε μὴ βουλόμενοι τοὺς πολεμίους τιμωρήσασθαι τὸ αὐτὸ πάθητε τῷ ἵππῳ. Arist. *Rh.* 1393[b]20.

πέμπω

1 LSJ distinguishes five main senses in the active and two in the middle, but devotes a great deal of space in sense **I** to the various constructions which may accompany it. Since these obviously cut across the semantic divisions, they are much better left to be exemplified under the different senses. As I shall demonstrate, sense **II** 'send forth or away' and sense **III** 'conduct, escort' conceal the existence of a sense *provide with means of travel*, which allows a regrouping of these examples into a better pattern. Nor is sense **IV** 'send as a present' properly distinguished; it comes under the heading of sending any tangible object, such as a letter, and is not

confined to presents. Sense **V** 'send up, produce' is a single poetic example which can be better interpreted in a way which allows us to relate it to at least one other example (see 3 below). I have therefore sorted the more important examples on semantic lines, ignoring in most cases the accompanying prepositions.

2 It will be as well to start with living creatures (thus including gods and animals as well as persons) who are able to move themselves. In this case πέμπω is semantically a causative verb and can be translated *make to go,* a definition we could hardly apply to sending a letter.

Ἕκτωρ δὲ προτὶ ἄστυ δύω κήρυκας ἔπεμπε. Il. 3. 116.

Here the destination is stated, and the fact that the next line contains two epexegetic infinitives does not affect the semantic analysis of the verb:

καρπαλίμως ἄρνας τε φέρειν Πρίαμόν τε καλέσσαι.

The use of the imperfect is interesting, for it is especially frequent with this verb, implying that the journey is regarded as a process, not an event; cf. πορεύομαι. Similarly:

οἱ δ' ἅμ' Ἀχιλλῆϊ ῥηξήνορι πέμπον ἕπεσθαι
Ἴλιον εἰς εὔπωλον, ἵνα Τρώεσσι μάχοιτο. Il. 16. 575.

τὴν μὲν Ἀχιλλῆος ῥηξήνορος υἱέϊ πέμπεν. Od. 4. 5.

Poetically:

πέμπειν μιν Θάνατόν τε φέρειν καὶ νήδυμον Ὕπνον 'send Death and sweet Sleep to carry him'. Il. 16. 454.

With the point of origin stated:

φράζεο μή τις ἔπειτα θεῶν ἐθέλησι καὶ ἄλλος
πέμπειν ὃν φίλον υἱὸν ἀπὸ κρατερῆς ὑσμίνης. Il. 16. 447.

ὣς εἰπὼν τὸν κριὸν ἀπὸ ἕο πέμπε θύραζε. Od. 9. 461.

Neither of these examples is placed by LSJ in sense **II** *send forth* or *away*. In later Greek:

τῶν δορυφόρων τινὰς πέμπει κελεύων φυλάξαι ὅ τι χρήσεται ἡ γυνή. Hdt. 5. 12. 3; 7. 15. 1; Th. 1. 129. 3.

μήτηρ με πέμπει πατρὶ τυμβεῦσαι χοάς. S. El. 406.

With internal accusative:

> βραδεῖαν ἡμᾶς ἆρ' ὁ τήνδε τὴν ὁδὸν
> πέμπων ἔπεμψεν. 'it was a slow journey then, this that we were
> sent on.' S. *Aj.* 739; *El.* 1163.

With accusative of destination:

> ἐξικέτευσε τῆς ἐμῆς χειρὸς θιγὼν
> ἀγρούς σφε πέμψαι κἀπὶ ποιμνίων νομάς.
> S. *OT* 761; *OC* 1770.

The middle is used in the same way with the usual additional
nuance of personal involvement.

> πῶς δῆτά σ' ἂν πεμψαίαθ', ὥστ' οἰκεῖν δίχα; 'How then could
> they make you go to live apart (for their own advantage)?'
> S. *OC* 602.

> τί χρῆμ' ἐπέμψω τὸν ἐμὸν ἐκ δόμων πόδα; literally 'why did
> you make my foot come out of the house?' E. *Hec.* 977.

These two examples are quoted by LSJ as meaning *send for*; the
second can certainly bear that meaning, but the first is surely not
to be so taken. It does not appear to be very different from this:

> ὡς χρείη μ' ἐπὶ
> τὸν σεμνόμαντιν ἄνδρα πέμψασθαί τινα; S. *OT* 556.

This is taken by LSJ as meaning *send in one's service* or *cause to be
sent*.

> συνεχῶς πεμπομένη τὴν ἄβραν, ὡς ἐδάκρυσε καὶ ἐπηγρύπνησε
> 'continually sending her maid (to say on her behalf) that she
> had wept and stayed awake'. Luc. *Tox.* 14.

3 A remarkable poetic use needs more comment than 'of troops',
since it is really a designation of origin, and so might be defined as
be the origin of. The second is given a special section by LSJ.

> ἄλλους δ' ὁ μέγας καὶ πολυθρέμμων
> Νεῖλος ἔπεμψεν. 'Others came from the mighty Nile.'
> A. *Pers.* 34.

> ὅσα πέμπει βιόδωρος αἶα. S. *Ph.* 1162.

4 As another special use we have expressions where the journey
involves engaging in an activity or suffering a change of state. If a

man is sent to Troy, this describes his physical movement, as in Il. 16. 575 quoted just above (2), but it may also imply his participation in the Trojan war.

πέμπε δέ μ' ἐς Τροίην.   Il. 6. 207.

πέμπε δέ μιν πόλεμόνδε.   Il. 18. 452.

οὕτω δ' Ἀτρέως παῖδας ὁ κρείσσων
ἐπ' Ἀλεξάνδρῳ πέμπει ξένιος
Ζεύς.   A. Ag. 61.

This is especially found in expressions implying death.

ὅς μιν ἔμελλε
πέμψειν εἰς Ἀΐδαο καὶ οὐκ ἐθέλοντα νέεσθαι.
Il. 21. 48; Od. 9. 524.

ὅς με κασίγνητον συλᾷς
Ἀΐδᾳ πέμψας.   E. IT 159.

Slightly different is the case where Achilles is conducting a funeral:

ὄπιθεν δὲ κάρη ἔχε δῖος Ἀχιλλεὺς
ἀχνύμενος· ἕταρον γὰρ ἀμύμονα πέμπ' Ἀϊδόσδε.   Il. 23. 137.

LSJ's spies also belong here:

σκοποὺς δὲ κἀγὼ καὶ κατοπτῆρας στρατοῦ
ἔπεμψα.   A. Th. 37.

τὸν οὖν παρόντα πέμψον ἐς κατασκοπήν.   S. Ph. 45.

οὓς ἐπεπόμφει Κῦρος ἐπὶ κατασκοπήν.   X. Cyr. 6. 2. 9.

For other purposes:

εἰς διδασκάλων πέμποντες.   Pl. Prt. 325d.

ὅταν πέμπωσιν (οἱ θεοὶ) ... συμβούλους.   X. Mem. 1. 4. 15.

γῆς μ' ὅπως πέμψεις ἄποικον.   S. OT 1518.

πέμψαι ... ἄνδρας οἵτινες ἀναγγελοῦσι σκεψάμενοι.
Th. 1. 91. 2.

5   To be distinguished from these is the use where πέμπω means *provide* persons *with means to travel, convey*. In such cases the person is regarded as a passenger to be carried, and is little different from a parcel. Moreover, it is irrelevant whether those doing the conveying accompany the traveller or not; or rather, this

is inherent in the context and is not expressed by the meaning of
the verb. So the alleged sense *escort* is unreal, for what the verb
describes is only the provision of means, though of course this
translation may still serve.

τὴν μὲν γὰρ σὺν νηὶ θοῇ ἑλίκωπες Ἀχαιοὶ
ἐς Χρύσην πέμπουσιν, ἄγουσι δὲ δῶρα ἄνακτι.   Il. 1. 390.

πέμπε δέ μιν πομποῖσιν ἅμα κραιπνοῖσι φέρεσθαι 'provided for
him to be conveyed by swift escorts'.   Il. 16. 681.

τὴν ἄρ' ὅ γ' ἔνθ' ἵπποισι καὶ ἅρμασι πέμπε νέεσθαι
Μυρμιδόνων προτὶ ἄστυ περίκλυτον.   Od. 4. 8.

ἢ ἄλλον πέμπωμεν ἱκανέμεν, ὅς κε φιλήσῃ 'or shall we send
them to someone else to entertain'.   Od. 4. 29.

οὐ γάρ οἱ πάρα νῆες ἐπήρετμοι καὶ ἑταῖροι
οἵ κέν μιν πέμποιεν ἐπ' εὐρέα νῶτα θαλάσσης.   Od. 4. 560.

                                   ἐκέλευον
πεμπέμεναι τὸν ξεῖνον.   Od. 7. 227.

Hercules loquitur:

τὸν (κύνα) μὲν ἐγὼν ἀνένεικα καὶ ἤγαγον ἐξ Ἀΐδαο.
Ἑρμείας δέ μ' ἔπεμψεν ἰδὲ γλαυκῶπις Ἀθήνη.   Od. 11. 626.

This is quoted as evidence for the sense *escort*, but it is irrelevant
whether Hermes and Athene were actually present; the point is
that they made his journey possible.

τύχησε γὰρ ἐρχομένη νηῦς
ἀνδρῶν Θεσπρωτῶν ἐς Δουλίχιον πολύπυρον,
ἔνθ' ὅ γέ μ' ἠνώγει πέμψαι βασιλῆϊ Ἀκάστῳ.   Od. 14. 336.

χρὴ ξεῖνον παρεόντα φιλεῖν, ἐθέλοντα δὲ πέμπειν.   Od. 15. 74.

This can fairly be translated 'send on his way', but it is still
covered by my proposed definition. Of the ferryman Nessus:

τοσόνδ' ὀνήσῃ τῶν ἐμῶν, ἐὰν πίθῃ,
πορθμῶν, ὁθούνεχ' ὑστάτην σ' ἔπεμψ' ἐγώ.   S. *Tr.* 571.

In the passive:

ὥσπερ ὁ (χορὸς) εἰς Δῆλον πεμπόμενος.   X. *Mem.* 3. 3. 12.

6   This same sense can be used of things which serve as a means
of conveyance:

ὄφρα σε τῇ πέμπωσι τιτυσκόμεναι φρεσὶ νῆες.   Od. 8. 556.

κλειναὶ νᾶες, αἵ ποτ' ἔβατε Τροίαν ...
πέμπουσαι χορούς.   E. El. 434.

πλάτα ...
ἀχείματόν μ' ἔπεμπε σὺν πνοαῖς.   A. Supp. 136.

κραιπνοφόροι δέ μ' ἔπεμψαν αὖραι.   A. Pr. 132.

In the passive:

σὺν Νότου δ' αὔραις ἐπ' Ἀξείνου στόμα πεμπόμενοι
ἤλυθον.   Pi. P. 4. 203.

7   From this it is a short step to sending tangible objects which
need to be carried: *have conveyed, despatch*. The first example
combines animate and inanimate objects.

πέμψον ἐπὶ Θρηκῶν ἀνδρῶν ἵππους τε καὶ εὐνάς.   Il. 10. 464.

εἵματα δ' ἐνθάδ' ἐγὼ πέμψω καὶ σῖτον ἅπαντα
ἔδμεναι.   Od. 16. 83.

τῷ μούνῳ Ξέρξης δῶρα πέμπεσκε.   Hdt. 7. 106. 1.

πέρσεις τε Τροίαν, σκῦλά τ' ἐς μέλαθρα σὰ
πέμψεις.   S. Ph. 1429.

Κύρῳ μὲν καὶ τῇ στρατιᾷ ἁπάσῃ ξένια ἔπεμπε.
X. Cyr. 3. 1. 42; An. 1. 9. 25.

χρὴ ... γράμματα πέμψαντα ἐμὲ ἐρέσθαι.   Pl. Ep. 310d; 323b.

In the passive, with the special sense *send in a procession* (cf. 9
below):

τὸν δ' ὦν φαλλὸν τῷ Διονύσῳ πεμπόμενον Μελάμπους ἐστὶ ὁ
κατηγησάμενος.   Hdt. 2. 49. 1.

ὁ ... πέπλος πεμπόμενος διὰ τοῦ Κεραμεικοῦ.
Plu. Demetr. 12.

In another special use it resembles ἵημι meaning *discharge, hurl*.

οἵ ῥα τριηκοσίας πέτρας στιβαρέων ἀπὸ χειρῶν
πέμπον ἐπασσυτέρας.   Hes. Th. 716.

This may be extended to looks, though in the context the look is
compared to an arrow, and to cries and noises.

καὶ παρθένων χλιδαῖσιν εὐμόρφοις ἔπι
πᾶς τις παρελθὼν ὄμματος θελκτήριον
τόξευμ' ἔπεμψεν ἱμέρου νικώμενος.   'cast a charming glance'.
A. Supp. 1005.

θνητὸς ὢν ἐς οὐρανὸν
πέμπει γεγωνὰ Ζηνὶ κυμαίνοντ' ἔπη.   A. Th. 443.

ὦ φθέγμα ποθεινὸν ἐμοὶ πέμψας.   S. Ph. 1445.

πύλας ἀράξας καὶ ψόφον πέμψας ἔσω.   E. IT 1308.

8   The next step is to abstract objects, where the sense may be
defined as *make to appear, send*. But the first two examples are
hardly to be distinguished from those placed in 2 above, since
Ὄνειρον is apparently personified.

πέμψαι ἐπ' Ἀτρεΐδη Ἀγαμέμνονι οὖλον Ὄνειρον.   Il. 2. 6.

πέμψον δ' οἰωνόν, ταχὺν ἄγγελον, ὅς τε σοὶ αὐτῷ
φίλτατος οἰωνῶν.   Il. 24. 310.

In the second it is hard to say whether οἰωνόν means 'bird' or
'omen'. More clearly immaterial is:

τῶ ἔχεθ' ὅττι κεν ὕμμι κακὸν πέμπησιν ἑκάστῳ.   Il. 15. 109.

Winds are hard to classify:

πέμψω δέ τοι οὖρον ὄπισθεν.   Od. 5. 167.

But the object may be more abstract, even if conceived as appear-
ing in human form:

ὑστερόποινον
πέμπει παραβᾶσιν Ἐρινύν.   A. Ag. 59.

ἀρωγὰς δ' ἐκ τάφου πέμπει πατήρ.
   A. Eu. 598; Ch. 477; S. OT 189.

Φοῖβος δ' ὁ πέμψας τάσδε τὰς μαντείας.   S. OT 149.

ἐν θέρει δ' ὕπνον
δι' ἀμφιτρῆτος αὐλίου πέμπει πνοή.   S. Ph. 19.

9   With the cognate accusative πομπήν the verb means *set in
motion* a procession. LSJ says *conduct* or *take part in,* since we have
here the same situation as in 5 above; the subject of the verb may
or may not be a part of the procession, though of course he usually
does take part himself.

μετὰ δὲ ἀπειπάμενος τὴν ὄψιν ἔπεμπε τὴν πομπήν, ἐν τῇ δὴ
τελευτᾷ.   Hdt. 5. 56. 2.

In this case it is clear that he did take part as well as being in control of it.

ἐν ὅπλοις τῶν πολιτῶν τοὺς τὴν πομπὴν πέμψαντας ἀθρόους γενέσθαι.   Th. 6. 56. 2.

In this case they were taking part, but not also in control.

οὔ τι μὴ
Ἱέρωνι τῷ κήρυκι πομπὴν πέμπετε;   Ar. Ec. 757.
ἔπεμψαν οἱ ἐκ Πειραιῶς τὴν πομπὴν εἰς πόλιν.
Lys. 13. 80; D. 4. 26.

In the passive:

τὲς δὲ πονπὲς hόπōς [ἂν hōς κάλ(λ)ιστα] πενφθêι, ho[ι
hι]εροπ[οι]οὶ ἐπιμελôσθôν.   IG ι². 84. 27.

LSJ adds to these cases where the accusative is not cognate, but may imply a procession. For E. El. 434 see 6 above. A better example is:

μικρὰ Παναθήναι᾽ ἐπει⟨δὴ⟩ δι᾽ ἀγορᾶς πέμποντά σε,
Μοσχίων, μήτηρ ἑώρα τῆς κόρης ἐφ᾽ ἅρματος.   Men. fr. 494.

10   From its frequent use of sending messengers arose the intransitive use where it means *send a message*. It may of course be accompanied by a statement of the content of the message.

ὁ Θεμιστοκλῆς τοῖς Ἀθηναίοις κρύφα πέμπει κελεύων ...
κατασχεῖν.   Th. 1. 91. 3.
παρά τε Φορμίωνα ἔπεμπον κελεύοντες ἀμύνειν.   Th. 2. 81. 1.
ἐπέμψαμεν ὡς ὑμᾶς περὶ ἀποστάσεως.   Th. 3. 13. 1; 8. 50. 2.
καὶ εἰς Πέρσας ἔπεμπε πρός τε τὸ κοινὸν καὶ πρὸς Καμβύσην.
X. Cyr. 1. 5. 4; 6. 2. 10; An. 2. 3. 1.

καὶ πέμπεις ἑκών,
οὐ βίᾳ—μὴ τοῦτο λέξῃς—σῇ δάμαρτι, παῖδα σὴν
δεῦρ᾽ ἀποστέλλειν.   E. IA 360.
ἀλλ᾽ οὐ γὰρ ἔμαθε ταῦτ᾽ ἐμοῦ πέμποντος.   Ar. fr. 216.
οὔτε τοὺς φρουροὺς ἀπέδοσαν πέμψαντος ὑπὲρ αὐτῶν ἐμοῦ
πολλάκις.   Epist. ap. D. 12. 12.

περ

1 This enclitic particle has been plausibly connected with the preposition περί, and since this in composition frequently has intensive value, great efforts have been made to discover such examples of περ too. It is a general rule that if you try hard enough to find something, you will succeed; but this runs counter to my lexicographical principle, that the meaning must be educed from the examples, and the examples must never be forced to conform to a preconceived notion. I hope I have been able to show that neither LSJ nor J. D. Denniston (*The Greek Particles*² (Oxford, 1954), 481–90) need to be followed in their belief in this intensive sense. The difficulty in handling a word of this type is that the meaning of many passages is open to several different interpretations; hence it is important to establish the meanings from clear examples, and then assign the doubtful ones to the pattern thus established. I have not attempted to quote every passage in Homer, simply because the word is too common; but I have examined every example quoted as evidence for a sense I do not recognise, and have convinced myself that this is a fair selection. In most cases I have appended a (sometimes abbreviated) translation, not as an elegant version, but to demonstrate how I think περ should here be understood. I observe that it is not infrequently ignored by translators, and like other such particles its force is often most naturally conveyed in English by tone of voice rather than specific words. In order to determine the classification of passages it is often necessary to study the wider context, which cannot be quoted *in extenso* here.

2 A preliminary point of order needs to be discussed. What is the historical development, from a qualifier of single words to a qualifier of participles, and from this to a qualifier of main clauses, or the reverse? Since all these uses are present in Homer, we have no objective criterion to apply. LSJ assumes that the participial use came first and the use with single words arose by the ellipse of the participle of εἰμί, and it ignores the use with main clauses. I prefer the order set out above, as being at least as plausible, and on lexical grounds slightly more likely.

3 The particle generally serves to qualify an element in the sentence as one which might have been expected to invalidate it.

Translations might be offered such as *in spite of being, even if, even though*.

οὐκέτι νῶϊ

ὀλλυμένων Δαναῶν κεκαδησόμεθ᾽ ὑστάτιόν περ.

'Are we no longer concerned about the Greeks perishing, even if this is the last chance?'   Il. 8. 353.

σφῶϊν δὲ πρίν περ τρόμος ἔλλαβε φαίδιμα γυῖα,
πρὶν πόλεμόν τε ἰδεῖν ...

'Trembling seized their shining limbs, even though it was before they set eyes on warfare.'   Il. 8. 452.

ἄνδρα φέριστον, ὃν ἀθάνατοί περ ἔτεισαν,
ἠτίμησας.

'You dishonoured a very brave man, whom the gods revered, gods though they are.'   Il. 9. 110.

μηδὲ μεγαλίζεο θυμῷ

ἀλλὰ καὶ αὐτοί περ πονώμεθα.

'Let us work on it even if we do it ourselves.'   Il. 10. 70.

ἀρίγνωτοι δὲ θεοί περ.   'Gods are easily recognised for all that they are gods.'   Il. 13. 72.

τί σευ ἄλλος ὀνήσεται ὀψίγονός περ;   'What profit will any other have of you, even if he is yet to be born?'   Il. 16. 31.

περὶ Πατρόκλοιο θανόντος

σπεύσομεν, αἴ κε νέκυν περ Ἀχιλλῆϊ προφέρωμεν
γυμνόν.

'Let us hasten to protect the dead Patroclus, to see if we can bring him as a present to Achilles, even though a corpse and stripped.'   Il. 17. 121.

οὐδ᾽ ὑμῖν ποταμός περ ἐΰρροος ἀργυροδίνης
ἀρκέσει.

'Nor will you find the river with its silver eddies enough to save you, even if it flows strongly.'   Il. 21. 130.

σθένος ἀνέρος ἀμφότεροί περ
σχῶμεν.

'Let us put a stop to this man's strength, even if it takes both of us to do it.'   Il. 21. 308.

τῷ νῦν μή ποτε καὶ σὺ γυναικί περ ἤπιος εἶναι.

'Do not ever be mild to a woman, just because she is a woman.'

Od. 11. 441.

The exempla cited are Helen and Clytaemnestra.

αὐτὰρ ἐγὼ κλαῖον καὶ ἐκώκυον ἔν περ ὀνείρῳ   'even though it was in a dream'.   Od. 19. 541.

ἐγὼ τόδε τοι
πέμπω μεμιγμένον μέλι λευκῷ
σὺν γάλακτι ...
ὀψέ περ 'even though late'.   Pi. N. 3. 80.

μένει τὸ θεῖον δουλίᾳ περ ἐν φρενί 'even though in a slave's
mind'.   A. Ag. 1084.

4   This use is frequently extended by adding a participle, sometimes with a preceding καί. This is of course the origin of the
normal classical usage of the compound καίπερ.

ἀγαθός περ ὤν.   Il. 1. 131.

ἐπεί μ' ἔτεκές γε μινυνθάδιόν περ ἐόντα 'since you are my
mother, short-lived though I may be'.   Il. 1. 352.

χαλεποί τοι ἔσοντ' ἀλόχῳ περ ἐούσῃ.   Il. 1. 546.

τέτλαθι, μῆτερ ἐμή, καὶ ἀνάσχεο κηδομένη περ,
μή σε φίλην περ ἐοῦσαν ἐν ὀφθαλοῖσιν ἴδωμαι
θεινομένην.   Il. 1. 586-7.

With preceding καί:

οἱ δὲ καὶ ἀχνύμενοί περ ἐπ' αὐτῷ ἡδὺ γέλασσαν.   Il. 2. 270.

βέλτερον, εἰ καὐτή περ ἐποιχομένη πόσιν εὗρεν 'It would be
better if she found a husband from elsewhere, even if she had to
go in search of one herself.'   Od. 6. 282.

In later Greek:

τάδε νῦν ἐπιδείξω
πιστὰ τεκμήρια, γαιονόμοισι δ' ἄελπτά περ ὄντα φανεῖται.
                                                    A. Supp. 55.

γυνή περ οὖσα.   A. Th. 1038.

καὶ θοῦρός περ ὤν.   A. fr. 199.2.

ἔργου εἴχοντο, ἐν ὀλίγῳ περ ἀπολαμφθέντες 'they set to their
task, even though restricted to a narrow space'.   Hdt. 8. 11. 1.

γενναῖός περ ὤν.   S. Ph. 1068.

ἡ σύμπασα θηρευτική, πολλή περ καὶ τεχνικὴ γεγονυῖα.
                                                    [Pl.] Epin. 975c.

5   Instead of qualifying a single word or phrase περ may apply to
a main clause; it will translate this notwithstanding, all the same,

nevertheless, still. In the first example it is the second περ which is classified here.

ἐπεί μ' ἔτεκές γε μινυνθάδιόν περ ἐόντα,
τιμήν πέρ μοι ὄφελλεν Ὀλύμπιος ἐγγυαλίξαι
Ζεὺς ὑψιβρεμέτης. 'Still Zeus ought to confer honour on me'.

Il. 1. 353.

οἴκαδέ περ σὺν νηυσὶ νεώμεθα, τόνδε δ' ἐῶμεν
αὐτοῦ ἐνὶ Τροίῃ γέρα πέσσεμεν.
'Nevertheless let us go home with our ships, and leave him to stay in Troy and gorge on his privileges.'   Il. 2. 236.

ἀλλά περ οἶος ἴτω Τελαμώνιος Αἴας 'but still let Ajax go alone'.   Il. 12. 349.

τὸν δ' οὔ περ ἔχει θράσος ὅς κεν ἴδηται 'nevertheless, if any see it, boldness is not enough to hold him'.   Il. 14. 416.

ἄλλοτέ περ καὶ μᾶλλον ὀφέλλετε ταῦτα πένεσθαι,
ὁππότε τις μεταπαυσωλὴ πολέμοιο γένηται.
(Achilles politely rejects Agamemnon's proposal) 'Nevertheless it is at a different time that you ought to do this.'   Il. 19. 200.

εἰ δὲ θεός περ
ἶσον τείνειεν πολέμου τέλος.
'nevertheless, if a god should hold the fortunes of battle equal'.

Il. 20. 100.

ἀγαθὸν δὲ γυναικί περ ἐν φιλότητι
μίσγεσθ'.
'(How long will you mourn and abstain from food and bed?) Despite your grief it is good to make love to a woman.'

Il. 24. 130.

αὐτὸν δ' ἐλέησον
μνησάμενος σοῦ πατρός· ἐγὼ δ' ἐλεεινότερός περ,
ἔτλην δ' οἷ' οὔ πώ τις ἐπιχθόνιός βροτὸς ἄλλος.
'Remember your father and pity me; nevertheless I am more to be pitied.'   Il. 24. 504.

This is Denniston's prime example of intensive περ: 'I am far more to be pitied.' But it is perfectly possible to take this (and all his other examples) in a different sense, so I cannot accept that the intensive use is proved to exist.

οὐδέ νυ σοί περ
ἐντρέπεται φίλον ἦτορ, Ὀλύμπιε.
'In spite of this your heart is not shamed.'   Od. 1. 59.

τῶν δ' ἄλλων οὔ πέρ τιν' ἀναίνομαι οὐδ' ἀθερίζω.
'Nevertheless of the rest there is none I despise or take lightly.'
Od. 8. 212.

ἡ δ' ἐμὴ οὐδέ περ υἷος ἐνιπλησθῆναι ἄκοιτις
ὀφθαλμοῖσιν ἔασε.
'Nevertheless my wife did not allow my eyes to have their fill of
my son.'   Od. 11. 452.

6   A rather different sense must be distinguished where it appears
to mean *if no other, if nothing else, at least*.

ἀλλὰ, Ζεῦ, τόδε πέρ μοι ἐπικρήηνον ἐέλδωρ·
αὐτοὺς δή περ ἔασον ὑπεκφυγέειν καὶ ἀλύξαι.
'Grant me at least this wish; let them at least get from under
and escape.'   Il. 8. 242–3.

εἰ δέ τοι Ἀτρείδης μὲν ἀπήχθετο κηρόθι μᾶλλον,
αὐτὸς καὶ τοῦ δῶρα, σὺ δ' ἄλλους περ Παναχαίους
τειρομένους ἐλέαιρε κατὰ στρατόν. 'Do you at least pity the
other Greeks.'   Il. 9. 301.

ὁ δὲ πείσεται εἰς ἀγαθόν περ. 'He will be persuaded at least if
it is to his advantage.'   Il. 11. 789.

ἀνὴρ δ' ὤριστος ὄλωλε
Σαρπηδών, Διὸς υἷός· ὃ δ' οὐδ' οὗ παιδὸς ἀμύνει.
ἀλλὰ σύ πέρ μοι, ἄναξ, τόδε κάρτερον ἕλκος ἄκεσσαι.
'Zeus' son is dead, but he does not even defend his own son.
But at least do you, king Apollo, heal this grievous wound for
me.'   Il. 16. 523.

οὐκέτι νῶϊ
ἔλπομαι αὐτώ περ νοστήσεμεν ἐκ πολέμοιο.
'I no longer expect the two of us to get ourselves, let alone any
other, home from the war'; the other is here the corpse of
Patroclus.   Il. 17. 239; 17. 712; 20. 300.

αἴ κέ ποθι Ζεὺς
ἐξοπίσω περ παύσῃ ὀϊζύος 'at least for the future'.
Od. 4.35; 18. 122.

ἀλλὰ σύ πέρ μοι εἰπέ, θεοὶ δέ τε πάντα ἴσασιν 'but do you, if
no other, tell me—the gods know everything'.   Od. 4. 379.

σὺ γὰρ αὖτε τά τ' ἄλλα περ ἄγγελός ἐσσι 'for you again are a
messenger at least for other news'.   Od. 5. 29; 15. 540.

νῦν δή πέρ μευ ἄκουσον, ἐπεὶ πάρος οὔ ποτ' ἄκουσας 'now at
least listen to me, since you never did before'.   Od. 6. 325.

In later Greek:

—ἦ καὶ δοκεῖτε τοῦ τυφλοῦ τιν' ἐντροπὴν
ἢ φροντίδ' ἕξειν, αὐτὸν ὥστ' ἐλθεῖν πέλας;
—καὶ κάρθ', ὅταν περ τοὔνομ' αἴσθηται τὸ σόν.   S. OC 301.

7   To express exactness or identity, *in fact, just*.

κρείσσων εἰς ἐμέθεν καὶ φέρτερος οὐκ ὀλίγον περ
ἔγχεϊ.
'You are stronger and not just a little braver with the spear.'
Il. 19. 217.

δίσκον
μείζονα καὶ πάχετον, στιβαρώτερον οὐκ ὀλίγον περ.
Od. 8. 187.

In later Greek of course this develops into the compounds with
relative words such as ὅσπερ, ἐπείπερ, etc. to emphasise identity. In
Homer the elements can still be separated.

τιμήν, ἥ τ' ἄλλων περ ἐπιγνάμπτει νόον ἐσθλῶν 'the very same
that ...'   Il. 9. 514.

ταὶ δ' ἐκ μεγάροιο γυναῖκες
ἤϊσαν, αἳ μνηστῆρσιν ἐμισγέσκοντο πάρος περ 'the same
women who used previously to consort with the suitors'.
Od. 20. 7.

It is also possible to take this as qualifying πάρος 'who at least
before used to ...' Denniston sees it as 'a grim hint that the intercourse will not continue much longer.' But I think it makes better
sense to connect περ with the relative, as I have indicated.

ὥς μιν ἔρως πυκινὰς φρένας ἀμφεκάλυψεν,
οἷον ὅτε πρῶτόν περ ἐμισγέσθην φιλότητι 'exactly as when I
made love for the first time'.   Il. 14. 295.

Again Denniston disagrees, taking περ with πρῶτον 'the very first
time'.

ἀλλ' ἐμὲ μὲν κὴρ
ἀμφέχανε στυγερή, ἥ περ λάχε γιγνόμενόν περ.   Il. 23. 79.

Here the repetition of περ creates difficulties. ἥ περ must express
identity 'the very same fate which befell me'. But what does
γιγνόμενόν περ mean? I would suggest 'at the very moment I was

born'; it is well known that a person's fate is determined at the moment of his birth. So too with conditional particles:

ἐπεὶ σύ περ εὔχεαι οὕτω 'since this is your boast'.

II. 13. 447.

ἢν μή περ ὁ πατὴρ αὐτὴν ἐγγυήσῃ 'unless in fact her father has betrothed her'.   Hdt. 6. 57. 4.

The later development of the compounds lies outside the scope of this note.

ῥέω

1   This is an attempt to remedy some of the manifest ambiguities of LSJ's treatment of this word, which has the disadvantage that English *flow* will translate many of its senses (cf. *BICS* (1994), 4–5). The obvious discriminant is the subject of the verb, but there are several other differences to be observed. There does not seem any reason to doubt that the matter of forms is adequately treated in LSJ; there seems to be no semantic difference implied by voice, and the variations are merely formal. I have added a number of examples to those cited by LSJ and the Supplements; these have * prefixed to their references. But I have no doubt that more might profitably be added.

2   We may begin therefore with rivers, streams, and the like, where the meaning is to *contain running water, flow, run*.

ἀλλ᾽ ὅτε δὴ Τροίην ἷξον ποταμώ τε ῥέοντε.
*Il. 5. 773; 6. 172.

τῶν δέ τε πάντες μὲν ποταμοὶ πλήθουσι ῥέοντες.
*Il. 16. 389.

οὐδέ τέ μιν σθένεϊ ῥηγνῦσι ῥέοντες.   *Il. 17. 751; *21. 256.

ὅστις Ἑλλήσποντον ἱρὸν δοῦλον ὣς δεσμώμασιν
ἤλπισε σχήσειν ῥέοντα.   *A. Pers. 746.

hόπōς ἂν ῥέōσ[ιν οἱ ὀχετοὶ κάλλιστα].   IG i². 54. 7.

3   A special use of this is to indicate the place or course of the stream.

αὐτὰρ ἐπὶ κρατὸς λιμένος ῥέει ἀγλαὸν ὕδωρ
κρήνη ὑπὸ σπείους.   *Od. 9. 140.

I assume that κρήνη is here in apposition to ὕδωρ, but if ὕδωρ is an internal accusative it must be classified elsewhere (see 4 below); this usage, however, seems to be confined to Hellenistic Greek.

> ἀμφὶ δ' ἴτυν ῥέεν Ὠκεανὸς πλήθοντι ἐοικώς.   *Hes. Sc. 314.

> Ἅλυος ποταμοῦ, ὃς ῥέων ἀπὸ μεσημβρίης μεταξὺ Συρίων ⟨τε⟩ καὶ Παφλαγόνων ἐξίει πρὸς βορῆν ἄνεμον ἐς τὸν Εὔξεινον καλεόμενον πόντον.   *Hdt. 1. 6. 1; 1. 72. 2.

> φαμένη τὸν Νεῖλον ῥέειν ἀπὸ τηκομένης χιόνος.   Hdt. 2. 22. 1.

This is perhaps a statement of the cause rather than the location, in which case it would come into the uses discussed at the end of 4 below.

> ῥεῖ γὰρ ἀπ' ἄκρας
> Πίνδου Λάκμου τ' ἀπὸ Περραιβῶν
> εἰς Ἀμφιλόχους.   *S. fr. 271.1.

> διὰ δὲ τῆς Θεσπρωτίδος Ἀχέρων ποταμὸς ῥέων.
> > *Th. 1. 46. 4.

> συμβαίνει δὲ τοὺς ποταμοὺς ῥεῖν οὐκ ἐπὶ ταὐτὸν ἀεί 'do not always flow in the same direction'.

> > Arist. Mete. 356ᵃ16; 361ᵃ33; Str. 7. 5. 8.

4   Another special use is where the manner of flow is specified. This may be by an adverb or adverbial expression, but there is also an idiomatic use where an adjective is used in apposition to the subject. Adverbially:

> ἀπ' Ἀξιοῦ εὐρὺ ῥέοντος.   Il. 2. 849.

> λέγεται ... τοὺς ποταμοὺς τούτους ῥέειν ... οὐδὲν ἧσσον ἢ νῦν.
> > Hdt. 7. 129. 3.

With dative:

> ἡ μὲν γὰρ (πηγή) θ' ὕδατι λιαρῷ ῥέει.   Il. 22. 149; Od. 5. 70.

> φάραγγες ...
> ὕδατι χειμάρρῳ ῥέουσαι.   E. Tr. 449.

With genitive in later Greek:

> οἱ ποταμοὶ ... πολλοῦ τε ὕδατος καὶ θολεροῦ ἔρρεον καὶ ὀξέος τοῦ ῥεύματος.   Arr. An. 5. 9. 4.

With internal accusative:

> Ἱμέρα ἀνθ' ὕδατος ῥείτω γάλα.   Theoc. 5. 124; 5. 126.

καὶ οἱ βουνοὶ ῥυήσονται γάλα, καὶ πᾶσαι αἱ ἀφέσεις Ἰούδα
ῥυήσονται ὕδατα.   LXX Jl. 3(4). 18.

πρῶτον μὲν αἷμα ποτάμιον ῥυήσεται
πηγαί τε πᾶσαι.   Ezek. Exag. 133.

ἐφιστάμεθα ποταμῷ οἶνον ῥέοντι.   Luc. VH 1. 7.

λέγεται δὲ τούτῳ (sc. for Midas) τὸν Πακτωλὸν χρυσὸν ῥεῦσαι.
                                        Sch. Ar. Pl. 287.

With adjective:

    περὶ δὲ ῥόος Ὠκεανοῖο
ἀφρῷ μορμύρων ῥέεν ἄσπετος.   Il. 18. 403.

τέως δὲ οἱ μὲν ... ῥέουσι μεγάλοι, τοῦ δὲ θέρεος ἀσθενέες εἰσί.
                                        Hdt. 2. 25. 4; 4. 53. 2.

μέγας οὕτως ἐρρύη ὥστε τοὺς ἱππέας μὴ οἵους τε γενέσθαι
διαβῆναι.   Hdt. 8. 138. 2; Th. 2. 5. 2.

For an extension of this idiom see 10 below.

5   Where the subject is a liquid, the verb may mean flow forth, be
shed.

    καλῇ ὑπὸ πλατανίστῳ, ὅθεν ῥέεν ἀγλαὸν ὕδωρ.   *Il. 2. 307.

    ὧδέ σφ' ἐγκεφαλὸς χαμάδις ῥέοι ὡς ὅδε οἶνος.
                                        Il. 3. 300; *Od. 9. 290.

    ῥέε δ' ἄμβροτον αἷμα θεοῖο.   *Il. 5.339; 17. 86.

                                    δάκρυα δέ σφι
    θερμὰ κατὰ βλεφάρων χαμάδις ῥέε μυρομένοισιν.
                                        *Il. 17. 438; Od. 19. 204.

    ῥεῖ μοι τὸ δάκρυον πολύ.   Ar. Lys. 1034.

                        ἔρρεε δ' ἵδρως
    πάντοθεν ἐκ μελέων.   *Il. 23. 688.

                        κεφαλῆς ἀμίαντον ἀπ' ἄκρης
    αἰεὶ λευκὸν ὕδωρ ῥεύσεται ἡμετέρης.   Thgn. 448.

    ὁ μὲν παῖς (sc. the statue of a boy), δι' οὗ τῆς χειρὸς ῥέει τὸ
    ὕδωρ.   Hdt. 1. 51. 4.

    ἐρρύη δὲ περὶ αὐτὸ τὸ ἔαρ τοῦτο ὁ ῥύαξ τοῦ πυρὸς ἐκ τῆς
    Αἴτνης.   Th. 3. 116. 1.

6   Where the subject is a person or a thing, the verb may mean
produce a liquid, have a discharge.

πρώτῃ καὶ ὀγδοηκόστῃ Ὀλυμπιάδι φασὶ τὴν Αἴτνην ῥυῆναι.
Ael. fr. 2.

This is especially used in a medical context.

Φίλωνος γὰρ θυγάτηρ ἐκ ῥινῶν λάβρον ἐρρύη 'had a copious epistaxis'. Hp. Epid. 1. 19.

πρὸς τὰς κοιλίας τὰς ῥεούσας φαρμάκῳ. D. S. 5. 41. 6.

Impersonally:

ἐρρύη γὰρ αὐτῷ ἐκ τῆς ῥινὸς βληθέντι. X. Cyr. 8. 3. 30.

7 Of things or places with the dative, be covered with, run with a liquid.

ῥέε δ' αἵματι γαῖα. *Il. 4. 451; 8. 65.

ῥεῖ δὲ γάλακτι πέδον, ῥεῖ δ' οἴνῳ, ῥεῖ δὲ μελισσᾶν
νέκταρι. E. Ba. 142.

οἴνῳ γὰρ ἅπασ' ἔρρει χαράδρα. Telecl. 1. 4.

In the middle voice:

οἵ που (νηοὶ) νῦν ἱδρῶτι ῥεούμενοι ἑστήκασι.
Orac. ap. Hdt. 7. 140. 3.

φόνῳ δὲ ναῦς ἐρρεῖτο. E. Hel. 1602.

ῥεομένοις ἱδρῶτι τοῖς ἵπποις. Plu. Cor. 3.

8 Used of things other than liquids, fall as if in a stream or shower, be shed abundantly.

ὡς τῶν ἐκ χειρῶν βέλεα ῥέεν. Il. 12. 159.

τῶν δ' ἐκ μὲν μελέων τρίχες ἔρρεον. Od. 10. 393.

αἱ δέ νυ χαῖται
ἔρρεον ἐκ κεφαλέων. Hes. fr. 133 M–W; Theoc. 2. 89.

ῥέεσκε δὲ καρπὸς ἔραζε.
Hes. fr. 204. 125 M–W.

περὶ τὸν καρπὸν, ὅταν ἀκμὴν ἄρχηται ῥεῖν. Plb. 12. 4. 14.

Of Zeus descending to Danae in a shower of gold:

ὡς γενόμενος χρυσὸς ὁ Ζεὺς ἐρρύη
διὰ τέγεος. *Men. Sam. 590.

ἐς Δανάην ἔρρευσας, Ὀλύμπιε, χρυσός. AP 5. 33(32).

οὐ μέλλω ῥεύσειν χρυσός ποτε. AP 5. 125(124).

9 Similarly of sounds (also, poetically, of a tongue), *be uttered in profusion, flow forth.*

τοῦ καὶ ἀπὸ γλώσσης μέλιτος γλυκίων ῥέεν αὐδή.
    Il. 1. 249; Hes. *Th.* 39; 97; *h. Ven.* 237.
τοῦ δὲ ἔπε' ἐκ στόματος ῥεῖ μείλιχα.   Hes. *Th.* 84.
ὃς οὐκ ἐάσει γλῶσσαν ἐργμάτων ἄτερ
ἔσω πυλῶν ῥέουσαν ἀλδαίνειν κακά.   A. *Th.* 557.

Similarly of reports or rumours, *be divulged, spread.*

τὸν μέν τε ῥέει φάτις οὕνεκ' Ἀχαιὴ
Δημήτηρ ἔβλαψεν.   Nic. *Th.* 484.

10 The phrase πολὺς ῥεῖν (see 4 above) is also used metaphorically, either as meaning *come in large quantity:*

ῥεῖ πολὺς ὅδε λεὼς πρόδρομος ἱππότας.   A. *Th.* 80.

or *exercise a powerful influence, be in full flow:*

Κύπρις γὰρ οὐ φορητός, ἢν πολλὴ ῥύῃ.   E. *Hipp.* 443.
τότ' ἐγὼ μὲν τῷ Πύθωνι θρασυνομένῳ καὶ πολλῷ ῥέοντι καθ'
ὑμῶν οὐχ ὑπεχώρησα.   D. 18. 136.

11 Of things, *move like a liquid, spread.*

λοιμοῦ ῥέοντος διὰ τῆς βαρβάρου.   Hp. *Ep.* 27 (9. 418 L).
ἡ φλὸξ ῥυεῖσα καὶ διαζώσασα πανταχόθεν τὴν πόλιν διέλαμψε
πολλή.   Plu. *Bru.* 31. 2.

Poetically, *run away, be lost* (cf. 17 below).

                    ἀλλὰ ταῦτα μὲν
ῥείτω κατ' οὖρον.   S. *Tr.* 468.

12 Of abstract things, *progress, develop.*

πολλάκι πὰρ δόξαν καὶ ἐλπίδα γίνεται εὖ ῥεῖν
ἔργ' ἀνδρῶν.   Thgn. 639.
            ἄνω γὰρ ἂν ῥέοι
τὰ πράγμαθ' οὕτως, εἰ 'πιταξόμεσθα δή.   E. *Supp.* 520.
ἀλλὰ δῆτ' ἄνω ποταμῶν ... πάντες οἱ περὶ πορνείας ἐρρύησαν
λόγοι.   D. 19. 287.
ῥέων δὲ ὁ μῦθος ἦλθε μέχρις ἡρώων.   Babr. 15. 3.

Of time, *progress, run on*.

οὐ πολλοῦ δὲ πάνυ ῥυέντος χρόνου.   Memn. 14. 1 J.

13   Metaphorically, with dative, *abound in*.

τῶν Φρυγῶν πόλιν
χρυσῷ ῥέουσαν ἤλπισας κατακλύσειν
δαπάναισιν.   E. *Tr.* 995.

εἶτα Κρατίνου μεμνημένος, ὃς πολλῷ ῥεύσας ποτ᾽ ἐπαίνῳ
διὰ τῶν ἀφελῶν πεδίων ἔρρει.   Ar. *Eq.* 526.

The underlined example is that for which the passage is quoted.

14   Metaphorically, of persons, *have a strong feeling* towards or against.

πρὸς τὰ μαθήματα καὶ πᾶν τὸ τοιοῦτο ἐρρυήκασιν.
                                              Pl. *R.* 485d.
οἳ ἂν ταύτῃ τύχωσι ῥυέντες.   Pl. *R.* 495b.

In a hostile sense:

ὅ γε δῆμος ... ὥσπερ σχολάζοντι τῷ θυμῷ πρὸς τὸν
Ἀλκιβιάδην ὅλος ἐρρύη.   Plu. *Alc.* 21. 5.

15   In a different metaphorical development, *lose consistency, fall apart, collapse*.

ὡς δ᾽ ἐθάλπετο
ῥεῖ πᾶν ἄδηλον καὶ κατέψηκται χθονί.   S. *Tr.* 698.

εἰ γὰρ ῥέοι τὸ σῶμα καὶ ἀπολλύοιτο ἔτι ζῶντος τοῦ ἀνθρώπου.
Pl. *Phd.* 87d.

πάσης ἀνάπαλιν τῆς τοῦ σώματος φύσεως ἐξ ἀνάγκης ῥυείσης.
                                              Pl. *Ti.* 84c.

τοῦ τέγους εἴ σοι μέρος τι ῥεῖ.   *Men. *Sam.* 593.

τήκεται δὲ καὶ ὁ λίθος ὁ πυρίμαχος ὥστε στάζειν καὶ ῥεῖν.
                              Arist. *Mete.* 383^{b}6; Thphr. *Lap.* 9.

ὡς δ᾽ αὖτις ἦλθεν, ἡλίου δ᾽ ὑπ᾽ ἀκτίνων
ἤδη ῥέοντα τὸν στάχυν θεωρήσας ...   Babr. 88. 14.

ῥέουσαν σύγκρισιν στῆσαι 'to stay a failing constitution'.
                              Herod. Med. ap. Orib. 5. 27. 1.

στιγμῆς γὰρ ῥυείσης γραμμὴν φαντασιούμεθα ... γραμμῆς δὲ
ῥυείσης πλάτος ἐποιήσαμεν ... ἐπιφανείας δὲ ῥυείσης στερεὸν
ἐγένετο σῶμα.   S. E. *M.* 7. 99.

This last example is given a special section by LSJ, as meaning *'run,* of ink, metaph.', but it clearly refers to the geometric definition of a line as a moving point, a surface as a moving line, etc.

16 As a special use of this last we may classify, of boats or vessels *leak.*

προφασιζόμενοι ... τὰ πλοῖα ῥεῖν. Arist. *fr.* 554.

ἀλλ' ὅταν ἐγχείῃς, φαίνεται τὸ ῥέον (ἀγγεῖον). Plu. 2. 782e.

17 Finally, we have an example of its transference to a purely abstract subject, *fall apart, be destroyed.*

τί δῆτα δόξης, ἢ τί κληδόνος καλῆς
μάτην ῥυείσης ὠφέλημα γίγνεται; S. *OC* 259.

σταθμός

1 I have briefly discussed this word in F. Létoublon (ed.), *La Langue et les Textes en grec ancien*, (Amsterdam, 1992), 283–7, and I had hoped simply to add some further comments. But as all too often, research only discloses the need for more research, and matters I had thought established prove to be still uncertain. I doubt whether this note is still an adequate treatment of the word, but I hope that it will at least serve to clear up some of the difficulties.

2 A preliminary discussion must be devoted to forms. LSJ records that σταθμός has as well as σταθμοί a heteroclite plural σταθμά. But there is also an article on σταθμόν, and it is obvious that many inflected forms are common to these two words. In some such cases it is possible to discriminate on semantic grounds; thus if all neuter examples had a meaning not found in securely masculine ones, it would be safe to distinguish these as two lexical items. In this case, though there is certainly a preponderance of the neuter in one sense, neuter forms are widely distributed over the various senses. I believe therefore the correct solution for a lexicon is to make a single article in which the neuters are treated as formal variants, calling attention to the apparent restrictions as

necessary. If two articles are written, there will inevitably be a large number of ambiguous examples, which must be assigned on an arbitrary basis. LSJ ought at least to call attention to the problem; it is no help to our understanding to pretend that it does not exist. In all such cases failure to observe accurately the distinctions often leads to their loss, and the forms become interchangeable; thus the record is always likely to show examples which breach the rules laid down by grammarians. Here it is significant that Hesychius' entry for σταθμοί has no mention of weighing, the sense in which the neuter is predominantly used.

σταθμοί· ἐπαύλεις, ὅπου ἵστανται ἵπποι καὶ βόες· καὶ στρατιωτικὴ κατάλυσις· καὶ ἡ τῶν θυρῶν παράστασις· καὶ τὰ ἑκατέρωθεν τῶν θυρῶν ξύλα, ἃ νῦν πήγματα καλοῦμεν.

3   It is obvious that σταθμός is in origin a verbal noun describing the action of the verb ἵστημι, so its etymological sense must be a 'standing'. But this is realised in three different ways. It is therefore somewhat arbitrary which we choose to put first, especially since all three branches appear to be attested in the Mycenaean documents of xiii BC. But we may assume its leading sense in Homer as a starting-point. In this it serves to mean a *rustic building for sheltering sheep and cattle and their minders, steading, sheep-station, byre, stable.*

κατὰ σταθμὸν ποιμνήϊον.   Il. 2. 470.

ἀλλὰ κατὰ σταθμοὺς δύεται, τὰ δ᾽ ἐρῆμα φοβεῖται.   Il. 5. 140.

τὼ (λέοντε) μὲν ἄρ᾽ ἁρπάζοντε βόας καὶ ἴφια μῆλα
σταθμοὺς ἀνθρώπων κεραΐζετον.   Il. 5. 557.

This does not imply that the σταθμοί plundered by the lions were only for human habitation; ἀνθρώπων can mean 'constructed by' as well as 'used by men'.

ὡς ὅτε μυῖαι
σταθμῷ ἔνι βρομέωσι περιγλαγέας κατὰ πέλλας.   Il. 16. 642.

Polyphemus addressing his ram:

πρῶτος δὲ σταθμόνδε λιλαίεαι ἀπονέεσθαι
ἑσπέριος.   Od. 9. 451.

ἐνὶ σταθμοῖσι συφορβῶν.   Od. 14. 504.

οὐ γὰρ ἐπὶ σταθμοῖσι μένειν ἔτι τηλίκος εἰμί. 'I am no longer young enough to live on a farm.' Od. 17. 20.

ἐσθλὴ (Ἑκάτη) δ' ἐν σταθμοῖσι σὺν Ἑρμῇ ληΐδ' ἀρήξειν 'she is good in the byres at helping the cattle'. Hes. Th. 444.

Certainly neuter:

ἐς τὰ Λαΐου σταθμά. S. OT 1139; E. Rh. 293.

For horses:

τὰ μὲν τοίνυν ὑγρά τε καὶ λεῖα τῶν σταθμῶν λυμαίνεται καὶ ταῖς εὐφυέσιν ὁπλαῖς. X. Eq. 4. 3.

By an understandable extension it can be used of a natural shelter used by a wild animal, *lair*, *den*.

εἴθισται δ' (ἡ ἔλαφος) ἄγειν τοὺς νεβροὺς ἐπὶ τοὺς σταθμούς· ἔστι δὲ τοῦτο τὸ χωρίον αὐταῖς καταφυγή, πέτρα περιρραγεῖσα μίαν ἔχουσα εἴσοδον. Arist. HA 578ᵇ21; 611ᵃ20.

4 Since a shelter of this kind is not normally a well-constructed, permanent building, it is easy to see how it came to be used for a simple lodging-place at which one might spend the night on a journey. These were constructed at regular intervals on the 'royal' roads of the Persian empire, and might of course be far more luxurious. It is doubtful whether the word developed the generalised sense of 'abode', as claimed by LSJ; there is always an implication of impermanence or at least poor quality. Thus we might define this sense as *stopping-place*, *staging-post*, *lodging*.

σταθμοί τε πανταχῇ εἰσι βασιλήιοι καὶ καταλύσιες κάλλισται.
Hdt. 5. 52. 1.

ἀλλά σφεας τῆς Κισσίης χώρης κατοίκισε ἐν σταθμῷ ἑωυτοῦ.
Hdt. 6. 119. 2.

πλησίον ἦν ὁ σταθμὸς ἔνθα ἔμελλε καταλύειν. X. An. 1. 8. 1.

εἰς σταθμὸν κατέβη βασιλικὸν παραδείσους ἔχοντα θαυμαστοὺς καὶ κεκοσμημένους διαπρεπῶς. Plu. Art. 25. 1.

The phrase σταθμὸν ποιεῖσθαι thus means 'to make a stop', 'spend the night'.

σκήνη μὲν ἔσκε πεπηγυῖα ἑτοίμη ἐς τὴν αὐτὸς σταθμὸν ποιεέσκετο Ξέρξης. Hdt. 7. 119. 3.

It can also stand for the distance between stops.

ἐντεῦθεν ἐξελαύνει σταθμοὺς δύο παρασάγγας δέκα εἰς
Πέλτας. X. *An.* 1. 2. 10.

In a more general sense, especially in verse:

εὖτ' ἂν αἰπεινῶν ἀπὸ σταθμῶν ἐς εὐδείελον
χθόνα μόλῃ κλειτᾶς Ἰαολκοῦ. Pi. *P.* 4. 76.
                    ὅ τοι πτερόεις
ἔρριψε Πάγασος
δεσπόταν ἐθέλοντ' ἐς οὐρανοῦ σταθμοὺς
ἐλθεῖν. P. *I.* 7(6). 45.

Here the reference to the winged horse makes the word sound
more natural, since the stables in the sky were where Pegasus
wanted to go.

ὅταν ... εἰς Ἀΐδα σταθμὸν
ἀνὴρ ἵκηται. Pi. *O.* 10. 92.

The abode of Hades might not be impermanent, but was certainly
an inferior lodging for men. In the neuter form:

ἀλλ' ἢ πρὸς οἶκον τὸν σὸν ἔκσωσόν μ' ἄγων,
ἢ πρὸς τὰ Χαλκώδοντος Εὐβοίας σταθμά. S. *Ph.* 489.

There is clearly a contrast between the οἶκος and the huts on
Euboea.

[τὸν Θεο]πόμπου σταθμὸν ὅπως ἔχωμεν ἐνοικεῖν.
                        P. Cair. Zen. 344. 2.

There are other examples in the papyri where it is part of an
address, but LSJ does not appear to be justified in giving these a
new sense, *quarter of town*.

5   A special use of this is to describe a building for housing ships,
ship-shed, boat-house. In the neuter plural:

ναῶν πυρσοῖς σταθμά. E. *Rh.* 43.

Ambiguously:
                    ναυλόχων σταθμῶν
πρόβλημα. Lyc. 290.

This is of course used in prose in the compound ναύσταθμον or
ναύσταθμος.

6 We may now pass to the second major line of development, where it denotes an *upright member of a structure, column, pillar, post*. This occurs in two contexts, and it is not always possible to assign individual examples securely; those quoted are those where it seems clear. First, as the support of a roof:

στῆ ῥα παρὰ σταθμὸν τέγεος πύκα ποιητοῖο.
Od. 1. 333 et alibi.

θριγκὸν εἰσιδεῖν
δόμων πίτνοντα, πᾶν δ' ἐρείψιμον στέγος
βεβλημένων πρὸς οὖδας ἐξ ἀκρῶν σταθμῶν. E. *IT* 49.

7 Secondly, as either of the uprights of a door-frame, door-post, jamb:

πυκινὰς δὲ θύρας σταθμοῖσιν ἐπῆρσε
κληῖδι κρυπτῇ. Il. 14. 167.

χρύσειαι δὲ θύραι πυκινὸν δόμον ἐντὸς ἔεργον·
ἀργύρεοι σταθμοὶ δ' ἐν χαλκέῳ ἕστασαν οὐδῷ
ἀργύρεον δ' ἐφ' ὑπερθύριον, χρυσέη δὲ κορώνη. Od. 7. 89.

πὰρ δὲ δύ' ἀμφίπολοι ...
σταθμοῖιν ἑκάτερθε. Od. 6. 19.

ἐν δὲ (οὐδῷ) σταθμοὺς ἄρσε, θύρας δ' ἐπέθηκε φαεινάς.
Od. 21. 45.

πύλαι δὲ ἐνεστᾶσι πέριξ τοῦ τείχεος ἑκατόν, χαλκέαι πᾶσαι,
καὶ σταθμοί τε καὶ ὑπέρθυρα ὡσαύτως. Hdt. 1. 179. 3.

δόμων θύρετρα καὶ σταθμοὺς
μοχλοῖσιν ἐκβαλόντες. E. *Or.* 1474; *HF* 999.

A puzzling passage using the neuter plural, which has not in my opinion been correctly understood:

ἐπὶ πλατὺν οὐδόν, ὅθι σταθμὰ κοῖλα θυράων
οἴκου. Theoc. 24. 15.

There can be little doubt what σταθμά means here, but κοῖλα has given trouble. I understand it as referring to the concave channel cut vertically into the door-posts, in which the rounded inside edge of the door fits so as to make a tight seal. This too may be what is meant in this inscriptional example:

τῶγ καταγλυμμάτων ἐν τοῖν σταθμοῖν.
IG 4² (1). 103. 94 (Epidaurus, iv BC).

8   Arising from this we find it used, perhaps originally only in the plural, to mean *doorway, entrance*.

> ἀλλ' εἰ σταθμοῖσι τοῖσδε μὴ 'κύρουν ἐγὼ
> πάλαι φυλάσσων.   S. *El.* 1331.
> τουτὶ λαβὼν ἄπελθε λαΐνων σταθμῶν.   Ar. *Ach.* 449.

The phrase is here probably mock-tragic. In the singular:

> οἱ ἱερεῖς οἱ φυλάσσοντες τὸν σταθμόν.   LXX *4 Ki.* 12. 9.

9   When we turn to the examples which relate to weighing, the difficulty of separating σταθμός and σταθμόν becomes acute. Four senses can be distinguished: (*a*) weight in abstract as a property of objects; (*b*) a quantity measured by weight; (*c*) a weighing instrument, balance (in this sense apparently always masculine); (*d*) an object, usually a piece of lead, having a known weight and used as a standard of measurement, a weight (in this sense σταθμόν is predominant and may be assumed where the form is ambiguous). It is difficult to see which of these was the earliest, and they will be treated in the order here shown.

10   *Weight* as a property of objects (only one of these examples can be proved to be masculine):

> σταθμὸν ἔχοντες τριήκοντα τάλαντα 'weighing 30 talents'.
>   Hdt. 1. 14. 2.
> ἀναθήματα ... ἴσα τε σταθμὸν καὶ ὅμοια τοῖσι ἐν Δελφοῖσι.
>   Hdt. 1. 92. 2.
> ἀπέφαινε δ' ἔχον τὸ ἄγαλμα τεσσεράκοντα τάλαντα σταθμὸν
> χρυσίου.   Th. 2. 13. 5.

These examples might all be neuter, and this is certain in the case of the numerous inscriptions which record weights; the phrase σταθμὸν τούτῶν is common in early Attic inscriptions.

> ὥσπερ γὰρ ἐν τῷ στόματι διαφέρουσι (ὑδάτων αἱ δυνάμεις)
> καὶ ἐν τῷ σταθμῷ.   Hp. *Aër.* 1.
> τὸ μὲν πρῶτον ἁπλῶς ὁρισθὲν μεγέθει καὶ σταθμῷ.
>   Arist. *Pol.* 1257ᵃ 39.
> θύννος οὗ σταθμὸς μὲν ἦν τάλαντα πεντεκαίδεκα.
>   Arist. *HA* 607ᵇ32.

Since there were several standards of weight in use, σταθμός is used to denote the *system of weights* (one example is clearly masculine).

τοῖσι μὲν αὐτῶν ἀργύριον ἀπαγινέουσι εἴρητο Βαβυλώνιον
σταθμὸν τάλαντον ἀπαγινέειν. Hdt. 3. 89. 2.

μέτρον δὲ οὔτε ἀριθμὸν οὔτε σταθμὸν ἄλλον ... οὐκ ἂν εὔροις
ἀλλ᾽ ἢ τοῦ σώματος τὴν αἴσθησιν. Hp. VM 9.

11 A *quantity measured by weight, weight of*. Again two examples
are clearly masculine.

ὀπτοῦ σίτου σταθμὸς πέντε μνέαι ἑκάστῳ. Hdt. 2. 168. 2.

μάλιστα, μυρίον γε δοὺς χρυσοῦ σταθμόν. E. Ba. 812.

πλείω παρὰ τὸν σταθμόν. P. Cair. Zen. 782 (a). 141 (iii BC).

12 LSJ quotes four examples of the sense *balance*, to which is
added the phrase ἕλκειν σταθμόν, *weigh* so much. But it is evident
that the object being weighed does not pull the balance, but the
weight against which it is being measured. More seriously it
attributes this sense to a passage in Homer (Il. 12. 434), and in my
earlier discussion I accepted this interpretation. I now believe I
was wrong to do so, and I therefore postpone discussion of this
now (see 13 below). The first example is then in Herodotus.

ξυρῶντες τῶν παιδίων ἢ πᾶσαν τὴν κεφαλὴν ἢ τὸ ἥμισυ ἢ τὸ
τρίτον μέρος τῆς κεφαλῆς, ἱστασι σταθμῷ πρὸς ἀργύριον τὰς
τρίχας. Hdt. 2. 65. 4.

The simplest interpretation of this appears to be 'place the hair in
the balance against silver', though it might conceivably mean 'in
the process of weighing.' Unambiguous evidence is provided by
the famous scene in Aristophanes' *Frogs*, where nothing but
weighing-device, balance will make sense. Here the σταθμός is distinguished from the two scale-pans, which are called πλάστιγγε.

ἐπὶ τὸν σταθμὸν γὰρ αὐτὸν ἀγαγεῖν βούλομαι,
ὅπερ ἐξελέγξει τὴν ποίησιν νῷν μόνον. Ar. Ra. 1365.

Then a little later the contestants are told to speak εἰς τὸν σταθμόν.

τοὔπος νῦν λέγετον εἰς τὸν σταθμόν. ibid. 1381.

Finally Aeschylus tells Euripides to get in the σταθμός himself,
together with his household and his library.

καὶ μηκέτ᾽ ἔμοιγε κατ᾽ ἔπος, ἀλλ᾽ ἐς τὸν σταθμὸν
αὐτὸς τὰ παιδί᾽ ἡ γυνὴ Κηφισοφῶν
ἐμβὰς καθήσθω, συλλαβὼν τὰ βιβλία. ibid. 1407.

In the second and third of these the sense of σταθμός is clear, and these carry the first with them. This then is likely to be the sense in the passage of Herodotus quoted above.

13 Finally we reach the sense which is or may be exclusively neuter. These examples therefore belong to the article σταθμόν, but are not all placed there by LSJ. This admits no example earlier than v BC, so it will be necessary to examine carefully the Homeric instance, which, since it is accusative singular, might belong to either σταθμός or σταθμόν. We may define this sense as an *object having a known weight used as a standard of measurement, weight.*

> ἀλλ' ἔχον ὥς τε τάλαντα γυνὴ χερνῆτις ἀληθής,
> ἥ τε σταθμὸν ἔχουσα καὶ εἴριον ἀμφὶς ἀνέλκει
> ἰσάζουσ', ἵνα παισὶν ἀεικέα μισθὸν ἄρηται·
> ὡς μὲν τῶν ἐπὶ ἶσα μάχη τέτατο πτόλεμός τε.   Il. 12. 434.

The meaning of χερνῆτις here has been disputed, largely because ancient sources give it a meaning 'poor', though this is probably only a reflection of the pittance (ἀεικέα μισθόν 435) she earns for her children. It is hard to see how ἀληθής will fit if this is the meaning; so it is more likely a compound of χείρ 'hand' and means 'one who works with the hands', 'artisan'. The epithet ἀληθής must then mean effectively 'not cheating', 'honest', the opposite of ψευδής. It would appear that τάλαντα here means the balance, and if so, σταθμόν must have some other meaning, *pace* LSJ, and this can hardly be other than the weight which the woman places on one scale and then balances by adding wool to the other. In order to see when they balance, she needs to lift the whole balance enough for the scales to leave the ground, and this is accurately described as ἀμφὶς ἀνέλκει, since she must grasp the beam by a support attached at its mid-point, so that the weight and the wool will be on either side of her. As always in Homeric similes, the picture is carefully observed and economically described.

14 Other examples of this sense often refer to the invention of weights attributed to Palamedes.

> εὑρὼν ... μέτρα τε καὶ σταθμά.   Gorg. Pal. 30.

> οὗτος δέ γ' ηὗρε ...
> σταθμῶν ἀριθμῶν καὶ μέτρων εὑρήματα.   S. fr. 432.

Euripides, as might be expected, rationalises.

καὶ γὰρ μέτρ' ἀνθρώποισι καὶ μέρη σταθμῶν
Ἰσότης ἔταξε.   E. Ph. 541.

There are also references to the public weights and measures
established by law.

πρός τε τὰ ὑγρὰ καὶ τὰ ξηρὰ καὶ τὰ σταθμὰ ἀν[αγκ]αζέτω[σαν
τοὺ]ς πωλοῦν[τ]άς τι ἐν τῆι ἀγορᾶι.   IG 2². 1013. 8.

and a few lines below:

[χ]ρῆσθαι τοῖς μέτροις καὶ τοῖς σταθμοῖς τούτοις.   ibid. 10.
νόμοις δὲ χρῆσθαι τοῖς Σόλωνος, καὶ μέτροις καὶ σταθμοῖς.
                              Decret. ap. And. 1. 83; Arist. Ath. 10. 1.

15   The phrase σταθμὸν ἕλκειν surely belongs in this division,
since the action of pulling the weight must refer to the weighed
object lifting the opposite scale off the ground. Thus this too, *pace*
LSJ, must be treated as an example of σταθμόν.

εἰκόνα ... ἕλκουσαν σταθμὸν τάλαντα δέκα.   Hdt. 1. 50. 3.

16   To sum up, it seems that the tripartite grouping of senses is
very ancient, since the word appears in the spelling *ta-to-mo* on the
Mycenaean documents in association with sheep, architecture and
weighed   commodities.   The   neuter   singular   is   especially
associated with the sense of weight used on a balance; the neuter
plural is, however, widespread and seems to have been a convenient metrical alternative for poets. The lexical pattern might be
established as follows (the numbers refer to the paragraphs above):

1   *rustic shelter, steading, sheep-station, byre, stable*; also, *lair,
den* of a wild animal (3).
2   *stopping-place, staging-post, lodging*; *the distance between
stops* (4). **b** *housing for ships, ship-shed, boat-house* (5).
3   *upright member* of a structure, *column, pillar, post*: **a** as support of a roof (6). **b** *either of the uprights of a door-frame, door-
post, jamb* (7).
4   usu. plur. *doorway, entrance* (8).
5   *weight* as a property of objects; *system of weights* (10).
6   *quantity measured by weight, weight* of (11).
7   *weighing device, balance* (12).
8   probably always neuter, *weight* used on a balance; σταθμὸν
ἕλκειν have the *weight of, weigh* (13, 14, 15).

τάλας

1   I had no intention of writing about this word until my attention was called to an article by J. R. Wilson (*American Journal of Philology*, 92 (1971), 292–300), which claims that the etymological connexion with τόλμα favours the existence of a sense *criminally daring, insolent*. My reaction on reading this was that although a case can be made, the examples quoted are perfectly capable of being understood otherwise. It is in fact a good example of my general principle, that if you look hard enough for something you want to find, there will usually be some evidence to support your theory. I conclude therefore that this is going beyond what the material justifies; but at the same time LSJ's rather cavalier treatment, with the translations *suffering, wretched, sorry*, is also unsatisfactory. I believe three senses need to be distinguished, and as so often, other interesting details emerge.

2   The closest etymological connexion is undoubtedly with τλάω, and a basic meaning of *enduring misfortune, unlucky, unhappy* is a plausible starting-point.

> ὁ τάλαις ἐγώ
> ζώω μοῖραν ἔχων ἀγροϊωτίκαν.   Alc. 130. 16 L-P.

> ἦλθες δή, Κλεάριστε, βαθὺν διὰ πόντον ἀνύσσας
>   ἐνθάδ' ἐπ' οὐδὲν ἔχοντ', ὦ τάλαν, οὐδὲν ἔχων.   Thgn. 512.

> ἆ τάλας ἀνήρ,
> ὅστις κακὸν τοιοῦτον ἀγκαλίζεται.   Sem. 7. 76.

> οἳ 'γὼ τάλαινα συμφορᾶς κακῆς, φίλοι.   A. Pers. 445; 517.

> σίγησον, ὦ τάλαινα, μὴ φίλον φόβει.   A. Th. 262; Ag. 1247.

> βᾶθί νυν, ὦ τάλαν, ὥς σε κελεύομεν.   S. Ph. 1196.

> δεῖξόν νυν, ὦ τάλαινα, σὴν νικηφόρον
> ἀστοῖσιν ἄγραν, ἣν φέρουσ' ἐλήλυθας.   E. Ba. 1200; Or. 526.

> φόνον ταλαίναις χερσὶν ἐξειργασμένων.   E. Ba. 1245.

> τάλαινα φρήν, παρ' ἡμῶν λαβοῦσα τὰς πίστεις ἡμέας
> καταβάλλεις;   Democr. fr. 125 B.

> κἀγὼ μὲν ὁ τάλας νεκρὸν ἀντὶ νυμφίου ἐκομισάμην καὶ ἔθαψα.
>   X. Cyr. 4. 6. 5.

> ἄγε νυν, ὦ τάλαινα καρδία,
> ἄπελθ' ἐκεῖσε.   Ar. Ach. 485.

3 The previous section includes not only persons but also parts of the body; but a further extension of meaning is detectable, when the adjective is applied to other things which can cause misfortune, though much the same translations can often be used. A formal definition might be *having unfortunate effects, damaging*.

βροτοὺς θρασύνει γὰρ αἰσχρόμητις
τάλαινα παρακοπὰ πρωτοπήμων. A. *Ag.* 223.

βιᾶται δ᾽ ἁ τάλαινα Πειθώ. A. *Ag.* 385.

οὐδ᾽ ἀγύμναστόν μ᾽ ἐᾶν
ἔοικεν ἡ τάλαινα διάβορος νόσος. S. *Tr.* 1084.

τὰ τῆς ταλαίνης νηδύος θρεπτήρια. S. *OC* 1263.

τάνδε γαῖαν εἰς ἄνολβον
ἔριν ἔριν τάλαιναν ἔθετο. E. *Hel.* 248.

πέπονθα ...
ἀπὸ δὲ συγγόνων τάλαν᾽ ἄνομα πάθεα. Ar. *Th.* 1039.

4 It is not always easy to detect when the basic sense of *unfortunate* passes over into a term of opprobrium, implying a wish for someone's misfortune; but there are certainly clear examples, especially in colloquial usage. It is this which has, I believe, misled J. R. Wilson into identifying a sense of 'criminally daring'. In all cases its force seems to me to be considerably weaker. It may be coupled with κατάρατος (E. *Hec.* 1064–5, see 5 below), but it is a milder reproach, especially in the vocative. This is sufficiently distinct to call for separate treatment, so I will begin with the more general examples where I think it means rather more than *unhappy* and rather less than *accursed*. The nearest English equivalent is *wretched*.

τὸν αὐτοφόντην ἡμὶν ἐν κοίτῃ πατρὸς
ξὺν τῇ ταλαίνῃ μητρί, μητέρ᾽ εἰ χρεὼν
ταύτην προσαυδᾶν. S. *El.* 273.

It is evident that Electra is not pitying her mother, but cursing her. So Menelaus on Helen:

ἥκω δὲ τὴν τάλαιναν—οὐ γὰρ ἡδέως
ὄνομα δάμαρτος ἥ ποτ᾽ ἦν ἐμὴ λέγω—
ἄξων. E. *Tr.* 869.

5   This is far more common in the vocative, and in fact the two earliest examples of this word, both from the Odyssey, belong here. It has been remarked that although not unused by men it is much more often put into the mouths of women. This is, I think, due to the fact that it is a relatively mild expression; strong language was never associated with women, and in a society where women were treated as inferiors it is not surprising that it should be a favourite word of theirs. The tone of the first example is given by the preceding line; in the second the context makes the feeling clear.

> ἦ ῥ' Ὀδυσῆ' ἐνένιπεν ὀνειδείοις ἐπέεσσι·
> ξεῖνε τάλαν, σύ γέ τις φρένας ἐκπεπαταγμένος ἐσσί.
> Od. 18. 327.

> ἀλλ' ἔξελθε θύραζε, τάλαν, καὶ δαιτὸς ὄνησο.   Od. 19. 68.

Cassandra in her prophecy addressing Clytaemnestra:

> ἰὼ τάλαινα, τόδε γὰρ τελεῖς;   A. Ag. 1107.

This is one of Wilson's prime examples; but even if the sense proposed is apposite, it is not strictly necessary. The blinded Polymestor:

> τάλαιναι κόραι τάλαιναι Φρυγῶν,
>   ὦ κατάρατοι,
> ποῖ καί με φυγᾷ πτώσσουσι μυχῶν;   E. Hec. 1064.

> ὦ καρδία τάλαινα, πρὶν μὲν ἐς ξένους
> γαληνὸς ἦσθα καὶ φιλοικτίρμων ἀεί.   E. IT 344.

> σὺ γάρ νιν, ὦ τάλαινα,
> θωΰξασ' ἔβαλες ἐξ ὕπνου.   E. Or. 167.

In Aristophanes it is a frequent mode of address by women to men, usually expressing irritation.

> τί δ'; οὐχὶ βινεῖται γυνὴ κἄνευ μύρου;
> —οὐ δῆτα τάλαν ἔγωγε.   Ar. Ec. 526.

> ἔπειτ' ὀμόσασα δῆτ' ἐπιορκήσω τάλαν;   Ar. Lys. 914.

> μὴ σκῶπτέ μ' ὦ τάλαν, ἀλλ' ἕπου δεῦρ' ὡς ἐμέ.   Ar. Ec. 1005.

> τοδὶ διέκυψε καὶ μάλ' εὔχρων ὦ τάλαν.   Ar. Th. 644.

> βούλει διὰ χρόνον πρός με παῖσαι; —ποῖ τάλαν.   Ar. Pl. 1055.

> ταλάντατ' ἀνδρῶν οὐκ ἐδεδοίκεις τὸν θεόν;
>   Ar. Pl. 684; 1046; 1060.

From one woman to another:

νὴ τὴν Ἀφροδίτην εὖ γε ταυταγὶ λέγεις.
—τάλαιν' Ἀφροδίτην ὤμοσας;   Ar. Ec. 190; 242; 919.

5 There is, however, a curious feature about this use which needs to be noticed. The vocative τάλαν or ὦ τάλαν is used in Aristophanes by one woman addressing another, where we should expect τάλαινα. LSJ treats this as a grammatical quirk, as if τάλας might be optionally used with two terminations; but such a feature is unlikely to have been strictly confined to the vocative singular. The ancient grammarians seem to have thought it might be neuter, and it is of course quite normal for neuter nouns to refer to human beings. But the most likely explanation is that this is a stereotyped expression, like expletives in modern languages, which are used in invariable form, and the speaker is unaware of any grammatical inconsistency. In the *Frogs* Plathane speaking to the πανδοκεύτρια:

μὰ Δί' οὐδὲ τὸν τυρόν γε τὸν χλωρὸν τάλαν
ὃν οὗτος αὐτοῖς τοῖς ταλάροις κατήσθιεν.   Ar. Ra. 559.

In *Lysistrata,* Callonice to Myrrhine:

ὁ γοῦν ἐμὸς ἀνὴρ πέντε μῆνας ὦ τάλαν
ἄπεστιν ἐπὶ Θρᾴκης φυλάττων Εὐκράτη.   Ar. Lys. 102.

In *Ecclesiazusae,* the first woman to Praxagora:

σκέψαι τάλαν
ὡς καὶ καταγέλαστον τὸ πρᾶγμα φαίνεται.   Ar. Ec. 124.

6 A footnote might be added on the mysterious form τάλης which occurs twice in our text of Herondas. As a hyper-Ionicism it is not necessarily incorrect, since it is put in the mouths of women, though it is perhaps a mistake on the part of the writer rather than the speaker. But it would appear that, whatever its explanation, it serves here too as an invariable expletive, and this accounts for the neglect of the vocative. The two passages are:

τοῦτο, φημί, χἠ μάμμη,
τάλης, ἐρεῖ σοι.   Herod. 3. 35.

τάχ' οὖν, τάλης, ἄξουσι σὺν τύχῃ πρός σε,
μᾶλλον δὲ πάντως.   Herod. 7. 88.

Attempts have of course been made to emend it, e.g. to τὰ λῇς. There is also an instance of the normal τάλας:

Πυρρίης, τάλας, κωφέ,
καλεῖ σε. Herod. 5. 55.

τέλειος, τέλεος

1 Since this is the adjective derived from τέλος, it ought really to be studied in conjunction with that word. It is quite possible that a better arrangement of the senses would emerge from such a study. I have not investigated the various forms, beyond establishing that τέλεος is not merely a poetic variant, but is used frequently in prose including inscriptions. It is remarkable that the two forms have their appropriate superlatives, τελειότατος and τελεώτατος. But there is no reason to believe that there is any difference in meaning, as will be evident from the examples quoted.

2 Of living things, whether persons, animals or plants, *fully-grown, adult.*

τοῦδ' ὁ παλαιὸς δριμὺς ἀλάστωρ ...
τόνδ' ἀπέτεισεν
τέλεον νεάροις ἐπιθύσας. A. *Ag.* 1504.

ἕν μὲν (μέρος) παισίν, ἓν δ' ἐφήβοις, ἄλλο τελείοις ἀνδράσιν. X. *Cyr.* 1. 2. 4.

πώλοις τε ἀβόλοις καὶ τελείων τε καὶ ἀβόλων τοῖς μέσοις καὶ αὐτοῖς δὴ τοῖς τέλος ἔχουσιν. Pl. *Lg.* 834c.

ὁπόσοιπερ ἂν ὦσιν γυναικῶν εἴτε ἀνδρῶν τέλειοι.
Pl. *Lg.* 929c.

τὸ τέλεον ἀπεργάσασθαι τὸ γεννώμενον, εἴτ' οὖν φυτὸν, εἴτε καὶ ζῷον. Gal. 7. 677.

συνωρί(δι) τελείᾳ. 'with a pair of full-grown horses'.
IG 4²(1). 101. 47; *IG* 5(2). 549. 2.

δρόμος δὲ δύο ἵππων τελείων συνωρὶς κληθεῖσα.
Paus. 5. 8. 10.

τελείῳ ἅρματι καὶ συνωρίδι πωλικῇ. Luc. *Tim.* 50.

πρόβατα τέλεια ἀριθμῶι ο̄ζ̄ *SB* 5277. 5.

τέλειος, τέλεος

Of trees:

τελείων ὄντων τῶν δένδρων.   Thphr. *CP* 3. 7. 5.

ἀκάνθας τελείας δεκατέσσαρας.   *P. Oxy.* 909. 18 (iii AD).

It is also used in scaling up a model, to mean *full size.*

ἐὰν ἀπὸ παραδειγματίου μικροῦ βουλώμεθα τέλειον ποιῆσαι.
                                   Ph. *Bel.* 13 D–S (= p. 55, 20 W).

The New Supplement adds some examples of *full-sized* αὐλοί.

3   The word is used especially of sacrificial victims, but the sense
is not immediately apparent. No doubt it excluded young animals,
but since there was an obligation to sacrifice unblemished animals
(called ἀνασκεθέα in Tegea, Schwyzer 654. 6) it presumably means
here not only full-grown, but complete in all respects. If so, these
examples might be better treated under the sense discussed in 8
below.

ἀρνῶν κνίσης αἰγῶν τε τελείων.   Il. 1. 66; 24. 34.

βωμὸς μέγας, ἐπ᾽ οὗ θύεται τὰ τέλεα τῶν προβάτων.
                                   Hdt. 1. 183. 2.

ℎῖ κα τôι Μαχανεῖ θύōμες τὸνς Ϝεξέκοντα τελέονς ὄϝινς. 'when
we sacrifice to Machaneus the sixty complete sheep'.
                                   Schwyzer 83. B. 10 (Argos, v BC).

This occurs several times in the formula used in solemn oaths:

ὀμνύντων δὲ τὸν ἐπιχώριον ὅρκον ἕκαστοι τὸν μέγιστον κατὰ
ἱερῶν τελείων.
                                   Foed. ap. Th. 5. 47. 8; Lex ap. And. 1. 97; D. 59. 60.

4   As an epithet of gods, *bringing about fulfilment of prayers,
accomplishing.*

Ζεῦ τέλει᾽, αἰδῶ δίδοι.   Pi.O. 13. 115; *P.* 1. 67.

Ἥβα τελείᾳ παρὰ ματέρι βαίνοισ᾽
ἔστι.   Pi. *N.* 10 .18.

Ζεῦ, Ζεῦ τέλειε, τὰς ἐμὰς εὐχὰς τέλει.
                                   A. *Ag.* 973; 1432; *Eu.* 28.

ἄναξ ἀνάκτων, μακάρων
μακάρτατε καὶ τελέων
τελειότατον κράτος, ὄλβιε Ζεῦ.   A. *Supp.* 526; *Th.* 167.

Ήραν δὲ τὴν τελείαν
μέλψωμεν. Ar. Th. 973.

Ἀπόλλωνος νομίοιο
ἱερὸν ἁγνόν, ξεῖνε, τελειοτάτοιο θεοῖο.   Theoc. 25. 22.

Μοιρῶν τε τελείων.   SEG 3. 400. 9 (Delphi, iii BC).

5   Hence of prayers, omens, dreams, etc, *leading to fulfilment,
reliable, true.*

αὐτίκα δ᾽ αἰετὸν ἧκε, τελειότατον πετεηνῶν.
                                    Il. 8. 247; 24. 315.

                                    ἐκ δὲ τέλειον
σύμβολον ἀθανάτων ποιήσομαι ἠδ᾽ ἅμα πάντων
πιστὸν ἐμῷ θυμῷ καὶ τίμιον.   h. Merc. 526.

Some editors suppose a lacuna after τέλειον.

τοῖσι τέλειον ἐπ᾽ εὐχᾷ κωμάσομαί τι παθὼν ἐ-
σλόν. 'To them I shall sing in triumph at receiving a fine
answer to my prayer.'   Pi. P. 9. 89.

τελείαις ... εὐχωλαῖς.   Pi. fr. 122. 15.

ὦ μέλαινα καὶ τελεία
γένεος Οἰδίπου τ᾽ ἀρά.   A. Th. 832.

ξυνευχόμεσθα τέλεα μὲν
πόλει τέλεα δὲ δήμῳ
τάδ᾽ εὔγματα γενέσθαι.   Ar. Th. 352-3.

σὲ γὰρ ἐγὼ δι᾽ ὄψιν ὀνείρου οὐ τελέην ἠδίκεον.   Hdt. 1. 121.

τέλεον ἄρα ἡμῖν τὸ ἐνύπνιον ἀποτετέλεσται.   Pl. R. 443b.

6   Of decisions, votes, syllogisms, etc., *conclusive, decisive, final.*

ἐπεὶ τελεία ψῆφος Ἀργείων, τέκνα,
θάρσει.   A. Supp. 739.

ὦ παῖ, τελείαν ψῆφον ἆρα μὴ κλύων
τῆς μελλονύμφου πατρὶ λυσσαίνων πάρει;   S. Ant. 632.

καὶ τὸ θέθμιον τοῖς Ὑποκναμιδίοις Λοϙροῖς ταῦτα τέλεον
εἶμεν Χαλείοις 'and the ordinance for the Hypocnemidian
Locrians is to be decisive in the same way for the Chaleians'.
                    Schwyzer 362. 47. (=IG 9(1). 334. 47, v BC).

τέλειος μὲν οὖν οὐκ ἔσται συλλογισμὸς οὐδάμως ἐν τούτῳ τῷ
σχήματι, δυνατὸς δ᾽ ἔσται.   Arist. A. Pr. 27ᵃ1.

7   Of a person, *effective, decisive.*

> ψῦχος ἐν δόμοις πέλει,
> ἀνδρὸς τελείου δῶμ᾽ ἐπιστρωφωμένου.   A. *Ag.* 972.

The choice of the word is obviously to pave the way for the appeal to Ζεὺς τέλειος in the next line (see 4 above). So of drugs:

> φάρμακον ἡμῖν αὐτὸ τελειότατον καὶ ἄριστον φαρμάκων
> ἐπιστήμην εὐχόμεθα διδόναι.
> Pl. *Criti.* 106b; cf. Scribonius Largus 177.

8   As applied to things, whether concrete or abstract, *having no part missing, complete, entire, whole.*

> οἴκατε πανδαισίῃ τελείῃ ἱστιῆσθαι.   Hdt. 5. 20. 4; 9. 110. 2.

> ὁ δ᾽ ἐμός γε (ἀνὴρ) τελέους ἑπτὰ μῆνας ἐν Πύλῳ.
> Ar. *Lys.* 104.

> ὅ γε τέλεος ἀριθμὸς χρόνου τὸν τέλεον ἐνιαυτὸν πληροῖ τότε.
> Pl. *Ti.* 39d.

> βοῖ κα θōᾱ(δ)δοι καὶ κοθάρσι τελείαι. 'let him make expiation with an ox and complete purification.'
> Schwyzer 412. 1 (Olympia, v BC).

> τούτους δὲ κόρυζαι μὲν τέλειαι μάλιστα ἀπαλλάσσουσι,
> ὠφελέουσι δὲ καὶ πταρμοί.   Hp. *Prorrh.* 2. 30 (9, 60 L).

> ἐν ἀγοράι τελείωι.   *SEG* 27. 124 (Delphi).

> ἁλιαίαι ἔδοξε τελείαι.   *SEG* 30. 355. 2 (Argos, iv BC).

> συνθέσις τελείας λευκὰς δεκατρεῖς 'thirteen complete white suits of clothes'.   *P. Hamb.* 10. 14 (ii AD).

> τελείαν ἀποζυγήν 'complete separation (of a married couple)'.
> *P. Grenf.* 2. 76. 19 (iv AD).

9   It is used also in the superlative of qualities, *approximating to the ultimate, complete, perfect.*

> τὴν τελέαν ἀδικίαν τελέας οὔσης δικαιοσύνης λυσιτελεστέραν
> φῂς εἶναι;   Pl. *R.* 348b.

> ἐπὶ τὴν τελεωτάτην ἀδικίαν.   Pl. *R.* 344a.

> καὶ τελεία μάλιστα ἀρετή, ὅτι τῆς τελείας ἀρετῆς χρῆσίς
> ἐστιν.   Arist. *EN* 1129ᵇ30; 1156ᵇ34.

> τελειοτάτη κακία.   Gal. 16. 500.

10 Of persons, *possessing the quality indicated in the highest degree, accomplished, perfect*.

καὶ ἔστιν ... ὁ θεὸς τέλεος σοφιστής. Pl. *Cra.* 403e.

κινδυνεύει ... εἰκότως ὁ Περικλῆς πάντων τελεώτατος εἰς τὴν ῥητορικὴν γενέσθαι. Pl. *Phdr.* 269e.

δεῖ τέλεον οὕτω γίγνεσθαι πρὸς ἀνδρείαν. Pl. *Lg.* 647d; 678b.

τὴν δὲ φύσιν ... πρὸς ... τοὺς λόγους οὔτε τελείαν οὔτε πανταχῇ χρησίμην. Isoc. 12. 9.

τούτους φημὶ καὶ φρονίμους εἶναι καὶ τελέους ἄνδρας καὶ πάσας ἔχειν τὰς ἀρετάς. Isoc. 12. 32; 242.

κατὰ πάντας ἰατρούς τε καὶ φιλοσόφους τοὺς τελείους δογματικούς. Gal. 15. 60.

ἱστοριῶν συγγραφέα τέλειον. *SEG* 1. 400 (Samos, ii AD).

11 In the New Testament there is evidence of at least one sense unrecognised by LSJ, *perfect in goodness*. In some cases it appears to be used of true believers, and might perhaps indicate *initiated*.

ἔσεσθε οὖν ὑμεῖς τέλειοι ὡς ὁ πατὴρ ὑμῶν τέλειός ἐστιν.
Ev. Matt. 5. 48.

εἰ θέλεις τέλειος εἶναι, ὕπαγε πώλησόν σου τὰ ὑπάρχοντα καὶ δὸς πτωχοῖς. *Ev. Matt.* 19. 21.

σοφίαν δὲ λαλοῦμεν ἐν τοῖς τελείοις. *1 Ep. Cor.* 2. 6.

ὅσοι οὖν τέλειοι, τοῦτο φρονῶμεν. *Ep. Phil.* 3. 15.

12 The pattern thus revealed may be tabulated as follows:

1 of living things, whether persons, animals or plants, *fully-grown, adult*; also of things, *full size* (2).

2 of sacrificial victims, *full grown and complete* (3).

3 as an epithet of gods, *bringing about fulfilment of prayers, accomplishing* (4).

4 of prayers, omens, dreams, etc, *leading to fulfilment, reliable, true* (5).

5 of decisions, votes, syllogisms, etc., *conclusive, decisive, final* (6).

6 of persons, *effective, decisive* (7).

7 of things, *having no part missing, complete, entire, whole* (8).

8 of qualities, *approximating to the ultimate, complete, perfect* (9).

9 of persons, *possessing the quality indicated in the highest degree, accomplished, perfect* (10).

10 In N. T., *perfect in goodness;* also perhaps, *initiated* (11).

τέμνω

1 I devoted some space in my article in BICS (1994), 5–7 to a criticism of LSJ's treatment of this word, but I did not attempt to construct a replacement for it. The following is an outline of such an article, but it must not be taken as a full and definitive re-writing, which time and space prevent me from attempting. I have not, with one exception, concerned myself with the forms, since they do not affect the meaning. Nor have I specially noted the use of the middle voice, which appears to me to be in accordance with its usual value.

2 The first distinction to be made is between literal cutting with a sharp tool and figurative division. But even where the word refers to the literal action, there are many distinctions to be observed and special uses to be noted. We may begin with the simplest sense, *make an incision in, cut open.*

> ἵεντ᾽ ἀλλήλων ταμέειν χρόα νηλέϊ χαλκῷ.
> Il. 13. 501 (= 16. 761).

> σφάγι᾽ ἔχων κάμηλον ἀ-
> μνόν τιν᾽, ἧς λαιμοὺς τεμών ... ἀπῆλθε.   Ar. *Av.* 1560.

Absolutely:

> —εἰπεῖν γε μέντοι δεῖ σ᾽ ὅπως κατέκτανες.
> —λέγω· ξιφουλκῷ χειρὶ πρὸς δέρην τεμών.   A. *Eu.* 592.

> τοὺς μὲν πρόσθεν ὀδόντας πᾶσι ζῴοις οἵους τέμνειν εἶναι.
> X. *Mem.* 1. 4. 6.

Of narrow bandages:

> οἱ στενοὶ μὲν γὰρ (τελαμῶνες) τέμνουσι.
> Sor. 1. 83 (= 2. 14. 6 I).

3 As a special use we can distinguish, ignoring LSJ's classification, *cut open for remedial purposes, perform surgery on.* This is especially used absolutely.

οὐ τεμέω δὲ οὐδὲ μὴν λιθιῶντας. Hp. Jusj.

ὁκόσοι ἧπαρ διάπυον καίονται ἢ τέμνονται. Hp. Aph. 7. 44.

φοβούμενος ὡσπερανεὶ παῖς τὸ κάεσθαι καὶ τὸ τέμνεσθαι.
Pl. Grg. 479a.

ἐδόκ[ε]ι αὐτῶι ὁ θεὸς ποιτάξαι τοῖς ἑπομένοις ὑπηρέτα[ις
συ]λ(λ)αβόντας αὐτὸν ἴσχειν, ὅπως τάμηι οὐ τὰν κοιλίαν. 'It
seemed that the god ordered the attendants following him to
take hold of him and hold him so that he could cut open his
belly.' IG 4²(1). 122. 40 (= Schwyzer 109. 40, Epidaurus, iv BC).

Absolutely, especially coupled with cautery:

ἤτοι κέαντες ἢ τεμόντες εὐφρόνως
πειρασόμεσθα πῆμ' ἀποστρέψαι νόσου. A. Ag. 849.

καὶ γὰρ οἱ ἰατροὶ καίουσι καὶ τέμνουσι ἐπ' ἀγαθῷ.
X. An. 5. 8. 18.

παρέχειν μύσαντα εὖ καὶ ἀνδρείως ὥσπερ τέμνειν καὶ καίειν
ἰατρῷ. Pl. Grg. 480c.

4 A quite different type of surgery is where it means *castrate*,
geld.

ἐρίφους τέμνειν καὶ πώεα μήλων. Hes. Op. 786; 791.

ὡς γάρ μιν ἡ Ῥέη ἔτεμεν. Luc. Syr. D. 15.

5 In agriculture it may be used to mean *prune*.

ἓξ ἔτη τεμεῖς τὴν ἄμπελόν σου. LXX Le. 25. 3.

καὶ ἀνήσω τὸν ἀμπελῶνά μου, καὶ οὐ τμηθῇ οὐδὲ μὴ σκαφῇ.
LXX Is. 5. 6.

But also *plough* land.

ἵν' οὔτ' ἄροτρον οὔτε γατόμος
τέμνει δίκελλ' ἄρουραν. A. fr. 196.

6 Another special sense is where cutting is used to slaughter an
animal, usually as a sacrifice. A simple example of *slaughter* is:

ἀγνοοῦντες ὅτι τῷ ὄντι ὥσπερ Ὕδραν τέμνουσιν. Pl. R. 426e.

But elsewhere it is largely restricted to *slaughter in sacrifice*.

κάπρον ἑτοιμασάτω, ταμέειν Διί τ' Ἡελίῳ τε. Il. 19. 197.

σφάγιά θ' ἠτοιμασμένα
ἕστηκεν οἷς χρὴ ταῦτα τέμνεσθαι θεῶν.   E. Heracl. 400.
ἐν ᾧ δὲ τέμνειν σφάγια χρή σ', ἄκουέ μου.   E. Supp. 1196.

The use with ὅρκια must have begun while this word still meant
'victims sacrificed to solemnise an oath' and some of the examples
still seem to bear this sense; but as early as Homer ὅρκια τέμνειν had
acquired the sense *solemnise an agreement by a sacrifice.*

ὅρκια πιστὰ ταμόντες.   Il. 2. 124; 3. 73; Od. 24. 483.

With accusative:

θάνατόν νύ τοι ὅρκι' ἔταμνον.   Il. 4. 155.

αἷμα συμμίσγουσι τῶν τὸ ὅρκιον ταμνομένων.   Hdt. 4. 70.

ἐπὶ τῆς κρυπτῆς τάφρου τάμνοντες ὅρκια, ἔστ' ἂν ἡ γῆ αὕτη
οὕτως ἔχῃ, μένειν τὸ ὅρκιον.   Hdt. 4. 201. 2.

ἐπὶ τούτοισι οἱ Ἕλληνες ἔταμον ὅρκιον.   Hdt. 7. 132. 2.

ἔταμον ὅρκια περὶ τούτων πρὸς τοὺς περὶ τὸν Ἀντίπατρον.
                    Plb. 21. 24. 3; 21. 32. 15.

With other terms for an agreement:

σπονδὰς τέμωμεν καὶ διαλλάχθητί μου.   E. Hel. 1235.

                    ἆρα φίλιά μοι
τεμεῖ, καὶ τέκνοις ταφὰς ληψόμεσθα;   E. Supp. 376.

7   We can pass naturally from slaughter to butchery, where τέμνω
means *cut in pieces, cut up.*

ἐν δ' ἄρα νῶτον ἔθηκ' ὄϊος καὶ πίονος αἰγός,
ἐν δὲ συὸς σιάλοιο ῥάχιν τεθαλυῖαν ἀλοιφῇ.
τῷ ἔχεν Αὐτομέδων, τάμνεν δ' ἄρα δῖος Ἀχιλλεύς.   Il. 9. 209.

                    ἠέ μιν ἤδη
ᾗσι κυσὶν μελεϊστὶ ταμὼν προὔθηκεν Ἀχιλλεύς.   Il. 24. 409.

τοὺς δὲ διὰ μελεϊστὶ ταμὼν ὁπλίσσατο δόρπον.   Od. 9. 291.

In such lines it is always doubtful whether the verb should be
treated as τέμνω or διατέμνω with tmesis. In the middle voice:

ταμνομένους κρέα πολλά.   Od. 24. 364.

μαχαίρᾳ τάμον κατὰ μέλη.   Pi. O. 1. 49.

ἡ δ' ἀντ' αὐτοῦ τάμνουσα ἰχθῦς παρέχει βορὴν τοῖσι θηρίοισι.
                    Hdt. 2. 65. 4; 3. 42. 3.

Cutting up may be for other purposes:

αὐτὸς δ' ἀμφὶ πόδεσσιν ἑοῖς ἀράρισκε πέδιλα,
τάμνων δέρμα βόειον ἐϋχροές.   Od. 14. 24.

ἕκαστος οὖν ἡμῶν ἐστιν ἀνθρώπου σύμβολον, ἅτε τετμημένος
ὥσπερ αἱ ψῆτται ἐξ ἑνὸς δύο.   Pl. Smp. 191d.

8 Medicinal drugs were usually some part of a plant, which needed to be cut up for use; hence φάρμακον τέμνειν came to mean *administer a drug, apply a remedy*. Thus the phrase can be used figuratively.

καὶ τί τέμνων φάρμακον τούτοις ἑκάστοις τοῦ τοιούτου
κινδύνου διαφυγὴν εὑρήσει;   Pl. Lg. 836b; 919b.

τούτων δὴ χρὴ πάσῃ προθυμίᾳ πάντας τοὺς Ἕλληνας τέμνειν
φάρμακον.   Pl. Ep. 353e.

εἴ τί σοι δυναίμαν
ἄκος τῶν δυσλύτων πόνων τεμεῖν.   E. Andr. 121.

This is probably the explanation of a possibly corrupt line in Aeschylus:

ἀμφυγᾶς τίν' ἔτι πόρον
τέμνω γάμου λυτῆρα;   A. Supp. 807.

9 Another major division is where the purpose of cutting is to remove something: *cut off, cut out*.

ἀρνῶν ἐκ κεφαλέων τάμνε τρίχας.   Il. 3. 273.

τάμνε μαχαίρῃ
ὀξὺ βέλος περιπευκές.   Il. 11. 844.

LSJ classifies this with the examples of surgery given in 3 above, but the essential difference is the nature of the object.

κεφαλὴν δέ ἑ θυμὸς ἄνωγε
πῆξαι ἀνὰ σκολόπεσσι ταμόνθ' ἀπαλῆς ἀπὸ δειρῆς.
    Il. 18. 177.

δυοῖν δρακόντοιν εὐπετῶς τεμὼν κάρα.
    A. Ch. 1047; S. Ph. 619.

αὔτως ὅπωσπερ τόνδ' ἐγὼ τέμνω πλόκον.   S. Aj. 1179.

τεμοῦσα κρατὸς βοστρύχων ἄκρας φόβας.
    S. El. 449; 901; E. Tr. 480.

τράχηλον σώματος χωρὶς τεμών. E. *Ba.* 241.

τὸν δὲ λίθον ἔτεμνον ὑπὸ τῆς νήσου ... τέμνοντες δὲ ἅμ᾽
ἠργάζοντο νεωσοίκους κοίλους. Pl. *Criti.* 116a.

10 As a special sense of this we may put *cut down, fell* trees or
crops.

τάμνων δένδρεα μακρά. Il. 11. 88; 23. 119.

μελίη ὥς ...
χαλκῷ ταμνομένη. Il. 13. 180.

τῇ ὁδῷ ἣν πρότερον ἐποιήσατο τεμὼν τὴν ὕλην. Th. 2. 98. 1.

ἢ σῆς ἔμελλον γῆς τεμεῖν βλαστήματα
πλεύσαντες αὖθις; E. *Hec.* 1204.

οἱ ἄλλων σπειράντων καὶ φυτευσάντων τόν τε σῖτον τέμνοντες
καὶ δενδροκοποῦντες. X. *Mem.* 2. 1. 13.

11 This can usefully be distinguished from the examples in
which the purpose of cutting is to acquire what is cut, especially
gather, cull, reap plants. The middle is particularly used in this
sense, i.e. gather for oneself.

ὁ δ᾽ ἐρινεὸν ὀξέϊ χαλκῷ
τάμνε νέους ὄρπηκας, ἵν᾽ ἅρματος ἄντυγες εἶεν. Il. 21. 38.

αὐτὰρ ὁ τάμνετο δοῦρα. Od. 5. 243.

φιτροὺς δ᾽ αἶψα ταμόντες. Od. 12. 11.

εἴ ποθί τοι ῥόπαλον τετμημένον ἐστί. Od. 17. 195.

ὑλοτόμον τε ταμεῖν θαλαμήϊα δοῦρα
νήϊά τε ξύλα πολλά. Hes. *Op.* 807.

ἐπεὰν ... νομέας εἰτέης ταμόμενοι ποιήσωνται 'cut and make
ribs of willow'. Hdt. 1. 194. 2.

ξύλα μὲν οὖν τεμόντες ἐκ τοῦ Κιθαιρῶνος. Th. 2. 75. 2.

φάσκων τέμνειν χάρακας ἐκ τοῦ ... Διὸς τεμένους.
Th. 3. 70. 4.

Ἰδαίαν ὅτε πρῶτον ὕλαν
Ἀλεξάνδρας εἰλατίναν
ἐτάμεθ᾽. E. *Hec.* 634.

ἢ τίς Ἑλλανίας ἀπὸ χθονὸς
ἔτεμε τὰν δακρυόεσσαν
Ἰλίῳ πεύκαν; E. *Hel.* 231.

τὴν ὕλην τὴν τετμημένην πεπρακότα. D. 42. 30.

ῥίζα μέλαινα ... ἥτις τέμνεται φθινοπώρῳ. Dsc. 3. 132. 1.

Similarly, *make by cutting*.

σπαδίξας δὲ αὐτοῦ τὸ δέρμα ἱμάντας ἐξ αὐτοῦ ἔταμε.
Hdt. 1. 194. 2.

Where it is used of stone, we should translate *quarry*.

ἐτάμνετο λίθους περιμήκεας. Hdt. 1. 186. 2.

μεδὲ τὸς λίθος τέμνεν ἐκ τὸ [Π]ελαργικô.
IG 1². 76. 56. (Epidaurus, v BC).

πέτραν γὰρ ἔχει πολλὴν σιδηρῖτιν, ἣν τέμνουσιν ἐπὶ τὴν χωνείαν καὶ κατασκευὴν τοῦ σιδήρου. D. S. 5. 13. 1.

12 Where the object is land, τέμνω means *clear of vegetation, lay bare*. This may be an agricultural operation, but is much more often military, where we should translate *ravage*.

ἄλλους γῆν τέμνων πολυδένδρεον εἰς ἐνιαυτὸν
λατρεύει, τοῖσιν καμπύλ' ἄροτρα μέλει. Sol. 13. 47.

τήν τε γῆν αὐτῶν ἔταμνον καὶ προσέβαλλον πρὸς τὸ τεῖχος.
Hdt. 9. 86. 2.

περιδεῖν αὐτὴν (sc. τὴν γῆν) τμηθεῖσαν.
Th. 2. 18. 5; 2. 20. 2; And. 3. 8.

ἔτεμνον ... Ἐλευσῖνα καὶ τὸ Θριάσιον πεδίον. Th. 2. 19. 2.

τῆς τε γῆς ἔτεμον οὐ πολλὴν καὶ σῖτον ἀνεκομίσαντο.
Th. 6. 7. 1.

13 Similar to this is where the object is a road, a channel, or a mine: *open up by cutting, cut*.

μυρίαι δ' ἔργον καλῶν τέ-
τμανθ' ἑκατόμπεδοι ἐν σχερῷ κέλευθοι. Pi. I. 6. 22.

τοῦ Περσικοῦ ... ἐόντος πεζοῦ στρατοῦ καὶ τὰς ὁδοὺς οὐκ
ἐπισταμένου ὥστε οὐ τετμημένων ὁδῶν. Hdt. 4. 136. 2.

ὁδοὺς εὐθείας ἔτεμε. Th. 2. 100. 2.

διάπλους ἐκ τῶν διωρύχων ... τεμόντες. Pl. Criti. 118e.

διὸ δὴ τῆς ἀρτηρίας ὀχετοὺς ἐπὶ τὸν πλεύμονα ἔτεμον.
Pl. Ti. 70d; 77c.

φήναντος γὰρ Λυσάνδρου τὸ Ἐπικράτους μέταλλον ... ⟨ὡς⟩
ἐ⟨κ⟩τὸς τῶν μέτρων τετμημένον. Hyp. Eux. 35.

14 This naturally leads to the extension of sense where the object is the medium of travel or the route pursued. Where it is the sea or air, it is possible to regard this as a simple extension of the idea of cutting through, and we might translate *cleave*. But we find also examples with ὁδόν and similar objects, where it seems to mean no more than *make one's way through, pursue*.

> ἠνώγει πέλαγος μέσον εἰς Εὔβοιαν
> τέμνειν. Od. 3. 175.

> ὡς ἡ ῥίμφα θέουσα θαλάσσης κύματ' ἔταμνεν. Od. 13. 88.

> βαθὺν ἠέρα τέμνον ἰόντες. h.Cer. 383.

> καί κεν ἐν ναυσὶν μόλον Ἰονίαν τάμνων θάλασσαν.
> Pi. P. 3. 68.

> ὁ πεζὸς στρατὸς ἐπορεύετο ἐκ τῆς Ἀκάνθου τὴν μεσόγαιαν
> τέμνων τῆς ὁδοῦ. Hdt. 7. 124; 9. 89. 4.

> ὦ τὴν ἐν ἄστροις οὐρανοῦ τέμνων ὁδὸν ...
> Ἥλιε. E. Ph. 1; Epigr. 2.

> ἀλίμενον αἰθέρος αὔλακα τέμνων. Ar. Av. 1400.

> διὰ μέσου γὰρ αἰθέρος
> τέμνων κέλευθον. Ar. Th. 1100.

Absolutely:

> ἐπιπρὸ γὰρ αἰὲν ἔτεμνον
> ἐσσυμένως, λιαροῖο φορεύμενοι ἐξ ἀνέμοιο.
> A. R. 2. 1244; 4. 771.

Figuratively:

> αἵ γε μὲν ἀνδρῶν
> πόλλ' ἄνω, τὰ δ' αὖ κάτω ψεύδη μεταμώνια τάμνοι-
> σαι κυλίνδοντ' ἐλπίδες. Pi. O. 12. 6.

> ποίην τις βιότοιο τάμοι τρίβον; AP 9. 359. 1; 360. 1.

> οὐδὲ ἐγὼ πρῶτος ταύτην ἐτεμόμην τὴν ὁδόν. Luc. Pr. Im. 24.

15 A special use of this, in the examples always figurative, is the phrase μέσον or τὴν μέσην τέμνειν, *pursue a middle course*.

> δέομαι ... μήτ' αὖ Πρωταγόραν ... φεύγειν εἰς τὸ πέλαγος
> τῶν λόγων ἀποκρύψαντα γῆν, ἀλλὰ μέσον τι ἀμφοτέρους
> τεμεῖν. 'I beg you ... both to keep to a middle course.'
> Pl. Prt. 338a; Lg. 793a.

> ἔντεχνον δὲ τὸ τὴν μέσην ἐν ἅπασι τέμνειν ἐμμελές τε.
> Plu. 2. 7b.

16 Finally there are uses where no physical cutting is intended, but an analogous action: *separate, divide*. This may be by marking out an area.

καὶ μέν οἱ Λύκιοι τέμενος τέμον ἔξοχον ἄλλων.
Il. 6. 194; 9. 580.

LSJ quotes under this heading:

τέμει δέ τε (ζυγὸν) τέλσον ἀρούρης. Il. 13. 707.

But τέμει is now better interpreted as the present to ἔτετμον *reach*, so it does not belong to this word.

ἐλθὼν δ᾽ εἰς τὴν ἀρχὴν καὶ λαβὼν αὐτὴν ἔβδομος, διείλετο ἑπτὰ μέρη τεμόμενος. Pl. *Lg.* 695c.

Also, by coming between so as to separate off:

ὦκα δ᾽ ἔπειτα
τάμνοντ᾽ ἀμφὶ βοῶν ἀγέλας καὶ πώεα καλὰ
ἀργεννέων οἰῶν. Il. 18. 528.

ῥέει γὰρ ἐκ Λιβύης ὁ Νεῖλος καὶ μέσην τάμνων τὴν Λιβύην.
Hdt. 2. 33. 2.

ἀμφὶ ποταμὸν Τάναον Ἀργείας ὄρους
τέμνοντα γαίας Σπαρτιάτιδός τε γῆς. E. *El.* 411.

By making a division in a line or other things:

ὥσπερ τοίνυν γραμμὴν δίχα τετμημένην λαβὼν ἄνισα τμήματα. Pl. *R.* 509d.

τοῦτο τοίνυν ἔτι διαιρετέον ... πῶς οὖν τέμνομεν δίχα, λέγεις;
Pl. *Phlb.* 49a; *Plt.* 287b; *Sph.* 223c.

τινὲς μὲν οὖν εἰς δύο μέρη τέμνουσιν αὐτὴν (*sc.* τὴν παράδοσιν). Sor. 1. 1.

17 It may also mean *act violently upon so as to lessen, cut down*.

ἐπεὶ δὲ καὶ τέμνει (ἡ πτισάνη) καὶ ὑγραίνει τὰ ἀναπτύσεως δεόμενα. Gal. 15. 507.

τούτοις γὰρ (φαρμάκοις) ἔργον ἐστὶν ... τέμνειν ... καὶ λεπτύνειν τὰ πάχεα τῶν ὑγρῶν. Gal. 6. 760; Sor. 1. 98.

τροφαί τε ὁμοίως διαχέουσαι καὶ τέμνουσαι τὸ φλέγμα.
Gal. 14. 472; 6. 352.

18 Used by poets and late prose in a transferred sense, *put an end to, do away with, resolve.*

ἐδόκησαν
ἐπ' ἀμφότερα μαχᾶν τάμνειν τέλος.   Pi. *O.* 13. 57.

μέλλω καὶ ὑπὲρ δόμων
  ἱκετὰς ὑποδεχθεὶς
κίνδυνον πολιῷ τεμεῖν σιδάρῳ.   E. *Heracl.* 758.

λόγῳ τὰ διάφορα τεμεῖν.   Lib. *Or.* 18. 164.

19 I have already in the article quoted at the beginning of this note drawn attention to the new sense created by LSJ as **VIII** 'metaph. for ἀρύσας' on the evidence of a single line cited unmetrically from Empedocles:

κρηνάων ἄπο πέντε ταμόντ' ⟨ἐν⟩ ἀτειρέϊ χαλκῷ.   Emp. 143.

While 'draw water' might seem a possible translation, a fuller context might well reveal a noun such as ὀχετούς allowing τέμνω to have a normal sense (see 13 above). The emendation is far from certain, since ἀτειρής may have an artificially lengthened first syllable on the (false) analogy of ἀκάματος, etc.

τοπαδειν

This word appears in an inscription of ii AD apparently erected by Herodes Atticus, which begins:

Μέμνων
τοπαδειν
Ἀρτέμιδος φίλος ...   *IG* 2². 13196.

Various suggestions have been made, the most favoured of which is to regard it as a spelling of τοπάζειν, understood to mean 'as one may guess'. This has been rightly criticised by R. Merkelbach, *ZPE* 48 (1982), 218, who suggests that it is a spelling for τοπάζιον. The diminutive of τόπαζος may well have been used as a term of endearment, and the spelling of -ιον as -ιν or -ειν is common. But on the change of consonant Merkelbach casually remarks: '-ζ- und -δ- gehen leicht ineinander über.' However, L. Threatte, *The Grammar of Attic Inscriptions,* i. 550, correctly states: 'The use of Δ for Z is foreign to Attic. There is a peculiar τοπαδειν (for τοπάζειν) in [this text]; none of the other similar texts has τοπάζειν or any related word. There are rare cases of Δ for Z in graffiti from the Agora ...' A much simpler remedy would be to suppose an engraver's error, the omission of I. The mysterious word will then be read τὸ πα⟨ι⟩δείν = τὸ παιδίον. We know that Memnon died young.

τόπος

1 There is a problem about the origin of this word, since it is absent from early epic and it appears first in Attic tragedy, where it is regularly used by all three tragedians. It is however rare in prose in v BC, and only becomes common and develops new senses from iv onwards. This distribution hardly supports Frisk's qualification of it as 'Wort der Alltagssprache' (*GEW*). The cognates proposed (see Frisk) are uncertain and semantically remote; there no evidence of any similar noun in other languages. Chantraine (*DELG*) has no hesitation in brushing them aside with the simple comment 'étymologie inconnue'. But these facts would be easily explained if the word were in fact a new coinage of Greek, perhaps an Atticism of the later vi century. I am therefore tempted to suggest, though very tentatively, that it began with a reply to a question containing the interrogative ποῦ with an expression such as περὶ τὸ ποῦ ἀπορῶ. This might have been misinterpreted with a change of accent as the genitive of a noun τόπος, which was thus created by back-formation. The new coinage filled a very useful function in the language, which down to this date appears to have had no single noun to describe location in space. For nouns created from interrogatives compare English *whereabouts, the why and wherefore,* Italian *ubicazione.*

2 The earliest uses seem to be fairly restricted. I have added a certain number of examples, prefixed with *, to those in LSJ; but I have ignored some of the very specialised meanings attributed to late authors. The simplest meaning appears to be a *point or region in space, geographical locality, place, spot.*

> χθονὸς γὰρ πᾶς πεποίμναται τόπος 'every spot on earth has been traversed'. A. *Eu.* 249.

· ἴσως γὰρ τόπον ἐσχατιᾶς
προιδεῖν ἐθέλεις ὄντινα κεῖται.   *S. *Ph.* 144.

εἰς ἐπόψιον τόπον.   *S. *Ant.* 1110.

ὡς δ' ἐν γαλήνῃ πάντ' ἐδερκόμην τόπον.   *S. *El.* 899.

κοὐδεὶς ἐπισπᾶταί με συμμαθεῖν τόπος.   *S. *Aj.* 869.

ἦν μὲν Κιθαιρών, ἦν δὲ πρόσχωρος τόπος.   *S. *OT* 1127.

εἴτε δὴ ὦν ἐς Σαρδὼ ἐκ τοῦ τόπου τούτου ἄγοι ἐς ἀποικίην.
                                            *Hdt. 5. 124. 2.

ἐν τόπῳ (*prob. corrupt, perhaps for* τρόπῳ) δέ τινι ἀφανεῖ.
                                            Th. 6. 54. 4.

ὁ δὲ τόπος οὗτος Ἀρμενία ἐκαλεῖτο ἡ πρὸς ἑσπέραν.
                                            X. *An.* 4. 4. 4.

ναυπηγησίμης ὕλης ὁ τόπος ἡμῖν τῆς χώρας πῶς ἔχει;
Pl. *Lg.* 705c; 760c; D. 4. 31.

ὥσθ' ὅλον τόπον καὶ πλεῖν ἢ μυρίους ... ὁπλίτας ...
συμπαρεσκεύασεν.   D. 19. 230.

Often qualified by a geographical term:

τὸν Κιθαιρῶνος τόπον.   *S. *OT* 1134.

            τὸν αὐτὸν ἐς τόπον
Τροίας ἐπελθών.   *S. *Aj.* 437.

τὸν μὲν τόπον τὸν Ἑλληνικόν.   Isoc. 5. 107.

τὸν ἐπὶ Θρᾴκης τόπον.   Aeschin. 2. 9; 3. 73.

τὸν περὶ Θρᾴκην τόπον.   D. 20. 59.

So of places outside this world:

τὸν δὲ ὑπερουράνιον τόπον οὔτε τις ὕμνησέ πω τῶν τῇδε
ποιητὴς οὔτε ποτὲ ὑμνήσει κατ' ἀξίαν.   *Pl. *Phdr.* 247c.

ἐλπίζομεν ... ὅτι ταχέως ἡμᾶς ἐλεήσει, καὶ ἐπισυνάξει ... εἰς
τὸν ἅγιον τόπον.   LXX 2 *Ma.* 2. 18.

3   A special use is found in the medical writers to indicate a
particular *part or area of the body*.

δύο πόνων ἅμα γινομένων μὴ κατὰ τὸν αὐτὸν τόπον.
                                            Hp. *Aph.* 2. 46.

This occurs in the title of several works both in this Corpus and in
Galen. LSJ records a further specialisation of this to mean *puden-·
dum muliebre*. This is alleged to occur in this passage:

ἔπαρσις μὲν οὖν τοῖς θήλεσι (ζῴοις) γίγνεται τῶν αἰδοίων,
ὅταν πρὸς τὴν ὀχείαν ὀργῶσι, καὶ ὑγρασία περὶ τὸν τόπον.

Arist. *HA* 572ᵇ28.

But it is evident that τὸν τόπον here might mean 'the part in question', which is in fact τὰ αἰδοῖα. But in a second reference it is clear
that this specialised sense had in fact developed:

γίγνεται δὲ σημεῖον τοῦ συνειληφέναι ταῖς γυναιξίν, ὅταν
εὐθὺς γένηται μετὰ τὴν ὁμιλίαν ὁ τόπος ξηρός.

Arist. *HA* 583ᵃ15.

The plural is frequently used in this sense by Soranus, e.g.:

ὕδωρ δὲ θερμὸν χάριν τοῦ ἀποπλυθῆναι τοὺς τόπους.

Sor. 2. 2 (= p. 51. 3 I).

4   When used in the plural it naturally acquires a wider meaning,
vicinity, region, area. In later Greek the sense of *region* becomes
frequent also in the singular, and this gives rise to some late uses,
such as when it refers to an administrative district or τοπαρχία.

παλιρρόχθοις ἐν Αὐλίδος τόποις.   A. *Ag.* 191.

χώρας ἐν τόποις Λιβυστικῆς.   A. *Eu.* 292.

οὔτ' ἐν Σκύθησιν οὔτε Πέλοπος ἐν τόποις.   A. *Eu.* 703.

πρόσθε Σαλαμῖνος τόπων.   A. *Pers.* 447.

ἐν Ἑλλάδος τόποις.   A. *Pers.* 796.

πρὸς ἑσπέρους τόπους.   A. *Pr.* 348.

ἐν τοῖσι αὐτοῖσι τόποισι κατοικημένοι εἰσί.   *Hdt. 4. 22. 2.

ἀνὴρ κατοικεῖ τούσδε τοὺς τόπους σαφῶς.   *S. *Ph.* 40.

ἤ που τῇδ' ἢ τῇδε τόπων.   *S. *Ph.* 204.

ὡδοιπόρεις δὲ πρὸς τί τούσδε τοὺς τόπους;
        *S. *OT* 1027; *OC* 64; *OC* 1020.

οἰκητῆρα ... τόπων
τῶν ἐνθάδ'.   *S. *OC* 627.

μήθ' οὗ κέκευθε μήτ' ἐν οἷς κεῖται τόποις.   *S. *OC* 1523.

        αὖρα
ἥτις μ' ἀποικίσειεν ἐκ τόπων.   *S. *Tr.* 955; E. *Ph.* 1027.

ἐπ' ἐσχάτοις τόποις.   *S. *Tr.* 1100.

Θρήκης ἐκ τόπων δυσχειμέρων.   E. *Alc.* 67; *Hipp. 53.

πέραν γε πόντου καὶ τόπων Ἀτλαντικῶν.   *E. *Hipp.* 1053.

ἢ κατ' οἶκον; ἢ ποίοις τόποις; *E. Ba. 1290.

ἐς τοὺς περὶ Οἰνάδας τόπους. *Th. 2. 102. 6.

πολλοὶ γὰρ ἐν τούτοις τοῖς τόποις ὄνοι καὶ νῦν ἔτι γίγνονται.
X. Cyr. 2. 4. 20.

τινὰ δὲ ἐπισκευάζοντος τῶν κοινῶν τόπων. IG 4²(1). 65. 8.

ἐκ τῶν ὑπαρχόντων ἀσύλων τόπων. P. Teb. 5. 83 (iii BC).

ἐν τοῖς ἔξω τόποις. BGU 1114. 6 (i BC).

5 Position in space can be regarded as a property of an object, *place occupied, position, location.*

ἐς τὸν Ἑλλήνων τόπον. A. Pers. 790.

τίς τόπος, ἢ τίς ἕδρα, τίν' ἔχει στίβον. *S. Ph. 157.

ὃν δ' ἐπιστείβεις τόπον
χθονὸς καλεῖται τῆσδε χαλκόπους ὁδός. *S. OC 56.

τὸν τόπον δ' ἵνα
χρῇσται μ' ἐφευρεῖν, τοῦτο βούλομαι μαθεῖν. *S. OC 503.

ἀλλὰ μήτε μοι χοὰς
μήθ' αἷμ' ἐάσῃς εἰς ἐμὸν στάξαι τόπον (s.v.l.).
E. Heracl. 1041.

ἀπέραντος μὲν ἀριθμὸς ἀνθρώπων ἐλέγετο, κατὰ δὲ τόπους
καὶ κώμας ... διενενέμηντο. Pl. Criti. 119a.

οὐ γὰρ τὸν τρόπον, ἀλλὰ τὸν τόπον μετήλλαξαν.
Aeschin. 3. 78.

καὶ γὰρ οἱ τόποι δύο, τὸ μέσον καὶ τὸ ἔσχατον.
Arist. Cael. 312a8; IA 707ᵇ3; PA 666ᵃ15.

ἴδε ὁ τόπος ὅπου ἔθηκαν αὐτόν. Ev. Marc. 16. 6.

6 To this may be attached the phrases ἐπὶ τόπου or τόπων, ἐν τόπῳ
in that place, on the spot.

ἵνα τὸ ... δίκαιον αὐτοῖς ἐπὶ τόπου διεξάγηται. Plb. 4. 73. 8.

ἐπὶ τῶν τόπων γενόμενος. CIL 3. 567. 3. (Delphi, ii BC).

ἵνα ἐπὶ τῶν τόπων τὸ τίμημα τούτων καταβληθείη.
P. Oxy. 2106. 24 (iv AD).

καταναλισκέτωσαν παραχρῆμα καὶ ταῦτα ἐν τόπῳ.
IG 12(7). 515. 63.

7 In later Greek this use is extended to places which are allocated to persons, whether as a dwelling or to occupy at table, etc., *place allocated, allotted place*.

δώσω σοι τόπον, οὗ φεύξεται ἐκεῖ ὁ φονεύσας.
*LXX *Ex*. 21. 13.

εἰσάξουσιν (αὐτοὺς) εἰς τὸν τόπον αὐτῶν. *LXX *Is*. 14. 2.

στενός μοι ὁ τόπος, ποίησόν μοι τόπον ἵνα κατοικήσω.
*LXX *Is*. 49. 20.

δώσω αὐτοῖς ἐν τῷ οἴκῳ μου καὶ ἐν τῷ τείχει μου τόπον ὀνομαστόν. *LXX *Is*. 56. 5.

ἀνέκλινεν αὐτὸν ἐν φάτνῃ, διότι οὐκ ἦν αὐτοῖς τόπος ἐν τῷ καταλύματι. *Ev. *Luc*. 2. 7.

ἐρεῖ σοι, δὸς τούτῳ τόπον, καὶ τότε ἄρξῃ μετὰ αἰσχύνης τὸν ἔσχατον τόπον κατέχειν. *Ev. *Luc*. 14. 9.

πορεύομαι ἑτοιμάσαι τόπον ὑμῖν. *Ev. *Jo*. 14. 2.

νυνὶ δὲ μηκέτι τόπον ἔχων ἐν τοῖς κλίμασι τούτοις.
*Ep. *Rom*. 15. 23.

οὐδὲ τόπος εὑρέθη αὐτοῖς ἔτι ἐν τῷ οὐρανῷ.
Apoc. 12. 8; 20. 11.

ἵνα πέτηται (ἡ γυνὴ) εἰς τὴν ἔρημον εἰς τὸν τόπον αὐτῆς.
Apoc. 12. 14.

δοῦναι δὲ αὐτῇ τόπον (*for burial*). *IG* 12(7). 401. 14.

This is quoted by LSJ as evidence for a sense 'burial-place' together with *Ev. Marc*. 16. 6 (for which see 5 above). There does not appear to be any very clear evidence for such a sense, though it would not be impossible.

8 Arising from this it was extended to mean a *room in a building*.

εἰς οἴκησιν αὐτῆς τόπον ἕνα ἄνευ ἐνο[ικίου.
BGU 896. 4 (ii AD).

θύρας καὶ κλεῖς πάντων τῶν τόπων. P. Oxy. 502. 34 (ii AD).

μισθώσει ... οἰκίας τὸ ἐνὸν κατάγειον καὶ τὸν ἐπάνω τῆς ἐξέδρας τόπον. P. Oxy. 912. 13 (iii AD).

δύο τόπους ἤτοι συμπόσια. P. Oxy. 1129. 10 (v AD).

9 Another extension is to mean a *place* for a thing, *proper place*. The phrase παρὰ τόπον means *out of place*.

ἐπειδὰν ὁ τόπος (sc. around a plant) ᾖ κενὸς καὶ μηδὲν τὸ ἀντιστατοῦν. Thphr. HP 1. 7. 1.

καὶ ἦν ὁ τόπος τόπος κτήνεσι. *LXX Nu. 32. 1.

ἔστι γὰρ ἀργυρίῳ τόπος ὅθεν γίνεται. *LXX Jb. 28. 1.

καὶ ποῖος τόπος τῆς καταπαύσεώς μου;
*LXX Is. 66. 1 (Act. Ap. 7. 49).

ὑπολιποῦ τόπον. 'leave a space' in writing.
P. Cair. Zen. 327. 83 (iii BC).

εὐθείας τόπος. In geometry, 'the space described by a straight line moving round a point'. Plu. 2. 1003e.

ἐξορχῇ παρὰ καιρὸν, παρὰ τόπον, ἄνευ θυμάτων, ἄνευ ἀγνείας.
Arr. Epict. 3. 21. 16.

τοὺς Ἡρακλέους ἄθλους (a statue) ... παρὰ τόπον κειμένους διὰ τὴν ἐρημίαν. Str. 10. 2. 21.

10 This can be used metaphorically to mean *position in a list or class, place;* so τόπον ἔχειν to be admitted to a class.

ὁ ἀναπληρῶν τὸν τόπον τοῦ ἰδιώτου. 1 Ep. Cor. 14. 16.

ὁ αἱρεθεὶς ὕπατος εἰς τὸν τοῦ Κίννα τόπον. D. S. 38/39. 3.

ἕτερος εἰς τὸ ἐκείνου καθίσταται τόπον. D. H. 2. 73. 3.

τόπῳ τῶν ἀπεζωσμένων. Hdn. 2. 14. 5.

φίλου οὐ δύνασαι τόπον ἔχειν. Arr. Epict. 2. 4. 5.

οὔτ' ἐν λόγοις τόπον ἔχων οὔτ' ἐν διαλόγοις. (The reference is to Plato's *Apology of Socrates,* which is neither a forensic speech nor a dialogue.) D. H. Dem. 23.

11 *Opportunity for action, scope.*

μὴ δῷς τόπον ἀνθρώπῳ καταράσασθαί σε. LXX Si. 4. 5.

διὰ τὸ μὴ καταλείπεσθαι σφίσι τόπον ἐλέους μηδὲ συγγνώμης.
Plb. 1. 88. 2.

μηδὲ δίδοτε τόπον τῷ διαβόλῳ. Ep. Eph. 4. 27.

δότε τόπον τῇ ὀργῇ (sc. τοῦ θεοῦ).
Ep. Rom. 12. 19; Plu. 2. 462b.

μετανοίας γὰρ τόπον οὐχ εὗρεν. Ep. Hebr. 12. 17.

κυκλωθέντες καὶ οὐδὲ φυγῆς τόπον εὐμοιρήσαντες.
Hld. 6. 13. 3.

12 A matter under discussion, point in an argument, subject, topic.
This tends to become a technical term of oratory.

ἵνα μηδεὶς αὐτῷ τόπος ἀσυκοφάντητος παραλείπηται.
Aeschin. 3. 216.

τόπον ἴδιον καὶ παντάπασιν ἀδιεξέργαστον. Isoc. 5. 109.

περὶ τὸν αὐτὸν τόπον διατρίβειν. Isoc. 10. 38.

οἷον ὁ τοῦ μᾶλλον καὶ ἧττον τόπος. Arist. Rh. 1358ᵃ14.

σχεδὸν μὲν οὖν ἡμῖν περὶ ἑκάστου τῶν εἰδῶν τῶν χρησίμων
καὶ ἀναγκαίων ἔχονται οἱ τόποι. Arist. Rh. 1396ᵇ30; 1397ᵃ7.

ἔστιν γὰρ στοιχεῖον καὶ τόπος εἰς ὃ πολλὰ ἐνθυμήματα
ἐμπίπτει. Arist. Rh. 1403ᵃ18; D. H. Comp. 1; Hermog. Prog.
6 (= 29 R); 11 (= 52 R).

ἕνα δὲ τόπον ἀγωνιᾶν τὸν κατὰ τοὺς Ῥοδίους. 'that he was
worried about one point, that concerning the Rhodians'.
Plb. 21. 18. 2; Ph. 2. 63 (= de Josepho 151).

13 Finally it may mean a place or passage in a book. If the first
example is not valid, this is a late development.

ἐν ἄλλῳ δὲ τόπῳ φησίν (τόπῳ is not needed here and has been
deleted as an interpolation). X. Mem. 2. 1. 20.

κατὰ τόπους τινὰς τῆς ἱστορίας. Plb. 12. 25ᶠ. 1.

ἀναπτύξας τὸ βιβλίον εὗρεν τὸν τόπον οὗ ἦν γεγραμμένον ...
Ev. Luc. 4. 17.

τραχαίοις

1 This is recorded as a new word by the editors of P. Oxy. 2728,
a letter of iii/iv AD. The relevant passage runs:

τὴν τούτων οὖν τιμὴν ἀπόστειλόν μοι ἐν μαρσιππίῳ ἐσφραγισμένον ἐν τραχαίοις· χρία γάρ ἐστιν ἀργυρίου.

'Send me therefore the price, sealed in a purse in ...' The
grammar of ἐσφραγισμένον is faulty, but no doubt the writer had
ἀργύριον in mind. The editors' note on this passage reads: 'The
next sentence suggests that he is asking either for cash or a quick
delivery. τροχίας means a messenger (Hesych.) and τροχίας χαλκός
means cast bronze (Poll. 7. 105). One of these may be relevant;

τραχύς seems not to be.' Their search of LSJ having proved disappointing, I should like to offer another suggestion.

2   At this date αι and ε are alternative spellings; τραχαίοις is equivalent to τραχέοις. This enables us to understand it as a new dative based on the neuter plural τὰ τραχέα, no doubt part of the process by which u-stem adjectives were eventually eliminated. 'Heteroclitic o-stem forms appear occasionally in the gen. and dat. sg. [of u-stem adjectives]' (F. T. Gignac, *Grammar of Greek Papyri*, ii. 127). We can add on this evidence in the dative plural also. There is thus no problem about the form of this word.

3   But if τραχαίοις is equivalent to τραχέσι, what does 'rough ones' mean in this context? The answer is provided by the Latin *asper*, which was used of coins to mean 'having rough edges', i.e. not smoothed by wear but in mint condition. Such coins would of course still have their full value as silver; we hear that Nero insisted on being paid in them: *exegitque ingenti fastidio et acerbitate nummum asperum* Suet. *Nero* 44. This use was so familiar that it was borrowed by Greek as ἄσπρον, and indeed the plural ἄσπρα remains in use down to the present day meaning 'money'. This word was discussed at length by E. Schwyzer (*IF* 49. 1–45, see especially p. 29), and he quotes other late examples of τραχύς used of coins, such as δηνάριον τραχύ (Gloss. ii. 269. 57) and τραχέα νομίσματα in Byzantine Greek. Perhaps even more significant is the use of ἄσπρος at a date earlier than this papyrus: δώσει τῇ πόλε[ι] χρυσοῦς ἑκατὸν ἄσπρους *IG* 12(8). 569 (Thasos, ii/iii AD). The example of this adjective quoted by LSJ from Aelian (*NA* 1. 26) meaning 'rough' is probably unsound; it is emended to λεπροῖς by modern editors.

τρώγω

1   LSJ gives a fair enough picture of this word, but some notes need to be added. Sense **III** *eat* is correctly reported, τρώγω having replaced ἐσθίω as present to ἔφαγον; but there is no hint that this is one of the important vocabulary changes which distinguish modern from ancient Greek, and therefore its appearance in the New Testament marks the beginning of the change. As so often, a

knowledge of modern Greek is indispensable for understanding the language of the gospels.

2 Again it is noted that the simple verb is not used in the aorist, either the inherited ἔτραγον or the analogical ἔτρωξα. This strongly suggests that it properly denoted a continued or repeated action, and the compound κατατρώγω was employed when it meant *consume*. For the one exception, see below.

3 The ancient grammarians observed that τρώγω was generally used of animals, and then went on to quote examples where it was used of human beings. It should be clear that this means it denoted an action typical of animals, but also on occasion taken by humans. Taken together with the aspectual point made in 2 above, it would appear that a satisfactory definition of its use in the present system would be *take repeated small bites at, nibble, gnaw*. This then explains the sense given by LSJ as **II** 'of men, *eat* vegetables or fruit'. It is not the object that defines the use, but the kind of eating. In any case the objects quoted range beyond fruit and vegetables to cakes and fish. It is predominantly used of consuming dessert after dinner, something which is usually taken in small quantities and eaten raw, especially to accompany drinks. It is therefore what we are accustomed to do at cocktail and similar parties.

> πίνουσι καὶ τρώγουσιν, οἱ μὲν ἴτρια,
> οἱ δ' ἄρτον αὐτῶν, οἱ δὲ συμμεμιγμένους
> γούρους φακοῖσι. Sol. 38. 1.

The ἴτρια were apparently something made with sesame like the modern *halvá*; γοῦροι were some other kind of sweetmeat or cake. It is obvious that these are things nibbled for pleasure, not consumed as a food.

> οὐ σῦκα ἔχουσι τρώγειν, οὐκ ἄλλο ἀγαθὸν οὐδέν.
> Hdt. 1. 71. 3; cf.

> κἀπευξαμένους τοῖσι θεοῖσιν
> διδόναι πλοῦτον τοῖς Ἕλλησιν,
> κριθάς τε ποιεῖν ἡμᾶς πολλὰς
> πάντας ὁμοίως οἶνόν τε πολὺν
> σῦκά τε τρώγειν. Ar. Pax 1324.

τούς τε γενομένους (κυάμους) οὔτε τρώγουσι οὔτε ἕψοντες
πατέονται. Hdt. 2. 37. 5; cf. 2. 92. 4.

Here there is a clear contrast between nibbling beans raw and eating them in quantity when cooked. It might be tempting to assign
the next example to the later sense *eat*, but the idea of eating
uncooked food is still appropriate.

Λωτοφάγοι, οἳ τὸν καρπὸν μοῦνον τοῦ λωτοῦ τρώγοντες
ζώουσι. Hdt. 4. 177.

εἰ δὲ δὴ τοῦτο (ὄψον) καὶ μετὰ δεῖπνον τρωξόμεθα.
X. *Smp.* 4. 8.

τρώγων ἐρεβίνθους ἀπεπνίγη πεφρυγμένους.
Pherecr. 170 K–A.

                                  κἂν ποίᾳ πόλει
τοσοῦτος ⟨ὢν⟩ τὸ μέγεθος ἰχθῦς τρώγεται;   Eup. 335 K-A.

— μελίπηκτα δ' εἴ σοι προσφέροι; — τρώγοιμι καὶ
ᾠὸν δὲ καταπίνοιμ' ἄν. Antiph. 138. 4 K-A.

We can explain the solitary example of an aorist:

μή μοι φακούς, μὰ τὸν Δί', οὐ γὰρ ἥδομαι·
ἢν γὰρ τράγῃ τις, τοῦ στόματος ὄζει κακόν.
Pherecr. 73. 5 K-A.

The reason for not using φάγῃ here must be the implication that
lentils if eaten raw will make one's breath smell bad. There is a
good example where it is used absolutely clearly meaning 'take
delicacies with a drink'.

ταύτην (τὴν γυναῖκα) τὸ μὲν οὑτωσὶ πίνειν ἡσυχῇ καὶ τρώγειν
ἠνάγκαζον. D. 19. 197.

The παρὰ προσδοκίαν joke in the *Clouds* again depends upon the
meaning being *nibble at*, rather than *eat*.

ἐκ πηριδίου
γνώμας τρώγων Πανδελετείους. Ar. *Nu.* 924.

4   The example of *eat* quoted by LSJ in sense **III** from
Batrachomyomachia belongs properly to the section dealing with
animals, for which I have not thought it necessary to quote the
examples. The speaker is a mouse, who claims significantly to be
the son of Τρωξάρτης.

σοὶ μὲν γὰρ βίος ἐστὶν ἐν ὕδασιν· αὐτὰρ ἔγωγε
ὅσσα παρ' ἀνθρώποις τρώγειν ἔθος. 'My habit is to nibble the
same things as human beings have.' *Batr.* 34.

τυφλός

1 This looks like a simple word, but as usual careful research and
analysis disclose a rather different pattern. We begin obviously
with the literal sense *unable to see, blind*.

καί μιν τυφλὸν ἔθηκε Κρόνου πάϊς. Il. 6. 139.

τυφλὸς ἀνήρ, οἰκεῖ δὲ Χίῳ ἔνι παιπαλοέσσῃ. *h. Ap.* 172.

τυφλὸς γὰρ ἐκ δεδορκότος. S. *OT* 454.

τυφλὴν γὰρ ὄψιν ἐκ σέθεν σχήσειν μ' ἔφη. E. *Cyc.* 697.

τυφλὸς δὲ τῶν ἄλλων ἁπάντων μᾶλλον δεξαίμην ἂν εἶναι.
X. *Smp.* 4. 12.

τυφλοῖς ὀφθαλμοῖς ὄψιν ἐντιθέντες. Pl. *R.* 518c.

2 This is extended to cases where the adjective is applied to parts
of the body or other objects which are *not guided by sight*.

ὄψῃ νιν αὐτίκ' ὄντα δωμάτων πάρος
τυφλὸν τυφλῷ στείχοντα παραφόρῳ ποδί. E. *Hec.* 1050.

ἡγοῦ πάροιθε, θύγατερ· ὡς τυφλῷ ποδὶ
ὀφθαλμὸς εἶ σύ. E. *Ph.* 834.

πρόσθεν τυφλὴν χεῖρ' ἐπὶ πρόσωπα δυστυχῆ. E. *Ph.* 1699.

—βάκτρῳ δ' ἐρείδου περιφερῆ στίβον χθονός.
—καὶ τοῦτο τυφλόν, ὅταν ἐγὼ βλέπω βραχύ. E. *Ion* 744.

πολεμίους ἀμύνεται
τυφλοῖς ὁρῶντας οὐτάσας τοξεύμασιν. E. *HF* 199.

τὰ τυφλὰ τοῦ σώματος καὶ ἄοπλα καὶ ἄχειρα.
X. *Cyr.* 3. 3. 45.

τυφλὴ δ' ἔδραμε πᾶσα τρόπις
χοιράδας ἐς πέτρας. *AP* 9. 289. 4.

Neuter as adverb:

τυφλὸν φέρεσθαι πάγκαλον πέλει λίαν. Anon. ap. Suid.

3 These examples, which are literal, need to be separated from
the next where the adjective is applied in a metaphorical sense to

mean *lacking mental perception, devoid of understanding*. The transference can be seen in progress in the first example.

τυφλὸς τά τ' ὦτα τόν τε νοῦν τά τ' ὄμματ' εἶ.   S. *OT* 371.

δόλιον ἀγύρτην, ὅστις ἐν τοῖς κέρδεσιν
μόνον δέδορκε, τὴν τέχνην δ' ἔφυ τυφλός.   S. *OT* 389.

τυφλὸς γάρ, ὦ γυναῖκες, οὐδ' ὁρῶν Ἄρης.   S. *fr.* 838.

καὶ μὴν ... καὶ τυφλῷ γε δῆλον ὡς μεταβαίνει.   Pl. *R.* 550d.

τυφλὸς δ' οὐκ αὐτὸς ὁ Πλοῦτος,
ἀλλὰ καὶ ὠφρόντιστος Ἔρως.   Theoc. 10. 19.

ὡς τυφλόν ἐστι τοῦ μέλλοντος ἄνθρωπος.   Plu. *Sol.* 12. 5.

ἣν (τύχην) τυφλὴν λοιδοροῦμεν.   Plu. 2. 98a.

Applied to mental powers or activities:

τυφλὸν δ' ἔχει
ἦτορ ὅμιλος ἀνδρῶν ὁ πλεῖστος.   Pi. *N.* 7. 23.

τυφλὰς ἐν αὐτοῖς ἐλπίδας κατῴκισα.   A. *Pr.* 250.

ἀρ' ὄλβος αὐτοῖς ὅτι τυφλὸς συνηρετεῖ,
τυφλὰς ἔχουσι τὰς φρένας ...;   E. *fr.* 776 (= *Phaëth.* 167).

ἡ μὲν γὰρ φύσις ἄνευ μαθήσεως τυφλόν.   Plu. 2. 2b.

4   *Acting without direction, unpredictable.*

τυφλῆς ὑπ' ἄτης ἐκπεπόρθημαι τάλας.   S. *Tr.* 1104.

τὸ δ' ἐς αὔριον αἰ-
εὶ τυφλὸν ἕρπει.   S. *fr.* 593. 6.

ἔμπορος ἢ τυφλοῦ κύματος ἰχθυβόλος.   *AP* 7. 400.

ὧν (δοξῶν) αἱ βέλτισται τυφλαί.   Pl. *R.* 506c.

τυφλὴν ὑπόνοιαν.   Plu. 2. 687c; 975b.

5   In later Greek it is used of things which can be entered such as roads, straits, etc. *having no (other) exit, blind.*

τοὺς πορθμοὺς ὑπονοήσαντες εἶναι τυφλοὺς στενωπούς.
Str. 1. 1. 17.

(ποταμὸς) εἰς λίμνας τυφλὰς καὶ ἑλώδεις ἀφανίζεται.
Plu. *Sull.* 20. 5.

τὰ τυφλὰ καὶ δύσορμα τῆς Ὠστιανῆς ἠϊόνος ἀνακαθηράμενος.
Plu. *Caes.* 58. 5.

ἀνὰ μέσον οὔσης τυφλῆς ῥύμης. 'separated by a blind alley.'
P. Oxy. 99.9 (i AD).

In anatomy, referring to the caecum:

καὶ τοῦ ἐντέρου τυφλόν τι καὶ ὀγκῶδες.
Arist. *PA* 675ᵇ7; 676ᵃ5.

τὸ καλούμενον τυφλὸν ἔντερον.   Ruf. ap. Orib. 7. 26. 25.

Of knots in trees:

εἰσὶ δὲ τῶν ὄζων οἱ μὲν τυφλοί, οἱ δὲ γόνιμοι. λέγω δὲ
τυφλοὺς ἀφ' ὧν μηδεὶς βλαστός.
Thphr. *HP* 1. 8. 4; *CP* 3. 2. 8.

Of a hook, *having a rounded end, blunt.*

καὶ ἕτερον (ἄγκιστρον) τυφλὸν καθήσομεν.   Orib. 45. 18. 9.

6   *Invisible on the surface, hidden, concealed.*

ὤλεσε Κρῆτα
καὶ Μαλέου τυφλαὶ καμπτομένου σπιλάδες
Δάμιδος Ἀστυδάμαντα.   *AP* 7. 275.

τὴν σάρκα φοινίξαι τυφλῷ μώλωπι.   Plu. *Aem.* 19. 9.

τῶν δεσμῶν τυφλὰς ἐχόντων τὰς ἀρχάς.   Plu. *Alex.* 18. 2; cf.

ὡς τό γε τυφλὸν ἄμμα καλούμενον.   Gal. 2. 669.

τοῖς δ' ἄλλοις τυφλὸν εἶναι πάντῃ καὶ κρύφιον.   Plu. 2. 983d.

Metaphorically:

ἀλλὰ τὸ μὲν ἐν Ῥώμῃ τυφλὸν ἦν ἔτι κίνημα.   Plu. *Galb.* 18. 3.

ὕβρις

1   This is a word every Greek scholar thinks he understands;
indeed it is such a familiar concept as to have invaded the English
vocabulary. A whole book has recently been devoted to showing
that it does not mean what most of us think (N. R. E. Fisher,
Warminster, 1992). But it may be worth while reviewing its *lexical* meaning, while leaving the philosophical ideas behind it for
others to debate. LSJ attempts to divide the senses into **I** 'wanton
violence', **II** 'an outrage', admitting that it is often difficult to distinguish the concrete sense from the abstract. This is of course a
regular phenomenon in such abstract words, which acquire a
plural when used to mean an instance of whatever is the basic

meaning. While not ignoring this, it does seem that a further important distinction of meaning has been overlooked.

2   As a quality of persons or their behaviour ὕβρις is regularly used to mean *conduct amounting to contempt, insolence, arrogance,* a quality which renders the person so designated odious, especially to inferiors. For a more detailed analysis see the book by Fisher just mentioned.

μητρὸς ἐμῆς μνηστῆρες, ὑπέρβιον ὕβριν ἔχοντες.

Od. 1. 368; 16. 86.

τῶν ὕβρις τε βίη τε σιδήρεον οὐρανὸν ἵκει.   Od. 15. 329.

It is here coupled with βίη, the use of force, in a way which implies it is not simply (as LSJ says) 'wanton violence'. Similarly with μένος:

οἱ δ᾽ ὕβρει εἴξαντες, ἐπισπόμενοι μένεϊ σφῷ.   Od. 14. 262.

ἀνθρώπων ὕβριν τε καὶ εὐνομίην ἐφορῶντες.   Od. 17. 487.

Here the opposite 'obedience to law' characterises it as the attitude of one who regards himself as above the law.

εἰ ἐτεὸν μνηστῆρες ἀτάσθαλον ὕβριν ἔτεισαν.   Od. 24. 352.

It is curious that this sense is well represented in the Odyssey, whereas the specific instance (see 3 below) is the only way the word is used by the Iliad.

σὺ δ᾽ ἄκουε δίκης μηδ᾽ ὕβριν ὄφελλε.   Hes. *Op.* 213.

δίκη δ᾽ ὑπὲρ ὕβριος ἴσχει
ἐς τέλος ἐξελθοῦσα.   Hes. *Op.* 217.

ἀλλά νιν ὕβρις εἰς ἀυάταν ὑπεράφανον
ὦρσεν.   Pi. *P.* 2. 28.

ἤν τ᾽ ἐπὶ σωφροσύνην τρεφθῇ νόος ἤν τε πρὸς ὕβριν.
Thgn. 379.

δεσμῷ ἐν ἀχλυόεντι σιδηρέῳ ἔσβεσαν ὕβριν.
Epigram ap. Hdt. 5. 77. 4 (also preserved
in fragmentary form *IG* 1². 394).

Of a horse, or perhaps rather its rider:

τῶν τις ἱρῶν ἵππων ... ὑπὸ ὕβριος ἐσβὰς ἐς τὸν ποταμὸν
διαβαίνειν ἐπειρᾶτο.   Hdt. 1. 189. 1.

λῆξον δ᾽ ὑβρίζουσ᾽· οὐ γὰρ ἄλλο πλὴν ὕβρις
τάδ᾽ ἐστί, κρείσσω δαιμόνων εἶναι θέλειν.   E. *Hipp.* 474.

This might be classified as an act, but attitude or behaviour also seems appropriate. Plato attempts a definition.

ἐπιθυμίας δὲ ἀλόγως ἑλκούσης ἐπὶ ἡδονὰς καὶ ἀρξάσης ἐν ἡμῖν
τῇ ἀρχῇ ὕβρις ἐπωνομάσθη. ὕβρις δὲ δὴ πολυώνυμον.

Pl. *Phdr.* 238a.

τὰ μὲν γὰρ (ἀγαθὰ) ὕβριν τοῖς πολλοῖς, τὰ δὲ (κακὰ)
σωφροσύνην τοῖς πᾶσιν ἐμποεῖ. X. *Cyr.* 8. 4. 14.

ἀλλὰ διὰ τὴν ὕβριν ἠδίκου ἀνθρώπους μικροπολίτας.

X. *HG* 2. 2. 10.

3 When used with a plural it means an instance of such behaviour, *insult, abuse*.

ἦ ἵνα ὕβριν ἴδῃ Ἀγαμέμνονος Ἀτρεΐδαο; Il. 1. 203.

ὕβριος εἵνεκα τῆσδε. Il. 1. 214.

οἷσιν Ἄρηος
ἔργ' ἔμελε στονόεντα καὶ ὕβριες. Hes. *Op.* 146.

μᾶλλον δὲ κακῶν ῥεκτῆρα καὶ ὕβριν
ἀνέρα τιμήσουσι. 'a man who is an example of arrogance'.

Hes. *Op.* 191.

οὐχ ὕβρις πίνειν ὁπόσον κεν ἔχων ἀφίκοιο
οἴκαδ' ἄνευ προπόλου. Xenoph. 1. 17.

ὑπὸ γυναικὸς ἄρχεσθαι ὕβρις εἴη ἂν ἀνδρὶ ἐσχάτη.

Democr. 111.

—ἆρ' οὐχ ὕβρις τάδ'; —ὕβρις, ἀλλ' ἀνεκτέα. S. *OC* 883.

ταῦτ' οὐχὶ δεινῆς ἀγκόνης ἔστ' ἄξια,
ὕβρεις ὑβρίζειν ... ; E. *Ba.* 247; *HF* 741.

ταῦτ' οὐχ ὕβρις δῆτ' ἐστίν; Ar. *Nu.* 1299; *Ra.* 21; *Pl.* 886.

αἱ τῶν νέων ἀκολασίαι τε καὶ ὕβρεις. Pl. *Lg.* 884a.

4 As an appendage to this we may add the adverbial expressions ὕβρει, ἐφ' ὕβρει or πρὸς ὕβριν, *by way of insult, offensively*.

ἀλλ' οὐχ ὕβρει
λέγω τάδ'. S. *El.* 881.

ἀρνῇ κατακτὰς κἀφ' ὕβρει λέγεις τάδε; E. *Or.* 1581.

ἐμοὶ γὰρ δοκεῖς ... τὴν γραφὴν ταύτην ὕβρει τινὶ καὶ ἀκολασίᾳ
καὶ νεότητι γράψασθαι. Pl. *Ap.* 26e.

οὐδ' ἐφ' ὕβρει τοῦτ' ἐποίησεν. D. 21. 38.

ὕβρει πεποιηκώς. D. 21. 42.

ἵνα μὴ {με} ἐφ᾽ ὕβρει με [ἐ]ξορκίζειν αὐτόν.
P. Cair. Zen. 462. 9 (iii BC).

Τυδεὺς δὲ καὶ πρὸς ὕβριν ἐκέλευσεν ἀποχωρεῖν.   Plu. Alc. 37.

5   It is an easy step from threatening behaviour to actual physical
violence, though it is not always clear from the context which is
intended. I quote here examples where the mental attitude is less
relevant and actual damage is inflicted. We may define this sense
as *physical violence, assault, attack*.

γελᾷ θ᾽ ὁρῶν ὕβριν ὀρθίαν κνωδάλων. (The beasts in question
are asses.)   Pi. P. 10. 36.

Similarly of snakes:

ἀπὸ στρωμνᾶς ὅμως ἄμυνεν ὕβριν κνωδάλων.   Pi. N. 1. 50.

ναυσίστονον ὕβριν ἰδὼν τὰν πρὸ Κύμας.   Pi. P. 1. 72.

καὶ τὰ πάντα σφι ὑπό τε ὕβριος καὶ ὀλιγωρίης ἀνάστατα ἦν.
Hdt. 1. 106. 1.

The context here shows that the Scythians did not merely treat
their subjects as inferiors but inflicted violence on them.

ἄρξασι Φρυξὶ τὴν κατ᾽ Ἀργείων ὕβριν.   S. fr. 368.

ἀθάνατον Ἥρας μητέρ᾽ εἰς ἐμὴν ὕβριν.   E. Ba. 9.

The reference is to the violent death of Semele.

τᾶς ὕβριος ποινὰς λαμβάνω[ν].
IG 4²(1). 122. 98 (= Schwyzer 109. 98, Epidaurus iv BC).

αἷμα δὲ ἐπιρραινούσης τῷ ἀφρῷ ἐκ τοῦ χαλίνου ὕβρεως.
D. Chr. 63. 5.

6   This sense was adopted as a legal term found in the Attic
orators. The exact definition of the term was perhaps vague; for a
discussion see Fisher, op. cit. But it would appear to have been a
general term for all kinds of physical assault, as the first quotation
shows.

τὸν τῆς ὕβρεως (νόμον), ὃς ἑνὶ κεφαλαίῳ ἅπαντα τὰ τοιαῦτα
συλλαβὼν ἔχει.   Aeschin. 1. 15.

It was distinguished from βλάβη 'damage' and αἰκία 'maltreat-
ment'.

ἦν ὁ τῆς βλάβης ὑμῖν νόμος πάλαι, ἦν ὁ τῆς αἰκείας, ἦν ὁ τῆς
ὕβρεως. D. 21. 35.

It is the circumstances of this speech against Meidias which prove
the meaning of ὕβρις. Meidias admitted having punched Demosthenes in the theatre while he was discharging his duties as
χορηγός. The point at issue in this case was whether it was simple
assault (clearly defined as ὕβρις in the ὑπόθεσις to this speech) or
ἀσέβεια 'impiety' as a result of the religious character of the office.

ἐνταυθὶ πόλλ᾽ ἄττα καὶ δεινά μοι ἐγκαλεῖ· καὶ γὰρ αἰκείαν καὶ
ὕβριν καὶ βιαίων καὶ πρὸς ἐπικλήρους ἀδικήματα. D. 37. 33.

The seriousness of the offence is clear from a passage in Isocrates,
which recalls our distinction between civil and criminal actions.

ἔπειτα τῶν μὲν ἄλλων ἐγκλημάτων αὐτῷ τῷ παθόντι ὁ δράσας
ὑπόδικός ἐστιν· περὶ δὲ τῆς ὕβρεως, ὡς κοινοῦ τοῦ πράγματος
ὄντος, ἔξεστι τῷ βουλομένῳ τῶν πολιτῶν γραψαμένῳ πρὸς
τοὺς θεσμοθέτας εἰσελθεῖν εἰς ὑμᾶς. Isoc. 20. 2.

πρὸς καταδίκην ἔρημον ὕβρεως 'condemned by default for
assault'. P. Hib. 1. 32. 8 (iii BC).

7 The abuse of a woman or a child may obviously have sexual
connotations, but it is a mistake to regard ὕβρις as actually meaning rape, even where this is probably the act intended. That it is a
wider term is evident from this passage:

ἐάν τις ὑβρίζῃ εἴς τινα, ἢ παῖδα ἢ γυναῖκα ἢ ἄνδρα, τῶν
ἐλευθέρων ἢ τῶν δούλων, ἢ παράνομόν τι ποιήσῃ εἰς τούτων
τινὰ γραφέσθω. ἐὰν δὲ ἀργυρίου τιμηθῇ τῆς ὕβρεως, δεδέσθω.
Lex ap. D. 21. 47.

Clearly sexual offences are implied by the following:

ἔτι δὲ παίδων ὕβρεις καὶ γυναικῶν αἰσχύνας. Isoc. 4. 114.

ταύτην τὴν ὕβριν ἅπαντες ἄνθρωποι δεινοτάτην ἡγοῦνται.
Lys. 1. 2.

The crime here was the seduction of the speaker's wife.

καὶ ὅσα αἰσχύνονται οἱ ἀδικηθέντες λέγειν, οἷον γυναικῶν
οἰκείων ὕβρεις ἢ εἰς αὐτοὺς ἢ εἰς υἱεῖς. Arist. Rh. 1373ᵃ35.

ἐπὶ τὰς τῶν γυναικῶν ὕβρεις καὶ παίδων ἁρπαγάς.
Plb. 6. 8. 5.

It is also used to refer to voluntary sexual abuse in the case of prostitution.

τὸν γὰρ τὸ σῶμα τὸ ἑαυτοῦ ἐφ' ὕβρει πεπρακότα.
Aeschin. 1. 29; 1. 116; 1. 188.

ὑγρός

1 The obvious starting-point is *composed of liquid, running, watery*.

ἐπέπλεον ὑγρὰ κέλευθα. Il. 1. 312; Od. 3. 71.

γίγνετο δ' ὑγρὸν ὕδωρ καὶ δένδρεον ὑψιπέτηλον. Od. 4. 458.

Stock epithets may be obvious, but are surely never otiose; so presumably ὑγρόν here means something more than 'wet'. Hence I suggest that *running* as opposed to stagnant water is meant. In the following example the other possible sense of ἅλς justifies the epithet; but in the next two it is more difficult to see its force.

βλάστε μὲν ἐξ ἁλὸς ὑγρᾶς
νᾶσος. Pi. O. 7. 69.

ὑγρῷ πελάγει. Pi. P. 4. 40.

συντέμνει δ' ὄρος
ὑγρᾶς θαλάσσης. A. Supp. 259.

Here the word is so obviously otiose that I am tempted to understand it as a transferred epithet belonging rather with ὄρος; and if so, it is also tempting to emend ὑγρᾶς to ὑγρός, for the corruption would be almost inevitable if the conjecture is correct; 'the watery boundary of the sea cuts it short.' Since a ὄρος would be expected to be on land, the epithet has immediate point. There is a point in the epithet of πῶμα in the following passage, since as Dodds remarks it is based on the opposition between the dry and the wet.

ὃς δ' ἦλθ' ἔπειτ', ἀντίπαλον ὁ Σεμέλης γόνος
βότρυος ὑγρὸν πῶμ' ηὗρε κεἰσηνέγκατο
θνητοῖς, ὃ παύει τοὺς ταλαιπώρους βροτοὺς
λύπης. E. Ba. 279.

Applied to olive oil or pitch, it serves to distinguish the fluid from a solidified form.

ὅς σφῶϊν μάλα πολλάκις ὑγρὸν ἔλαιον
χαιτάων κατέχευε, λοέσσας ὕδατι λευκῷ.
Il. 23. 281; Od. 6. 79.

πίσσαν ὑγράν.   *I Cret.* 1. 17. 17. 14 (Lebena, i BC).

Used of liquids in general:

τὰ μὲν ὑπὸ τοῦ ψυχροῦ τε καὶ ὑγροῦ πιεζόμενα 'some parts
oppressed by coldness and wetness'.   Hdt. 1. 142. 2.

ἢν δὲ μὴ ἔχωσι ὑγρὸν μηδέν 'if they have no liquid available'.
Hdt. 4. 172. 4.

γῇ ὑγρῷ φυραθεῖσα πηλὸς ἂν εἴη.   Pl. *Tht.* 147c.

ὅταν ... τὸ ὑγρὸν θερμανθὲν λεπτότερον γένηται.
Hp. *Loc. Hom.* 9.

περὶ ὑγρῶν χρήσιος.   Hp. title.

ὡς δ' ἐξερρύα συχνὸν ὑγ[ρό]ν.
Schwyzer 109. 4 (Epidaurus, iv BC).

The expression ἐφ' ὑγροῖς ζωγραφεῖν, Plu. 2. 759c, has been taken
to mean 'paint on a wet surface' with fresco technique, and this
view is adopted by LSJ. But since there seems to be no other
example of ὑγρός meaning 'having a wet surface', it is easier to take
it as a variant of the idiom ἐν ὕδατι γράφειν, Pl. *Phdr.* 276c, a
proverbial expression for transience. The feminine as substantive
is a poetic expression for the sea.

                              πουλὺν ἐφ' ὑγρὴν
ἤλυθον ἐς Τροίην.   Il. 10. 27.

οἵ μ' οἴσουσιν ἐπὶ τραφερήν τε καὶ ὑγρήν.   Il. 14. 308; 24. 341.

Its reappearance in Aristophanes must be mock-epic.

πολλὰ μὲν ἐν γῇ, πολλὰ δ' ἐφ' ὑγρᾷ πιτυλεύσας.   Ar. *V.* 678.

2   *Abounding in moisture, wet.*

μία γενομένη νὺξ ὑγρὰ διαφερόντως γῆς αὐτὴν (sc. τὴν
ἀκρόπολιν) ψιλὴν περιτήξασα πεποίηκε.   Pl. *Criti.* 112a.

Neuter as substantive:

τὰ ... ὑγρά τε καὶ λεῖα τῶν σταθμῶν.   X. *Eq.* 4. 3.

Neuter as adverb:

οὔτ' ἀνέμων διάη μένος ὑγρὸν ἀέντων.   Od. 5. 478; 19. 440.
ὄφρ' ἴσχωσ' ἀνέμων μένος ὑγρὸν ἀέντων.
Hes. *Op.* 625; *Th.* 869.

Perhaps here belong examples where it is applied to air.

γαῖά τε καὶ πόντος πολυκύμων ἠδ᾽ ὑγρὸς ἀήρ. Emp. 38.3.

ἐν δὲ τῷ ἔαρι ὑγρὸς (ὁ ἀήρ), ἐν δὲ τῷ μετοπώρῳ ἤδη ὑγραίνεται. Arist. Mete. 348ᵇ28.

Of timber, *unseasoned, green*.

ὅτι ἐν τῷ ὑγρῷ ξύλῳ ταῦτα ποιοῦσιν, ἐν τῷ ξηρῷ τί γένηται;
Ev. Luc. 23. 31.

3   *Used for liquids*.

μέτρα ξηρά τε καὶ ὑγρά. Pl. Lg. 746e.

Of animals, *living in water, aquatic*.

τὸν Νυμφῶν θεράποντα, φιλόμβριον, ὑγρὸν ἀοιδόν
... βάτραχον. AP 6. 43.
θῆρες
ὑγροὶ καὶ πεζοί. AP 9. 18.

τοῖς ὄρνισι τοῖς ὑγροῖς. Philostr. Im. 1. 9. 1.

4   In the sense of *unstable* it is applied by grammarians to *sonant* consonants, not restricted to the modern significance of *liquid*.

ἀμετάβολα τέσσαρα· λ μ ν ρ. ... τὰ δὲ αὐτὰ καὶ ὑγρὰ καλεῖται. D. T. 632. 9 (p. 14 U).

δεῖ παρατηρεῖν μὴ τὸ μὲν πρῶτον (σύμφωνον) ἄφωνον ᾖ, τὸ δὲ δεύτερον ὑγρόν (the rule of 'mute + liquid'). Heph. 1. 3.

But it is also used of vowels to mean *variable in quantity*.

τρία δὲ (φωνήεντα) κοινὰ μήκους τε καὶ βραχύτητος, α ι υ, ἅπερ δίχρονα καὶ ὑγρὰ καὶ ἀμφίβολα καὶ μεταβολικὰ καλοῦσιν. S.E. M. 1. 100.

5   Of sounds, *uncertain in pitch, wavering, wailing*; in the examples only used adverbially.

σαλπιγκτῶν ... πλῆθος, παρὰ μέρος ὑγρότατα καὶ πένθιμα μελῳδούντων. App. BC 1. 106.

καί ῥ᾽ ὁ μὲν οἰνοβαρὴς ἕρπει πάρος ὑγρὸν ἀείδων,
οὐ μάλα νηφάλιον κλάζων μέλος. Opp. H. 2. 412.

The second example is given by LSJ under the heading '*moist with wine, tipsy*'; but the drunkenness is indicated twice in the rest of

the context, so it would make better sense if ὑγρόν here referred to
the habit of drunks of singing out of tune. The sense alleged by
LSJ probably does not exist; see 8 below.

6 Applied to living organisms ὑγρός means *supple, flexible*.

> ὁ δὲ (αἰετὸς) κνώσσων
> ὑγρὸν νῶτον αἰωρεῖ. Pi. *P*. 1. 9.

> χορῷ δ' ἕτερ-
> πον κέαρ ὑγροῖσι ποσσίν. B. 17. 108.

δεῖ δὲ τὸν ἱππέα καὶ τὸ ἄνωθεν τῶν ἑαυτοῦ ἰσχίων σῶμα ὡς
ὑγρότατον ἐθίζειν εἶναι. X. *Eq*. 7. 7.

καὶ μὴ ἕλκειν πρὸς τὸ γυμνάσιον σκληρὸν ἤδη ὄντα, τῷ δὲ δὴ
νεωτέρῳ τε καὶ ὑγροτέρῳ ὄντι προσπαλαίειν. Pl. *Tht*. 162b.

νεώτατος μὲν δή ἐστι καὶ ἁπαλώτατος, πρὸς δὲ τούτοις ὑγρὸς
τὸ εἶδος. Pl. *Smp*. 196a.

τραχήλους μακρούς, ὑγρούς, περιφερεῖς. X. *Cyn*. 4. 1; 5. 31.

διὰ τὸ ὑγρὸς εἶναι καὶ πηδᾶν πόρρω. Arist. *HA* 580ᵃ30.

Of a plant:

> πάντα δ' ἀμφὶ δέπας περιπέπταται ὑγρὸς ἄκανθος.
> Theoc. 1. 55.

Of movement:

> ὑγροτέραν τε γὰρ ἀναγκαῖον αὐτῶν εἶναι τὴν κίνησιν.
> Arist. *PA* 655ᵃ24.

Similarly in a transferred sense, of diction.

> τραχεῖαν γὰρ ἔδει καὶ πικρὰν εἶναι (τὴν λέξιν) ... ἡ δ' ἔστιν
> ὑγρὰ καὶ ὁμαλὴ καὶ ὥσπερ ἔλαιον ἀψοφητὶ διὰ τῆς ἀκοῆς
> ῥέουσα. D. H. *Dem*. 20.

7 *Yielding to the touch like a liquid, tender, pliant.*

> ἐς δ' ὑγρὸν
> ἀγκῶν' ἔτ' ἔμφρων παρθένῳ προσπτύσσεται. S. *Ant*. 1236.

> ὁρᾷς τὸν ὑψοῦ τόνδ' ἄπειρον αἰθέρα
> καὶ γῆν πέριξ ἔχονθ' ὑγραῖς ἐν ἀγκάλαις; E. *fr*. 941.

> χὠ μὲν οἰστὸς ἐκρύφθη
> λέοντος ὑγραῖς χολάσιν. Babr. 1. 10.

πεσὼν δ᾽ ἐφ᾽ ὑγραῖς μητρὸς ἀγκάλαις.   Babr. 34. 7.

τροφὴν ἀπαλὴν νεοττοῖς ὑγροῖς.   Ael. NA 7. 9.

τὸν ἐκ πυρὸς ὑγρὸν ἀείρας
Ζεὺς βρέφος ... λόχευσε.   Nonn. D. 1. 4.

Transferred to an abstract substantive:

θάλε γὰρ πόθος ὑγρὸς ἐπελθὼν
νύμφῃ ἐϋπλοκάμῳ Δρύοπος φιλότητι μιγῆναι.   h. Pan. 33.

So of looks, *melting, languishing:*

τὸ δὲ βλέμμα νῦν ἀληθῶς
ἀπὸ τοῦ πυρὸς ποίησον,
ἅμα γλαυκὸν ὡς Ἀθήνης,
ἅμα δ᾽ ὑγρὸν ὡς Κυθήρης.   Anacreont. 15. 21.

ὑγρὰ δὲ δερκομένοισιν ἐν ὄμμασιν.   AP 7. 27.

καὶ τῶν ὀφθαλμῶν δὲ τὸ ὑγρὸν ἅμα τῷ φαιδρῷ καὶ
κεχαρισμένῳ.   Luc. Im. 6.

The adverb is so used in Philostr. Ep. 33.

8   *Free from tension, slack, loose.*

κἀπιθεὶς ὑγρὰν χέρα
φωνὴν μὲν οὐκ ἀφῆκεν, ὀμμάτων δ᾽ ἄπο
προσεῖπε δακρύοις.   E. Ph. 1439.

τὰ γόνατ᾽ ἔκτεινε καὶ γυμναστικῶς
ὑγρὸν χύτλασον σεαυτὸν ἐν τοῖς στρώμασιν.   Ar. V. 1213.

The exact meaning of χύτλασον is unclear; perhaps the idea is 'pour
yourself out slack in the blankets.'

εἰκάζοις ἂν καὶ ἱππεύοντα ὑγρὰ ἕξειν τὰ σκέλη.   X. Eq. 1. 6.

αἴρει δὲ ἄνω τὰ σκέλη ὀργιζόμενος, οὐ μέντοι ὑγρά γε.
X. Eq. 10. 15.

καὶ τὸ σύμπαν σῶμα ὑγρὸν κείμενον.   Hp. Prog. 3.

Of a bow:

αὐτὰρ ἐγὼ κέρας ὑγρὸν ἑλών.   Theoc. 25. 206.

τῶν δὲ πελαγίων (ἰχθύων αἱ σάρκες) ὑγραί εἰσι καὶ κεχυμέναι.
Arist. HA 598ᵃ9; 603ᵇ32.

ὑγρὸς σφυγμός ἐστιν ὁ ἀπαλὸς οὔσης καὶ τῆς ἐν αὐτῷ οὐσίας
προσηνοῦς τῇ ἁφῇ ὑγρασίαν καί τινα προσβάλλων.

Gal. 19. 405.

I should be inclined to place in this section a well-known fragment
of Heraclitus:

ἀνὴρ ὁκόταν μεθυσθῇ, ἄγεται ὑπὸ παιδὸς ἀνήβου σφαλλόμενος,
οὐκ ἐπαΐων ὅκη βαίνει, ὑγρὴν τὴν ψυχὴν ἔχων. Heracl. 117.

There is no reason to assume that ὑγρός here means 'tipsy'; the
slackness of the mental faculties is the result of drink. The famous
commendation of the 'driest soul' (*fr.* 118) no doubt has the same
explanation. The same is true of the following passage.

τὴν διάνοιαν ὑγρὰν ὑπὸ τῆς μέθης καὶ ἀκροσφαλῆ γεγενημένον.

Plu. 2. 713a.

There is thus no reason to invent a special sense 'tipsy'; for the
Oppian passage see 5 above. The word is sometimes used in
medical language of the κοιλία, a regular term for the bowels, so
it is difficult to distinguish here between slackness and a watery
discharge.

ὁκόσοισι νέοισιν ἐοῦσιν αἱ κοιλίαι ὑγραί εἰσι, τούτοισιν
ἀπογηράσκουσι ξηραίνονται. Hp. *Aph.* 2. 20.

τὴν μέντοι χροίαν ἔχει (ὁ πελλὸς ἐρῳδιὸς) φαύλην καὶ τὴν
κοιλίαν ἀεὶ ὑγράν. Arist. *HA* 617ᵃ1.

9 *Easily influenced, compliant.*

ἐπαινεῖ δὲ τὸ Κίμωνος ἐμμελὲς καὶ ὑγρόν 'tact and complai-
sance'. Plu. *Per.* 5. 3.

παρὰ τὴν αὐτοῦ φύσιν ὑγρός τις εἶναι βουλόμενος καὶ
δημοτικός. Plu. *Mar.* 28. 1.

With a construction, *prone (to)*.

λεγόμενος μὲν ὑγρότατος ἐς ταῦτα ἀεὶ φῦναι. App. *BC* 5. 8.

πρὸς δὲ τοὺς συνήθεις ὑγρότερον τῷ γελοίῳ καὶ φιλοσκώπτην
'in dealing with familiar friends more given to laughter and
fond of jokes'. Plu. *Brut.* 29. 1.

ὁ κόλαξ ... ὑγρὸς ὢν μεταβάλλεσθαι. Plu. 2. 51c.

10 *Given to pleasure, luxurious, soft*. This definition is in Hesychius (ὁ εὐκαταφερὴς εἰς ἡδονάς).

πεῖραν ἐπεθύμουν θατέρου βίου λαβεῖν,
ὃν πάντες εἰώθασιν ὀνομάζειν ὑγρόν. Alex. 206 K.–A.

τὸ δ' οὖν εὐδάπανον καὶ ὑγρὸν πρὸς τὴν δίαιταν.
Plu. *Sol*. 3. 1.

τὸν δ' ὑγρὸν τοῦτον (ἔρωτα) καὶ οἰκουρὸν ἐν κόλποις
διατρίβοντα καὶ κλινιδίοις γυναικῶν. Plu. 2. 751a.

ὕλη

1 There are several problems connected with this word, not least the absence of any satisfactory etymology; but there can be no doubt that the earliest examples all refer to *wood*. This may be growing vegetation or cut for use, but in either case it is generally distinguished from ξύλον, which is always wood from grown trees or *timber* (cf. however 6 below). This makes it clear that ὕλη is not in origin a general word for stands of trees or woods, though it later may have acquired that sense. Its primary use must have been to describe the dense, low vegetation which covers much of the mountainsides of Greece. This is technically known to botanists as *garrigue*. I have added a certain number of examples, marked with an asterisk, to LSJ's collection, and omitted a few which it cites.

2 The original use seems to have been as a collective noun, to refer to growing plants rather than the area they occupy, *low, bushy vegetation, scrub, brush*.

βάλλειν ἄγρια πάντα, τά τε τρέφει οὔρεσιν ὕλη. *Il. 5. 52.

φύλλα τὰ μέν τ' ἄνεμος χαμάδις χέει, ἄλλα δέ θ' ὕλη
τηλεθόωσα φύει. *Il. 6. 147.

ὡς δ' ὅτε πῦρ ἀΐδηλον ἐν ἀξύλῳ ἐμπέσῃ ὕλῃ.
Il. 11. 155; *20. 491; *Hes. *Th*. 694.

δοχμώ τ' ἀΐσσοντε (σύε) περὶ σφίσιν ἄγνυτον ὕλην
πρύμνην ἐκτάμνοντες. Il. 12. 148.

τὼ (sc. *Hera and Hypnos*) δ' ἐπὶ χέρσου
βήτην, ἀκροτάτη δὲ ποδῶν ὕπο σείετο ὕλη. Il. 14. 285.

ἔστι μὲν ὕλη
παντοίη, ἐν δ' ἀρδμοὶ ἐπηετανοὶ πάρεασι.
*Od. 13. 246; 13. 351.

οὐ μὲν γάρ τι φύγεσκε βαθείης βένθεσιν ὕλης
κνώδαλον. Od. 17. 316.

τῆμος ἀδηκτοτάτη πέλεται τμηθεῖσα σιδήρῳ
ὕλη, φύλλα δ' ἔραζε χέει, πτόρθοιό τε λήγει. *Hes. Op. 421.

μέμυκε δὲ γαῖα καὶ ὕλη (sc. in a wind). *Hes. Op. 508; 511.

ἔθνεα ... ἀπ' ὕλης ἀγρίης ζώοντα. Hdt. 1. 203. 1.

γῆν νεμόμενοι πᾶσαν δασέαν ὕλῃ παντοίῃ. Hdt. 4. 21.

φοιτᾷ γὰρ ὑπ' ἀγρίαν
ὕλαν. *S. OT 477; *OC 349.

πᾶσαν αἰκίζων φόβην
ὕλης πεδιάδος. *S. Ant. 420.

θηρᾶν καθ' ὕλην. *E. Ba. 688.

ὕλης ἐν βαθυξύλῳ φόβῃ. *E. Ba. 1138.

χλωρὰν δ' ἀν' ὕλην. *E. Hipp. 17.

εἰ δέ τι καὶ ἄλλο ἐνῆν ὕλης ἢ καλάμου, ἅπαντα ἦσαν εὐωδῆ
ὥσπερ ἀρώματα. X. An. 1. 5. 1.

εἰ μέλλει ἀγαθὴ ἡ νεὸς ἔσεσθαι, ὕλης τε καθαρὰν αὐτὴν δεῖ
εἶναι καὶ ὀπτὴν ... πρὸς τὸν ἥλιον. X. Oec. 16. 13.

καὶ ὕλη δὲ πολλάκις ὑπὸ τῶν ὑδάτων δήπου συνεξορμᾷ τῷ
σίτῳ. X. Oec. 17. 12.

Distinguished from trees (cf. the end of 4):

καρποὺς δὲ ἀφθόνους εἶχον ἀπό τε δένδρων καὶ πολλῆς ὕλης
ἄλλης. *Pl. Plt. 272a.

3 The plural is rare in early Greek:

ἤϊξ' ἠΰτε μαινὰς ὄρος κάτα δάσκιον ὕλης. h. Cer. 386.

It is perhaps not impossible that ὕλῃ should be read here; and in
the following example we may doubt the accuracy of the citation.

οὔρεα ὑψηλὰ καὶ δασέα ὕλῃσιν. Hecat. 291 J.

More frequent in later Greek:

Βοιωτίδες ὗλαι. Mosch. 3. 88.

τόπος ὀρεινὸς καὶ τραχὺς, συνηγμένος ταῖς ὕλαις.
Plb. 5. 7. 10.

ἐγκαθημένην ὕλαις
ἀηδόν' ὀξύφωνον. Babr. 12. 2.

αἱ ὕλαι τοσαύτην ἔχουσι βάλανον ὥστε ... Str. 5. 1. 12.

ἐν ὕλαις καὶ νάπαις. D. H. Th. 6.

δασεῖαν ὕλαις ὁδόν. Plu. Pyrrh. 25. 3.

ἡ γῆ δὲ ἄγριόν τι χρῆμα καὶ ἄμορφον, ὕλαις ἅπασα καὶ
ταύταις ἀνημέροις λάσιος. Luc. Prom. 12.

ὑπὸ ταῖς ἄγαν παλινσκίοις ὕλαις. Luc. Am. 12.

καὶ νοερῷ σείοντο τινάγματι θυιάδες ὗλαι.
Nonn. D. 3. 69; 3. 252; 16. 91.

4   The result of cutting such material is to produce quantities of
twigs, brushwood. So Odysseus building his raft surrounds it with
willow bulwarks and backs this with brushwood.

φράξε δέ μιν ῥίπεσσι διαμπερὲς οἰσυΐνῃσι
κύματος εἶλαρ ἔμεν· πολλὴν δ' ἐπεχεύατο ὕλην. Od. 5. 257.

In building the bridge of boats:

ποιήσαντες δὲ ταῦτα ὕλην ἐπεφόρησαν, κόσμῳ δὲ θέντες καὶ
τὴν ὕλην γῆν ἐπεφόρησαν. Hdt. 7. 36. 5.

To reinforce a palisade:

ἐφοροῦν δὲ ὕλην ἐς αὐτὸ (sc. τὸ χῶμα) καὶ λίθους καὶ γῆν.
Th. 2. 75. 2.

Distinguished from trees:

κόπτοντες τὰ δένδρα καὶ ὕλην. Th. 4. 69. 2.

Of birds concealing their eggs by screening them with twigs:

ἐπηλυγαζόμενα ὕλην. Arist. HA 559ᵃ2.

5   It has remained down to modern times the custom in Greece
to cut brushwood from the hillsides for use as *fuel*. This may
include branches from large trees.

τοὶ δ' ὁπλίζοντο μάλ' ὦκα,
ἀμφότερον, νέκυάς τ' ἀγέμεν, ἕτεροι δὲ μεθ' ὕλην.
Il. 7. 418; 23. 50; 23. 111.

For cooking:

φέρε δ' ὄβριμον ἄχθος
ὕλης ἀζαλέης, ἵνα οἱ ποτιδόρπιον εἴη. Od. 9. 234.

For other purposes:

ὥς οὔτ᾽ ἄναυδος οὔτε σοι δαίων φλόγα
ὕλης ὀρείας σημανεῖ καπνῷ πυρός.   *A. Ag. 497.

ἐς πύργον ... καταφυγόντας ἰδιωτικὸν ὕλην περινήσας ...
ἐνέπρησε.   Hdt. 4. 164. 2; 6. 80.

πολλὴν μὲν ὕλην τῆς βαθυρρίζου δρυὸς
κείραντα, πολλὸν δ᾽ ἀρσέν᾽ ἐκτεμόνθ᾽ ὁμοῦ
ἄγριον ἔλαιον.   *S. Tr. 1195.

The use of κείρω here indicates that this is cropping the foliage, not
cutting down the oak.

ὕλην παρατιθέντας αὔην καὶ ξηρὰν ἄφθονον.
                                        *Pl. Lg. 761c; *849d.

ἰδοὺ ἡλίκον πῦρ ἡλίκην ὕλην ἀνάπτει.   Ep. Jac. 3. 5.

6   From the classical period ὕλη is also used to mean *cut wood suitable for building, timber*.

Ἰδαίαν ὅτε πρῶτον ὕλαν
Ἀλέξανδρος εἰλατίναν
ἐτάμεθ᾽.   *E. Hec. 631.

ὅτ᾽ οὖν δὴ τὰ νῦν οἷα τέκτοσιν ἡμῖν ὕλη παράκειται.
                                        *Pl. Ti. 69a.

ναυπηγησίμης ὕλης ὁ τόπος τῆς χώρας πῶς ἔχει;
                                        Pl. Lg. 705c.

πρὸς ποῖα τῆς ὕλης ἑκάστη χρησίμη.   Thphr. HP 5. 7. 1.

7   Especially in later Greek this developed to denote *material*
employed for any purpose or of which anything was made.

φάρμακά τε καὶ πάντα ὄργανα καὶ πᾶσαν ὕλην παρατίθεσθαι
πᾶσιν.   *Pl. Phlb. 54c.

περὶ ὕλης ἰατρικῆς.   Diosc. Title.

βασιλικαῖς ὕλαις καὶ παρασκευαῖς περιουσιάζοντα τὸν
ἀθλητήν.   Ph. 1. 640 (= de Somniis 1. 126).

πληγαῖς ὑπακούουσαν ὕλην ἄψυχον δημιουργοῦντες.
                                        Plu. 2. 802b.

εἰς σύνοψιν ἀγαγεῖν ἠβουλήθην ἅπασαν τὴν πραγματείαν, ὡς
μηδεμίαν ὕλην λαθεῖν.   Gal. 6. 77; 6. 157.

τὴν ... τῆς ὕλης τῶν ἐμπυημάτων οὐσίαν.   Gal. 18(2). 256.

πάσης δὲ ὕλης τμητικώτατός ὁ σίδηρος.

Sor. 2. 11 (= 58, 14 I).

ἐρεοῦς ... διὰ τὸ τῆς ὕλης προσηνές. Sor. 2. 14 (= 61, 14 I).

8   As an abstraction from this we find the philosophical use of ὕλη to mean *matter*.

ἔστι δὲ ὕλη μάλιστα μὲν καὶ κυρίως τὸ ὑποκείμενον γενέσεως καὶ φθορᾶς δεκτικόν. Arist. *GC* 320ᵃ2.

τὸ δ' ἐξ οὗ γίγνεται ἣν λέγομεν ὕλην.

Arist. *Metaph.* 1032ᵃ17.

9   Finally the *subject-matter* of a book, discussion, etc.

εἰ κατὰ τὴν ὑποκειμένην ὕλην διασαφηθείη (ἡ μέθοδος).

Arist. *EN* 1094ᵇ12.

πᾶσαν δὴ τὴν τραγικὴν καὶ ταύτῃ προσεοικυῖαν ὕλην ... ὑπερθησόμεθα. Plb. 2. 16. 14.

εἰς ποιητικὰς ὕλας. Longin. 13. 4; 43. 1.

ὑγρᾷ τινι παντάπασι καὶ εὐπλαδεῖ ὕλῃ.

Iamb. *Comm. Math.* 4.

ὑπομονή

1   On reading this article in LSJ I was struck by two things. I observed that nowhere is the English word *patience* proposed as a translation; yet this is its normal significance in modern Greek, and most of the semantic developments of the present day are, if not exemplified, at least foreshadowed in late antiquity. Secondly, there is no reference to the New Testament, which is strange for a word which plays such a prominent part in Christian writings. It therefore appeared to be worth further investigation, especially as it has been variously translated where it occurs in the New Testament. I fully expect to be told I have misinterpreted some of the passages I have quoted, but a fresh approach seems to be needed here. Where ὑπομονή occurs in a list of virtues, it is hard to be sure what precise meaning is intended, but I feel obliged to question whether *steadfastness* is always the meaning.

2   LSJ begins rightly with the sense derived from the verb
ὑπομένω, the *act of remaining behind, stay*.

ἐναντία ὑπομονὴ ἀκολούθησις.   Arist. *Rh.* 1410ᵃ4.

Πελοποννησίων ὑπομονῆς ἐν Ἰταλίᾳ.   D. H. 1. 44. 2.

But from this we can see a development to mean *stay on earth,
survival*.

τῆς δ᾽ ὑπομονῆς (*sc. of a damaged tree*) αἴτιον ἡ ὑγρότης καὶ ἡ
φύσει μανότης.   Thphr. *CP* 5. 16. 3.

ὡς σκιὰ αἱ ἡμέραι ἡμῶν ἐπὶ γῆς, καὶ οὐκ ἔστιν ὑπομονή.
LXX 1 *Ch.* 29. 15.

3   There appears to be another sense which might be predicted
from the verb, where it means the *act of waiting for, expectation*.

ὑπομονητικοὶ πρὸς καιροῦ τὴν ὑπομονήν 'patient in waiting for
the opportune moment'.   Hp. *Decent.* 9. 228, 17.

Once recognised it offers a likely interpretation of other passages.

οἵτινες ἐν καρδίᾳ καλῇ καὶ ἀγαθῇ ἀκούσαντες τὸν λόγον
κατέχουσι καὶ καρποφοροῦσιν ἐν ὑπομονῇ 'bring forth fruit by
waiting patiently for it'.   *Ev. Luc.* 8. 15.

ὁ δὲ κύριος κατευθύναι ὑμῶν τὰς καρδίας εἰς τὴν ἀγάπην τοῦ
θεοῦ καὶ εἰς ὑπομονὴν Χριστοῦ 'towards the love of God and
the expectation of Christ's coming'.   2 *Ep. Thess.* 3. 5.

Other interpretations have been given of these passages; for
instance in the last the *New English Bible* has 'the steadfastness of
Christ', presumably meaning 'as displayed by Christ'; but the
expectation of the Second Coming is a constant theme of the New
Testament.

4   More often the word is found with a genitive to mean
endurance or *tolerance* of something unpleasant.

οἱ ἑκούσιοι πόνοι τὴν τῶν ἀκουσίων ὑπομονὴν ἐλαφροτέρην
παρασκευάζουσι.   Democr. 240.

καρτερία ὑπομονὴ λύπης ἕνεκα τοῦ καλοῦ· ὑπομονὴ πόνων
ἕνεκα τοῦ καλοῦ.   [Pl.] *Def.* 412c.

ἡ μὴ ὑπομονὴ ἀτιμαζομένων.   Arist. *A. Po.* 97ᵇ24.

ἡ δὲ ἀπόνοιά ἐστιν ὑπομονὴ αἰσχρῶν ἔργων καὶ λόγων.
Thphr. *Char.* 6.1.

LSJ gives this a separate section '*enduring to do*', but this simply results from the genitives which follow it, 'tolerance of [doing] disgraceful deeds and [speaking] disgraceful words'.

τῆς ὑπομονῆς τοῦ πολέμου.   Plb. 4. 51. 1.

ἐν ὑπομονῇ τῶν αὐτῶν παθημάτων.   2 *Ep. Cor.* 1. 6.

οὔτε γὰρ φυγὴ θανάτου μεμπτόν ... οὔτε ὑπομονὴ καλόν.
Plu. *Pel.* 1. 4.

εἰς εὐχερῆ τῆς ἀποτέξεως ὑπομονήν.   Sor. 1. 46. 1.

Predicated of a thing, *ability to resist:*

τὴν τῆς μαχαίρας ὑπομονὴν τῶν πληγῶν 'the sword's tolerance of the blows (inflicted on it)'.   Plb. 15. 15. 8.

5   It is easy to see how from this sense there could be a development where there is no genitive, but suffering is understood. We can define this as *willingness to endure* or *calm toleration of adversity, patience, fortitude.*

ἀπὸ ἀνανδρείας γὰρ ἢ δειλίας ἡ ὑπομονὴ καὶ τὸ μὴ ἀμύνεσθαι.
Arist. *Rh.* 1384ᵃ21.

διὰ τῆσδε τῆς κακοπαθείας καὶ ὑπομονῆς τὰ τῆς ἀρετῆς ἆθλα οἴσομεν.   LXX 4 *Ma.* 9. 8.

ἐν τῇ ὑπομονῇ ὑμῶν κτήσασθε (*v. l.* κτήσεσθε) τὰς ψυχὰς ὑμῶ
ν.   *Ev. Luc.* 21. 19.

The meaning of this last sentence is far from self-evident. The words come at the end of a prophecy of disasters, followed by a promise that 'not a hair of your head shall be lost'. This might support the view that here too we have a promise rather than an injunction, and the future is the reading favoured by most modern translators and commentators. The difficulty lies in the second rather than the first part of the sentence, and if we can be sure of that the meaning of ὑπομονή here may become clearer. It is questionable whether κτῶμαι can ever mean 'possess', a meaning normally restricted to the perfect. However, LSJ quotes for this:

ἀποδεκατῶ πάντα ὅσα κτῶμαι.   *Ev. Luc.* 18. 12.

But this surely means 'I pay a tenth of my income', not 'of my property'. Thus we must doubt the translation 'possess' here, familiar though it is from the Authorised Version. So what does τὰς ψυχὰς ὑμῶν mean? The experts are inclined to give this an eschatological interpretation 'immortal life'; e.g. 'by standing firm you will win true life for yourselves' (*New English Bible*). If correct, this appears to be a new sense of ψυχή which needs to be added to my note on this word, and to LSJ. I should therefore prefer to give it the sense discussed in section 10 of my note on this word, 'strength of character'. If so, there appears to be no reason why ὑπομονή should not mean here 'endurance of adversity', 'patience'; ἐν as frequently in the New Testament will mean 'by means of'.

εἰδότες ὅτι ἡ θλῖψις ὑπομονὴν κατεργάζεται. *Ep. Rom.* 5. 3.

εἰ δὲ ὃ οὐ βλέπομεν ἐλπίζομεν, δι' ὑπομονῆς ἀπεκδεχόμεθα 'but if our hoping is for what we do not see, we wait for it patiently'. *Ep. Rom.* 8. 25.

ἐν ὑπομονῇ πολλῇ, ἐν θλίψεσι, ἐν ἀνάγκαις... 2 *Ep. Cor.* 6. 4.

ἐν πάσῃ δυνάμει δυναμούμενοι ... εἰς πᾶσαν ὑπομονὴν καὶ μακροθυμίαν. *Ep. Col.* 1. 11.

ὑπομονῆς γὰρ ἔχετε χρείαν ἵνα τὸ θέλημα τοῦ θεοῦ ποιήσαντες κομίσθησθε τὴν ἐπαγγελίαν. *Ep. Heb.* 10. 36.

τὴν ὑπομονὴν Ἰὼβ ἠκούσατε. *Ep. Jac.* 5. 11.

ὅτι ἐτήρησας τὸν λόγον τῆς ὑπομονῆς μου 'you have observed my command to be patient.' *Apoc.* 3. 10.

ὧδέ ἐστιν ἡ ὑπομονὴ καὶ ἡ πίστις τῶν ἁγίων.
Apoc. 13. 10; 14. 12.

6   In the Septuagint the word seems to be extended to mean *that which gives strength to endure, support*.

ἡ ὑπομονὴ τῶν πενήτων οὐκ ἀπολεῖται εἰς τὸν αἰῶνα.
LXX *Ps.* 9. 19.

πλὴν τῷ θεῷ ὑποτάγηθι ἡ ψυχή μου, ὅτι παρ' αὐτοῦ ἡ ὑπομονή μου. LXX *Ps.* 61. 5.

καὶ ὑπομονὴν ἀνθρώπου ἀπώλεσας. LXX *Jb.* 14. 19.

ὑπομονὴ Ἰσραὴλ Κύριε, καὶ σώζεις ἐν καιρῷ κακῶν.
LXX *Je.* 14. 8; 17. 13.

7   LSJ alleges a sense of *obstinacy* on the basis of a single reference from Demetrius Lacon in a Herculaneum papyrus. The passage in question runs

τὸ μὲν] βλεπόμενον ὥς εἰσίν τινες ὑπομενετικαὶ διδασκαλίαι
πολλῆς εὐοδίας ἡμᾶς κατὰ τὴν ἀνάγνωσιν πληρώσει,
βλέποντας ὡς οὐχ ὁμολογεῖται τὰ ἄτοπα, δι' ὑπομονῆς δὲ τῆς
τούτων ἐλέγχει τοὺς κα[τ]ὰ τοῦτον τὸν τρόπον διακαμό[ν]τας.
                                          Demetr. Lac. *Herc.* 1012. 69.

The Italian translation given by E. Puglia (*Aporie testuali ed
esegetiche in Epicuro,* Naples, 1988) can be rendered into English
thus: 'The fact of seeing that there are some teachings (of
Epicurus) which firmly resist will fill us with great happiness while
reading, because we see that the absurdities are not confirmed, and
also by means of the firm resistance of these teachings, a fact which
refutes those who expatiate at length in this direction.' This
should be sufficient to disprove the existence of the alleged sense
of obstinacy; it would appear that ὑπομονή here has its usual sense
of endurance, though here applied to something as abstract as a
philosophical doctrine.

ψυχή

1   This is of course a word with very high frequency of usage at
all periods, but it may be doubted whether this justifies the length
of the article on it in LSJ, which runs to more than two columns.
Contrast this with the partial synonym θυμός, which is less than
one column. The length of a dictionary entry should depend upon
the diversity of usage, and since this is generally proportionate to
its frequency, some correlation is to be expected. The existing
article is not only too long, but goes into philosophical distinctions
which are, in my opinion, the matter of philosophy, and no direct
concern of the lexicographer. The concept of the ψυχή has of
course been discussed in countless books and articles, and those
who wish to study the subject will not think of turning to an
article in a lexicon for enlightenment. The lexicographer's task is
to present an overview of the different ways in which the word is
used, so as to give an idea of the range of meanings which it was
used to convey. For instance, the concept of *the immortal soul* does
not appear to be a meaning conveyed by the word alone; thus it
should not appear as one of the definitions. What is significant is
that the soul was conceived as continuing to exist after separation
from the mortal body; and this is an idea already well represented

in Homer. It hardly needs to be added that all languages offer
a subjective view of the world around us, as it appears to its
speakers; so there is no need to become involved in arguments
about the real existence of the soul.

2 The etymology of ψυχή indicates that it was originally a word
for *breath*, but this is not in fact how it was used. The association
of breathing with the living body had already led to a development
in its meaning by the time of our earliest texts. It might therefore
be defined as the entity which animates the living body and distinguishes it from a dead one. As I have said, it is unnecessary to
speculate on the nature of such an entity; it was sufficient to
inspect living and lifeless forms to infer that the living ones contained something which was absent from the dead or lifeless. We
might therefore begin with a definition: *animating principle, life-
force*.

> τοῦ δ' αὖθι λύθη ψυχή τε μένος τε. Il. 5. 196.
>
> τοὺς μὲν Τυδεΐδης δουρικλειτὸς Διομήδης
> θυμοῦ καὶ ψυχῆς κεκαδὼν κλυτὰ τεύχε' ἀπηύρα.
> Il. 11. 334; Od. 21. 154.
>
> ψυχὴ δὲ κατ' οὐταμένην ὠτειλὴν
> ἔσσυτ' ἐπειγομένη. Il. 14. 518.
>
> αὐτὰρ ἐπὴν δὴ τόν γε λίπῃ ψυχή τε καὶ αἰών.
> Il. 16. 453; Od. 9. 523.
>
> τοῖο δ' ἅμα ψυχήν τε καὶ ἔγχεος ἐξέρυσ' αἰχμήν. Il. 16. 505.
>
> λίσσομ' ὑπὲρ ψυχῆς καὶ γούνων σῶν τε τοκήων. Il. 22. 338.

This might be taken as the developed sense of *life* discussed in 4
below, but the fact that it is coupled with knees suggests that it is
still thought of as a part, even if invisible, of the living body. It is
used of animals as well as human beings.

> τὸν (sc. ὗν) ἔλιπε ψυχή. Od. 14. 426.
>
> ἀμφὶ δὲ κάπροι
> δοιοί, ἀπουράμενοι ψυχάς. Hes. Sc. 173.

This simplistic concept continues to be found in poetry, but in
prose it usually develops to the more abstract idea of life.
Significantly the early idea recurs in the Septuagint.

> ψυχὰν ἀποπνέοντα. Simon. 52 (48 P).

ἀγχομένοις δὲ βρόχος
ψυχὰς ἀπέπνευσεν μελέων ἀφάτων (of snakes).
Pi. N. 1. 47; O. 8. 39.

In both these examples the original idea of breath might be present; but it seems more likely that the connexion with ψύχω had by this date been lost.

βλάβην ... τοὐμὸν ἐκπίνουσ᾽ ἀεὶ
ψυχῆς ἄκρατον αἷμα.   S. El. 786; cf.
καὶ τὰς πλευρὰς δαρδάπτουσιν
καὶ τὴν ψυχὴν ἐκπίνουσιν.   Ar. Nu. 712.
ἀλλ᾽ ἐλευθέρως
ψυχὴν ἀφήσω.   E. Or. 1171.
πρὸς δὲ καὶ ψυχὴν σέθεν
ἔκτεινε.   E. Tr. 1214.

One can hardly kill a person's life; something more concrete must be intended here. In prose:

τὰ ἄλλα ζῷα ὅσα ψυχὴν ἔχει.   Anaxag. 4; Democr. 278.
ἡ ψυχή, ἕως μὲν ἂν ἐν θνητῷ σώματι ᾖ, ζῇ.   X. Cyr. 8. 7. 19.
παντὶ τῷ ἑρπετῷ ἕρποντι ἐπὶ τῆς γῆς, ὃ ἔχει ἐν ἑαυτῷ ψυχὴν
ζωῆς.   LXX Ge. 1. 30.

3   In some cases the loss of the ψυχή may be temporary, leading to unconsciousness, but not death. The basic sense here is unchanged, but the context shows the distinction.

τὸν δὲ λίπε ψυχή, κατὰ δ᾽ ὀφθαλμῶν κέχυτ᾽ ἀχλύς·
αὖτις δ᾽ ἐμπνύνθη, περὶ δὲ πνοιὴ Βορέαο
ζώγρει ἐπιπνείουσα κακῶς κεκαφηότα θυμόν.   Il. 5. 696.
τὴν δὲ (Ἀνδρομάχην) κατ᾽ ὀφθαλμῶν ἐρεβεννὴ νὺξ ἐκάλυψεν,
ἤριπε δ᾽ ἐξοπίσω, ἀπὸ δὲ ψυχὴν ἐκάπυσσε.   Il. 22. 467.

This sense appears not to have survived into later Greek.

4   The ψυχή was believed to continue in existence after the death of the body, being carried to the realm of Hades, but in some circumstances capable of re-appearing on earth. In this sense it may be translated *spirit, ghost*.

πολλὰς ἰφθίμους ψυχὰς Ἄϊδι προΐαψεν.   Il. 1. 3.

ψυχαὶ δ᾽ Ἀϊδόσδε κατῆλθον. Il. 7. 330.

ὢ πόποι, ἦ ῥά τίς ἐστι καὶ εἰν Ἀΐδαο δόμοισι
ψυχὴ καὶ εἴδωλον, ἀτὰρ φρένες οὐ ἔνι πάμπαν. Il. 23. 104.

ἦλθε δ᾽ ἐπὶ ψυχὴ Πατροκλῆος δειλοῖο. Il. 23. 65; Od. 11. 387.

κέλεται γὰρ ἑὰν ψυχὰν κομίξαι
Φρίξος. Pi. P. 4. 159; N. 8. 44.

σὺν Ἀγαμεμνονίᾳ
ψυχᾷ. Pi. P. 11. 21.

αἰθὲρ μὲμ φσυχὰς ὑπεδέχσατο. IG 1². 945.

πέμψατ᾽ ἔνερθεν ψυχὴν εἰς φῶς. A. Pers. 630.

εἴτ᾽ ἄρα ἐν Ἅιδου εἰσὶν αἱ ψυχαὶ τελευτησάντων τῶν
ἀνθρώπων εἴτε καὶ οὔ. Pl. Phd. 70c; Lg. 927b.

δὶς ἀποθανουμένη ψυχή (addressed to a ghost about to be
speared). Anon. ap. Plu. 2. 236d.

The disembodied spirit might be regarded as immortal and able
to inhabit other bodies, but the sense of the word remains
unchanged.

ἐς τὸν ὕπερθεν ἅλιον κείνων ἐνάτῳ ἔτει
ἀνδιδοῖ (Φερσεφόνα) πάλιν. Pi. fr. 133 (137T).

τόνδε τὸν λόγον Αἰγύπτιοί εἰσι οἱ εἰπόντες, ὡς ἀνθρώπου
ψυχὴ ἀθάνατός ἐστι. Hdt. 2. 123. 2.

οὐκ ᾔσθησαι ... ὅτι ἀθάνατος ἡμῶν ἡ ψυχὴ καὶ οὐδέποτε
ἀπόλλυται; Pl. R. 608d; Men. 81b.

ἔνθα καὶ εἰς θηρίου βίον ἀνθρωπινὴ ψυχὴ ἀφικνεῖται.
Pl. Phdr. 249b.

ὥσπερ ἐνδεχόμενον κατὰ τοὺς Πυθαγορικοὺς μύθους τὴν
τυχοῦσαν ψυχὴν εἰς τὸ τυχὸν ἐνδύεσθαι σῶμα.
Arist. de. An. 407ᵇ22.

5 It is a short step from the simple sense (2 above) to the more
abstract concept of ψυχή as meaning *a person's continued existence,
life*. This is something that can be taken away, fought for, put at
risk, granted to suppliants, and so forth.

οἷά τε ληϊστῆρες ὑπεὶρ ἅλα τοί τ᾽ ἀλόωνται
ψυχὰς παρθέμενοι. Od. 3. 74.

φροντίδες ἀνθρώπων ...
μυρόμεναι ψυχῆς εἴνεκα καὶ βιότου. Thgn. 730.

ψυχὰς ἔχοντες κυμάτων ἐν ἀγκάλαις. Archil. 23 (= 213 W).

ψυχέων μηκέτι φειδόμενοι.   Tyrt. 10. 14; Sol. 13. 46.

λίσσεσθαι, χρήματα μέν σφι προϊέντα, ψυχὴν δὲ παραιτεόμενον.
                                              Hdt. 1. 24. 2.

οἵ σ' ἀντὶ παίδων τῶνδε καὶ ψυχῆς, πάτερ,
ἱκετεύομεν.   S. OC 1326.

ἐκεῖνον ... σωτηρίας ἂν τῆς ψυχῆς ἀποστερῆσαι.
                                              Th. 1. 136. 4.

ἐγὼ μὲν ... κἂν τῆς ψυχῆς πριαίμην ὥστε μήποτε λατρεῦσαι
ταύτην. 'I would pay with my life to prevent her from being a
servant.'   X. Cyr. 3. 1. 36.

τὴν ψυχὴν ἢ τὴν οὐσίαν ἢ τὴν ἐπιτιμίαν ἀφελόμενος.
                      Aeschin. 2. 88; Antipho 4. 1. 6; 4. 1. 7.

              ἄχρις ἡ ψυχὴ
αὐτοῦ ἐπὶ χειλέων μοῦνον ἡ κακὴ λειφθῇ.   Herod. 3. 3.

ἡ ψυχή μου ἐν ταῖς χερσί σου διάπαντος.
        LXX Ps. 118. 109; 1 Ki. 19. 5; 1 Ki. 28. 21.

An example of this idiom in Xenarch. 4. 20 is unlikely to be
genuine.

ζητοῦσι τὴν ψυχήν μου λαβεῖν αὐτήν.   LXX 3 Ki. 19. 10.

οἱ ζητοῦντες τὴν ψυχὴν τοῦ παιδίου.   Ev. Matt. 2. 20.

τί γὰρ ὠφελεῖ ἄνθρωπον κερδῆσαι τὸν κόσμον ὅλον καὶ
ζημιωθῆναι τὴν ψυχὴν αὐτοῦ;   Ev. Marc. 8. 36.

The phrase περὶ ψυχῆς accordingly means *for one's life, at risk of
death*.

ἀλλὰ περὶ ψυχῆς θέον Ἕκτορος ἱπποδάμοιο.
Il. 22. 161; Od. 9. 423; 22. 245.

τρέχων περὶ τῆς ψυχῆς.   Hdt. 9. 37. 2.

              λόγων γὰρ οὐ
νῦν ἐστιν ἀγών, ἀλλὰ σῆς ψυχῆς πέρι.
S. El. 1492; E. Ph. 1330; Or. 847.

περὶ τῆς ψυχῆς δι' ἐκείνους κινδυνεύοντι.
Th. 8. 50. 5; Antipho 2. 1. 4.

            τὸν περὶ ψυ-
χῆς δρόμον δραμεῖν.   Ar. V. 375.

But in the following example it means 'whether he is alive or not'.

            τοὺς δὲ Μενέλεω ποθῶ
λόγους ἀκοῦσαι τίνας ἐρεῖ ψυχῆς πέρι.   E. Hel. 946.

6   In one example it appears to mean *the taking of life*.

ὃς βούλοιτο ποινὴν τῆς Αἰσώπου ψυχῆς ἀνελέσθαι.
Hdt. 2. 134. 4.

7   As a periphrasis for a *living creature or person*, especially in counting.

Ἑλένα,
μία τὰς πολλάς, τὰς πάνυ πολλὰς
ψυχὰς ὀλέσασ' ὑπὸ Τροίᾳ.   A. *Ag.* 1457; Ar. *Th.* 864.
πρὶν φόνον φόνῳ ὁμοίῳ ὅμοιον ἡ δράσασα ψυχὴ τείσῃ.
Pl. *Lg.* 873a.
ἐξαγέτω ἡ γῆ ψυχὴν ζῶσαν κατὰ γένος.
LXX *Ge.* 46. 15; 1 *Ep. Pet.* 3. 20.
πᾶσα ψυχὴ ἐξουσίαις ὑπερεχούσαις ὑποτασσέσθω.
Ep. Rom. 13. 1.

8   A person's ψυχή may be regarded as a sentient being resident within the body, thus capable of thought and feeling. Translations such as *personality, self, heart, soul* may be appropriate.

ψυχῇ διδόντες ἡδονὴν καθ' ἡμέραν.   A. *Pers.* 841.

The conjecture ψυχήν ... ἡδονῇ seems to be unnecessary.

ψυχὴ γὰρ ηὔδα πολλά μοι μυθουμένη,
τάλας, τί χωρεῖς οἳ μολὼν δώσεις δίκην;   S. *Ant.* 227.
τῆς ἐμῆς ψυχῆς γεγώς 'born of myself'.   S. *El.* 775.
          ἐμπαίει τί μοι
ψυχῇ συνηθὲς ὄμμα.   S. *El.* 903.
ὦ φιλτάτου μνημεῖον ἀνθρώπων ἐμοὶ
ψυχῆς Ὀρέστου λοιπόν.   S. *El.* 1127.

This obviously does not mean 'O memorial remaining of the life of Orestes'.

          τὴν Φιλοκτήτου σε δεῖ
ψυχὴν ὅπως λόγοισιν ἐκκλέψεις λέγων.   S. *Ph.* 55.
τί ποτ' ἔστι μαθεῖν ἔραται ψυχή; 'I long to know ...'
E. *Hipp.* 173.
          ὡς ὑπείργασμαι μὲν εὖ
ψυχὴν ἔρωτι.
'My soul is all made ready by desire' (W. S. Barrett).
E. *Hipp.* 505.

Ἔρως ... εἰσάγων γλυκεῖαν
ψυχᾷ χάριν.   E. *Hipp*. 527.

ταῦτ' ἄρ' ἀκούσασ' αὐτῶν τὸ φθέγμ' ἡ ψυχή μου πεπότηται.
                                                    Ar. *Nu*. 319.

ὅτι σοι ἐκ τῆς ψυχῆς φίλος ἦν.   X. *An*. 7. 7. 43; cf.

βόσκοιτ' ἐκ ψυχᾶς τὰς ἀμνάδας.   Theoc. 8. 35.

ἀπὸ τῆς ψυχῆς 'from the heart'.   Thphr. *Char*. 17. 3.

τῷ δὲ ἡ ψυχὴ σῖτον μὲν οὐ προίετο, διψῆν δ' ἐδόκει.
                                                    X. *Cyr*. 8. 7. 4.

καὶ ἀνθρώπου γε ψυχή, ἣ ... τοῦ θείου μετέχει, ὅτι μὲν
βασιλεύει ἐν ἡμῖν φανερόν, ὁρᾶται δὲ οὐδ' αὐτή.
                                                    X. *Mem*. 4. 3. 14.

πάνυ μοι ἡ ψυχὴ ἐπεθύμει αὐτῶν τινι συγγενέσθαι.
                                                    X. *Oec*. 6. 14.

σοφία μὴν καὶ νοῦς ἄνευ ψυχῆς οὐκ ἄν ποτε γενοίσθην.
                                                    Pl. *Phlb*. 30c.

λίχνῳ δὲ ὄντι αὐτῷ τὴν ψυχὴν μόνῳ τῶν ἐν τῇ πόλει οὔτε
ἀποδημῆσαι ἔξεστιν οὐδαμόσε ... 'however much he longs in
his heart to do so, he alone in the city is not allowed to travel
elsewhere ...'   Pl. *R*. 579b.

ἀλλ' ἄλλο τι βουλομένη ἑκατέρου ἡ ψυχὴ δήλη ἐστίν.
                                                    Pl. *Smp*. 192c.

καὶ τὸ σῶμα ἀπειρηκὸς ἡ ψυχὴ συνεξέσωσεν 'the soul has
rescued the body too when it had given up'.   Antipho 5. 93.

      οὐχ ἅδε πλούτου φρονέουσιν ὄνασις,
ἀλλὰ τὸ μὲν ψυχᾷ, τὸ δέ πού τινι δοῦναι ἀοιδῶν.
                                                    Theoc. 16. 24.

καὶ ἐρῶ τῇ ψυχῇ μου, ψυχή, ἔχεις πολλὰ ἀγαθὰ κείμενα εἰς
ἔτη πολλά.   Ev. *Luc*. 12. 19.

εἰς τὰ ὑπὸ ψυχῆς, οἷον ποίμνας, ἀγέλας (i.e. sentient beings).
                                                    M. Ant. 6. 14.

9   The personality can be regarded from the point of view of its
moral attributes, so that here ψυχή comes to mean *character*.

              ἀπὸ πάμπαν ἀδίκων ἔχειν
ψυχάν.   Pi. *O*. 2. 70.

              κτεάνων ψυ-
χὰς ἔχοντες κρέσσονας
ἄνδρες.   Pi. *N*. 9. 32.

διεπειρᾶτο αὐτοῦ τῆς ψυχῆς. Hdt. 3. 14. 1; 5. 124. 1.

ἀμήχανον δὲ παντὸς ἀνδρὸς ἐκμαθεῖν
ψυχήν τε καὶ φρόνημα καὶ γνώμην. S. Ant. 176.

ἀλλ' ἡ κακὴ σὴ διὰ μυχῶν βλέπουσ' ἀεὶ
ψυχή νιν ἀφυῆ τ' ὄντα κοὐ θέλονθ' ὅμως
εὖ προὐδίδαξεν ἐν κακοῖς εἶναι σοφόν. S. Ph. 1014.

κράτιστοι δ' ἂν τὴν ψυχὴν δικαίως κριθεῖεν οἱ τά τε δεινὰ καὶ
ἡδέα σαφέστατα γιγνώσκοντες. Th. 2. 40. 3.

μηδ' ἄλλο μηδὲν τῆς ἐμῆς ψυχῆς πέρι
λέξονθ' ὅθεν χρὴ δειλίαν ὀφλεῖν τινα. E. Heracl. 984.

ψυχῶν σοφῶν τοῦτ' ἐστὶ φροντιστήριον. Ar. Nu. 94.

μοχθηροὺς ὄντας τὰς ψυχάς. X. Oec. 6. 16.

ἡ ἐν γῇ ἀργία ἐστὶ σαφὴς ψυχῆς κατήγορος κακῆς.
X. Oec. 20. 15.

τὴν τῆς ψυχῆς ἐπιμέλειαν. Isoc. 15. 304; 15. 290.

ἐπιμελεῖσθαι ... τῆς ψυχῆς, ὅπως ἀρίστη ἔσται. Pl. Ap. 30b.

ἀνάγκη ἄρα κακῇ ψυχῇ κακῶς ἄρχειν. Pl. R. 353e.

ἤρετο ... τίνα ποτε ψυχὴν ἀξιοῖ ... τοιαύτῃ γνώμῃ χρῆσθαι.
Lys. 32. 12.

τίν' οἴεσθε αὐτὴν ψυχὴν ἔχειν; D. 28. 21.

ἔστι δὲ ἡ κακολογία ἀγωγὴ τῆς ψυχῆς εἰς τὸ χεῖρον ἐν λόγοις.
Thphr. Char. 28. 1.

ἔπειτα ἂν μὲν αἱ χάριτες αἱ τῆς λέξεως ἐπικοσμεῖν δοκῶσί μοι
τὴν γραφήν, τῆς Λυσίου ψυχῆς αὐτὴν τίθεμαι. D.H. Lys. 11.

10   As a positive quality, *strength of character, courage, spirit*. It is
this sense which gave rise to the adjective μεγαλόψυχος.

οἵαις ἐν πολέμοιο μάχαις
τλάμονι ψυχᾷ παρέμειν'. Pi. P. 1. 48.

χερσὶ καὶ ψυχᾷ δυνατοί. Pi. N. 9. 39.

θάρσει· σὺ μὲν ζῇς, ἡ δ' ἐμὴ ψυχὴ πάλαι
τέθνηκεν, ὥστε τοῖς θανοῦσιν ὠφελεῖν. S. Ant. 559.

ψυχήν τ' ἄριστε πάντων. Ar. Eq. 457.

ὁ γὰρ λόγχην ἀκονῶν ἐκεῖνος καὶ τὴν ψυχήν τι παρακονᾷ 'the
man who sharpens his spear also makes his spirit a bit sharper'.
X. Cyr. 6. 2. 33.

δεῖ ὑπάρξαι αὐτῷ (sc. ἵππῳ) καὶ τὴν ψυχὴν μεγαλόφρονα καὶ
τὸ σῶμα εὔρωστον. X. Eq. 11. 1.

ἐν σμικρᾷ πόλει ὅταν μεγάλη ψυχὴ φυῇ.   Pl. R. 496b.
ἡ πάσης τῆς Ἑλλάδος ἄρ᾽ ἐλευθερία ἐν ταῖς τῶνδε τῶν
ἀνδρῶν ψυχαῖς διεσῴζετο.   [D.] 60. 23.

11   In the philosophers there are numerous attempts at defining
the ψυχή, most of which can be happily fitted into the scheme proposed here. But in a few cases it appears to refer to a sentient being
external to the individual, hence some kind of divine or world-
soul.

καὶ τὴν τῶν ἄλλων ἁπάντων φύσιν οὐ πιστεύεις Ἀναξαγόρᾳ
νοῦν καὶ ψυχὴν εἶναι τὴν διακοσμοῦσαν καὶ ἔχουσαν;
                                        Pl. Cra. 400a; Arist. de An. 404ᵃ25.

ψυχὴ δ᾽ ἐν πρώτοις γεγενημένη.   Pl. Lg. 892c.

διὰ τίνα γὰρ αἰτίαν ἐν μὲν τῷ ἀέρι ἢ τῷ πυρὶ οὖσα ψυχὴ οὐ
ποιεῖ ζῷον, ἐν δὲ τοῖς μικτοῖς …;   Arist. de An. 411ᵃ10.

ὡς ἓν ζῷον τὸν κόσμον μίαν οὐσίαν καὶ ψυχὴν μίαν ἐπέχον
συνεχῶς ἐπινοεῖν.   M. Ant. 4. 40.

τήν τε τοῦ κόσμου τήν τε τῆς ψυχῆς αὐτοῦ γένεσιν καὶ
σύστασιν.   Plu. 2. 1013e.

12   Since one's life is obviously one's dearest possession, the
word can also be used as a type or model of what is dearest, and
thus as a term of endearment or even a proper name, as in the case
of Cupid's lover in Apuleius.

χρήματα γὰρ ψυχὴ πέλεται δειλοῖσι βροτοῖσιν.   Hes. Op. 686.
                πᾶσι δ᾽ ἀνθρώποις ἄρ᾽ ἦν
ψυχὴ τέκν᾽.   E. Andr. 419.

As a term of endearment:

μή, φίλα ψυχά, βίον ἀθάνατον
σπεῦδε.   Pi. P. 3. 61.

ὦ μελέα ψυχά.   S. Ph. 712.

φεῦ, ὦ ἀγαθὴ καὶ πιστὴ ψυχή, οἴχῃ δὴ ἀπολιπὼν ἡμᾶς;
                                        X. Cyr. 7. 3. 8.

οἴμοι ψυχή, ὅτι ἀπόλωλεν εὐσεβὴς ἀπὸ τῆς γῆς.
                                        LXX Mi. 7. 2.

This is presumably what is meant in the Latin satirists:

quotiens lasciuum interuenit illud
ζωὴ καὶ ψυχή.   Juv. 6. 195; Mart. 10. 68.

ὦ φιλτάτη καὶ ψυχὴ ἐμὴ Χαρίκλεια. Hld. 1. 8. 4.

13 In a completely transferred sense ψυχή can be used to mean the *animating force* or *life* of other things.

πᾶσα πολιτεία ψυχὴ πόλεώς ἐστι. Isoc. 12. 138.

ἀρχὴ μὲν οὖν καὶ οἷον ψυχὴ ὁ μῦθος τῆς τραγῳδίας.

Arist. *Po.* 1450ᵃ38.

ἡ γὰρ ψυχὴ πάσης σαρκὸς αἷμα αὐτοῦ ἐστι.

LXX *Le.* 17. 11; *De.* 12. 23.

14 Finally, starting from the analogy between the emergence of the soul from the body, it comes to be used of the *butterfly* which emerges from the chrysalis.

γίγνονται δ᾽ αἱ μὲν καλούμεναι ψυχαὶ ἐκ τῶν καμπῶν, αἳ γίγνονται ἐπὶ τῶν φύλλων τῶν χλωρῶν. Arist. *HA* 551ᵃ14.

οἷον ἐκ κάμπης γίνεται χρυσαλλὶς εἶτ᾽ ἐκ ταύτης ψυχή.

Thphr. *HP* 2. 4. 4.

ἕτερον πτερωθὲν δι᾽ αὐτῆς τὴν καλουμένην ψυχὴν μεθίησιν (κάμπη). Plu. 2. 636c.

15 A table of the meanings discussed may be presented as follows.

1 *animating principle, life-force* (2). **b** as lost in unconsciousness (3).
2 as surviving the body, *spirit, ghost* (4).
3 *continued existence, life* (5). **b** *the taking of life* (6).
4 *living creature, person* (7).
5 *personality, self, heart, soul* (8).
6 *character* (9).
7 *strength of character, courage, spirit* (10).
8 *world-soul* (11).
9 as a type of what is dearest (12). **b** as a term of endearment (12).
10 *animating force* of things (13).
11 *butterfly* (14).

INDEX OF GREEK WORDS

Entries and references in bold type refer to the page on which the main notes in the book begin, the remainder to words which are discussed in passing.

ἀάατος 31
ἀβλεμής 76
ἀγαπητός 16, **32**
ἀγοράζω 21, **34**
ἀϝλανέος 39
αἰκία 295
ἀλανής 39
ἀλλ' ἤ 126
ἄνερμα 40
ἀνόστεος 15
ἀντία, ἀντίον 41
ἄντομος 43
ἀολλής 39
ἀπέχω 45
ἁπλόος 46
ἀραιός 14, **46**
ἀργύριος 54
ἁρπακτός 54
ἄσπρος 287
ἀσσκονικτεί 55
ἀτεχνῶς 56
ἄχυρον 56

βάπτω 59
βαρέω 62
βαρύς **64**
βεβαρημένος 62
βινέω 21, **73**, 187
βλαβή 295
βλεμεαίνω **76**
βλέπω 76
βόρηται 64
βωμός 113

γαμέω 74
γερός **77**
γλεῦκος **78**
γράφω **79**

δεῖνα 209

δέλλιν 115
διαβάλλω **87**
διάβολος 92
διατρίβω 51
δίζημαι **94**
δισκυροῦσι 16, **95**

ἔγρω **95**
εἶδον 8
εἰκῆ 23, **96**
εἰκότως 98
ἐκτός **100**
ἐλύμνιαι 13
ἐλύς **105**
ἐμβατεύω 21
ἐμέτερος 134
ἔμη 116
ἐνδαής 16, **107**
ἐξῆς, ἐξείης **107**
ἐπηρασία 116
ἐπιγράφω 79
ἐσχάρα **111**
ἔτυς **115**
ἔχω 23
ἕως ὅσου 116

ϝάγανον 1, **117**

ζῆλος **119**
ζωγράφος 81

ἤ, ἦ (ἤέ) **123**
ἠάν 116
ἤγανον 118
ἡμέτερος **134**
ἡμιεκτάνιον
 (-οκτάνιον) **134**
ἤρυς 13, **137**

θάλασσα **138**
θάλος (θάλεα) **140**

θᾶς **142**
θυμός **143**
θωράκιον 171

ἱερός 78, **150**, 226
ἶνες 140
ἴς 157
ἱπνός **161**
ἱππεύς 117
ἰσχυρός **165**

καίπερ 243
καρχήσιον **170**
καταλαμβάνω **172**
καταχαρίζομαι **173**
καταχράομαι **174**
κατειλέω 173
κεφαλή **177**
κινέω **183**
κλακτός 11
κοῖλος 257
κονίαλος 221
κοντός 22
κρίβανος 162

μαλακός 19
μέγας 197
μένος 157, **189**
μέξ, μές **195**
μέσποδι 196
μέσφα 196
μέττ(α) 196
μέχρι 197
ναύσταθμον 256
νέμω **198**
νόμος 206

ξύλον 303

ὄβδη	208	προσθάλπω	10		τόλμα	262	
ὅδε	208				τραχαίοις	286	
οἶδα	8	ῥέω	247		τρώγω	287	
ὀλερός (ὀλός)	210				τυφλός	290	
ὀξύς	211	συκοφάντης	22				
ὀπυίω	21, 74	σταθμός	22, 253		ὕβρις	292	
ὀργάω	217	στέργω	32		ὑγρός	297	
ὅρκια	273	στοργή	32		ὕλη	303	
ὀρχηστής	218				ὕπερθεν	52	
ὅσιος (ὁσία)	221	τάγηνον	118		ὑπομονή	307	
οὐλή	39	τάλας	16, 262				
		τάλης	265		φθόνος	120–1	
παίζω	220	τέλειος, τέλεος	266		φορμός	42–3	
παρθένος	226	τέμνω	271		φρήν	146	
πάσχω	229	τένδει	15				
πατάσσω	144	τέως	142		χάος	22	
πεδά	10	τήγανον	118		χερνῆτις	260	
πέμπω	233	τοπαδειν	279				
περ	241	τόπος	280		ψεῦδος	52	
					ψυχή	311	

INDEX OF GREEK CITATIONS

Inscriptions and papyri will be found at the end.

ÆLIAN

NA 1. 26	287	733	40	Pr. 77	68
2. 8	165	802	202	92	230
4. 46	213	849	272	132	238
7. 9	301	972	269	250	291
15. 10	173	973	267	292	204
VH 1. 23	174	1067	190	330	104
9. 1	67	1084	243	348	282
11. 9	174	1107	264	450	96
12. 1	72	1247	262	526	202
14. 5	174	1388	144	529	225
fr. 2	250	1389	215	706	146
		1432	267	720	194
		1457	316	759	231
		1504	266	863	61

ÆSCHINES

1. 15	295	Ch. 289	183	Supp. 27	223
1. 29	297	450	83	55	243
1. 52	97	477	239	136	238
1. 116	297	1011	61	259	297
1. 122	176	1047	274	302	167
1. 188	297	1076	195	403	204
2. 9	281	Eu. 28	267	415	68
2. 21	68	50	82	526	267
2. 22	99	108	113	739	268
2. 50	45	249	280	807	274
2. 70	176	292	282	1005	238
2. 88	315	592	271	Th. 37	236
3. 53	174	598	239	80	251
3. 62	85	624	204	167	267
3. 66	169	703	282	202	127
3. 73	281	747	204	262	262
3. 78	283	868	231	265	101
3. 177	97	Pers. 34	235	332	68
3. 216	286	205	113	393	195

ÆSCHYLUS

Ag. 59	239	445	262	443	239
61	236	447	282	557	251
191	282	517	262	590	202
206	68	572	69	767	68
223	263	630	314	832	268
238	195	746	247	954	213
269	129	790	283	983	230
385	263	796	282	1010	224
497	306	828	68	1038	243
685	202	841	316	fr. 69	89
		1044	68	196	272

AESCHYLUS *fr. (cont.)*
199	243
323	155
353	165

AESOP
2. 2	122
40	59

AGATHARCHIDES
61	99

ALCAEUS
69. 5	230
70. 8	142
72. 6	207
129. 10	147
129. 22	149
129. 25	207
130. 16	262
206. 6	142
308. 2(b)	148
346. 5	178
351	160, 185
358	148
424	153

ALCMAN
1. 55	54
15	141
26	156
40. 1	207

ALEXIS
178. 15	182
206. 2	303

ANACREON
26	118

ANACREONTEA
15. 21	301

ANAXAGORAS
4	313

ANAXIPPUS
2	186

ANDOCIDES
1. 83	209, 261
1. 96	223
1. 97	267
2. 24	91
3. 8	276
3. 22	32
3. 31	149

ANTHOLOGIA PALATINA
2. 1. 216	121–2
5. 33 (32)	250
5. 125 (124)	250
5. 190 (189). 2	122
5. 228. 5	120
6. 43.1	299
7. 27. 3	301
7. 275. 2	292
7. 400. 2	291
9. 18	299
9. 91	222
9. 248. 5	121
9. 289. 4	290
9. 345. 3	121
9. 359. 1	277
9. 360. 1	277
11. 7	187
15. 25. 1	211

ANTIPHANES
138. 4	289
174. 3	162
216. 7	99
225. 2	59

ANTIPHO
1. 25	225
2. 1. 4	315
2. 2. 2	225
2. 4. 4	98
4. 1. 6, 7	315
5. 10	205
5. 11	168
5. 93	317

APOLLONIUS DYSCOLUS
Pron. 104. 15	188

APOLLONIUS RHODIUS
1. 616	121
2. 77	31
2. 1244	277
4. 771	277

APPIAN
BC 1. 106	299
4. 4. 22	163
5. 8	302
5. 128	121
Mac. 14	67

ARATUS
858	62
951	62

ARCHESTRATUS
46. 4	162

ARCHILOCHUS
23 (213 W)	314
63	212

ARCHIMEDES
Spir. 16	212

ARISTOPHANES
Ach. 112	62
193	214
449	258
485	262
508	59
591	166
625	36, 38
665	194
720	34
804	216
833	179
888	113
943	168
1052	187
1111–12	129
Av. 13	129
159	203
162	129
384	205
437	163
556	153
898	224
1095	213
1397	129
1400	277
1432	230
1560	271
1648	92
1652	128
Ec. 124	265
190	265
216	60
242	265
526	264
638	110
757	240
919	265
1005	264
Eq. 262	88
364	187
413	128
431	97
457	318

526	252	*Ra.* 21	294	*EE* 1216^{b}40	98
570	147	327	223	1240^{a}2	215
582	153	538	81	*EN* 1094^{b}12	307
864	233	559	265	1126^{a}18	215
953	129	652	158	1129^{b}30	269
1286	114	733	99	1141^{a}19	182
1373	35-6	765	108	1156^{b}34	269
1374	36	995	102	*GA* 752^{b}8	212
Lys. 102	265	1365	259	788^{a}22	72
104	269	1381	259	*GC* 320^{a}2	307
471	97	1407	259	*HA* 510^{a}14	181
633	37, 108	*Th.* 258	180	551^{a}14	320
		352-3	268	559^{a}2	305
743	225	644	264	572^{a}28	282
914	264	864	316	578^{b}21	255
928	129	912	114	580^{a}30	300
1034	249	973	268	583^{a}15	282
1202	215	1039	263	592^{a}18	62
Nu. 40	179	1100	277	596^{a}25	57
94	318	1214	92	598^{a}9	301
234	233	*V.* 375	315	603^{b}32	301
319	317	424	190	605^{a}29	60
483	130	567	149	607^{b}32	258
530	228	678	298	611^{a}20	255
712	313	837	163	612^b 22	58
816	230	881	86	617^{a}1	302
924	289	894	86	620^{b}35	156
1103	187	938	113	*IA* 707^{b}3	283
1299	294	946-7	233	*Metaph.*	
1369	149	1213	301	1032^{a}17	307
1429	85	*fr.* 33	155	*Mete.* 348^{b}28	299
1482	86	216	240	356^{a}16	248
Pax 643	89, 93	353	165	361^{a}33	248
		ARISTOTLE		364^{b}25	47
841	164	*A. Po.* 97^{b}24	308	383^{b}6	252
1063	179	*A. Pr.* 27^{a}1	268	*MM* 1203^{b}21	232
1173	213	*Ath.* 8. 3	204	*Mu.* 394^{a}21	47
1176	62	10. 1	261	*PA* 645^{a}20	163
1324	288	30. 3	206	655^{a}24	300
Pl. 210	215	31. 3	206	666^{a}15	283
526	179	63. 4	204	675^{b}7	292
650	182	*Aud.* 803^b 28	48	676^{a}5	292
682	222	*Cael.* 270^{b}24	176	*Ph.* 196^{a}5	36
684	264	271^{b}11	188	*Phgn.* 806^{b}4	213
718	180	310^{b}25	65	*Po.* 1450^{a}38	320
815	164	312^{a}8	283	*Pol.* 1257^{a}39	258
886	294	*Col.* 791^a 27	47	1268^{b}28	188
937	157	797^{b}27	47	1268^{b}35	188
946	167	*de An.* 404^{a}25	319	1271^{a}3	173
1046	264	407^{b}22	314	1272^{a}14	180
1048	215	411^{a}10	319	1275^{a}12	205
1055	264	421^{a}30	214	1311^{b}9	72
1060	264	435^{a}2	60	1313^{b}16	90

ARISTOTLE *Pol. (cont.)*
1335^b 13	52
Pr. 863^{a}12	114
901^{b}30	58
928^{a}20	59
931^{a}18	78
Protr. 23	97
Resp. 478^{b}5	212
Rh. 1358^{a}14	286
1373^{a}35	296
1384^{a}21	309
1388^{a}32	121
1388^{b}22	119
1390^{a}11	150
1391^{a}27	68
1393^{b}20	233
1396^{b}30	286
1397^{a}7	286
1403^{a}18	286
1403^{b}29	214
1403^{b}30	71
1404^{b}21	90
1406^{a}2	190
1410^{a}4	308

Rh. Al.
1424^{b}5	72
SE 178^{a}3	71
Top. 106^{a}13	213
107^{a}16	212
fr. 554	253
611	58

ARRIAN
An. 2. 3. 7	89
5. 9. 4	248
Cyn. 15	144
Epict. 2. 4. 5	285
2. 9. 20	60
3. 21. 16	285
Tact. 8. 3	182

ASCLEPIODOTUS
TACTICUS
4. 1	48

ATHENAEUS
2. 53b	72
2. 54a	162
3. 115e	67
7. 282e	156
7. 319e	162
11. 474f	172
11. 480e	61
14. 623a	99

BABRIUS
1. 10	300
12. 2	305
15. 3	251
34. 7	300
71. 2	62
88. 14	252

BACCHYLIDES
17 (16). 108	300
18 (17). 5, 8	127

*BATRACHOMYO-
MACHIA*
34	290

CALLIMACHUS
43. 46	181
75	161, 222
218	208
295	165
337	141
394	157
Aet. 31. 5	222
Del. 47	196
Epigr. 50	45
54	45

DEMETRIUS COMICUS
VET.
1	89

DEMETRIUS LACON
Herc. 1012. 69	311

DEMOCRITUS
51	168
111	294
125	262
240	308
278	313

DEMOSTHENES
1. 19	85
2. 10	168
3. 15	217
3. 28	166
4. 11	231
4. 26	240
4. 31	281
4. 34	152
8. 50	166
9. 41	82
10. 55	86
12. 12	240
16. 24	167
18. 13	86
18. 14	93
18. 20	92
18. 28	85, 93
18. 59	86
18. 102	109
18. 103	87
18. 119	87
18. 120	120
18. 136	251
18. 150	175
18. 217	121
18. 222	86
18. 225	93
18. 241	68
18. 273	121
18. 290	179
18. 294	179
19. 55	86
19. 197	289
19. 208	168
19. 230	281
19. 277	176
19. 287	251
19. 297	167
20. 59	281
20. 146	86
21. 17	232
21. 35	153, 296
21. 38	294
21. 42	294
21. 47	296
21. 71	166
21. 104	222
21. 117	180
21. 149	38
21. 203	204
22. 73	119
23. 64	121
24. 9	226
24. 48	85–6
24. 83	85
24. 133	170
28. 1	93
28. 5	98
28. 21	318
30. 20	98
33. 1	98
35. 13	232
35. 44	175
37. 33	296
41. 12	173

42. 12	178	*Dem.* 20	300	EURIPIDES	
42. 15	168	23	285	*Alc.* 67	282
42. 30	276	*Lys.* 11	318	75	157
43. 39	176	*Th.* 6	305	*Andr.* 121	274
47. 50	175			419	319
48. 9	168	DIONYSIUS THRAX		607	187
48. 43	98	632. 9	299	1226	185
48. 44	176	674b. 3, 14	214	1240	113
49. 4	175			*Ba.* 9	295
49. 58	168	DIOSCORIDES		77	224
56. 6	83	*Title*	306	142	250
59. 46	38	2. 6	184	241	275
59. 60	267	2. 109. 2	187	247	294
59. 116	113	2. 127	187	279	297
60. 23	319	3. 120	181	370	222
60. 24	119	3. 132. 1	276	374	225
Ep. 5. 3	225	5. 88. 4	163	686	97
fr. 23	45	5. 121	60	688	304
				690	186
DINARCHUS		DIPHILUS		694	229
1. 70	86	18. 1	214	735	203
1. 105	174			812	259
		EMPEDOCLES		1138	304
DIO CASSIUS		3. 7	223	1200	262
49. 38. 2	122	11. 3	194	1245	262
78. 17. 3	64	27. 2	195	1290	283
		38. 3	299	*Cyc.* 28	199
DIO CHRYSOSTOMUS		111. 9	192	125	223
30. 20	89	112. 6	140	265	155
63. 5	295	115. 9	194	384	112
		143	279	697	290
DIODORUS SICULUS				*El.* 302	188
3. 14	47	EPHIPPUS		379	97
3. 22. 2	99	15. 4	222	411	278
5. 13. 1	276	16. 4	108	434	238,
5. 41. 6	250				240
26. 2	72	EPICHARMUS		1163	200
38/39. 3	285	13	1	1320	223
				Epigr. 2	277
DIOGENES LAERTIUS		EPICRATES		*Hec.* 352	120
1. 118	89	9	172	610	61
				614	230
DIOGENES		EUBULUS		631	306
OENOANDENSIS		40. 1	82	634	275
64	63	57. 1	160	868	205
		109. 2	222	940	184
DIONYSIUS				977	235
HALICARNASSENSIS		EUCLID		1050	290
1. 44. 2	308	1. 1	80	1064	263–
2. 73. 3	285	1. *Def.* 12	212		4
5. 15. 2	61	8. 1	109	1204	275
6. 30. 2	173			1261	172
7. 8. 4	157	EUNAPIUS		*Hel.* 231	275
7. 63. 3	173	*VS* p. 472 B	40		
Comp. 1	286				
16. 10	169	EUPOLIS			
22. 1	169	247. 3	187		
22. 12	169	335	289		

EURIPIDES *Hel. (cont.)*
248	263
566	114
946	315
1235	273
1602	250

Heracl. 400 273
428	194
719	223
758	279
984	318
1041	283

HF 199 290
741	294
771	103
999	257
1249	104

Hipp. 17 304
53	282
173	316
443	251
474	293
505	316
527	317
745	205
764	225
791	69
1053	282
1065	102
1081	224
1206	155

IA 249 108
360	240
1117	101

Ion 117 155
231	102
512	152
744	290
1285	152

IT 49 257
159	236
344	264
465	225
755	232
1045	225
1161	222
1308	239
1310	101
1461	222

Med. 8 148
99	187
410	155
1079	149

Or. 167 264
526	262
547	223
707	62
847	315
1171	313
1474	257
1581	294

Ph. 1 277
107	185
274	113
541	261
574	82
834	290
1027	282
1330	315
1439	301
1578	61
1699	290

Rh. 18 186
43	256
117	89
139	188
226	180
293	255

Supp. 40 224
376	273
447	167
520	251
931	89
1196	273

Tr. 449 248
480	274
869	263
995	252
1189	82
1214	313

fr. 290 166
308	178
672	110
776	291
941	300

EZEKIEL
Exag. 133 249

GALEN
1. 47	80
2. 669	292
3. 488	181
3. 568	181
4. 565	181
5. 289	91
5. 480	91
6. 77	306
6. 157	306
6. 352	278
6. 753	205
6. 760	278
7. 677	266
9. 444	48
9. 887	214
11. 182	159
14. 742	278
15. 60	270
15. 507	278
16. 500	269
18. (2). 256	306
19. 126	210
19. 405	302

UP 6. 16 181
7. 14	181

GORGIAS
6	223

Pal. 30 260

HARPOCRATIO 164

HECATAEUS
291	304

HELIODORUS
1. 8. 4	320
6. 13. 3	285
10. 5	104

HEPHAESTIO
GRAMMATICUS
1. 3	299

HERACLITUS
11	199
46	161
47	97
117	302
118	302

HERMOGENES
Prog. 6 286

HERO
Aut. 26. 6	71
Bel. 88.5-89.9	172
101. 12	89

HERODIAN
2. 6. 6	94
2. 14. 3	70
2. 14. 5	285
8. 8. 1	64

HERODOTUS

1. 1. 4	148	2. 41. 2	82
1. 6. 1	248	2. 42. 5	157
1. 14. 2	258	2. 45. 2	222
1. 19. 3	132	2. 49. 1	238
1. 24. 2	315	2. 65. 4	259,
1. 36. 1	230		273
1. 50. 3	261	2. 81. 2	152
1. 51. 4	249	2. 82. 2	83
1. 59. 6	202	2. 92. 4	289
1. 71. 3	288	2. 123. 2	316
1. 72. 2	248	2. 129. 2	150
1. 74. 4	168	2. 134. 4	314
1. 76. 1	169	2. 168. 2	259
1. 78. 1	200	2. 170. 1	225
1. 79. 1	131	2. 171. 2	222
1. 80. 1	153	3. 8. 1	211
1. 80. 4	41	3. 14. 1	318
1. 82. 8	176	3. 29. 2	180
1. 84. 3	40	3. 33	161
1. 84. 4	146	3. 35. 5	178
1. 92. 2	258	3. 36. 1	149
1. 94. 3	169	3. 42. 3	273
1. 106. 1	295	3. 80. 1	103
1. 117. 2	176	3. 80. 3	102
1. 120. 3	147	3. 80. 5	188
1. 121	268	3. 85. 2	147
1. 125. 2	83	3. 89. 2	259
1. 136. 1	167	3. 133. 1	200
1. 142. 2	298	3. 155. 1	72
1. 148. 2	233	3. 160. 2	42
1. 155. 3	179	4. 19	199
1. 179. 3	257	4. 21	304
1. 183. 2	267	4. 22. 2	282
1. 183. 3	185	4. 29	169
1. 186. 2	276	4. 36. 2	82
1. 189. 1	293	4. 53. 2	249
1. 194. 2	275–	4. 70	273
	6	4. 72. 2	58
		4. 88. 1	81
1. 203. 1	304	4. 91. 2	181
2. 2. 2	41	4. 117	228
2. 16. 2	212	4. 118. 3	230
2. 20. 3	233	4. 133. 3	104
2. 22. 1	248	4. 136. 2	276
2. 25. 4	249	4. 146. 3	176
2. 28. 2	212	4. 150. 3	65,
2. 33. 2	278		67
2. 35. 2	35	4. 164. 2	306
2. 36. 4	80,	4. 164. 4	35
	152	4. 165. 1	201
2. 37. 5	289	4. 168. 2	228
2. 39. 1	177	4. 172. 4	298
2. 41. 1	157	4. 177	289
4. 191. 3	199	5. 101. 2	203
4. 201. 2	273	5. 124. 1	318
4. 205	170	5. 124. 2	281
5. 6. 1	228	6. 11. 3	204
5. 9. 2	215	6. 33. 2	200
5. 12. 3	234	6. 34. 2	153
5. 19. 1	72	6. 57. 4	247
5. 20. 4	269	6. 64	91
5. 29. 2	202	6. 79. 2	101
5. 33. 1	88	6. 80	306
5. 34. 2	88	6. 86. a. 1	224
5. 35. 1	91	6. 98. 1	185
5. 49. 4	148	6. 109. 5	204
5. 50. 2	91	6. 119. 2	255
5. 52. 1	255	6. 119. 3	67
5. 56. 2	239	6. 134. 2	185
5. 58. 3	83	7. 15. 1	234
5. 71. 2	202	7. 23. 1	201
5. 77. 3	41	7. 36. 5	305
5. 77. 4	293	7. 51. 3	146
5. 92. η. 2	162	7. 52. 2	147
5. 96. 1	91,	7. 64. 2	212
	187	7. 67. 1	61
		7. 69. 1	211
		7. 85. 1	103
		7. 102. 1	170
		7. 106. 1	238
		7. 112	201
		7. 119. 3	255
		7. 123. 1	201

HERODOTUS *(cont.)*

7. 124	277
7. 129. 3	248
7. 132. 2	273
7. 136. 1	178
7. 140. 3	250
7. 158. 2	203
7. 160. 1	149
7. 209. 2	41
7. 214. 3	84
7. 220. 4	190
7. 236. 3	42
8. 11. 1	243
8. 47	102
8. 60. *a*	66
8. 65. 5	179
8. 68. γ	146
8. 77. 1	153
8. 90. 1	90
8. 102. 3	231
8. 110. 1	92
8. 115. 4	199
8. 116. 2	148
8. 130. 3	147
8. 137. 2	198
8. 138. 2	249
9. 7. *a*. 2	205
9. 23. 1	214
9. 37. 2	315
9. 41. 4	170
9. 79. 2	224
9. 86. 2	276
9. 89. 4	277
9. 99. 2	180
9. 110. 2	269
9. 116. 2	92
9. 120. 4	176

HERONDAS

1. 55	184
3. 3	315
3. 35	265
3. 49	184
3. 67	184
5. 2	184
5. 55	266
5. 74	128
7. 88	265

HESIOD

Op. 119	201
146	294
191	294
195	121

213	293
217	293
218	231
339	156
414	194
421	304
481	41–2
508	304
511	304
524–5	15
582–8	15
594	41
597	156
625	298
684	54
686	319
786	272
791	272
805	156
807	275
809	50
Sc. 173	312
233	213
235	191
314	248
348	213
364	193
429	190
457	211
Th. 21	152
39	251
57	152
66	206
84	251
93	152
97	251
384	121
444	255
492	193
688	190
694	303
716	238
832	190
869	298
896	189
fr. 133	250
204. 125	250
252. 6	192

HESYCHIUS

	13,
	44,
	74,
	76,
	94,

	105,
	107,
	124,
	165,
	254

HIPPOCRATES

Acut. 63	195
Acut. (Sp.) 4	169
Aër. 1	258
15	71
17	228
Aph. 1. 1	216
1. 22	217
2. 20	302
2. 46	281
4. 1	218
4. 10	218
5. 71	47
7. 44	272
Art. 30	181
43	172
45	160
50	167
Decent.	
9. 228. 17	308
Ep. 27	251
Epid. 1. 17	210
1. 19	250
1. 26. *a'*	48
3. 17. 2	228
4. 20	164,
	210
5. 50	228
7. 46	104
7. 90	104
Fract. 4	202
16	202
Jusj.	104,
	272
Liqu.	298
Loc. Hom. 9	298
Morb.	
2. (12(1). 6)	114
2. 47	162
2. 73	210
4. 49	63
Morb. Sacr. 10	145
21	161
Mul. 1. 1	47
1. 37 (8. 90)	218
1. 57 (8. 114)	217
1. 91 (8. 220)	163
Nat. Puer. 24	47

30	92	2. 236	244	5. 886	230
Prog. 3	301	2. 270	243	5. 892	189
4	58	2. 300	132	6. 17	144
8	148	2. 305	152	6. 27	192
12	210	2. 307	249	6. 89	152
Prorrh. 2. 30	269	2. 387	192	6. 139	290
2. 39	71	2. 409	145	6. 147	303
VC 1	80	2. 440	215	6. 169	79
VM 3	103	2. 470	254	6. 172	247
9	195, 259	2. 496	200	6. 182	194
16	214	2. 514	227	6. 194	278
22	47	2. 536	191	6. 207	236
[9. 420. 19]	121	2. 751	200	6. 241	109
		2. 776	105	6. 265	191
HIPPONAX		2. 780	200	6. 502	192
68	227	2. 849	248	7. 187	79
		3. 73	273	7. 210	192
HOMER		3. 116	234	7. 216	144
Iliad		3. 168	177	7. 330	314
1. 3	313	3. 193	177	7. 418	305
1. 47	184	3. 273	274	8. 65	250
1. 66	267	3. 294	144, 192	8. 66	156
1. 89	69			8. 111	132
1. 99	152	3. 300	249	8. 138	147
1. 103	190	3. 374	217	8. 242–3	245
1. 131	243	4. 151	101	8. 247	268
1. 173	148	4. 152	146	8. 281	180
1. 190	132	4. 155	273	8. 301	148
1. 193	149	4. 162	179	8. 334	69
1. 203	294	4. 163	145	8. 337	76
1. 205	143	4. 185	211	8. 353	242
1. 214	294	4. 263	148	8. 361	191
1. 219	66	4. 447	192	8. 452	242
1. 230	41	4. 451	250	9. 67	101
1. 249	251	5. 2	190	9. 110	242
1. 260	125	5. 52	303	9. 209	273
1. 312	297	5. 140	254	9. 217	203
1. 352	243	5. 196	312	9. 301	245
1. 353	244	5. 243	147	9. 343	147
1. 390	237	5. 288	131	9. 496	149
1. 429	147	5. 296	192	9. 514	246
1. 431	152	5. 339	249	9. 580	278
1. 546	243	5. 425	48	9. 598	149
1. 562	149	5. 470	190	10. 2	19
1. 586–7	243	5. 499	154	10. 27	298
1. 593	143	5. 506	192	10. 56	159
2. 6	239	5. 524	194	10. 70	242
2. 111	68	5. 531	125	10. 71	68
2. 124	273	5. 557	254	10. 335	211
2. 144	184	5. 648	153	10. 418	112
2. 147	183	5. 696	313	10. 464	238
2. 171	147	5. 773	247	11. 55	179
2. 196	149	5. 777	203	11. 88	275

HOMER *Iliad* (cont.)

11. 155	303	15. 710	148	18. 504	157
11. 162	126	16. 11–12	127	18. 528	278
11. 194	156	16. 31	242	19. 125	214
11. 268	191,	16. 100	153	19. 161	193
	214	16. 161	49	19. 197	272
		16. 189	192	19. 200	244
11. 272	214	16. 255	148	19. 217	246
11. 313	233	16. 264	186	19. 222	57
11. 334	144,	16. 280	184	20. 36	76
	312	16. 389	247	20. 37	49
11. 404	230	16. 407	156	20. 55	68
11. 631	156	16. 412	177	20. 100	244
11. 726	155	16. 447	234	20. 297	230
11. 789	245	16. 453	312	20. 300	245
11. 844	274	16. 454	234	20. 374	192
12. 18	194	16. 505	312	20. 491	303
12. 42	76	16. 523	245	21. 38	275
12. 56	211	16. 575	234	21. 48	236
12. 64	211	16. 602	192	21. 130	242
12. 148	303	16. 642	254	21. 173	211
12. 159	250	16. 646	146	21. 256	247
12. 313	201	16. 681	237	21. 308	242
12. 349	244	16. 688	125	21. 383	191,
12. 386	144	16. 739	211		194
12. 434	260	16. 761	271	21. 481	42
13. 60	190	17. 20	190	21. 608	101
13. 72	242	17. 22	73	22. 87	141
13. 180	275	17. 86	249	22. 141	213
13. 280	145–	17. 88–9	213	22. 149	248
	6	17. 121	242	22. 161	315
13. 282	144	17. 135	73	22. 263	148
13. 444	193	17. 239	245	22. 312	190
13. 447	247	17. 242	179	22. 338	312
13. 501	271	17. 256	217	22. 467	313
13. 634	189	17. 372	212	22. 504	141
13. 707	278	17. 438	249	23. 50	305
14. 13	101	17. 442	184	23. 65	314
14. 167	257	17. 456	191	23. 79	246
14. 271	31	17. 464	157	23. 94	180
14. 285	303	17. 476	191	23. 104	314
14. 295	246	17. 599	79	23. 111	305
14. 308	298	17. 675	215	23. 119	275
14. 345	212	17. 712	245	23. 137	236
14. 416	244	17. 751	247	23. 169	177
14. 418	192	18. 24	177	23. 177	203
14. 518	312	18. 71	213	23. 190	194
15. 94	146	18. 82	179	23. 238	194
15. 109	239	18. 114	180	23. 281	297
15. 143	102	18. 177	274	23. 370	144
15. 280	146	18. 264	192	23. 424	101
15. 313	213	18. 403	249	23. 468	191
15. 566	146	18. 411	49	23. 607	231
15. 631	200	18. 452	236	23. 688	249

23. 837	192	6. 19	257	11. 185	201
24. 34	267	6. 63	74	11. 220	194
24. 130	244	6. 72	101	11. 270	189
24. 310	239	6. 79	297	11. 323	153
24. 315	268	6. 109	229	11. 387	314
24. 341	298	6. 157	141	11. 441	242
24. 409	273	6. 188	204	11. 452	245
24. 504	244	6. 228	229	11. 502	192
24. 650	101	6. 282	243	11. 626	237
24. 681	159	6. 322	152	12. 11	275
24. 789	95	6. 325	245	12. 74	211
24. 792	194	7. 2	193	12. 219	102
Odyssey		7. 89	257	12. 279	189
1. 59	244	7. 153	112	13. 88	277
1. 321	190	7. 179	203	13. 104	152
1. 333	257	7. 197	68	13. 246	304
1. 343	180	7. 227	237	13. 351	304
1. 368	293	8. 2	157	13. 372	156
2. 167	201	8. 85	178	13. 407	200
2. 237	179	8. 95	69	14. 24	274
2. 365	33	8. 187	246	14. 79	41
2. 409	157	8. 212	245	14. 262	293
3. 27	153	8. 298	184	14. 336	237
3. 71	297	8. 359	192	14. 420	112
3. 72	127	8. 470	203	14. 426	312
3. 74	314	8. 534	69	14. 504	254
3. 104	189	8. 556	237	15. 48	41
3. 175	277	9. 140	247	15. 74	237
3. 278	153	9. 233	199	15. 329	293
3. 450	192	9. 234	305	15. 377	41
4. 5	234	9. 257	69	15. 540	245
4. 8	237	9. 290	249	16. 83	238
4. 29	237	9. 291	273	16. 86	293
4. 35	245	9. 302	148	16. 138	132
4. 363	193	9. 382	211	16. 269	192
4. 379	245	9. 392	60	16. 275	230
4. 408	108	9. 423	315	16. 423	221
4. 449	109	9. 449	203	17. 20	254
4. 458	297	9. 451	254	17. 195	275
4. 560	237	9. 457	192	17. 234	102
4. 580	109	9. 461	234	17. 316	304
4. 643	127	9. 523	312	17. 334	41
4. 678	101	9. 524	236	17. 487	293
5. 29	245	10. 78	146	17. 555	230
5. 59	112	10. 90	49	18. 34	158,
5. 70	248	10. 160	194		193
5. 167	239	10. 275	152		
5. 243	275	10. 351	155	18. 122	245
5. 257	305	10. 357	203	18. 327	264
5. 393	215	10. 393	250	19. 68	264
5. 411	211	10. 426	152	19. 204	249
5. 478	194,	10. 461	146	19. 440	298
	298	11. 58	128	19. 517	214
				19. 541	242

HOMER *Odyssey (cont.)*
20. 7	246
20. 19	190
20. 123	112
20. 336	201
21. 45	257
21. 91	31
21. 108	153
21. 154	312
21. 194	127
21. 289	32
22. 5	31
22. 203	191
22. 245	315
22. 280	79
22. 394	185
22. 412	222
23. 178	101
23. 214	32
24. 5	183
24. 81	159
24. 106	233
24. 193	129
24. 319	191
24. 352	293
24. 364	273
24. 483	273

h. Ap. 20	207
172	290
237	222
371	158, 194
374	212
h. Cer. 66	141
187	141
361	191
368	191
383	277
386	304
h. Hom. 8. 14	215
h. Merc. 130	222
173	222
349	51
470	222
526	268
h. Pan. 33	301
h. Ven. 82	228
237	251
278	141

HYPERIDES
| *Eux.* 35 | 276 |
| *Lyc.* 17 | 178 |

| *fr.* 21 | 205 |

IAMBLICHUS
| *Comm. Math.* 4 | 307 |
| *VP* 30. 184 | 223 |

IBYCUS
| 7 | 141 |

ISOCRATES
2. 48	84
4. 12	97
4. 74	175
4. 114	296
4. 136	97
5. 107	281
5. 109	286
7. 66	226
8. 10	174
8. 30	98
8. 53	205
10. 38	286
12. 9	270
12. 24	98
12. 32	270
12. 133	231
12. 138	320
12. 242	270
15. 157	98
15. 175	93
15. 290	318
15. 304	318
20. 2	296

JOSEPHUS
AJ 4. 8. 14	174
BJ 2. 14. 1	63
5. 10. 3	32
7. 357	119

LIBANIUS
| *Or.* 18. 164 | 279 |

LONGINUS
1. 3	84
4. 3	84
7. 4	123
9. 14	109
13. 4	307
23. 4	109
27. 2	216
29. 1	76
43. 1	307

LONGUS
| 4. 31 | 228 |

LUCIAN
| *Am.* 12 | 305 |

Cat. 21	83
Demon. 50	93
57	122
D. Mort. 4. 14	63
Fug. 13	160
Im. 6	301
Ind. 17	120
J. Tr. 51	160
Macr. 14	93
Merc. Cond. 1	172
Nig. 5	167
Pisc. 6	104
Pr. Im. 24	277
Prom. 12	305
Rh. Pr. 1	155
Salt. 81	217
Symp. 47	173
Syr. D. 15	272
23	84
Tim. 50	266
Tox. 14	235
VH 1. 7	249

LYCOPHRON
| 290 | 256 |

LYRICA ADESPOTA
| 111 | 141 |

LYSIAS
1. 2	296
1. 31	170
2. 48	120
6. 3	174
7. 27	91
7. 34	168
13. 80	240
15. 9	170
16. 10	204
19. 22	175
19. 46	204
19. 51	231
32. 12	318

MARCUS ANTONINUS
4. 5	110
4. 40	319
6. 14	317
8. 44	63

MEMNON
| 14. 1 | 252 |

MENANDER
Dysc. 775	40
869	40
Epit. 347	168
Kith. 49	231

Sam. 353	178	*Act. Ap.* 7. 49	285	ORPHICA	
590	250	18. 6	179	*fr.* 21a	183
593	252	25. 7	69	PARMENIDES	
fr. 462. 11	73	*Ep. Rom.* 5. 3	310	11. 3	194
494	240	8. 25	310	PARTHENIUS	
718	82	12. 19	285	9. 8	63
MICHAEL EPHESIUS		13. 1	316		
in PA 1. 4	163	13. 4	98	PAUSANIAS	
MOSCHUS		15. 23	284	1. 36. 3	153
3. 88	304	*1 Ep. Cor.* 2. 6	270	5. 8. 10	266
NICANDER		14. 16	285	8. 28. 6	173
Al. 82	76	15. 2	98,	PHERECRATES	
Th. 133	51		104	73. 5	289
484	251	*2 Ep. Cor.* 1. 6	309	75. 5	186
NONNUS		6. 4	310	170	289
D. 1. 4	301	10. 10	69	PHILO	
3. 69	305	*Ep. Gal.* 3. 4	98	*Bel.* 13	267
3. 252	305	4. 11	98	PHILO JUDAEUS	
16. 91	305	*Ep. Eph.* 4. 27	285	1. 640	306
NOVUM		*Ep. Phil.* 3. 15	270	2. 63	286
TESTAMENTUM		*Ep. Col.* 1. 11	310		
Ev. Matt.		2. 18	98	PHILODEMUS	
1. 22	229	*2 Ep. Thess.*		*Rh.* 1. 193	186
2. 20	315	3. 5	308	2. 53	120
3. 11	167	*1 Ep. Ti.* 3. 3	40	PHILOSTRATUS	
3. 12	56	*2 Ep. Ti.* 3. 15	153	*Ep.* 33	301
5. 48	270	*Ep. Tit.* 3. 2	40	*Gym.* 48	66
6. 2	45	*Ep. Heb.* 10. 27	122	PHILOSTRATUS JUNIOR	
12. 18	34	10. 36	310	*Im. Praef.*	81
19. 21	270	12. 17	285	1. 9. 1	299
23. 23	68	*Ep. Jac.* 3. 5	306	PHILOXENUS	
Ev. Marc.		4. 13	209	8	141
8. 36	315	5. 11	310	PHILUMENUS	
12. 6	33	*1 Ep. Pet.* 3. 20	316	*Ven.* 17. 1	200
16. 6	283	*Apoc.* 3. 10	310	PHRYNICHUS	
Ev. Luc. 1. 34	229	12. 8	284	*PS* p. 19 B	210
2. 7	284	12. 14	284	PHYLARCHUS	
4. 17	286	13. 10	310	36	184
4. 28	149	14. 10	150	PINDAR	
7. 11	109	14. 12	310	*O.* 1. 49	273
8. 15	308	20. 11	284	2. 12	202
9. 37	109	ONOSANDER		2. 45	141
12. 19	317	6. 1	216	2. 66	201
13. 8	116	10. 2	216	2. 70	317
14. 9	284	OPPIAN		3. 25	148
15. 14	169	*C.* 1. 326	82	3. 30	82
16. 1	91	*H.* 2. 412	299	6. 68	141
18. 12	309	5. 430	164	7. 67	180
21. 19	309	ORIBASIUS		7. 69	297
23. 31	299	5. 27. 1	252	7. 70	212
Ev. Jo. 6. 1	139	7. 26. 25	292		
14. 2	284	45. 18. 9	292		

PINDAR O. *(cont.)*

8. 39	317
8. 85	214
10. 3	83
10. 9	214
10. 92	256
12. 6	277
13. 27	202
13. 57	279
13. 115	267
P. 1. 9	300
1. 20	212
1. 48	318
1. 67	267
1. 72	295
2. 28	293
3. 61	319
3. 68	277
3. 70	202
3. 97	214
4. 40	297
4. 76	256
4. 150	201
4. 159	314
4. 203	238
4. 285	42
4. 289	102
5. 55	204
5. 97	157
9. 36	222
9. 89	230, 268
9. 96	147
10. 36	295
11. 21	314
11. 55	201
N. 1. 2	141
1. 25	42
1. 32	231
1. 47	313
1. 50	295
3. 80	243
3. 82	200
5. 51	171
6. 7	85
7. 23	291
8. 44	314
9. 32	317
9. 39	318
10. 18	267
10. 56	202
10. 62	215
11. 48	214

I. 1. 67	202
5. 52	204
6. 22	276
7. 24	141
7. 45	256
8. 28	146
fr. 70a. 14	140
75. 5	153
122. 15	268
133	314
169. 1	207

PLACITA
PHILOSOPHORUM

2. 32. 2	183

PLATO

Alc. 1. 116d	126
Ap. 17a	232
17c	97
23a	68
26e	294
30b	318
35c	174
39b	215
Cra. 399b	70
399d	109
400a	319
403e	270
419d	148
419e	143
426e	175
428b	85
Cri. 43c	69, 127
46e	104
Criti. 106b	268
109c	199
112a	298
116a	275
118e	276
119a	283
120c	83
Def. 412c	308
Ep. 310d	238
321c	155
323b	238
335a	152
353e	274
Epin. 975c	243
Euthd. 283e	179
302d	230
Euthphr. 2b	86
5d	225

12d	225
Grg. 449d	130
453e	81
463e	217
468d	130
474d	103
479a	272
480c	272
505d	182
513d	174
523b	104
Hipp. 225b	97
Lg. 629d	103
633d	147
647d	270
656a	185
678b	270
679c	122
695c	278
696a	205
700c	175
705c	281, 306
717d	150
746e	299
754e	87
755e	159
760c	281
761c	306
793a	277
834c	266
836b	274
842e	185
849d	306
850b	85
854d	82
857b	226
861d	225
863a	205
867b	149
873a	316
884a	294
888a	149
892c	319
908d	187
919b	274
923c	83–4
927b	217, 314
929c	266
955e	157
Men. 81b	314
Mx. 241a	109

242a	122	416e	226	*Ti.* 20b	109		
247b	176	420c	81	39d	182,		
Phd. 67e	92	426e	272		269		
70c	314	429d	61	69a	306		
85b	152	438c	65	69b	182		
87d	252	439e	101	70b	191		
98c	232	443b	268	70d	276		
Phdr. 233c	170	450a	188	73e	60		
237c	128	465a	150	74c	214		
238a	294	485d	252	77c	276		
245b	186	495b	252	80a	214		
247c	281	496b	319	84c	252		
249b	314	498c	90,				
250d	215		104	PLOTINUS			
258a	126	506c	291	2. 1. 6	188		
264a	180	509d	278	4. 4. 8	184		
268d	213	516c	215	5. 5. 8	190		
268e	71	518c	290				
269e	270	520a	175	PLUTARCH			
272a	208–	526b	217	*Aem.* 19. 9	292		
	9	528a	109	*Alc.* 21. 5	252		
276c	83,	541a	103	37	295		
	298	550d	291	*Alex.* 18. 2	292		
Phlb. 15e	188	550e	121	18. 4	200		
30c	317	552d	103	*Ant.* 2. 8	123		
40e	150	566b	91	58	46		
42c	109	566e	187	*Arist.* 4. 1	167		
49a	278	568d	152	*Art.* 25. 1	255		
51a	175	579b	317	*Brut.* 29. 1	302		
66d	182	600d	178	31. 2	251		
Plt. 271b	109	608d	314	*Caes.* 58. 5	291		
272a	304	616a	101	*Cam.* 6	98		
286c	109	*Smp.* 173a	128,	*Cat. Mi.* 6. 3	213		
287b	278		130	*Comp. Lyc.*			
295d	85	174e	230	*Num.* 3. 2	170		
299a	231	191d	274	*Cor.* 3	250		
Prm. 144d	204	191e	142	32	160		
Prt. 322e	103	192c	317	*Crass.* 23	52		
323e	150	196a	300	*Demetr.* 12	238		
325d	236	222c, d	90	*Dio* 27	186		
326d	82,	*Sph.* 223c	278	*Galb.* 18. 3	292		
	97,	253a	233	*Mar.* 28. 1	302		
	103	*Thg.* 122b	154	41. 6	148		
332c	70	*Tht.* 143a	83	*Marc.* 17. 11	112		
338a	277	147a	162	41. 6	148		
R. 329e	186	147c	298	*Num.* 15. 4	170		
344a	226,	152d	65	*Pel.* 1. 4	309		
	269	160e	130	*Per.* 2	122		
348b	269	162b	300	5. 3	302		
353e	318	163a	188	6. 2	168		
373d	199	189d	71	*Publ.* 7	174		
377e	81	210c	68	9. 4	149		
390a	109	210d	86	*Pyrrh.* 25. 3	305		
				Rom. Thes. 3. 2	150		

PLUTARCH *(cont.)*
Sol. 3. 1	303
12. 5	291
22. 4	45
Sull. 20. 5	291
TG 15. 2	158
Them. 12. 1	172
17	45
Thes. 25. 5	122
34. 1	91
2. 2b	291
2. 7b	277
2. 51c	302
2. 98a	291
2. 124e	45
2. 148d	90
2. 165a	200
2. 180e	113
2. 236d	314
2. 272f	90
2. 279c	69
2. 292d	224
2. 325c	152
2. 365a	224
2. 462b	285
2. 563d	92
2. 596a	67
2. 636c	320
2. 682b	232
2. 687c	291
2. 713a	302
2. 751a	303
2. 759c	298
2. 782e	253
2. 802b	306
2. 809f	93
2. 812c	160
2. 815d	160
2. 930b	94
2. 975b	291
2. 981d	157
2. 983d	292
2. 1003e	285
2. 1013e	319

POLLUX
1. 93	159
2. 94	47
2. 180	160
2. 186	181
7. 105	286
7. 121	182

POLYBIUS
1. 1. 4	84
1. 17. 5	66
1. 58. 5	161
1. 60. 3	153
1. 76. 3	65
1. 85. 1	176
1. 88. 2	285
2. 4. 8	102
2. 16. 14	307
2. 47. 10	103
2. 54. 2	185
4. 27. 8	123
4. 51. 1	309
4. 73. 8	283
5. 7. 10	304
6. 8. 5	296
6. 17. 4	38
6. 47. 8	206
8. 5. 10	172
9. 41. 4	115
12. 4. 14	250
12. 6. 4	180
12. 25^f. 1	286
15. 1. 1	72
15. 15. 8	309
21. 18. 2	286
21. 24. 3	273
21. 32. 15	273
29. 8. 9	161
30. 19. 2	91

PROCOPIUS
Arc. 14. 10	63
22. 19	94

QUINTUS SMYRNAEUS
4. 319	55

RUFINUS
Onom. 171	51

SAPPHO
1. 4	146
1. 18	148
44. 6	153
96. 17	64

SCHOLIA
Ar. *Pl.* 287	249

SEMONIDES
7. 61	163
7. 76	262

SEPTUAGINTA (LXX)
Ge. 1. 30	313
20. 1	185
46. 15	316
Ex. 5. 7	58
16. 16	180
21. 13	284
27. 4	115
Le. 4. 17	60
17. 11	320
25. 3	272
Nu. 32. 1	285
De. 12. 23	320
Jd. 11. 34	33
Ju. 9. 4	122
1 Ki. 19. 5	315
28. 21	315
2 Ki. 8. 8	139
3 Ki. 7. 16	182
3 Ki. 7. 23	139
18. 32, 35	140
19. 10	315
4 Ki. 12. 9	258
19. 31	122
1 Ch. 29. 15	308
2 Ch. 9. 20	172–3
Jb. 1. 17	182
14. 19	310
28. 1	285
Ps. 9. 19	310
29(30). 4	224
61. 5	310
78. 5	122
118. 109	315
Si. prol. 4	103
4. 5	285
Mi. 7. 2	319
Jl. 3(4). 18	249
Is. 5. 6	272
11. 7	58
14. 2	284
42. 1	34
49. 20	284
56. 5	284
66. 1	285
Je. 14. 8	310
17. 13	310
2 Ma. 2. 18	281
3 Ma. 3. 1	72
4 Ma. 9. 8	309

SEXTUS EMPIRICUS
adv. dogmat.
1. 6	187
M. 1. 100	299
1. 113	214

7. 99	252	273	263	546	68
8. 360	187	406	234	556	235
SIMONIDES		432	225	622	130
5. 9	206	449	274	636	188
52	312	598	205	676	101
SOLON		775	316	736	131
13. 46	315	786	313	761	235
13. 47	276	881	294	975	146
38. 1	288	899	281	979	96
fr. 52b	73	901	274	1027	282
SOPHOCLES		903	316	1127	281
Aj. 28	205	1127	316	1134	281
95	61	1163	235	1139	255
258	215	1319	148	1338	32
265	204	1331	258	1379	152
437	281	1333	128	1428	155
503	120	1347	146	1518	236
521	230	1402	101	1526	120
640	103	1492	315	*Ph.* 19	239
739	235	*OC* 56	283	40	282
869	281	64	282	45	236
998	216	259	253	55	316
1016	202	287	157	144	281
1017	68	301	246	157	283
1179	274	349	304	204	282
1221	153	469	155	208	69
1331	205	470	223	368	69
1405	224	503	283	393	201
1412	192	602	235	489	256
Ant. 18	102	627	282	504	104
108	212	883	294	582	91
109	184	943	119	619	274
112	213	1020	282	662	224
176	318	1193	149, 215	709	203
227	316			712	319
330	103	1204	68	808	216
392	103	1263	263	866	184
413	186	1276	186	945	166
420	304	1326	315	1014	318
424	213	1328	69	1045	68
559	318	1371	185	1068	243
614	104	1489	231	1162	235
632	268	1523	282	1196	262
718	149	1660	185	1215	155
1016	113	1770	235	1260	102
1110	281	*OT* 17	67	1325	83
1236	300	149	239	1330	67
1238	215	189	239	1429	238
El. 18	187	371	291	1445	239
26	147	389	291	*Tr.* 57	204
30	217	411	85	148	227
150	205	454	290	235	67
		477	304	269	101

SOPHOCLES *Tr. (cont.)*

398	205
468	251
483	205
571	237
574	60
580	60
698	252
955	282
966	67
974	187
1084	263
1100	282
1104	291
1189	102
1195	306
1219	228
fr. 24	204
144	205
271. 1	248
368	295
432	260
593. 6	291
724	104
811	83
838	290
844	69
933	69

SORANUS

1. 1	278
1. 46. 1	309
1. 83	271
1. 98	278
2. 2	282
2. 11	307
2. 14	307
Fasc. 4	202

STOBAEUS

3. 1. 117	194

STRABO

1. 1. 17	291
1. 2. 21	210
2. 1. 12	188
5. 1. 2	176
5. 1. 12	305
6. 2. 6	152
7. 3. 4	188
7. 5. 8	248
10. 2. 21	285
11. 13. 11	206
14. 1. 41	123
14. 2. 27	120

14. 3. 8	153

TELECLIDES

1. 4	250

TESTAMENTUM EPICTETI

8. 8	176

THEOCRITUS

1. 55	300
1. 96	70
1. 100	69
2. 89	250
5. 124	248
5. 126	248
5. 127	61
8. 10	232
8. 35	317
8. 87	181
10. 19	291
10. 49	56
12. 24	51
13. 59	53
16. 24	317
17. 130	147
18. 47	82
22. 14	97
24. 15	257
25. 22	268
25. 206	301

THEOGNIS

132	224
366	217
379	293
448	249
512	262
639	251
730	314
744	104
754	104
1009	231
1030	217

THEOPHRASTUS

Char. 6. 1	308
17. 3	317
28. 1	318
CP 2. 4. 7	47
3. 2. 8	292
3. 7. 5	267
5. 16. 3	308
HP 1. 7. 1	285
1. 8. 4	292
2. 4. 4	320

4. 4. 9	57
4. 10. 7	178
5. 7.1	306
5. 9. 3	214
5. 9. 7	114
7. 6. 1	167
8. 4. 1	58
9. 8. 2	181
9. 9. 5	200
9. 11. 3	161
Lap. 9	252

THUCYDIDES

1. 2. 2	201
1. 5. 3	203
1. 6. 2	203
1. 46. 4	248
1. 49. 3	147
1. 70. 2	217
1. 82. 1	187
1. 91. 2	236
1. 91. 3	240
1. 100. 2	201
1. 112. 5	153
1. 129. 3	234
1. 136. 4	315
2. 5. 2	249
2. 7. 1	104
2. 8. 3	185
2. 11. 7	149
2. 13. 5	258
2. 18. 5	276
2. 19. 2	276
2. 20. 2	276
2. 40. 3	318
2. 40. 4	231
2. 49. 2, 3	169
2. 52. 3	152, 226
2. 75. 2	275, 305
2. 81. 1	240
2. 83. 3	89
2. 98. 1	275
2. 100. 2	276
2. 102. 6	283
3. 4. 4	90
3. 6. 1	166
3. 13. 1	240
3. 48. 1	205
3. 70. 4	275
3. 85. 2	169
3. 88. 2	153
3. 105. 1	169

3. 109. 2	91	1. 8. 1	255	8. 7. 4	317
3. 114. 1	204	1. 9. 25	238	8. 7. 19	313
3. 116. 1	249	2. 1. 9	72	*Eq.* 1. 6	301
4. 9. 3	169	2. 3. 1	240	4. 3	255,
4. 14. 3	126	2. 6. 25	224		298
4. 24. 4	169	4. 4. 4	281	7. 7	300
4. 69. 2	305	4. 6. 11	169	9. 2	147
4. 126. 6	216	4. 6. 17	199	10. 7	173
5. 23. 1	166	5. 3. 13	154	10. 15	301
5. 42. 1	199	5. 6. 4	155	11. 1	318
5. 45. 3	91	5. 8. 14	169	*Eq. Mag.* 8. 24	169
5. 47. 8	267	5. 8. 18	272	*HG* 1. 2. 3	103
5. 77, 79	138	6. 4. 27	185	1. 7. 20	170
5. 104	224	7. 3. 21	204	1. 7. 34	85
5. 111. 2	166	7. 7. 43	317	2. 1. 22	185
6. 7. 1	276	*Ath.* 1. 14	167	2. 2. 10	294
6. 11. 5	230	*Cyn.* 4. 1	300	4. 4. 9	40
6. 30. 1	89	5. 31	300	6. 5. 18	166
6. 34. 3	187	6. 15	191	7. 1. 31	191
6. 51. 1	34,	6. 20	213	7. 2. 8	178
	38	7. 4	69	*Lac.* 11. 6	52
6. 54. 4	281	13. 2	83	*Mem.* 1. 2. 30	233
6. 56. 2	240	*Cyr.* 1. 2. 4	266	1. 2. 42	85
6. 88. 1	232	1. 4. 22	169	1. 4. 6	271
7. 14. 1	84	1. 4. 23	131	1. 4. 15	236
7. 29. 4	108,	1. 5. 4	240	2. 1. 13	275
	110	2. 4. 20	283	2. 1. 20	286
7. 72. 1	169	3. 1. 36	315	2. 6. 12	166
8. 46. 5	166	3. 1. 37	148	2. 9. 5	231
8. 50. 2	240	3. 1. 42	238	3. 3. 12	237
8. 50. 5	315	3. 2. 20	199	3. 6. 12	67
8. 81. 2	91	3. 3. 45	290	3. 9. 1	166
8. 96. 5	215	3. 3. 61	191	3. 9. 7	170
		3. 3. 66	181	3. 10. 10	168
TYRTAEUS		4. 1. 16	40	4. 2. 2	186
10. 14	315	4. 3. 21	85	4. 3. 14	317
		4. 5. 34	85	*Oec.* 6. 14	317
VETUS TESTAMENTUM		4. 6. 5	262	6. 16	318
see *SEPTUAGINTA*		4. 6. 6	230	8. 1	187
		5. 1. 23	97	16. 11	186
VETTIUS VALENS		5. 3. 37	67	16. 13	304
44. 22	186	6. 1. 36	40	17. 9	167
		6. 2. 9	236	17. 12	304
XENARCHUS		6. 2. 10	240	18. 2	56
4. 20	315	6. 2. 31	214	19. 10	166
		6. 2. 33	318	20. 15	318
XENOPHANES		7. 1. 30	166	20. 28	97
1. 17	294	7. 3. 8	319	*Smp.* 4. 8	289
		8. 3. 12	114	4. 11	232
XENOPHON		8. 3. 30	250	4. 12	290
An. 1. 2. 10	255	8. 4. 14	294	*Vect.* 5. 4	152
1. 3. 14	37				
1. 5. 1	304				
1. 5. 10	37				

INSCRIPTIONS

Buck, *Gr. Dial.*
39   117
CEG 372   55
CIG 2782. 31   182
CIL 3. 567. 3   283
Didyma   101
Dodona   132
Inscr. Cret.
  1. 1. 17. 14   298
  4. 78. 7   84
Inscr. Délos
  1417 C 58, 89   77
IG 1^2. 10. 3   204
  1^2. 45. 7   204
  1^2. 54. 7   247
  1^2. 76. 56   276
  1^2. 84. 27   240
  1^2. 186   225
  1^2. 394   293
  1^2. 893   206
  1^2. 920   158
  1^2. 945   314
  2. 4054   121
  2^2. 236   139
  2^2. 463. 42, 44   178
  2^2. 1013. 8, 10   261
  2^2. 1544. 24   40
  2^2. 1672. 304   175
  2^2. 13196   279
  4^2. (1). 65. 8   283
  4^2 (1). 101. 47   266
  4^2 (1). 103. 94   257
  4^2 (1). 122. 40   272
  4^2 (1). 122. 98   295
  5 (2). 549. 2   266
  9 (1). 334. 47   268
  12 (3). 536,
    540, 546   221

12 (3). 170. 12   132
12 (7). 401. 14   284
12 (7). 515. 63   283
12 (8). 569   287
12 (9). 7. 4   183
14. 830   63
14. 1183   180
Leg. Gort. 1. 51   130
  3. 21   84
  5. 9   130
  6. 31   133
  8. 18   130
  9. 23   133
  9. 25   92
LSAG pl. 1. 1   218
  pl. 7. 5   151
  pl. 26. 2   151
Marsala   137
Mon. Anc. Gr.
  5. 17   158
OGI 50. 3   202
Pech-Maho   134
Schwyzer
  51   133
  62, 63   43
  66   158
  74. 1   158
  83. B. 10   267
  90. 10   84
  109. 4   298
  109. 40   272
  109. 98   295
  135. 2   154
  175   84
  181. 7. 15   130
  186. 9   138
  214   221
  309   132
  362. 2   226

362. 47   268
409. 8   231
412. 1   75,
     269
412. 4   39
428. 13   121
509. 19   159
511. 2   159
654. 1, 11   199
679. 10   125,
     133
731. B. 7   232
758   218
App. I. a   218
SEG 1. 366. 58   226
  1. 400   270
  2. 710. 13   115
  3. 115. 18   37
  3. 400. 9   268
  10. 238. 51   105
  24. 361   117
  26. 461. 7   138
  27. 124   269
  30. 355   269
  30. 1352   46
  31. 2. C. 46   219
  32. 637   95
  37. 340. 23   131
SIG 685. 84   168
  888. 10   158
  1027. 13   164
  1073. 48   160
Tabulae Heracleenses
  1. 12–13   44
  1. 36   163
  1. 74   154
  1. 121   131
  1. 125   132
  2. 93   43
TAPhA 65. 105   56

PAPYRI

BGU 256. 9	201	*P. Grenf.*		900. 7	216
612	45	1. 1. 13	121	909. 18	267
896. 4	284	2. 76. 19	269	912. 13	284
1114. 6	283			1129. 10	284
		P. Hamb. 4. 8	158	2106. 24	283
P. Cair. Zen.		10. 14	269	2115. 6	216
327. 83	285			2728	286
344. 2	256	*P. Hib.* 1. 32. 8	296		
462. 9	295			*P. Oxy. Hels.*	134
692	113	*P. Oxy.* 99.9	291		
782(a). 141	259	239	84	*P. Teb.* 5. 83	283
		282. 7	111	23. 4	94
P. Giss. 6. 7	63	502. 34	284		
P. Goodsp. Cair.		525. 3	63	*SB* 5277. 5	266
15	66	474. 28	109	5343. 41	91